Cisco Cloud Infrastructure: Application, Security, and Data Center Architecture

Avinash Shukla, CCIE No. 28418

Jalpa Patel, CCIE No. 42465

Komal Panzade

Himanshu Sardana

I0131561

Cisco Press

Cisco Cloud Infrastructure: Application, Security, and Data Center Architecture

Avinash Shukla, Jalpa Patel, Komal Panzade, Himanshu Sardana

Copyright © 2023 Cisco Systems, Inc.

Cisco Press logo is a trademark of Cisco Systems, Inc.

Published by:
Cisco Press

ScoutAutomatedPrintCode

Library of Congress Cataloging-in-Publication Number: 2022920878

ISBN-13: 978-0-13-769012-1
ISBN-10: 0-13-769012-6

Warning and Disclaimer

This book is designed to provide information about Cisco Cloud Infrastructure for various Cisco Products, existing Cisco technologies in the "Data Center, Security, and Applications" domain which are available in the On-Prem environment and how the technology has evolved to fit in a Hybrid Cloud model, which facilitates the management and operation of On-Prem deployments and provides integration with Public Cloud. Every effort has been made to make this book as complete and as accurate as possible, but no warranty or fitness is implied.

The information is provided on an "as is" basis. The authors, Cisco Press, and Cisco Systems, Inc. shall have neither liability nor responsibility to any person or entity with respect to any loss or damages arising from the information contained in this book or from the use of the discs or programs that may accompany it.

The opinions expressed in this book belong to the author and are not necessarily those of Cisco Systems, Inc.

Trademark Acknowledgments

All terms mentioned in this book that are known to be trademarks or service marks have been appropriately capitalized. Cisco Press or Cisco Systems, Inc., cannot attest to the accuracy of this information. Use of a term in this book should not be regarded as affecting the validity of any trademark or service mark.

Special Sales

For information about buying this title in bulk quantities, or for special sales opportunities (which may include electronic versions; custom cover designs; and content particular to your business, training goals, marketing focus, or branding interests), please contact our corporate sales department at corpsales@pearsoned.com or (800) 382-3419.

For government sales inquiries, please contact governmentsales@pearsoned.com.

For questions about sales outside the U.S., please contact intlcs@pearson.com.

Feedback Information

At Cisco Press, our goal is to create in-depth technical books of the highest quality and value. Each book is crafted with care and precision, undergoing rigorous development that involves the unique expertise of members from the professional technical community.

Readers' feedback is a natural continuation of this process. If you have any comments regarding how we could improve the quality of this book, or otherwise alter it to better suit your needs, you can contact us through email at feedback@ciscopress.com. Please make sure to include the book title and ISBN in your message.

We greatly appreciate your assistance.

Editor-in-Chief: Mark Taub	**Technical Editors:** Manuel Velasco, Atul Khanna
Director, ITP Product Management: Brett Bartow	**Editorial Assistant:** Cindy Teeters
Executive Editor: James Manly	**Designer:** Chuti Prasertsith
Managing Editor: Sandra Schroeder	**Composition:** codeMantra
Development Editor: Ellie C. Bru	**Indexer:** Erika Millen
Project Editor: Mandie Frank	**Proofreader:** Donna E. Mulder
Copy Editor: Bart Reed	

Credits

Chapter 2, 3, 6, Logo of Google Cloud: Google

Chapter 2, 3, 8, Logo of Azure: Microsoft Corporation

Chapter 2, 3, 8, Logo of AWS: Amazon, Inc

Chapter 2, Logo of Alibaba: Alibaba

Chapter 3, Logo of VMware: VMware, Inc

Chapter 3, Logo of Windows Hyper V: Microsoft Corporation

Chapter 3, Logo of Red Hat: Red Hat, Inc

Chapter 3, Logo of F5: F5, Inc

Chapter 3, Logo of Citrix Systems: Citrix Systems, Inc

Chapter 3, Logo of Dell: Dell, Inc

Chapter 3, Logo of Brocade: Broadcom

Chapter 3, Logo of IBM: IBM

Chapter 3, Logo of Netapp: NetApp

Chapter 3, Logo of Pure Storage: Pure Storage, Inc

Chapter 3, Logo of Hitachi: Hitachi, Ltd

Chapter 6, Logo of OneDrive: Microsoft Corporation

Chapter 6, Logo of SharePoint: Microsoft Corporation

Chapter 6, Logo of Box: Box

Chapter 6, Logo of DropBox: DropBox

About the Authors

Avinash Shukla (CCIE No. 28418), Senior Leader in Cisco's US Customer Experience (CX) Organization, has 14 years of experience in Cisco CX roles spanning Professional and Technical Services, and extensive expertise in collaboration and data center technologies. He now leads a team of engineers working on Cisco Data Center Technology (Cisco Unified Computing Systems, Hyperconverged Infrastructure, Virtualization, and data center automation). He holds a B.Tech in ECE from IIIT, Hyderabad and has won numerous Cisco awards for customer focus, and has delivered many technical trainings for Cisco partners and customers.

Jalpa Patel (CCIE No. 42465) is a multidisciplinary technologist and a passionate leader with a strong track record of successful engineering executions and game-changing business achievements defining, building, and growing new products. Her domain knowledge of Data Center hardware infrastructure is focused on Compute, Networking, Storage, and Accelerators. Patel holds an MS degree in Telecommunication Networks from NYU, a BS degree from Government Engineering College, Gujarat, India, and an Advanced Program Management Certificate from Stanford.

Komal Panzade is a Senior Technical Consulting Engineer in Cisco's Customer Experience (CX) organization and has 6 years of experience working on different Data Center Technologies like Compute, Storage, and Virtualization. She currently works in the Hyperconverged Infrastructure (HCI) domain focusing on Distributed Systems and Automation. She is a Certified Kubernetes Administrator and helps Cisco customers with efficient management of their infrastructure using Cisco's SaaS platform called Intersight. Komal holds a Bachelor of Technology degree in Information Technology from Amity University, Noida, India.

Himanshu Sardana (CCNP, VCP, CKA), is a Senior Technical Consulting Engineer in Cisco's Customer Experience (CX) Org. He started his professional journey with Cisco and now has 6 years of experience in Data Center Compute and Storage space. His current area of focus is on Cisco's Hyperconverged business (Hyperflex) and Intersight, helping with high escalations and creating tools like Hypercheck to make customer interactions with Cisco Products better. He holds a BS degree in Computer Science from Chitkara University, Punjab, India.

About the Technical Reviewers

Manuel Velasco (CCIE No. 49401) is a Customer Success Specialist, in the Customer Experience group at Cisco Systems. In his previous role, he worked as TAC engineer at Cisco supporting multiple data center technologies, including Cisco Unified Computing System and Virtualization, Cisco Application Centric Infrastructure (ACI), and Cisco Hyperflex. He has over 11 years of experience in the data center technologies. Manuel holds a B.S. degree in Computer Engineering from CalPoly San Luis Obispo.

Atul Khanna (CCIE No. 35540) is working as Personalized Support Manager in Twilio Inc. Before joining Twilio, he was Data Center Networking Manager with Cisco Customer Experience Center Americas. He has extensive experience in directing and leading strategies to provide optimal technical services to Cisco Customers, with more than 12 years of experience at Cisco in enterprise support, network operations, manage/cloud services, data center networking, compute, and virtualization. Atul was a senior technical consulting engineer supporting Hyperflex solutions in Richardson, Texas; he facilitated Advanced Services (AS) team members for successful new customer deployments and upgrades; and he cultivated relationships with Cisco Partners and customers to meet organizational demands. He also presented a technical webinar for cloud services platform 2100. He attended Cisco Live in 2015 and 2018, interacting with Cisco customers and partners at the TAC booth. Atul lives with his wife and son in Frisco, Texas.

Dedications

Avinash Shukla: I would like to dedicate this book to my lil' baby girl Avira who was born during the time of writing the book, my son Aryav, my nieces Riddhi and Siddhi, my lovely wife Neelima, my sister Anubha, and my parents Kanak and Anil, for their unconditional love and support. Without their support, none of this would have been possible. I would also like to dedicate this book to one of my earliest inspirations while growing up, my beloved Bade Papa, Aravind Kumar Shukla (RIP). Lastly, I would like to thank everyone in my big extended family for their motivation and encouragement. All of you have inspired me in many ways and helped me in my professional endeavors.

Jalpa Patel: I would like to dedicate this book to my parents, Minaxi and Babubhai Patel, for their blessings and faith in me; and to Jigisha, Falguni, and Harish, for their guidance and encouragement. I also would like to dedicate this book to my brother, Hardik, and his wife, Dharmistha, who have been a great support to me throughout the complete process of writing of this book. Finally, thank you to Raj and Samaira for their love and inspiration.

Acknowledgments

We would like to thank and acknowledge several people who have helped us directly or indirectly with the necessary skills that enabled us to write this book.

This book couldn't have been possible without the support of many people in the CiscoPress team. A thank you goes to James Manly, Eleanor Bru, and everybody else at CiscoPress for believing in us and supporting us throughout this journey.

Also, much research for this book was done by sifting through heaps of design guides, specifications, and videos so many thanks to all of the technology professionals.

Finally, we would like to thank our technical reviewers Manuel Velasco, Vibhor Amrodia, and Atul Khanna, for their patience, commitment, and support in the adventure of writing this book.

Contents at a Glance

Reader Services

Register your copy at www.ciscopress.com/title/ISBN for convenient access to downloads, updates, and corrections as they become available. To start the registration process, go to www.ciscopress.com/register and log in or create an account.* Enter the product ISBN 9780137690121 and click Submit. When the process is complete, you will find any available bonus content under Registered Products.

*Be sure to check the box that you would like to hear from us to receive exclusive discounts on future editions of this product.

Contents

Icons Used in This Book

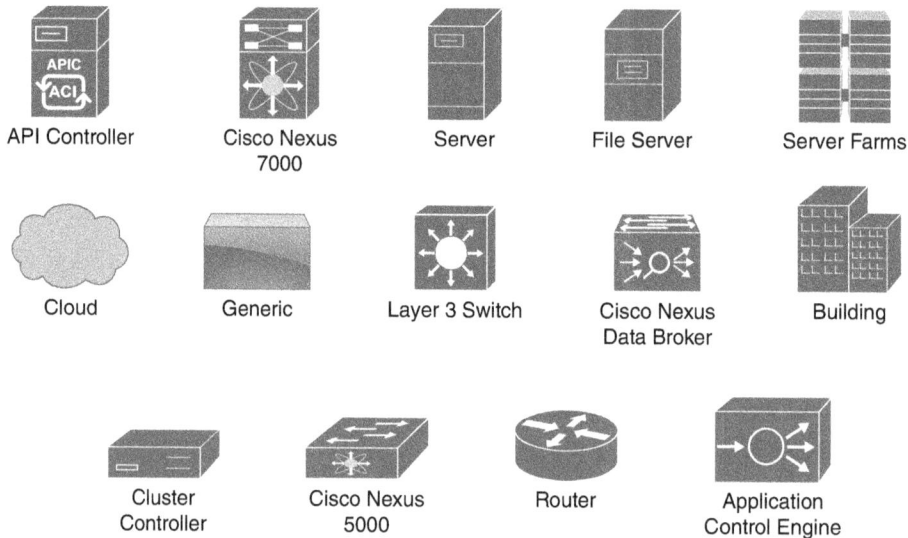

API Controller   Cisco Nexus 7000   Server   File Server   Server Farms

Cloud   Generic   Layer 3 Switch   Cisco Nexus Data Broker   Building

Cluster Controller   Cisco Nexus 5000   Router   Application Control Engine

Command Syntax Conventions

The conventions used to present command syntax in this book are the same conventions used in Cisco's Command Reference. The Command Reference describes these conventions as follows:

- **Boldface** indicates commands and keywords that are entered literally as shown. In actual configuration examples and output (not general command syntax), boldface indicates commands that are manually input by the user (such as a **show** command).

- *Italics* indicate arguments for which you supply actual values.

- Vertical bars (|) separate alternative, mutually exclusive elements.

- Square brackets [ ] indicate optional elements.

- Braces { } indicate a required choice.

- Braces within brackets [{ }] indicate a required choice within an optional element.

Note   This book covers multiple operating systems, and a differentiation of icons and router names indicates the appropriate OS that is being referenced. IOS and IOS XE use router names like **R1** and **R2** and are referenced by the IOS router icon. IOS XR routers will use router names like **XR1** and **XR2** are referenced by the IOS XR router icon.

Introduction

Almost every company is adopting hybrid cloud solutions as it provides decreased hosting costs, agility and scalability, and faster deployment ability and security. Using a hybrid cloud might be an investment upfront, but it will provide plenty of cost saving benefits down the road. For example, businesses that use public cloud without a hybrid might have a difficult and expensive time migrating information if they decide to make changes to their internal systems. Furthermore, because a hybrid cloud is scalable, it makes handling changes in business goals cheaper down the line. Only hybrid cloud technology can provide a blend of benefits that come from public and private servers. With a hybrid cloud, for instance, you can enjoy the scalability of a public cloud environment without forfeiting all control to a third party. In fact, with every hybrid cloud situation being different, a unique solution will have to be applied to each hybrid system in order to fulfill specific requirements. Because a hybrid cloud is designed around your organization's needs, it can be optimized with speed in mind. For example, because this system isn't entirely public, your IT staff will be able to minimize latency, which will make data transfers quicker and easier. The overall level of customization available for hybrid cloud also ensures your organization is agile enough to handle the needs of customers or clients. Not only does it connect old systems to new ones, but the hybrid cloud also allows businesses to create an overarching structure that meets the unique needs of a specific enterprise.

As we see an increasing trend in deployment of hybrid cloud with on-prem solutions, the book will be useful to both small-scale customers and large-scale data centers. It can be considered as one book for all who deal with Cisco Cloud Solutions on a daily basis. External references are provided wherever applicable, but readers are expected to be familiar with cloud-specific technologies, infrastructure concepts, networking connectivity, and security policies of the customer installation. Readers can gain knowledge about the benefits of cloud solutions, how to manage, operate, and integrate existing infrastructure in a hybrid/multicloud environment with minimum changes and leverage insights from the cloud for their business decisions.

Cisco doesn't have a public cloud offering like AWS but has many products that complement and facilitate cloud integration and use of hybrid cloud. The attempt of this book is to fill the gap where a user can find a one-stop book that details all such products and architecture and provides insights on how they can co-exist in a hybrid cloud environment.

The book helps IT professionals, CIOs, and IT managers in their decision to move into a hybrid cloud deployment vs. an on-prem deployment. It describes in detail and from a technical and business aspect the possible solutions and offerings from Cisco. The book also describes products such as the Cisco Nexus Dashboard, which facilitate the orchestration and insights about your deployment.

Last but not least, the book covers best practices and guidelines to make readers aware of known caveats prior to specific deployment, the do's and don'ts while designing complex hybrid cloud networks, how and why to design in a certain way for maximum efficiency.

Goals and Methods

CIOs and IT professionals who want to simplify their IT and networking environment are now challenged with the decision of whether to move fully into the cloud, build their own data centers, or go with hybrid solution. Making such decisions depends on a lot of factors that include the scale and complexity of their existing setup, the level of control over their own resources, security, availability of IT and networking resources, level of expertise, overall fixed and recurring costs, and so on.

As cloud is a new buzzword in industry and multiple vendors are introducing products that offer various infrastructure solutions and are challenging the existing network design, all the new technologies are getting confusing to IT professionals who are trying to move into next-generation architectures while maintaining a current setup that is generating revenue. This book will walk the reader through and provide a reference guide to understand and independently implement cloud solutions for Cisco Network, Compute, Storage, Application, and Security.

In this book we are covering Cisco Cloud Infrastructure for various Cisco Products. This book will cover existing Cisco technologies in the "Data Center, Security, and Applications" domain that are available in the on-prem environment and how the technology has evolved to fit in a hybrid cloud model that facilitates the management and operation of on-prem deployments and provides integration with public cloud. This gives you the tools to ask the right questions when you embark on the transformation of your data center into private and hybrid clouds.

Who Should Read This Book?

We see an increase in hybrid cloud adoption, which requires planning, designing, and execution strategy of on-prem and public cloud setups. In general IT professionals are divided in their areas of expertise. Individuals are spread into focus areas that overlap:

- Orchestration
- Analytics
- Cloud integration
- Virtualization
- Storage networking
- Security
- Software applications
- Automation
- DevOPs

Cisco is taking a network-centric approach to multi-cloud and hybrid deployments. Cisco has partnerships with Azure and AWS and has expanded a relationship with Google Cloud. Add in AppDynamics, which specializes in application and container management, and Cisco has the various parts to address hybrid and multi-cloud deployments. In addition, Cisco is a key hyper-converged infrastructure player and its servers and networking gear are staples in data centers. The audience of this book is the sum of all solution architects, deployment engineers, systems engineers, networking engineers, software virtualization engineers, network management engineers, sales engineers, field consultants, professional services, partner engineering, customers deploying the Cisco Cloud Solutions, and anyone who would like to know about Cisco's presence in cloud space. Also as the book touches on the business aspects of pros and cons of moving from private clouds to public clouds, IT managers and CIOs will benefit from understanding the impact of cloud solutions on the transformation of their data centers and the speed of deploying highly available applications.

How This Book Is Organized

For those who are familiar with the authors' writing style from previous books such as "Implementing Cisco HyperFlex Solutions," the authors put a big emphasis on easy reading and making the difficult look easy. The book goes through a smooth progression of the topics and a lot of the basic concepts are laid out in advance so you do not miss a beat and feel comfortable progressing through the chapters. It is recommended to go through the chapters in order to get the full benefit of the book.

Orchestration, analytics, management, security, and automation are not easy topics and are getting more complex every day. Boundaries between system administrators, networking engineers, and software engineers are getting blurred day by day and expectations are increasing to be an expert in all dimensions by a single individual.

The authors have put a lot of effort into putting you on the right track and giving you the launch pad into tackling cloud infrastructure. Their many years of experience in both the vendor and system integration track and across the different technology areas make this difficult topic sound simple. The advantages you see from this book follow:

- An easy reading style with no marketing fluff or heavy technical jargon

- Progression through the chapters from easy to advanced

- Comprehensive coverage of the topic at both a technical and business level

- First book to address Cisco cloud solutions in detail under one umbrella to bridge the technology gap between the different IT departments

- Beneficial to IT professionals trying to evaluate whether to move into the hybrid cloud solution

- Beneficial to IT management, CIO, and CTO evaluating various cloud applications

- Coverage of the latest cloud offerings by Cisco

- Discusses Automation and Orchestration solutions

- Compares and contrasts different implementations objectively and with vendor neutrality

Book Structure

The book is organized into three parts.

PART 1—Cisco Data Center Networking and Infrastructure

Chapter 1—Cisco Data Center Orchestration: This chapter talks about Cisco's data center orchestration software that uses the automation of tasks to implement processes, such as deploying new servers. Automation solutions that orchestrate data center operations enable an agile DevOps approach for continual improvements to applications running in the data center. Data center orchestration systems automate the configuration of L2-L7 network services, compute and storage for physical, virtual, and hybrid networks. New applications can be quickly deployed.

Chapter 2—Cisco Data Center Analytics and Insights: This chapter talks about Cisco's API-driven monitoring and assurance solutions that provide essential insights as well as add to an expansive and increasingly onerous toolset. These network insight solutions are bringing the ability to see the big picture, and if something goes wrong, they show exactly where to look instead of poking around and hoping to get lucky. This helps prepare companies to progressively transition from reactive to proactive and eventually predictive IT operations.

Chapter 3—Cisco Data Center Solutions for Hybrid Cloud: This chapter talks about the various hybrid cloud management platforms like ACI, UCS Director, CWOM, and Intersight that are provided by Cisco and offer flexible consumption for on-premises infrastructure in order to optimize workloads across clouds, on-premises data centers, labs, and co-location facilities for scale, performance, and agility with great value.

PART 2—Cisco Applications and Workload Management

Chapter 4—Application, Analytics, and Workload Performance Management with AppDynamics: This chapter describes Cisco's AppDynamics solution, cloud migration, and various monitoring such as Application Security Monitoring, End User monitoring and Browser monitoring. It also covers database and infrastructure visibility and cloud platforms.

Chapter 5—Management: This chapter describes the challenges that the IT teams face in managing the modern workloads and gives you various systematic Workload Management Solutions such as Intersight Workload Optimization Manager, Cisco Container Platform, and Cisco Intersight Kubernetes Service (IKS).

Chapter 6—Cisco Cloud Webex Applications: Collaboration is a key component of any IT solution and Cisco Webex provides an ideal platform for staying connected and collaborating with individuals, teams, and meetings to move projects forward faster. This chapter describes Cisco Webex Features and Cisco Webex Cloud Service Architecture in detail.

Chapter 7—Internet of Things (IoT): This chapter describes how well we can combine the Operational Technology hardware with IT and come up with amazing IoT solutions, which Cisco currently offers. These solutions can really help you get the best insights and increase efficiency.

PART 3—Cisco Cloud Security

Chapter 8— Cisco Cloud Security: This chapter talks about all the Cisco Cloud Security solutions like Cloudlock, Umbrella, Cloud Analytics, and Duo using which one can adopt the cloud with confidence and protect users, data, and applications, anywhere they are. Unlike traditional perimeter solutions, Cisco Cloud Security blocks threats over all ports and protocols for comprehensive coverage. Cisco Cloud Security also uses API-based integrations so that the existing security investments can be amplified.

Chapter 1

Cisco Data Center Orchestration

We are working in a multidimensional world of data and applications accessed by a workforce shifting among work-from-home offices to centralized campuses to work-from-anywhere setups. Data is widely distributed, and business-critical applications are becoming containerized microservices disseminated over on-premises, edge cloud, and public cloud data center locations. These applications rely on agile and resilient networks to provide the best level of experience for the workforce and customers.

It is therefore a multidimensional challenge for IT to keep applications and networks in sync. With the ever-increasing scope of the NetOps and DevOps roles, an automation toolset is needed to accelerate data center operations and securely manage the expansion to hybrid cloud and multicloud.

Data center orchestration software uses the automation of tasks to implement processes such as the deploying of new servers. Automation solutions that orchestrate data center operations enable an agile DevOps approach for continual improvements to applications running in the data center. Data center orchestration systems automate the configuration of L2–L7 network services as well as compute and storage for physical, virtual, and hybrid networks. New applications can be quickly deployed.

The Cisco Nexus Dashboard provides a single focal point to unite the disparate views of globe-spanning multicloud data center operations, application deployment, and performance.

This chapter will cover following topics:

- IT challenges and data center solutions
- Cisco Nexus Dashboard
- Cisco Nexus Dashboard Orchestrator
- Cisco Nexus Dashboard Fabric Controller
- Third-party applications and cloud-based services

IT Challenges and Data Center Solutions

Organizations are deploying applications in multiple public and private clouds, with more applications than ever. There are also more different classes of people and machines using these applications.

As a result of containers, which have microservices and are serverless, developers are constructing these highly distributed application constructs with workload tiers and data services spread across hybrid IT, spanning on-premises data centers and multiple public clouds. Because of these trends, multicloud data center operators are facing serious challenges, including the following:

- Approximately 40% of skilled IT staff time is spent on troubleshooting in break-fix mode.

- The majority of network outages are due to human error, leading to unplanned downtime.

These issues require network operators to have a high level of domain expertise and the ability to correlate complex IT environments to prevent or fix issues while upholding the infrastructure uptime to honor service level agreements (SLAs) with minimum disruptions.

Day 0 is design and procurement; Day 1 is installing, provisioning, and segmenting; and Day 2 is running a network. Most of the challenges currently faced by network operators are related to the Day 2 operations capabilities of running a network.

IT needs a way to transform and get past installing, provisioning, and segmenting. To make Day 2 operations easier, IT needs to be able to do the following:

- Analyze every component of a data center first.

- Ensure business intent.

- Guarantee reliability.

- Detect performance issues proactively in a network.

Figure 1-1 illustrates the main challenges in network operations.

To be successful, IT needs to be in a strategic partnership with business. Without this, it's impossible to efficiently help enable the changes necessary to enable business growth. Cisco believes analytics enable IT professionals to turn raw data into actionable insights that they can use to drive business growth. When IT practitioners move to a proactive operations approach for their data center, both sides win. Figure 1-2 illustrates the Cisco data center solutions.

Lacking pervasive
visibility and insights

No event and
issue correlation

Inability to understand
change impact

Limited performance
and availability

Figure 1-1   *Main challenges in network operations*

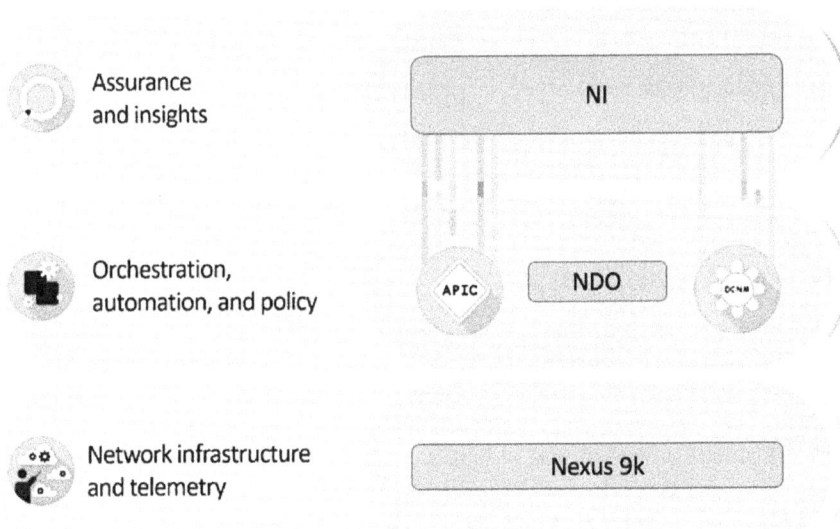

Assurance
and insights

NI

Orchestration,
automation, and policy

APIC

NDO

DCNM

Network infrastructure
and telemetry

Nexus 9k

Figure 1-2   *Cisco data center solutions*

Data center analytics and automation capabilities both within and across domains help in simplifying the network operations and attain the insights and assurance needed to continually evolve them. This is key for an intent-based networking (IBN) strategy.

The data center analytics and automation provide the following capabilities:

- To begin, pull critical telemetry information out of the data and control planes and make it available to the analytics layer. Cisco has done this through silicon innovation, turning every networking device into a sensor.

- Stitch together network, security, and application analytics to provide a single source of truth for IT operations teams and a unified view across data center, campus, WAN, branch office, and cloud environments.

- Provide artificial intelligence/machine learning–based decision support tools for a range of common operations activities such as upgrade planning and software release guidance, proactive service level monitoring, and smart troubleshooting based on graph-based search.

- Extend to cloud-based analytics and mobile phone dashboard option.

The business sees the following benefits:

- Highest operational uptime and outage mitigation to meet SLAs/SLOs

- Operational expenditure (OpEx) optimization and IT strategic agility enhancement

- Security compliance and assurance

And IT sees these benefits:

- Faster remediation of issues while increasing agility

- Engineers can focus on mission-critical work

- Greater confidence and less risk in operating the network

Cisco Nexus Dashboard

Cisco Nexus Dashboard revolutionizes operations in today's modern data center environments. Network operations teams are struggling to reconcile fragmented toolchains, an inconsistent user experience (UX), and siloed processes in order to manage complex data center environments that include on-premises infrastructure and public cloud sites. Cisco Nexus Dashboard specifically addresses this pain point by providing a single pane of glass from which to manage a unified operations infrastructure based on the Cisco Nexus Dashboard platform. Based on a horizontal, scale-out architecture, Cisco Nexus Dashboard can unify operations from the on-premises infrastructure (Cisco Application Centric Infrastructure [Cisco ACI] or Cisco NX-OS with Cisco Nexus Dashboard Fabric Controller [NDFC]) to co-locations and to the public cloud. Cisco Nexus Dashboard provides a seamless user experience for the operator, whether it is to rapidly troubleshoot issues or execute change window actions with a high degree of confidence. Operators spend more time on the "logistics ladder" of traditionally fragmented toolchains before any operational value is realized. With the frictionless user experience of Cisco Nexus Dashboard, operators can focus on what they do best—troubleshooting, triaging, and executing change windows with a high degree of confidence, rather than figuring out URLs, credentials, and access controls.

The intuitive Cisco Nexus Dashboard platform provides services such as Cisco Nexus Dashboard Insights, Cisco Nexus Dashboard Orchestrator, Cisco Nexus Dashboard Data

Broker, and a single operational view of geographically dispersed multicloud environments. The platform enables the acceleration of NetOps and DevOps capabilities while scaling into the cloud, and it aligns seamlessly with third-party ecosystem tools from HashiCorp Terraform, ServiceNow, and Splunk, with other integrations to come.

The Cisco Nexus Dashboard Orchestrator (formerly Cisco ACI Multi-Site Orchestrator [MSO]), Cisco Nexus Dashboard Insights (formerly Nexus Insights [NI]), and Cisco Nexus Dashboard Data Broker (formerly Nexus Data Broker) services are being integrated into the Cisco Nexus Dashboard as native services in order to simplify the customer experience:

- **Cisco Nexus Dashboard Orchestrator:** Formerly Cisco ACI Multi-Site Orchestrator, the Cisco Nexus Dashboard Orchestrator service allows operators to push policies and templates and set up intersite connectivity at scale. Besides delivering high-level policies to the local data center controller—also referred to as the *domain controller*—it enables separation of fault domains, federation of data center and cloud networks, and business resiliency at a global scale. Nexus Dashboard Orchestrator also enables end-to-end change management workflows, centralized fabric management and upgrades, multi/hybrid-cloud connectivity, normalized segmentation, and security policies across the data center, SD-WAN, and enterprise branch and campus networks. For example, the SD-WAN integration provides application-aware SLA-based routing (policy-based path selection and quality of service [QoS] treatment) in the SD-WAN infrastructure used for interconnecting sites.

- **Cisco Nexus Dashboard Insights:** Formerly Nexus Insights, the Cisco Nexus Dashboard Insights service allows operators to consume the entire insights and assurance stack as a unified offering but also to take advantage of the integrated services to set up automated workflows such as upgrade assist and automated Splunk SIEM (security information and event management) integration. It incorporates a set of advanced alerting, baselining, correlation, and forecasting algorithms to provide a deep understanding into the behavior of the network. It also analyzes flow telemetry data streamed from Cisco Nexus 9000 Series Switches to provide perfect introspection into hybrid cloud infrastructure. The Insights service and AppDynamics are tightly integrated to pinpoint exactly where and when an application issue originated from a network perspective.

- **Cisco Nexus Dashboard Data Broker:** Formerly Nexus Data Broker, the Cisco Nexus Dashboard Data Broker service is now a part of Cisco Nexus Dashboard, which provides pervasive packet and network visibility for NetOps and SecOps to programmatically manage aggregating, filtering, and forwarding complete workflows to custom analytics tools. It is a multitenant-capable solution that can be used with both Nexus and Cisco Catalyst fabrics. It replaces the traditional purpose-built network packet broker appliances with high-throughput Cisco Nexus switches, enabling IT to create cost-effective and scale-out packet broker fabrics.

- **Third-party applications:** Cisco Nexus Dashboard offers a rich suite of services for third-party developers to build applications. REST APIs allow third-party tools to authenticate and integrate with key services such as Nexus Dashboard Insights and Nexus Dashboard Orchestrator. Currently supported third-party integrations in the Nexus Dashboard ecosystem include ServiceNow ITSM/ITOM, Splunk SIEM, HashiCorp Terraform, and Red Hat Ansible.

■ **Cisco Nexus Dashboard Fabric Controller:** Cisco Nexus Dashboard can also host Cisco Nexus Dashboard Fabric Controller (NDFC), similar to the hosting of operational services. This unified capability gives customers a single touch point on their journey from installation to operations. This brings the controller for fabrics based on Cisco NX-OS under the Cisco Nexus Dashboard platform and unleashes the benefits of faster time to deploy and upgrade and an improved overall user experience to Cisco NDFC.

The operations team now has to deal with a single stack and one operations toolkit—whether they are running Cisco ACI or Cisco NDFC in their hybrid cloud infrastructures. Figure 1-3 illustrates the Cisco Nexus Dashboard graphical user interface (GUI).

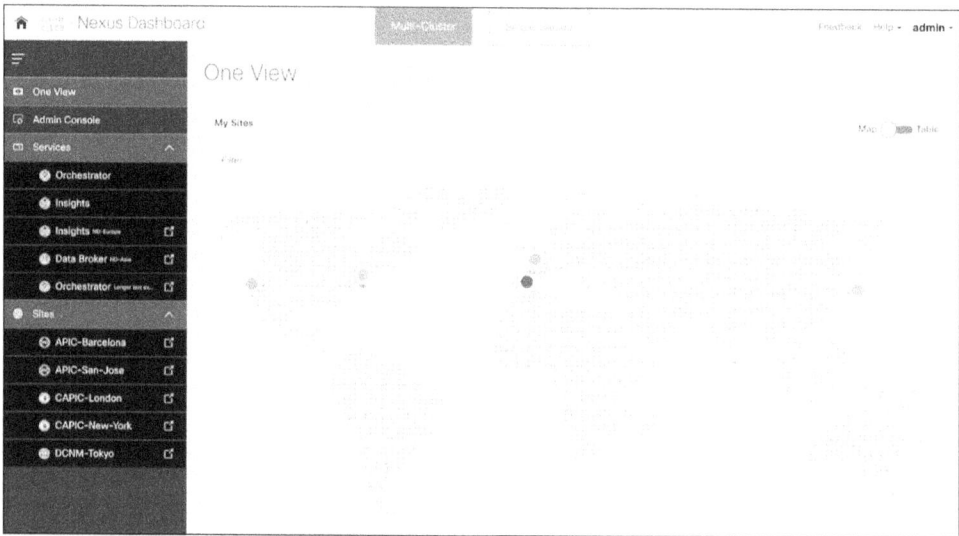

Figure 1-3   *Cisco Nexus Dashboard GUI*

Operational infrastructure standardization and toolchain unification directly lead to operational excellence and savings as well as free up resources for business innovation.

Features and Benefits

Table 1-1 lists the features and benefits of Cisco Nexus Dashboard.

Table 1-1 *Features and Benefits of Cisco Nexus Dashboard*

Feature	Benefit
Single sign-on (SSO)	Seamless user experience while using Cisco Nexus Dashboard Insights, Cisco Nexus Dashboard Data Broker, or Cisco Nexus Dashboard Orchestrator. Faster triaging and troubleshooting of issues.
Multifactor authentication	Reduced risk of static passwords and increased security with DUO-supported multifactor authentication.
Unified operations platform	Clustered, highly available, and scale-out platform infrastructure to host all applications. Minimizes maintenance and lifecycle management versus a siloed operations infrastructure.
Single pane of glass to manage the operations infrastructure	A single pane of glass to manage Cisco Nexus Dashboard services and infrastructure.
Cisco Nexus Dashboard One View	With Cisco Nexus Dashboard One View, operators seamlessly consume services they have access to, regardless of where the services are running.
Physical, virtual, and cloud form factors	Cisco Nexus Dashboard can be deployed in any form factor—physical, virtual, or cloud.
Prepackaged services	Jump-start installation with prepackaged Cisco Nexus Dashboard Insights, Cisco Nexus Dashboard Orchestrator, Cisco Nexus Dashboard Fabric Controller, and Cisco Nexus Dashboard Data Broker services.
Cloud site onboarding	Onboard and manage multicloud environment with site onboarding for Amazon AWS, Microsoft Azure, and Google Cloud.

Too often the network operations team spends most of its time gathering troubleshooting data to triage and root-cause an issue. The burden of tying together siloed insights from a fragmented operational toolkit often lies with the operations team. As the company's data center footprint extends from the on-premises data center to the cloud, and as modern application architectures become the de-facto standard, the operations team needs a unified operations toolchain with a seamless user experience to maintain and operate such complex environments.

Cisco Nexus Dashboard unifies these disparate toolsets and experiences for the operations teams to consume the rich and powerful capabilities of Day 2 operations solutions and executes multisite policies from a single pane of glass. Unnecessary handoffs between toolchains and dealing with multiple portals and credentials to get to troubleshooting data and insights have become a thing of the past. An operator logs in once to Cisco Nexus Dashboard and is able to go straight to the Discover, Analyze, Remediate,

Automate workflow from a single launchpad. Cisco Nexus Dashboard offers a powerful and rich set of capabilities, including the following:

■ **Single sign-on (SSO):** SSO powers the frictionless interaction between Cisco Nexus Dashboard and the hosted services. The operator logs in once and is able to switch seamlessly between services and also site controllers such as Cisco APIC, Cloud APIC, and NDFC.

■ **Unified operations platform:** The Cisco Nexus Dashboard platform is a powerful unified platform capable of scaling out horizontally to accommodate application needs. With a modern microservices infrastructure services stack on a clustered architecture, the same underlying platform can be used to co-host the entire Day 2 applications portfolio, thus reducing the burden of the underlying software and hardware lifecycle maintenance.

Figure 1-4 illustrates Cisco Nexus Dashboard components.

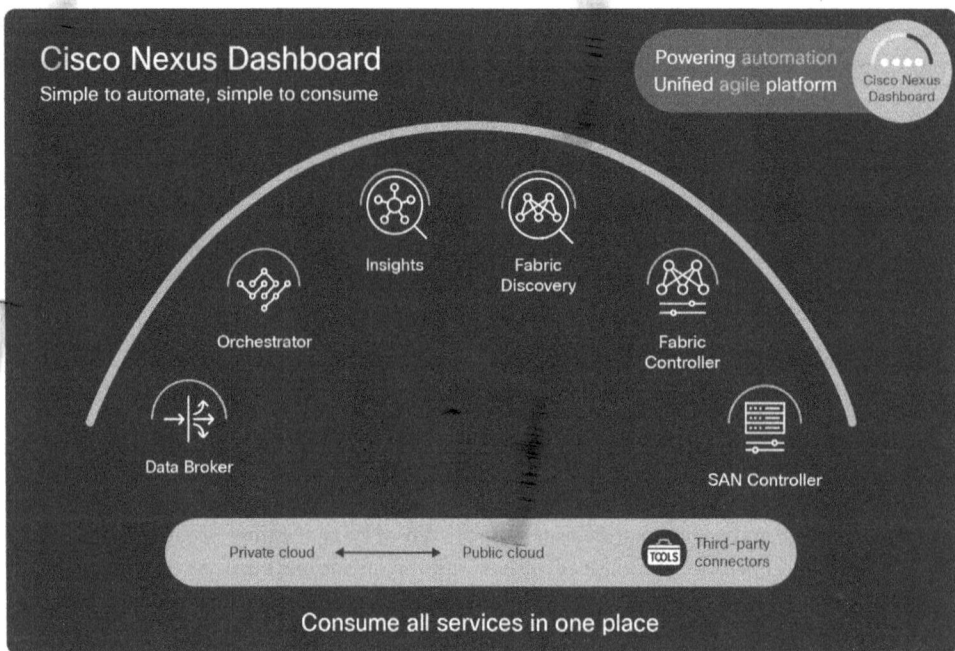

Figure 1-4   *Cisco Nexus Dashboard components*

■ **Persona-based dashboard:** Cisco Nexus Dashboard has two primary personas:

■ The administrator, who is able to manage all the Cisco Nexus Dashboard platform infrastructure services and hardware from a single pane of glass. The administrator is also able to install, upgrade, and launch all services on the Cisco Nexus Dashboard platform. This role can set up common sites and services for the applications to use from a single pane of glass. Figure 1-5 shows the Cisco Nexus

Dashboard System Overview, and Figure 1-6 shows common sites and services from a single pane of glass.

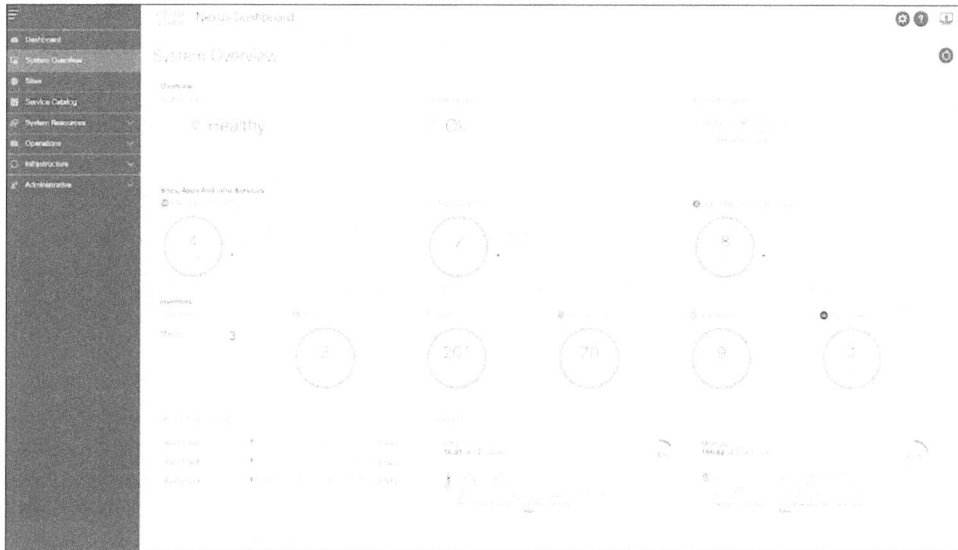

Figure 1-5   *Cisco Nexus Dashboard System Overview*

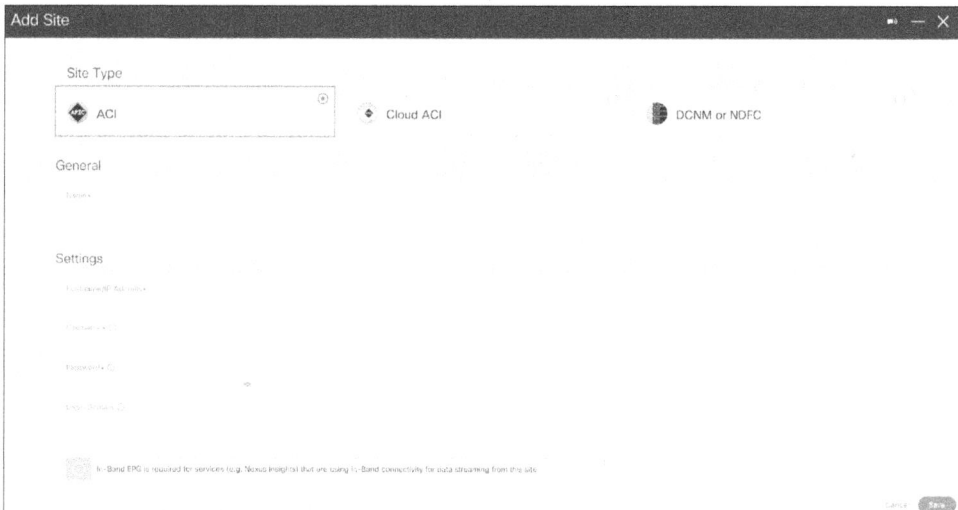

Figure 1-6   *Common sites and services from a single pane of glass*

■ The operator, who is able to get an aggregate view of the health of the sites and with a single click, navigate to the Insights service, gain more information about critical anomalies, and scroll through the temporal view to get historical context. If the operator then needs to make changes to policy, they can easily switch to the Cisco Nexus Dashboard Orchestrator and roll out changes to multiple sites, including public cloud environments, all from a single portal.

■ **Common infrastructure services:** Cisco Nexus Dashboard provides a host of common infrastructure services, such as common site onboarding, authentication domains, role-based access control (RBAC), notification services, and API services.

■ **Flexible deployment options:** The Cisco Nexus Dashboard portfolio is composed of physical, virtual, and cloud form factors, giving customers unprecedented flexibility while deploying their operations infrastructure and at the same time ensuring a common and unified operator experience through a single pane of glass.

■ **Programmable infrastructure:** Third-party automation tools are critical to improving reporting workflows and responding to issues encountered by distributed workloads. Cisco Nexus Dashboard has built-in integrations with many third-party services such as ServiceNow, one of the most prevalent IT service management platforms. With the ServiceNow integrations, NetOps and DevOps teams can open and track tickets from within Nexus Dashboard. From one portal, operations teams get visibility into the status of open tickets, resulting in the automation of troubleshooting for faster resolutions across fabrics.

■ **SR-MPLS with Nexus Dashboard Orchestrator:** With Cisco Nexus Dashboard Orchestrator, SR-MPLS (Segment Routing with Multiprotocol Label Switching) policies can be centrally automated across 5G telco cloud sites (central, regional, and edge data centers). Cisco Nexus Dashboard with Insights and Orchestrator services is the most comprehensive way to automate distributed data centers, overcoming the challenges of managing the infrastructure, applications, and data sources distributed over disparate locations.

With these services integrated into Cisco Nexus Dashboard, NetOps teams can achieve command and control over global network fabrics, optimizing performance and attaining insights into data center and cloud operations.

■ **Cisco Nexus Dashboard One View:** The Cisco Nexus Dashboard operations infrastructure can be deployed and managed at scale via a single pane of glass. Figure 1-7 illustrates Cisco Nexus Dashboard One View.

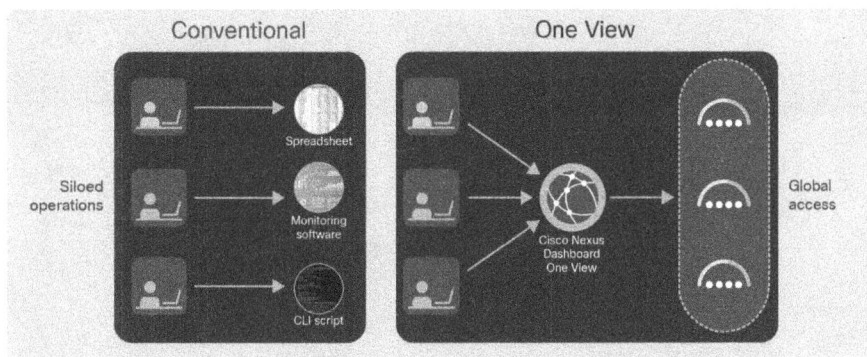

Figure 1-7   *Cisco Nexus Dashboard One View*

Hardware vs. Software Stack

Nexus Dashboard is offered as a cluster of specialized Cisco UCS (Unified Computing System) servers (Nexus Dashboard platform) with the software framework (Nexus Dashboard) pre-installed on it. The Cisco Nexus Dashboard software stack can be decoupled from the hardware and deployed in a number of virtual form factors.

Each Nexus Dashboard cluster consists of three master nodes. For physical Nexus Dashboard clusters, you can also provision up to four worker nodes to enable horizontal scaling and up to two standby nodes for easy cluster recovery in case of a master node failure. For virtual and cloud clusters, only the base three-node cluster is supported.

Cisco Data Center Networking (DCN) Licensing

Following are the licensing options for greenfield and brownfield deployments:

- **Cisco DCN Premier License (for greenfield):** Provides Cisco Nexus Dashboard, Cisco Nexus Insights (formerly Network Insights Resources and Network Insights Advisor), and Cisco Network Assurance Engine (NAE). Users with an existing Essentials or Advantage subscription can transition to Premier and receive the Cisco Nexus Insights capabilities.

- **Cisco DCN Day 2 Operations or D2Ops Solution Suite (for brownfield):** This is recommended for users who already have a Cisco DCN Advantage or Essentials license. The bundle provides Cisco Nexus Dashboard and Cisco Nexus Insights and Network Assurance Engine.

Figure 1-8 illustrates Cisco DCN licensing and Nexus Dashboard orderability.

Cisco Cloud Networking licensing
Cisco Nexus Dashboard and Apps Orderability*

Cisco DCN Essentials	Cisco DCN Advantage	Cisco DCN Premier	ND service add-on licenses
Cisco ACI Base	VPN fabric		Cisco Nexus Dashboard Insights (Day2Ops)
LAN Enterprise	Cisco ND Orchestrator	Cisco Nexus Dashboard Insights	
Cisco NDFC LAN	Physical remote leaf		Cisco Nexus Dashboard Data Broker (NDDB)
Network services			
Streaming telemetry	Cisco DCN Essentials	Cisco DCN Advantage	
Cisco ACI Multipod		Cisco DCN Essentials	
PTP			

| Single data center | Multiple data centers and/or clouds | Multiple data centers and/or clouds with highest innovations | Intelligent analytics, deep operational visibility reduce mean time to resolution |

Cisco Nexus 9000 Series - Cisco ACI or NX-OS

Cisco Software Support Service (SWSS) included in all subscriptions

*Virtual and cloud form factor offered at no cost. Physical paid or with promotion bundle through Cisco Enterprise Agreement (EA)

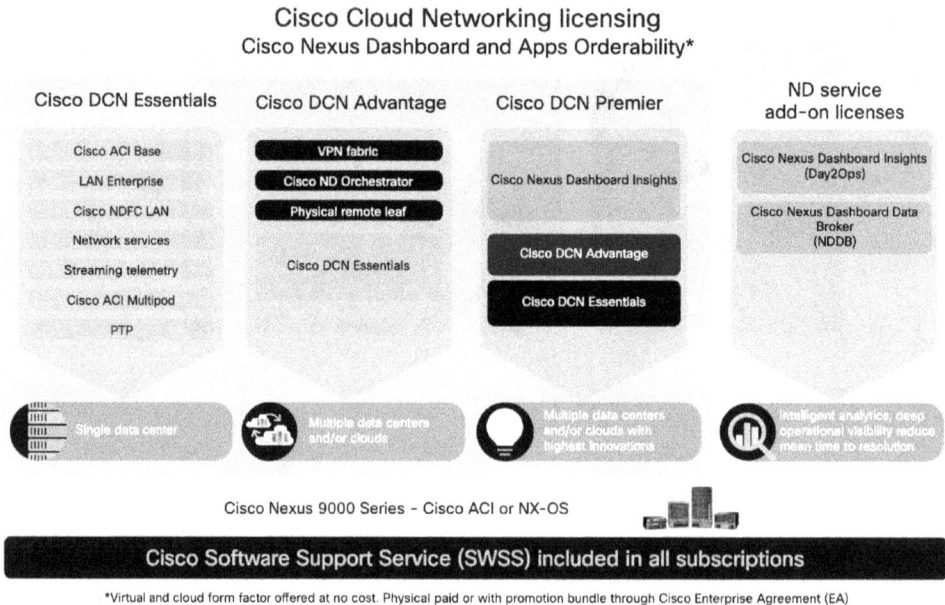

Figure 1-8 *Cisco DCN Licensing and Nexus Dashboard orderability*

Available Form Factors

Cisco Nexus Dashboard is available in physical, virtual, and cloud form factors:

- **Cisco Nexus Dashboard physical appliance (.iso):** This form factor refers to the original physical appliance hardware that you purchased with the Cisco Nexus Dashboard software stack pre-installed on it.

- **VMware ESX (.ova):** A virtual form factor that allows you to deploy a Nexus Dashboard cluster using three VMware ESX virtual machines.

- **Amazon Web Services (.ami):** A cloud form factor that allows you to deploy a Nexus Dashboard cluster using three AWS instances.

- **Microsoft Azure (.arm):** A cloud form factor that allows you to deploy a Nexus Dashboard cluster using three Azure instances.

After Cisco Nexus Dashboard cluster deployment, you can perform all remaining actions using its GUI. To access Cisco Nexus Dashboard GUI, simply browse to any one of the nodes' management IP addresses. Figure 1-9 shows the Cisco Nexus Dashboard general view.

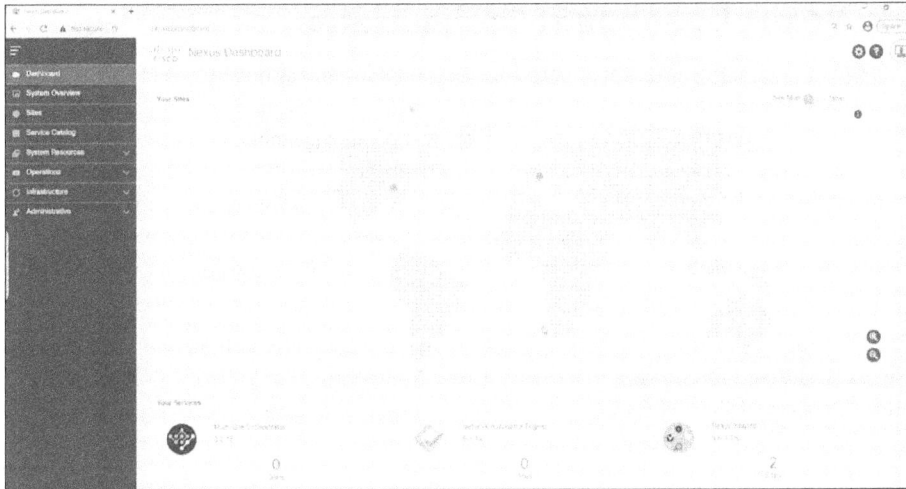

Figure 1-9 *Cisco Nexus Dashboard general view*

With Cisco Nexus Dashboard, you get a unified operations view across all your sites and services. Cisco Nexus Dashboard scales out based on the size, number of sites, and the operational services used to manage them.

The Dashboard provides a wholistic view of the Cisco Nexus Dashboard. You can use this view to monitor system health, sites, and the connectivity status of applications. Figure 1-10 shows the Cisco Nexus Dashboard One View GUI.

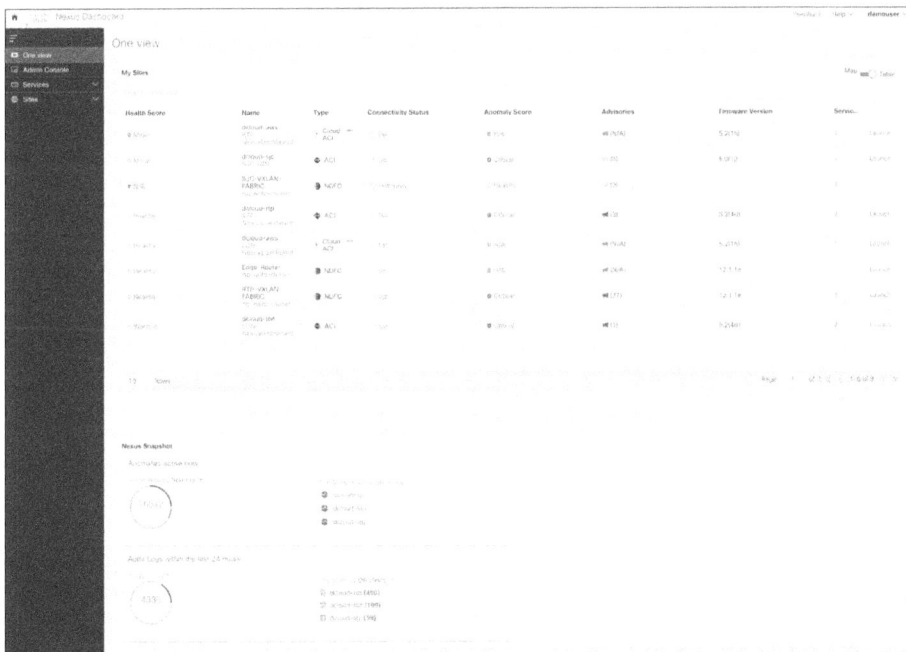

Figure 1-10 *Cisco Nexus Dashboard One View GUI*

Cisco Nexus Dashboard Orchestrator

More than ever, applications are critical for all global organizations. Applications and the data they carry are at the heart of digital transformation, providing not only essential back-office systems of record but also increasing frontline systems of engagement. As businesses grow, it is imperative to have agility in applications—to have the ability to move applications wherever the business needs them and to be sure that network security policies follow. With the unprecedented changes brought on recent years around the world, organizations see the necessity of having a connected and secure data center, wherever the data may exist.

Cisco Nexus Dashboard now supports onboarding of Cisco NX-OS/DCNM sites. Cisco Nexus Dashboard Orchestrator (formerly Cisco Multi-Site Orchestrator-MSO) offers multisite networking orchestration and policy management, disaster recovery and high availability, as well as provisioning and health monitoring.

Cisco Nexus Dashboard Orchestrator (NDO) allows operators to realize a true hybrid cloud scenario, defining and orchestrating network policy across DCNM, ACI, cloud, and edge domains. NDO will also be the first application to work across both Cisco ACI and DCNM sites, making Nexus Dashboard a single pane of glass across Cisco ACI/APIC and Cisco NX-OS/DCNM controllers. Figure 1-11 shows the Cisco Nexus Dashboard Orchestrator.

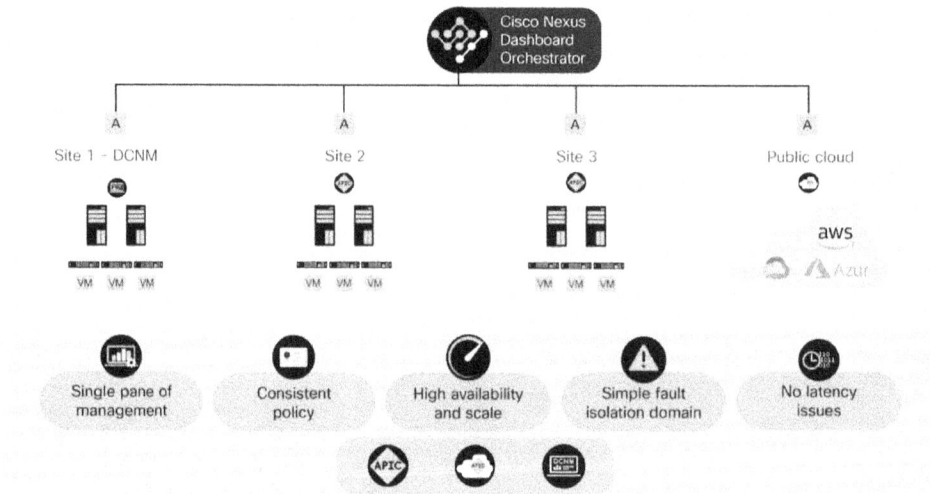

Figure 1-11 *Cisco Nexus Dashboard Orchestrator*

NDO allows you to interconnect separate Cisco ACI sites, Cisco Cloud ACI sites, and Cisco Data Center Network Manager (DCNM) sites, each managed by its own controller (APIC cluster, DCNM cluster, or Cloud APIC instances in a public cloud).

The on-premises sites (ACI or DCNM in the future) can be extended to different public clouds for hybrid-cloud deployments or for cloud-first multicloud-only deployments between cloud sites that do not have an on-premises site.

■ **Cisco ACI Multi-Site:** For Cisco ACI, Nexus Dashboard Orchestrator is the intersite policy manager. It provides single-pane management, enabling you to monitor the health-score state of all interconnected sites. It also allows you to define, in a centralized place, all intersite policies, which can then be pushed to different APIC domains for rendering them on the physical switches in those fabrics. This provides a high degree of control over when and where to deploy the policies, which in turn allows the tenant change domain separation that uniquely characterizes the Cisco Multi-Site architecture. With Nexus Dashboard Orchestrator, you can extend your policies to any site or multiple public clouds.

■ **Cisco DCNM Multi-Site:** Cisco Data Center Network Manager (DCNM) is the network management platform for all NX-OS-enabled deployments, spanning new fabric architectures, IP Fabric for Media, and storage networking deployments. It provides automation, visibility, and consistency within a DCNM-clustered fabric. Nexus Dashboard Orchestrator now enables network policy consistency and disaster recovery across multiple DCNM fabrics around the world through a single pane of glass and scale-out DCNM leaf switches to thousands of switches managed using one centralized policy.

Common Use Cases

This section discusses some of the several use cases of Nexus Dashboard Orchestrator, including large-scale data center deployment, data center interconnectivity, Cisco NDO multidomain integrations, hybrid cloud and multicloud, and service provider/5G telco.

Large-Scale Data Center Deployment

Some users require a data center solution based on software-defined networking (SDN) that consists of a higher number of leaf switches (for example, 20,000) with a single management console for provisioning, orchestration, and policy consistency. Cisco NDO can meet these requirements to help build these large-scale data centers through the following:

■ Easy provisioning and orchestration

■ Disaster recovery and high availability

■ Enhanced scale

■ Business continuity

Figure 1-12 illustrates a Cisco NDO large-scale data center deployment.

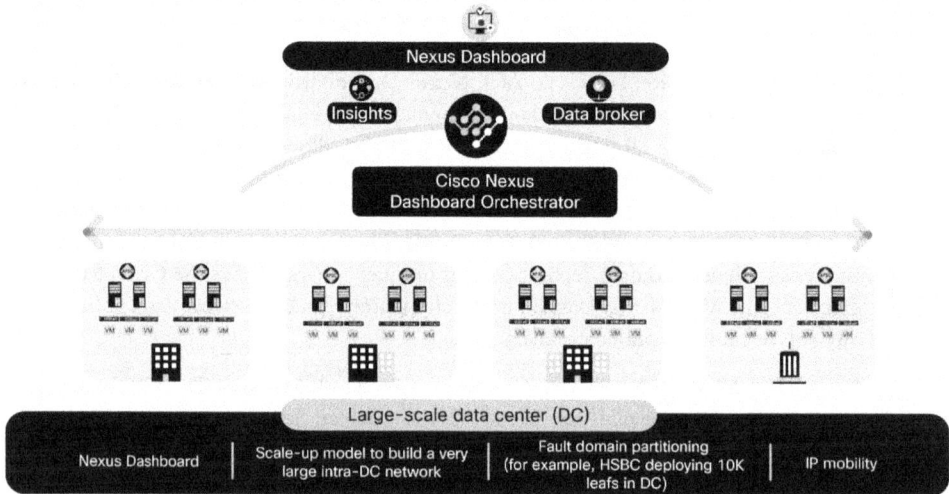

Figure 1-12   *Large-scale data center deployment*

Data Center Interconnectivity

Cisco NDO extends intersite connectivity and network policy segmentation between loosely coupled data centers across multiple geographies, enabling agile deployment where policies and security follow the movement of virtual machines across data centers. In addition, it enhances disaster recovery or active-active use cases spread across multiple sites and locations. Figure 1-13 illustrates data center interconnectivity using Cisco NDO.

Cisco NDO Multidomain Integrations

Large and medium-sized organizations that have adopted a multisite approach to their data centers have experienced performance degradation with unmanaged connections between the separate data centers. To assist customers with managing this, Cisco NDO has been integrated with Cisco's SD-WAN. Figure 1-14 illustrates multidomain integrations using Cisco NDO.

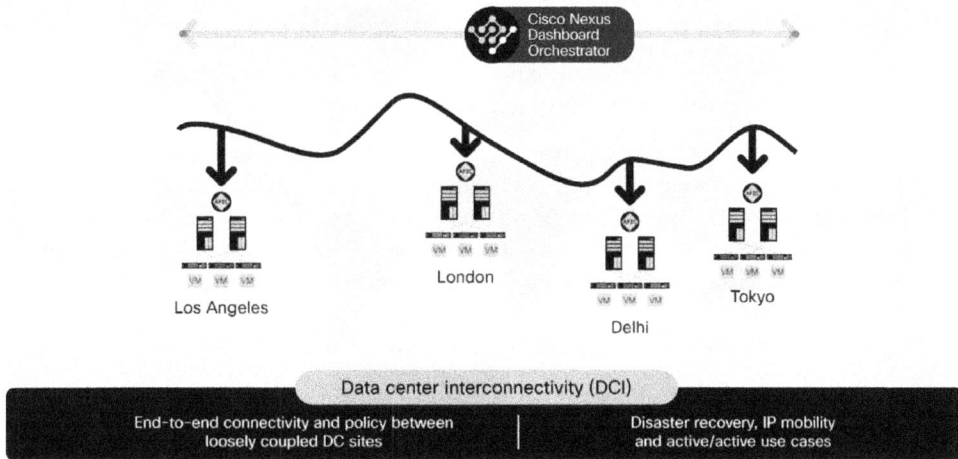

Figure 1-13 *Data center interconnectivity*

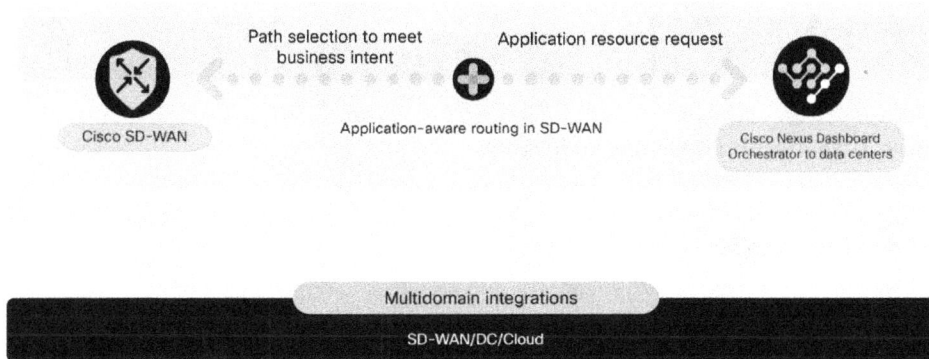

Figure 1-14 *Multidomain integrations*

Hybrid Cloud and Multicloud

Cisco NDO expands networking functions to cloud sites and automates the creation of overlay connectivity between all sites (on-premises and in the public cloud).

As the central orchestrator of intersite policies, Cisco NDO allows for pushing the same policies to multiple data centers and public clouds across the globe in a single step.

Cisco NDO supports Cisco ACI policy extensions to the public cloud (AWS and Azure), allowing for hybrid cloud and multicloud deployments. In both cases, NDO enables automated and secure interconnect provisioning, consistent policy enforcement for on-premises sites and the public cloud, and simplified operations for end-to-end visibility. Figure 1-15 illustrates hybrid cloud and multicloud orchestration using Cisco NDO.

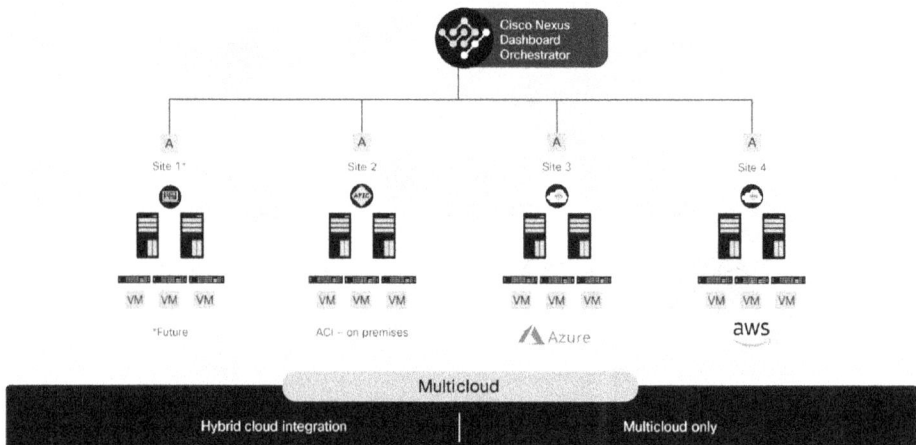

Figure 1-15 *Hybrid cloud and multicloud*

Service Provider/5G Telco

5G transformations are challenging telecom providers to develop data center networks of the future that can seamlessly scale, automate, and integrate their infrastructure from the central data center to the edge and across the transport network.

Cisco NDO provides the following:

- Automation of SR-MPLS policies that can be centrally orchestrated across the 5G telco cloud sites (central, regional, and edge data centers).

- Consistent SR-MPLS handoff transport and application slice interworking between 5G telco cloud sites and the service provider's transport backbone.

Figure 1-16 illustrates centralized DC orchestration for 5G using Cisco NDO.

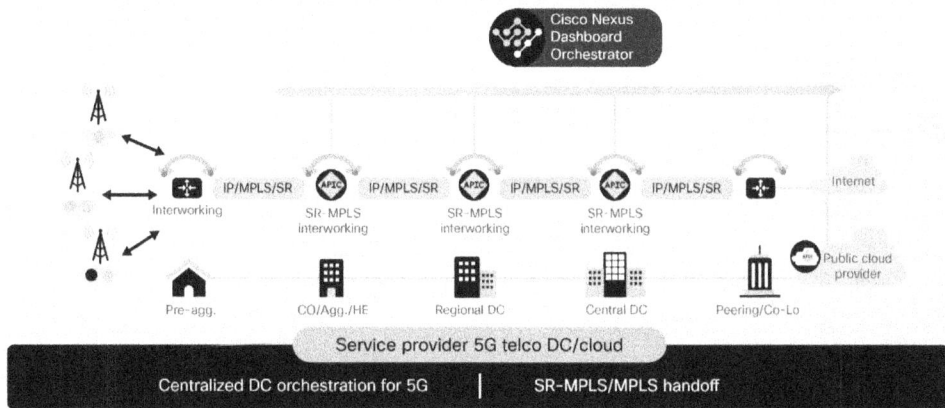

Figure 1-16 *Service provider/5G telco*

Functions Provided by the Nexus Dashboard Orchestrator

Cisco NDO provides the following main functions:

- Create and manage Cisco Multi-Site Orchestrator users and administrators through application of RBAC rules.

- Add, delete, and modify Cisco ACI/DCNM sites.

- Use the health dashboard to monitor the health, faults, and logs of intersite policies for all the Cisco ACI fabrics that are part of the Cisco Multi-Site domain. The health-score information is retrieved from each APIC domain and presented in a unified way.

  Figure 1-17 shows the Cisco NDO health-score information GUI.

- Provision Day 0 infrastructure to allow the spine switches at all Cisco ACI sites to peer and connect with each other. This feature allows the system to establish MP-BGP EVPN control-plane reachability and exchange endpoint host information (MAC and IPv4/IPv6 addresses).

- Create new tenants and deploy them in all the connected sites (or a subset of them).

- Define policy templates. Each template can be associated with and pushed to a specific set of fabrics.

Figure 1-18 illustrates the Cisco NDO schema, template, and sites.

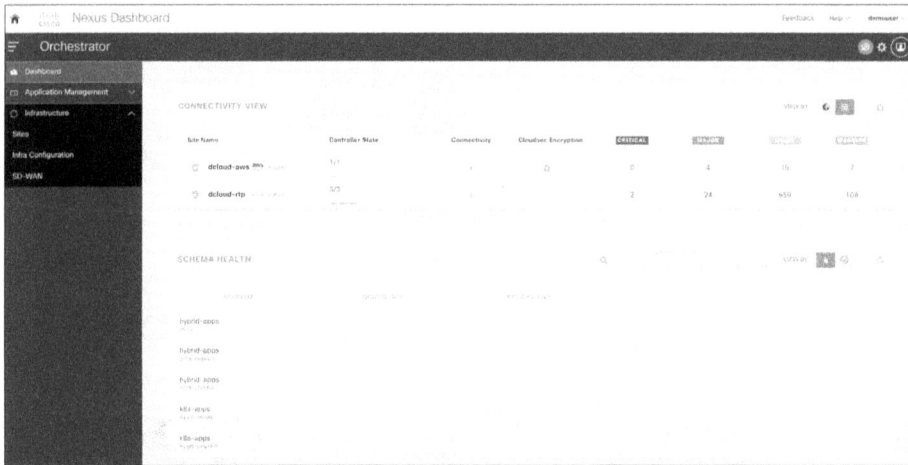

Figure 1-17   *Cisco NDO health-score information GUI*

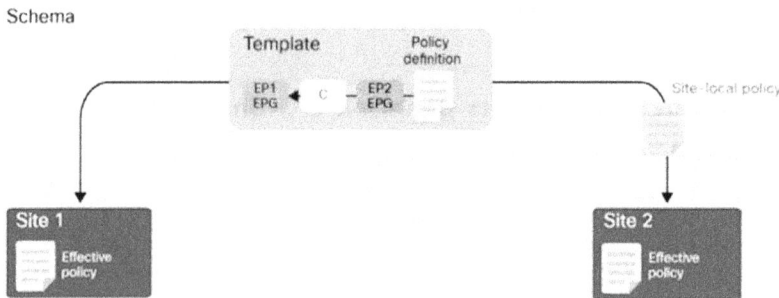

Figure 1-18   *Cisco NDO schema, template, and sites*

Note   One or more templates can be grouped together as part of a schema, which can be considered a "container" of policies. However, the association of policies to a given tenant is always done at the template level (not at the schema level). This feature is one of the most important that the Cisco Multi-Site Orchestrator offers, together with the capability to define and provision scoped policies for change management. When you define intersite policies, Cisco Multi-Site Orchestrator also properly programs the required namespace translation rules on the Multi-Site-capable spine switches across sites. As mentioned in the previous section, every intersite communication requires the creation of translation entries on the spine nodes of each fabric part of the Multi-Site domain. This happens only when the policy to allow intersite communication is defined on the Multi-Site Orchestrator and then pushed to the different APIC cluster managing the fabrics. As a consequence, the best-practice recommendation is to manage the configuration of all the tenant objects [EPGs (Endpoint Group), BDs (Bridge Domain), and so on] directly on MSO, independent from the fact that those objects are stretched across multiple sites or locally defined in a specific site.

■ Import tenant policies from an already deployed Cisco ACI fabric (a brownfield deployment) and stretch them to another, newly deployed site (a greenfield deployment).

Deployment of Cisco Nexus Dashboard Orchestrator

The Cisco Nexus Dashboard Orchestrator design is based on a microservices architecture in which the NDO functionalities are deployed across clustered nodes working together in an active-active fashion. The Cisco NDO services communicate with the interface of the APIC nodes deployed in different sites. Depending on the specific version of NDO deployed, the communication with the APIC clusters will be established to the out-of-band (OOB) interface, the in-band (IB) interface, or both. NDO also provides northbound access through Representational State Transfer (REST) APIs or the GUI (that is, HTTPS), which allows you to manage the full lifecycle of networking and tenant policies that need to be deployed across sites. Figure 1-19 illustrates Cisco NDO services communication with APIC nodes.

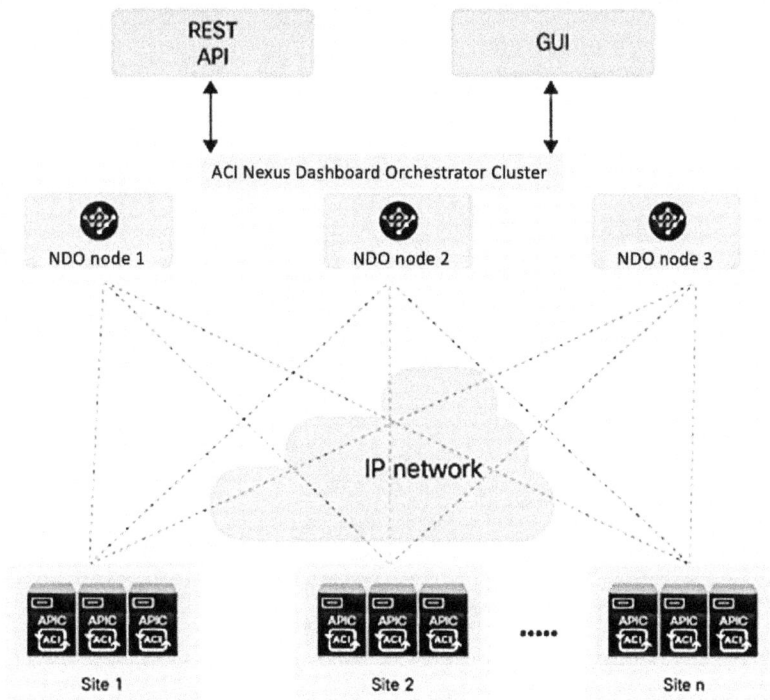

Figure 1-19   *Cisco NDO services communication with APIC nodes*

With Cisco NDO 3.2, you can deploy Cisco Orchestrator using the Cisco Nexus Dashboard platform. Figure 1-20 shows the Cisco NDO app on Nexus Dashboard.

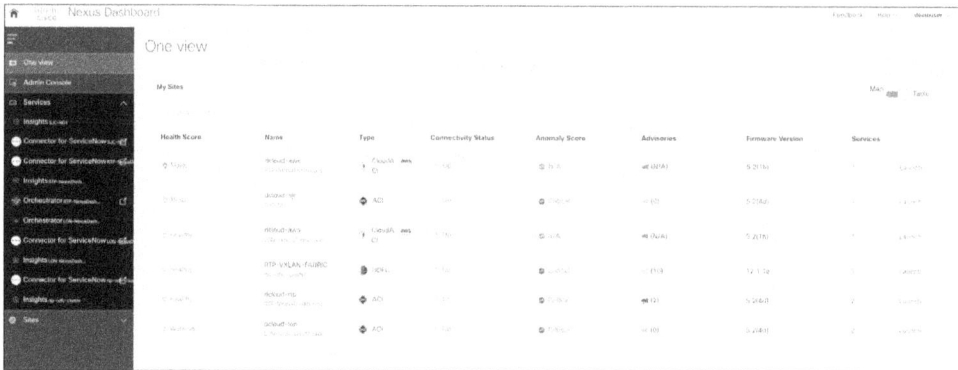

Figure 1-20   *Cisco NDO app on Nexus Dashboard*

You can view the installed NDO app on the Nexus Dashboard, as shown in Figure 1-21.

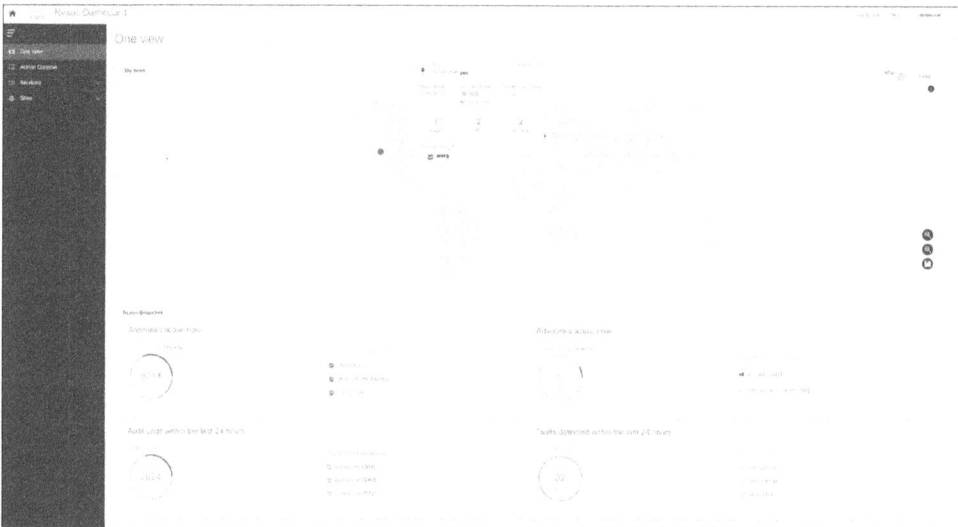

Figure 1-21   *Cisco NDO on Nexus Dashboard*

Add ACI/DCNM Sites

Use the following steps to add DCNM sites to Cisco Nexus Dashboard Orchestrator:

Step 1.   Log in to the Nexus Dashboard GUI.

Step 2.   Add a new site. Figure 1-22 shows the Cisco NDO Add Site feature.

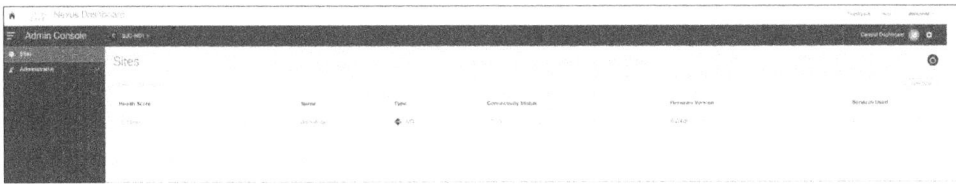

Figure 1-22 *Cisco NDO Add Site feature*

> **1.** From the left navigation menu, select **Admin Console > Sites.**
>
> **2.** In the top right of the main pane, select **Add Site.**

Step 3.   Provide site information, as shown in Figure 1-23.

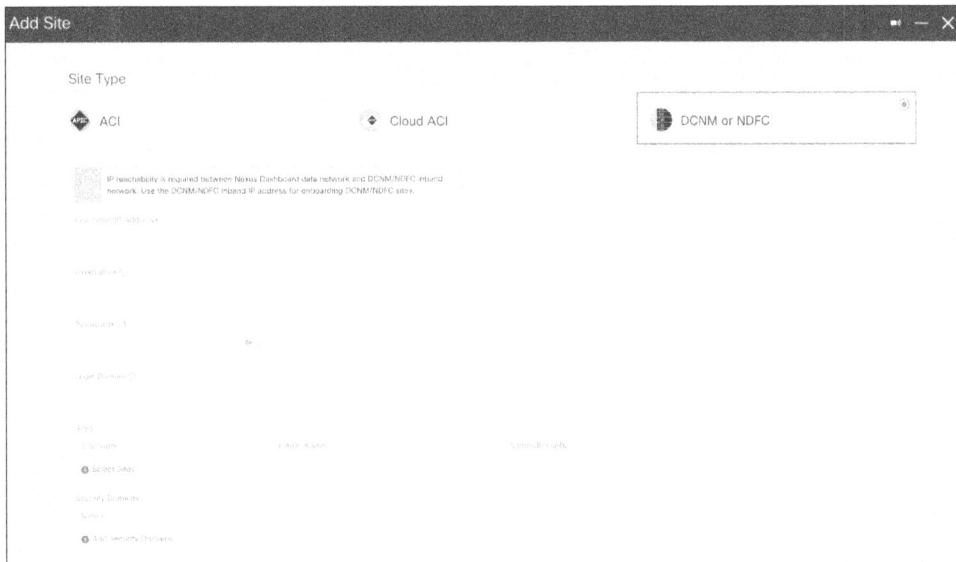

Figure 1-23 *Cisco NDO site information*

For Site Type, select **DCNM.**

> **1.** Provide the DCNM controller information.
>
> **2.** You need to provide the hostname/IP address of the in-band (eth2) interface as well as the username and password for the DCNM controller currently managing your DCNM fabrics.
>
> **3.** Click **Select Sites** to select the specific fabrics managed by the DCNM controller.

The fabric selection window will open.

Step 4.   Select the fabrics you want to add to the Nexus Dashboard.

Figure 1-24 illustrates Cisco NDO fabric selection.

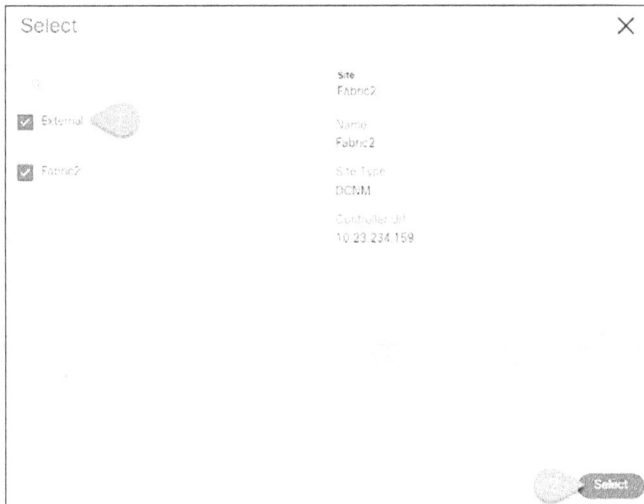

Figure 1-24   *Cisco NDO fabric selection*

1. Check one or more fabrics you want to be available to the applications running in your Nexus Dashboard.

2. Click **Select**.

Step 5.   In the Add Site window, click **Add** to finish adding the sites.

At this time, the sites will be available in the Nexus Dashboard, but you still need to enable them for Nexus Dashboard Orchestrator management, as described in the following section. Repeat the previous steps for any additional DCNM controllers.

Manage Sites Using Cisco Nexus Dashboard Orchestrator

Use the following steps to manage sites via Cisco Nexus Dashboard Orchestrator:

Step 1.   From the Nexus Dashboard's **Service** option, open the **Nexus Dashboard Orchestrator** service.

You will be automatically logged in using the Nexus Dashboard user's credentials.

Step 2.   In the **Nexus Dashboard Orchestrator** GUI, manage the sites, as shown in Figure 1-25.

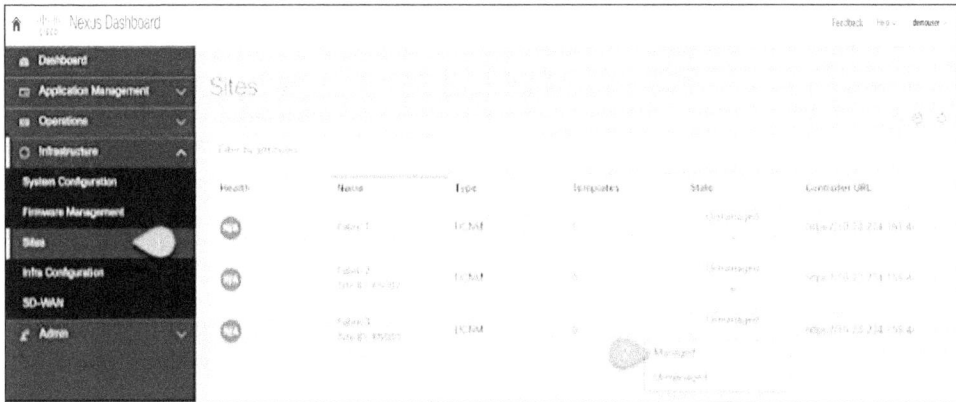

Figure 1-25 *Cisco NDO site management*

1. From the left navigation menu, select **Infrastructure > Sites**.

2. In the main pane, change the State from **Unmanaged** to **Managed** for each fabric that you want the NDO to manage.

   If the fabric you are managing is part of a DCNM Multi-Site Domain (MSD), it will have a Site ID already associated with it. In this case, simply changing the State to Managed will manage the fabric.

   However, if the fabric is not part of a DCNM MSD, you will also be prompted to provide a Fabric ID for the site when you change its state to Managed.

Cisco Nexus Dashboard Fabric Controller

Businesses are seeing enormous change, and to cope with this change they have relied on IT and especially on their network environments. Networks have had to become simpler, more agile, more proactive, and more intuitive. Long gone are the days when a network administrator manually configured every switch. Cisco Nexus Dashboard Fabric Controller (NDFC), formerly Cisco Data Center Network Manager (DCNM), has helped address many of the challenges of managing Cisco NX-OS switches. NDFC empowers IT to move at the increasing speed required of your business. With NDFC, you get complete automation, extensive visibility, and consistent operations for your data center.

Cisco Nexus Dashboard Fabric Controller (NDFC) provides granular, scalable visibility for deep-dive troubleshooting, functionality, and maintenance operations that benefit data center operation teams. Cisco NDFC makes fabric management simple and reliable. Also, Cisco NDFC meets ever-growing scalability needs with the integration of Cisco Nexus Dashboard Orchestrator (NDO).

NDFC is the comprehensive management and automation solution for all Cisco Nexus and Cisco Multilayer Distributed Switching (MDS) platforms powered by Cisco NX-OS.

NDFC provides management, automation, control, monitoring, and integration for deployments spanning LAN, SAN, and IP Fabric for Media (IPFM) fabrics. SAN administrators are some of the busiest engineers in the data center and need to manage and maintain a wide variety of storage networking switches, directors, and storage arrays. Cisco NDFC makes the management and maintenance of the data center easier and less complex for the administrators.

- **Management:** NDFC provides fabric-oriented configuration and operations management. It is optimized for large deployments with little overhead, but traditional deployments are supported and can be customized by the user to meet business needs. NDFC also provides representational state transfer (RESTful) APIs to allow easy integration from Cisco or third-party overlay managers and enable the automation to meet customers' needs.

- **Automation:** NDFC brings an easy-to-understand and simple deployment approach to bootstrapping new fabrics. Cisco's best practices are built into the fabric builder policy templates, and automatic bootstrap occurs with the click of a button, reducing provisioning times and simplifying deployments.

- **Monitoring and visualization:** NDFC maintains the active topology monitoring views per fabric into the new NDFC user interface (UI). When combined with Cisco's Nexus Dashboard Insights (NDI), customers can complement their solution with advanced support for Day 2 operations. Cisco Nexus Dashboard Orchestrator (NDO) allows operators to realize a true hybrid cloud scenario, defining and orchestrating network policy across DCNM, ACI, cloud, and edge domains. NDO will also be the first application to work across both Cisco ACI and DCNM sites, making Nexus Dashboard a single pane of glass across Cisco ACI/APIC and Cisco NX-OS/DCNM controllers.

Figure 1-26 illustrates Cisco NDFC comprehensive management.

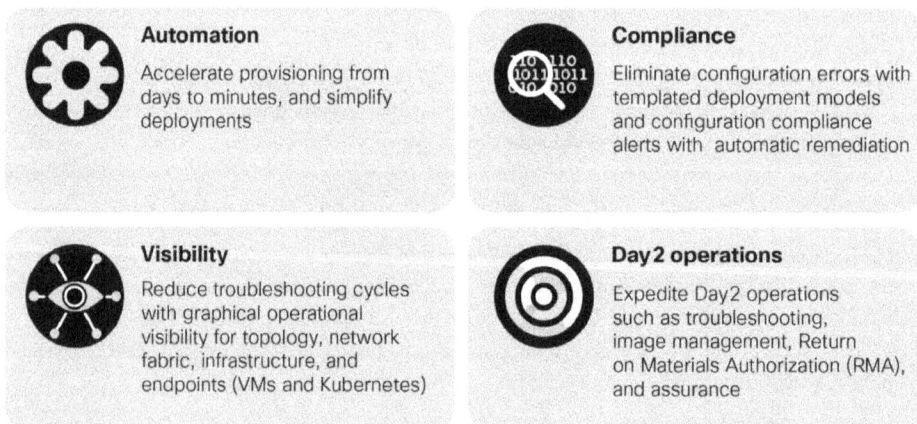

Automation
Accelerate provisioning from days to minutes, and simplify deployments

Compliance
Eliminate configuration errors with templated deployment models and configuration compliance alerts with automatic remediation

Visibility
Reduce troubleshooting cycles with graphical operational visibility for topology, network fabric, infrastructure, and endpoints (VMs and Kubernetes)

Day 2 operations
Expedite Day 2 operations such as troubleshooting, image management, Return on Materials Authorization (RMA), and assurance

Figure 1-26   *Cisco NDFC comprehensive management*

Cisco NDFC Benefits and Features

Cisco Nexus Dashboard Fabric Controller (NDFC) provides granular, scalable visibility for deep-dive troubleshooting, functionality, and maintenance operations that benefit data center operation teams. Cisco NDFC makes fabric management simple and reliable.

Benefits

Cisco NDFC empowers IT to move at the increasing speed required by the business.

- Provides complete lifecycle management and automation for Cisco Nexus and Cisco MDS platforms

- Streamlines data center automation and centralizes applications with Cisco Nexus Dashboard

- Reduces deployment time of VXLAN-EVPN fabrics to minutes

- Improves fabric reliability with constant monitoring of compliance and health

- Reduces operation errors with predefined deployment models

- Monitors and alerts operators to failure conditions

- Enables visualization of multiple fabrics with intuitive topology

Figure 1-27 illustrates Cisco NDFC Platform overview.

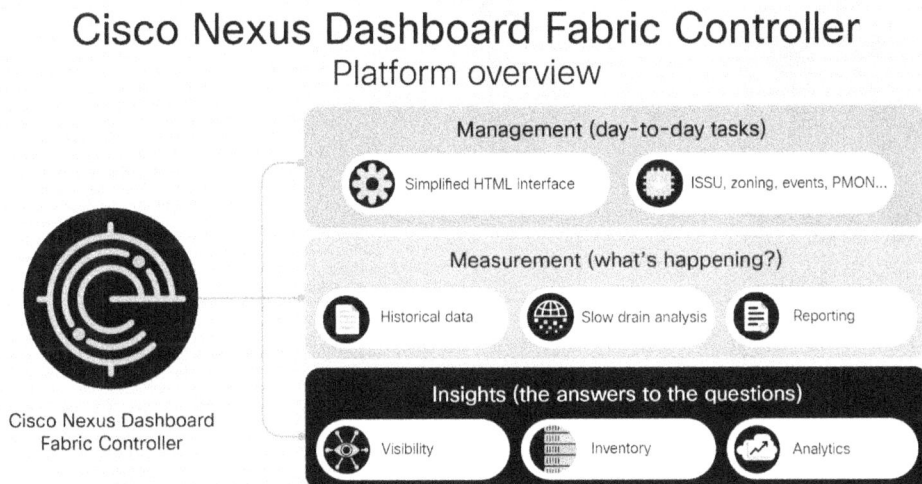

Figure 1-27   *Cisco NDFC Platform overview*

Features

With NDFC, you get complete automation, extensive visibility, and consistent operations for your data center.

■ **Cisco NDFC App:** Cisco NDFC is designed with an HTML-based web UI, which is the main interface for the product. NDFC 12.0 is fully integrated and will run exclusively as a service on the Cisco Nexus Dashboard (ND), providing a single sign-on and simplified user experience across the entire data center software portfolio. Scale and performance were top of mind in the development of NDFC and, as such, included modern architectures that incorporate microservices and containerization of functions to help ensure reliability and allow for growth over time.

Figure 1-28 shows the Cisco NDFC app.

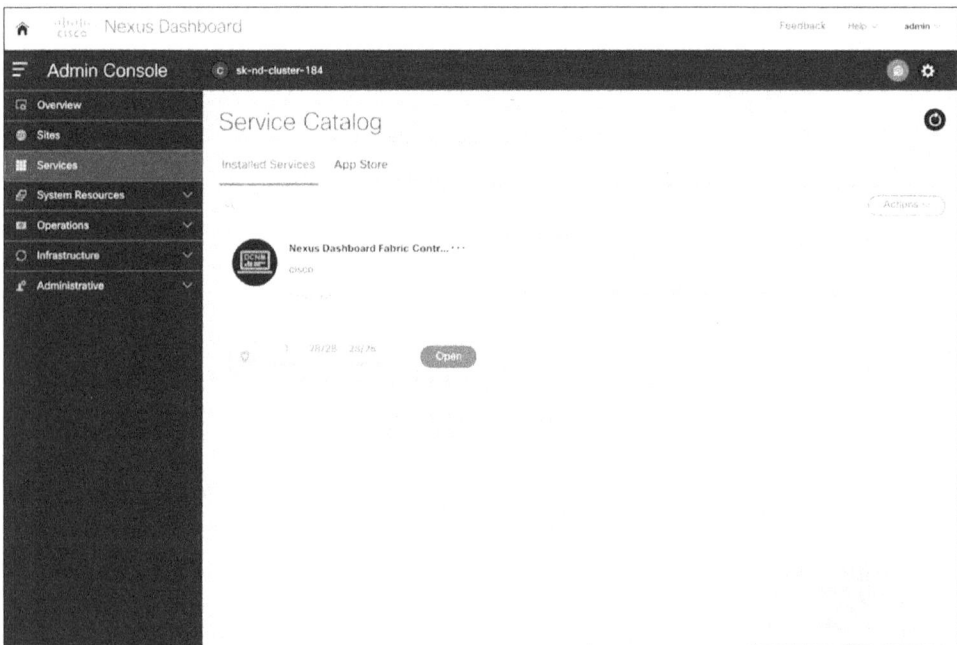

Figure 1-28   *Cisco NDFC app*

NDFC is now a complete microservices architecture on Nexus Dashboard that is based on Kubernetes. By moving away from a monolithic infrastructure to a containerized and modular one, users will be able to leverage this new model to enable elastic scale-out. NDFC will also support active-active high availability with L2 reachability for three-node clusters. Along with this update, NDFC will implement a new look and feel with an intuitive React JavaScript GUI that aligns with Nexus Dashboard GUI and supports modernized topology views. Figure 1-29 shows the Cisco NDFC Topology view.

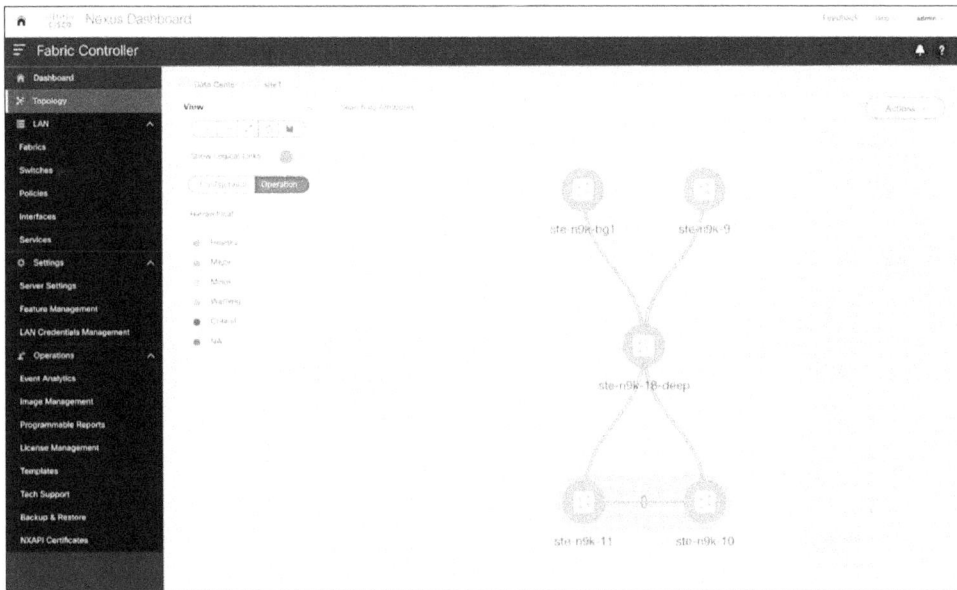

Figure 1-29 *Cisco NDFC Topology view*

■ **Feature manager:** With NDFC, you will no longer have to select a mode for LAN, SAN, or IPFM at the time of installation. Instead, NDFC has a runtime feature installer. This feature management capability will allow you to selectively enable or disable different features, including Fabric Controller (LAN), SAN, IPFM, and Fabric Discovery. Figure 1-30 illustrates enabling/disabling features from the NDFC feature manager.

■ **Nexus Dashboard Fabric Discovery capability:** NDFC now includes a base capability selection for Fabric Discovery. Fabric Discovery is a lightweight version of NDFC and, when enabled, will support monitoring, discovery, and inventory only. Configuration provisioning will not be supported when this option is selected. This option allows users who are using NDFC for monitoring or Day 2 Ops to minimize resource utilization and further customize NDFC for their specific needs.

■ **Compute visibility on Fabric Topology view:** NDFC integrates VMware topology onto its dynamic topology views. You simply "discover" a VCenter that controls the host-based networking on the fabric to show how the virtual machine, host, and virtual switches are interconnected. This is a great benefit for the network operator since it gives compute visibility, which is ordinarily the purview of compute administration. Figure 1-31 illustrates NDFC fabric view.

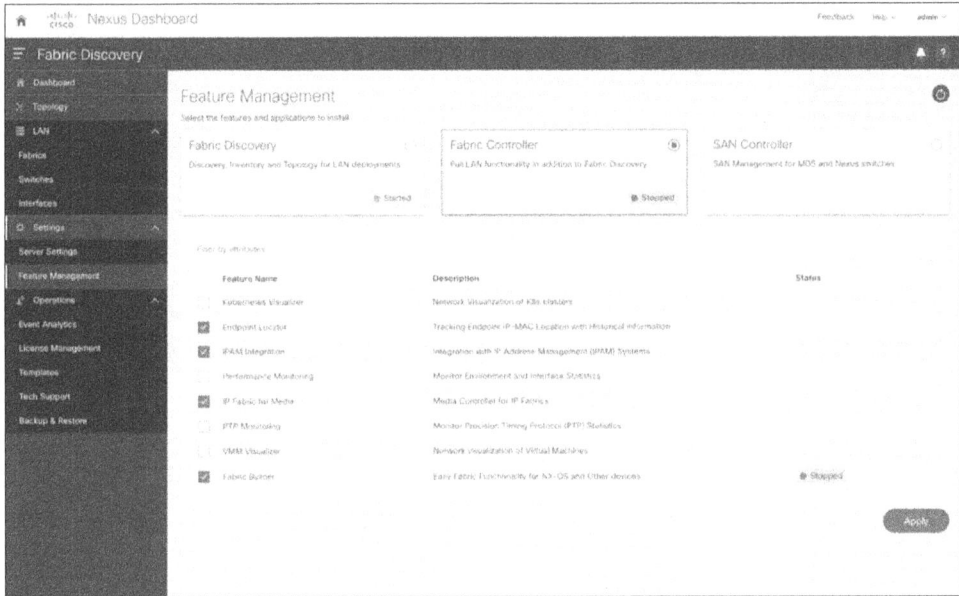

Figure 1-30   *Enabling/disabling features from the NDFC feature manager*

Cisco Nexus Dashboard Fabric Controller
Data center fabric view

Network: Cisco Nexus and MDS fabrics	Nexus 5K, 7K, 9K	MDS 9100, 9200, 9300, 9500, 9700
Compute: Cisco UCS	Visualize and gather data on fabric interconnect	
Virtual Compute: VMware	Visualize vCenter servers, virtual servers, CPU, disk latency network, and SAN traffic	
Storage arrays: Block and file	EMC, IBM, HDS, NetApp, PURESTORAGE	

Figure 1-31   *NDFC fabric view*

■ **Revamped image management:** Large networks need to be maintained efficiently. NDFC has fully redesigned image management, making upgrades easy and less time consuming. This new easy and customizable workflow will be for device upgrades/ downgrades, patching, EPLD (Electronic Programmable Logic Device) image upgrades, software maintenance updates (SMUs), and more. NDFC will continue to support maintenance-mode and RMA (Return Material Authorization) actions right on the actual topology display. You can put a switch into maintenance mode and swap serial numbers with a replacement unit with a few clicks.

- **Smart licensing policy:** Implementation of Smart Licensing Policy (SLP) with NDFC will further enhance the current smart licensing capabilities. SLP aims to increase ease of use by enforcing fewer restrictions with a goal of reducing the overall license friction.

- **Non-Nexus platform support (IOS-XE and IOS-XR):** For Cisco IOS XE platform Catalyst 9000 Series Switches, NDFC supports VXLAN EVPN automation. With this new fabric builder template with built-in best practices, you can extend your VXLAN EVPN overlay networks for greenfield deployments of Catalyst 9K switches.

  NDFC also provides additional support for IOS-XR devices, Cisco ASR 9000 Series Aggregation Services routers, and Cisco Network Convergence System (NCS) 5500 Series devices, to be managed in external fabric in managed mode. NDFC is now able to generate and push configurations to these switches, and configuration compliance will also be enabled for these platforms.

- **Granular role-based access control (RBAC) model for existing roles:** With NDFC, RBAC is orchestrated directly in the Nexus Dashboard. The current RBAC roles will continue to be supported, but the granularity for these roles will be increased, allowing you to assign different roles to various users on a per-fabric level. For example, one user could be a network administrator for one fabric while being a network stager for another.

- **Programmable reports for performance monitoring:** NDFC previously introduced programmable reports, which provided detailed information on devices. A new template will be added to support NDFC in generating these programmable reports for performance monitoring. These reports can be used for LAN, IPFM, and SAN deployments. You are also able to email these generated reports to users.

- **Multitenancy VRF:** This feature brings in VRF support for NBM deployments, where you can logically isolate multiple customers so that they can co-exist on the same fabric. Multiple VRFs can be enabled in IPFM NBM-active mode.

- **Fabric builder for IPFM:** To ease IPFM network provisioning, NDFC supports availability of preconfigured policy templates that were created with best practices in mind in order to build IPFM underlay in minutes. Using IP throughout your operation relieves you from the very rigid frame format dependency, creating a dynamic network that allows you to allocate resources upon need and future-proof your business!

- **NDFC SAN Insights brings SAN analytics to life:** One of NDFC's most important features is SAN Insights, which provides collection and visualization of the MDS SAN analytics capabilities. This feature provides insight into end-to-end flow-based metrics, custom graphing, outlier detection, ECT analysis, summary dashboards, and anomaly detection. Anomaly detection, the newest feature, provides a fully customizable infrastructure that can be used to identify and alert on issues captured by the SAN Insights capabilities. SAN Insights also includes new infrastructure to help consume all the new streaming telemetry data available on the new 64Gbps and 32Gbps MDS switches from Cisco. Figure 1-32 shows NDFC SAN Insights.

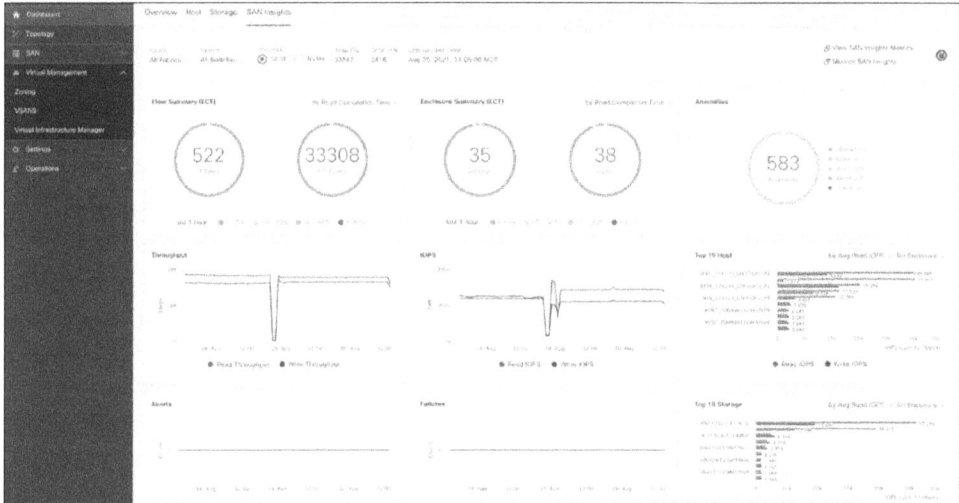

Figure 1-32 *NDFC SAN Insights*

Figure 1-33 illustrates NDFC SAN analysis.

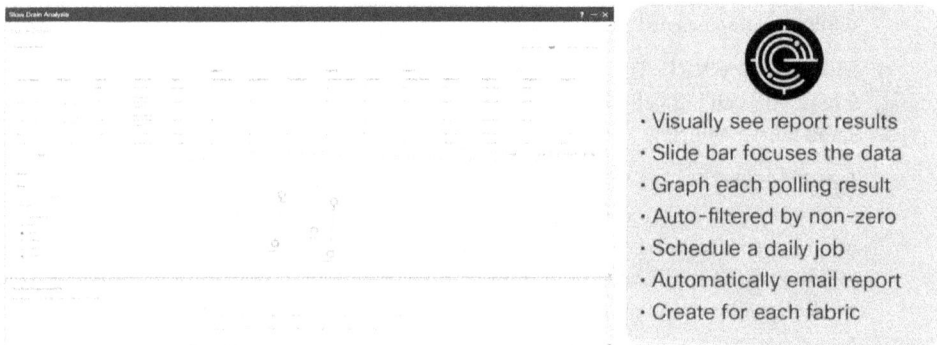

Cisco Nexus Dashboard Fabric Controller
Slow drain analysis

- Visually see report results
- Slide bar focuses the data
- Graph each polling result
- Auto-filtered by non-zero
- Schedule a daily job
- Automatically email report
- Create for each fabric

Figure 1-33 *NDFC SAN analysis*

■ **Dynamic ingress rate limiting:** NDFC also plays an important part of integrating some of the most modern software features Cisco has created that help to eliminate congestion in SAN fabrics. NDFC provides an interface to fully configure dynamic ingress rate limiting (DIRL) so that any congestion in the fabric can be eliminated automatically and with almost no impact on performance. DIRL can help with both credit starvation and over-utilization situations, which can have big implications on the SAN fabric, by controlling the rate of frames from the culprit in the fabric while at the same time reducing the impact to all of the victims. NDFC plays an important role in helping to simplify the deployment of DIRL so that it can be implemented quickly to easily solve the dreaded slow drain condition.

■ **Optics information for SAN interfaces:** NDFC introduces a new interface that allows customers to see trends in optics temperature and power over time. This is a powerful new feature that provides insight into how optics are working across time, and it can help to reduce individual outages that are so often due to optics failures. Figure 1-34 shows the NDFC SAN optics interface.

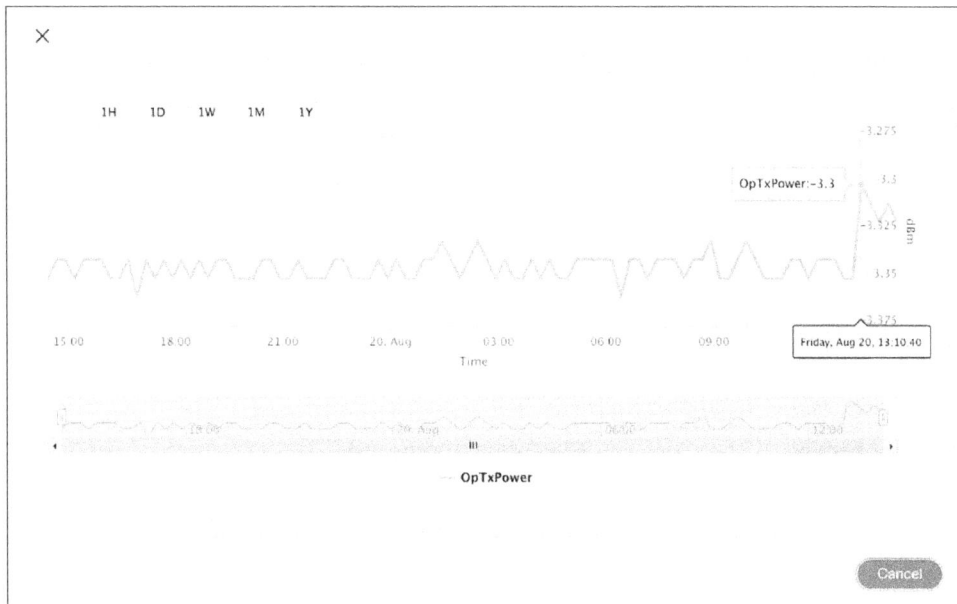

Figure 1-34   *NDFC SAN optics interface*

■ **New zoning interface:** NDFC has reinvented the way customers will perform SAN zoning in the future. This includes a new interface in the web UI that focuses on managing regular and IVR zones. This is a feature that many customers use every day, and, as such, Cisco worked on the look and feel and the navigation of the zoning interface to make the data easier to use and faster to deploy correctly. Figure 1-35 shows the NDFC SAN zoning interface.

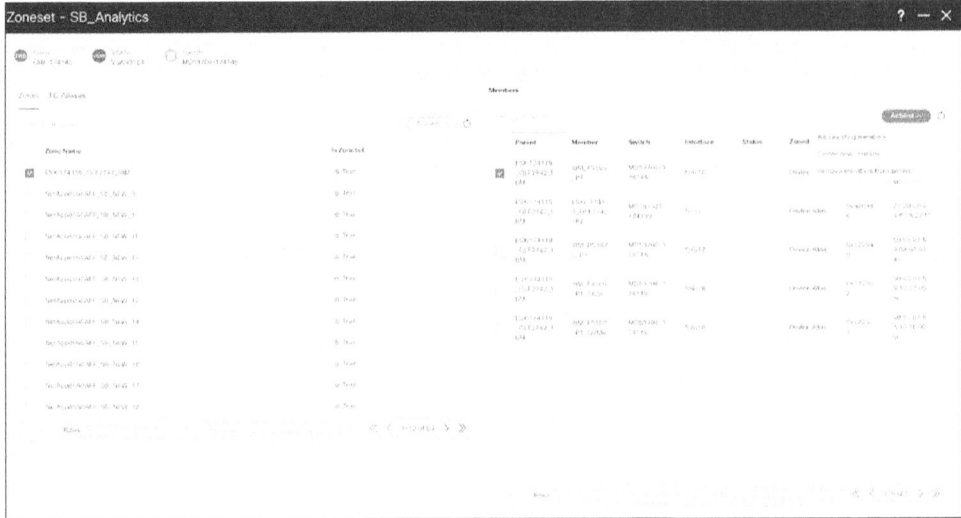

Figure 1-35 *NDFC SAN zoning interface*

Platform Support Information

Table 1-2 lists platform support details for Cisco Nexus switches and MDS storage switches.

Table 1-2 *Platform Support Information*

Product Family	Platforms Supported
Cisco Nexus switches	Cisco NDFC supports most current Nexus switch family product offerings.
Cisco MDS storage switches	Cisco NDFC supports most current MDS switch family product offerings.

Server Requirements

Cisco NDFC Release 12.x runs on the Nexus Dashboard platform. It is supported on:

- Virtual Nexus Dashboard for LAN, IPFM, and SAN deployments
- Physical Nexus Dashboard for LAN, IPFM, and SAN deployments

Third-party Applications and Cloud-based Services

The intuitive Cisco Nexus Dashboard platform provides services such as Cisco Nexus Dashboard Insights, Cisco Nexus Dashboard Orchestrator, Cisco Nexus Dashboard

Data Broker, and a single operational view of your geographically dispersed multicloud environments. The platform enables the acceleration of NetOps and DevOps capabilities while scaling into the cloud.

Cisco Nexus Dashboard offers a rich suite of services for third-party developers to build applications. REST APIs allow third-party tools to authenticate and integrate with key services such as Nexus Dashboard Insights and Nexus Dashboard Orchestrator. Currently supported third-party integrations in the Nexus Dashboard ecosystem include ServiceNow ITSM/ITOM, Splunk SIEM, HashiCorp Terraform, and RedHat Ansible.

With third-party services integrated in Nexus Dashboard, NetOps can achieve command and control over global network fabrics, optimizing performance and attaining insights into data center and cloud operations. Using Cisco Nexus Dashboard, DevOps can improve the application deployment experience for multicloud applications' Infrastructure as Code (IaC) integrations. Developers describe in code the networking components and resources needed to run an application in a data center or cloud.

Table 1-3 details the Cisco Nexus Dashboard third-party ecosystem.

Table 1-3   *Cisco Nexus Dashboard Third-Party Ecosystem*

Partner	Integration Capability	Applications Link
ServiceNow	Ticketing Automation for Cisco Nexus Dashboard Insights anomalies and advisories, including the ability to filter specific categories and severity.	Cisco Nexus Dashboard Insights App for ServiceNow Platform
	ServiceNow Incident visibility and management on Cisco Nexus Dashboard.	ServiceNow App for Nexus Dashboard
	Visibility into network and application entities and policies defined on the Cisco Nexus Dashboard Orchestrator and business service mapping.	Cisco ACI/Nexus Dashboard Orchestrator App for ServiceNow Platform
Splunk	Real-time and historical monitoring (organization-specific KPIs and dashboards), troubleshooting, cross-tier correlation, and alerting automation for Cisco Nexus Dashboard Insights.	Cisco Nexus Dashboard Insights App for Splunk Cisco Nexus Dashboard Insights Add-on for Splunk
HashiCorp Terraform	Terraform provider to support Cisco Nexus Dashboard Orchestrator Automation.	Terraform Provider for Nexus Dashboard Orchestrator Automation
Red Hat Ansible	Ansible module to support Cisco Nexus Dashboard Orchestrator Automation.	Ansible Collection for Nexus Dashboard Orchestrator Automation

Cisco Nexus Dashboard Open Ecosystem with Splunk

Cisco Nexus Dashboard, along with Nexus Dashboard Insights and Nexus Dashboard Orchestrator, offers a rich suite of platform services, open REST APIs, and Kafka subscription service for third-party developers to build custom applications and integrations. Leveraging these open APIs and platform services, Cisco has released out-of-the-box tools that unlock valuable use cases through integration with Splunk Enterprise.

The Nexus Dashboard Insights and Splunk integration enables customers to gain deeper insights into the operational state of their infrastructure, accelerate troubleshooting, and improve operational efficiency. Some of the benefits include the following:

- Get comprehensive network insights and simplified troubleshooting.

- Visualize real-time, contextually relevant network insights.

- Create automated alerts for network problems, errors, and conflicts.

- Correlate multitier and multidevice anomalies and advisories.

- Perform flexible, query-driven searches for anomalies and advisories over time.

- Analyze trends related to anomalies and advisories over a specified period.

- Create rules that automate the response of the network to recurring events.

Figure 1-36 illustrates Cisco Nexus Dashboard and Splunk integration.

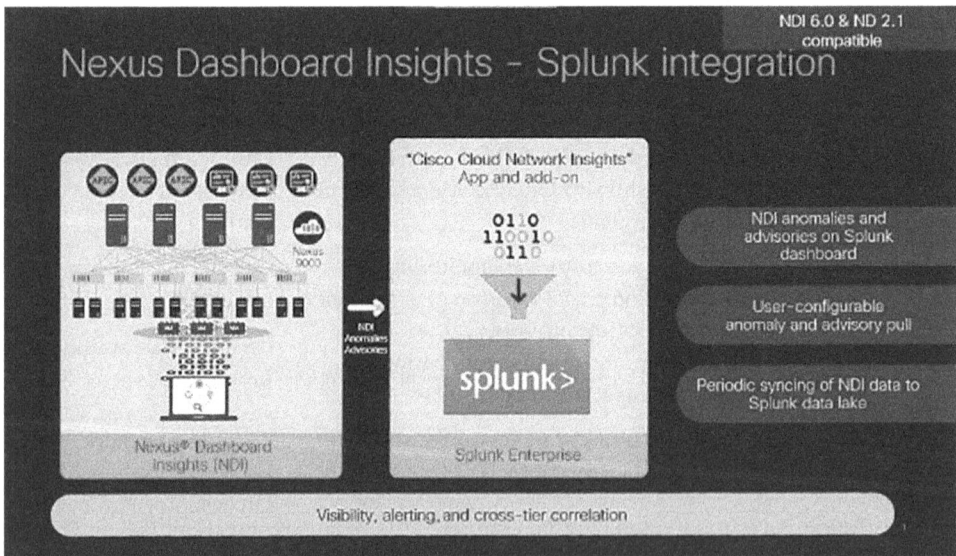

Figure 1-36 *Cisco Nexus Dashboard Splunk integration*

The solution consists of two components: the Cisco Cloud Network Insights add-on and the app for Splunk Enterprise. The add-on ingests rich data related to Nexus Dashboard Insights anomalies and advisories in a Common Information Model–compliant format that enables customers to do the following:

- Monitor unique KPIs and compliance metrics with custom dashboard and drilldowns to monitor specific anomalies and advisories.

- Prevent outages through custom alerting for specific anomalies and advisories.

- Build cross-tier correlations with the data from other tiers, such as applications, compute, and security.

Cisco Nexus Dashboard Open Ecosystem with ServiceNow

In monitoring service health, identifying service disruptions, and aiding problem resolution, cloud-based service management solutions offer critical insights and control. However, they don't have full visibility of the underlying network or all the variables that can cause service disruptions. When complex network problems arise, service management solutions need deeper insights into the intent of the network administrator to pinpoint, characterize, or resolve them. This resolution requires arduous investigation and troubleshooting. When the problem is identified and understood, network administrators must create a ticket, resolve the problem, verify the fix, and close the ticket.

What's needed is a solution involving continuous network insights, assurance, and analytics that can be coupled with cloud-based service-management tools—a solution that can align service and network insights and enable automated, closed-loop incident management, all through a single dashboard. Cisco Nexus Dashboard Insights and ServiceNow integration is that solution. This solution comprises two apps: namely, the ServiceNow app on Nexus Dashboard and the Nexus Insights app on ServiceNow. Some of the benefits of the solution are listed below:

- Comprehensive visibility across incidents over a given time span

- Automatic ticketing and downtime minimization and reduced time to resolution

- Single pane of unified ticket management for Nexus Dashboard operators

Cisco Nexus Dashboard Insights integrates with ServiceNow to provide comprehensive visibility and incident management capabilities spanning IT services as well as the underlying network. Figure 1-37 illustrates Nexus Dashboard Insights ServiceNow integration.

Nexus Dashboard Insights

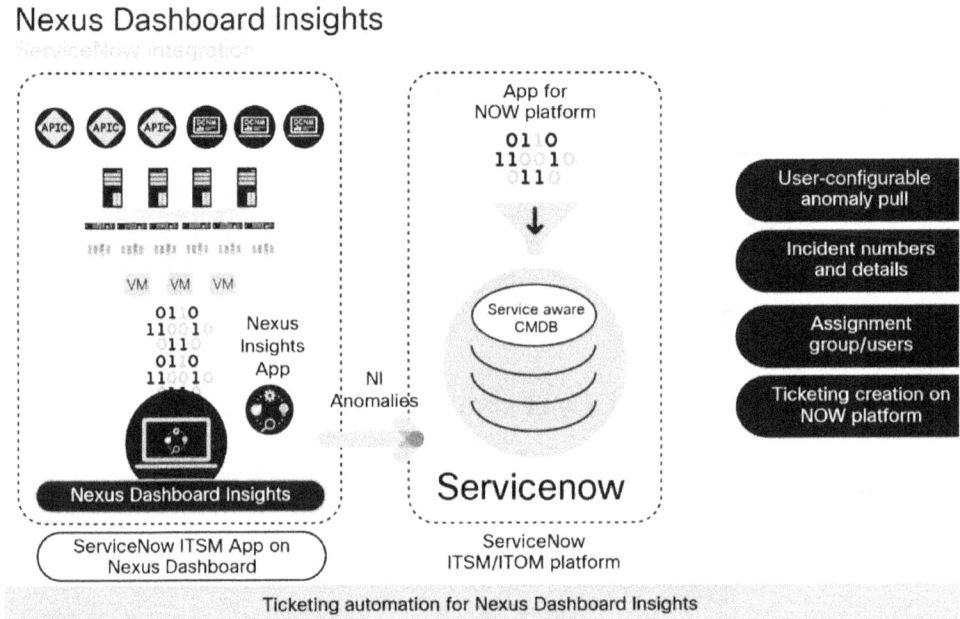

Figure 1-37 *Nexus Dashboard Insights ServiceNow integration*

Nexus Dashboard Insights–generated anomalies are fetched by the ServiceNow ITOM/ITSM platform, and incident tickets are created. The anomalies pulled can be configured by the user. Incidents include incident number, the state of the ticket, details from the anomaly, and assignment group/user. The application extends support for correlating multiple Nexus Dashboard Insights on a single ServiceNow instance. Also, ticketing information is uniform across multiple Nexus Dashboard instances.

With Cisco Nexus Dashboard Insights integration, ServiceNow administrators can predict network outages and vulnerabilities before they affect service performance and can accelerate changes while reducing risk.

The ServiceNow app on Nexus Dashboard (ND) helps manage ServiceNow incidents directly from ND for single pane of glass operations and quicker time to resolution.

Figure 1-38 illustrates the ServiceNow app on Nexus Dashboard.

ServiceNow App (SNA) on Nexus Dashboard (ND)

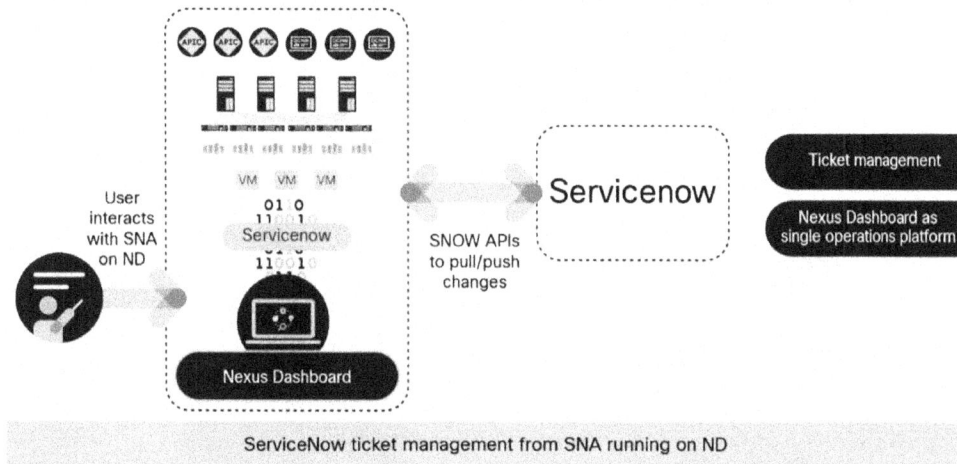

Figure 1-38 *ServiceNow App on Nexus Dashboard*

Summary

Are your operations teams tasked with delivering security, uptime, and business continuity on a complex data center infrastructure? Do they have the right tools that provide proactive change management and precise troubleshooting information tied together in a unified, easy-to-consume user experience? Start powering the transformation of the networking operations teams by standardizing on the Cisco Nexus Dashboard experience. Meet and exceed critical business mandates of agility and availability as you operate your secure, intent-based data center from Cisco Nexus Dashboard.

The new Cisco Nexus Dashboard unleashes a unified experience and automation workflows by standardizing on the Cisco Nexus Dashboard platform (physical/virtual/cloud). Customers can now standardize operations' processes on a single platform, and teams can use advanced visibility, monitoring, orchestration, and deployment services from a unified pane of glass. The Cisco Nexus Dashboard platform can be deployed across the hybrid cloud infrastructure in the form factor of your choosing (physical/virtual or cloud). The Nexus Dashboard platform is extensible. The Cisco Nexus Dashboard platform integrates with third-party services such as ServiceNow and Splunk and also provides the central point for cross-domain integrations.

With Cisco Nexus Dashboard, you can do the following:

■ **Improve experience:** Reduce the time to value for powerful operations capabilities with a consistent UX and a single pane of glass for all native and fabric-agnostic applications.

■ **Increase cost savings and revenue:** Reduce overall network total cost of ownership (TCO) by scaling on a uniform operations infrastructure, and reduce management screen sprawl across data center sites.

■ **Ensure business continuity and compliance:** Quickly debug and resolve root-cause issues.

References/Additional Reading

https://www.cisco.com/c/en/us/support/cloud-systems-management/prime-data-center-network-manager/products-release-notes-list.html

https://www.cisco.com/c/en/us/support/cloud-systems-management/prime-data-center-network-manager/products-device-support-tables-list.html

https://www.cisco.com/c/en/us/support/cloud-systems-management/multi-site-orchestrator/series.html

https://store.servicenow.com/sn_appstore_store.do#!/store/application/56fe817b0f4 caa003ac788cce1050e4d/4.0.0?referer=%2Fstore%2Fsearch%3Flistingtype%3Dall integrations%25253Bancillary_app%25253Bcertified_apps%25253Bcontent%25253 Bindustry_solution%25253Boem%25253Butility%25253Btemplate%26q%3Daci& sl=sh

https://developer.cisco.com/nexusapi/#terraform

https://developer.cisco.com/nexusapi/#ansible

Chapter 2

Cisco Data Center Analytics and Insights

When you have hundreds of network fabrics spread across multiple data centers, it can be extremely challenging to get a full picture of what's happening with contextual details about where, when, and why it's happening. It is critical for IT to have a solution that provides a unified and correlated view of its network infrastructure, endpoints, and events as well as helps prepare companies to progressively transition from reactive to proactive and eventually predictive IT operations.

The networking team should not spend time on understanding data like a data science team. Cisco's API-driven monitoring and assurance solutions provide essential insights along with security compliance benefits. These network insight solutions bring the ability to see the big picture, and if something goes wrong, they show you exactly where to look instead of you poking around and hoping to get lucky.

This chapter will cover following solutions:

- Cisco Nexus Dashboard Insights

- Cisco Network Assurance Engine

- Cisco Nexus Dashboard Data Broker

- Cisco Meraki vMX

Cisco Nexus Dashboard Insights

Intent-based policies can be extended to multiple data center sites, branches, and the public cloud to provide centralized control. Cisco Nexus Dashboard Insights helps with Day 2 operations of these network sites to provide visibility, assurance, proactive detection of anomalies with correlated network, and application view. This helps identify issues, accelerate troubleshooting, and then remediate issues on these sites. Cisco Nexus Dashboard Insights was designed with the following network characteristics and architecture in mind:

■ **Built-in automation:** The network configuration is centrally managed by a controller; therefore, the network operators no longer need to manage the device configuration on a box-by-box basis. With the centralized controller method, it is easier to maintain features and configuration consistency across the network.

■ **Scalable architecture:** For different reasons, such as scale, disaster avoidance, and disaster recovery, modern data centers often expand beyond a single site to multiple geographically dispersed locations, sometimes even to the public cloud. As data centers scale out, the complexity of collecting and analyzing data to understand the operational state of the networks increases. At the same time, with the increasingly distributed application workload, a data center infrastructure can be running anywhere from a few thousand to a few million flows at a time. In addition, at times there may be a few hundred messages or events being logged every second. Manually correlating these flows and logs, switch by switch, in order to troubleshoot issues can be very challenging and time consuming.

■ **Operations challenges:** The challenge faced by operators is to comprehend and correlate the data collected from each switch in the fabric to a particular problem, such as slowness in a web application. This implies a stringent expectation that an operator has the required knowledge and expertise (which usually takes time to build) about most, if not all, of what's happening in the infrastructure.

Cisco Nexus Dashboard Insights addresses these challenges to bring about the following benefits:

■ **Increased operational efficiency and network availability with proactive monitoring and alerts:** Cisco Nexus Dashboard Insights learns and analyzes network behaviors to recognize anomalies before end users do and then generates proactive alerts useful in preventing outages. Cisco Nexus Dashboard Insights also proactively identifies vulnerability exposures of the networks to known defaults, PSIRTs (Product Security Incident Response Teams), and field notices and recommends the best course for proactive remediation.

■ **Shortened mean time to resolution (MTTR) for troubleshooting:** Cisco Nexus Dashboard Insights minimizes the critical troubleshooting time through automated root-cause analysis of data-plane anomalies, such as packet drops, latency, workload movements, routing issues, ACL drops, and so on. Additionally, Cisco Nexus Dashboard Insights provides assisted auditing and compliance checks using searchable historical data presented in time-series format.

■ **Increased speed and agility for capacity planning:** Cisco Nexus Dashboard Insights detects and highlights components exceeding capacity thresholds through fabric-wide visibility of resource utilization and historical trends. The captured resource utilization shows time series–based trends of capacity utilization so that the network operation team can plan for resizing, restructuring, and repurposing.

■ **Increased efficiency and reduced risks in network operations, such as configuration change management and software upgrades:** Starting with the 6.0 release, Nexus Dashboard Insights provides a dry-run place for network operators to test and validate their intended configuration changes against a snapshot of the actual network, allowing them to understand the impacts of the changes to the network and to have the opportunity to catch and correct any errors in the changes before entering them into the production network. It also minimizes the risk of the network configuration changes.

Cisco Nexus Dashboard Insights is a microservices-based modern service for network operations. It is hosted on Cisco Nexus Dashboard, where Cisco ACI and Cisco DCNM sites are onboarded and the respective data from these sites is ingested and correlated by Cisco Nexus Dashboard Insights.

Cisco Nexus Dashboard Insights directs operators' attention to the significant matters relevant to the task at hand, such as troubleshooting, monitoring, auditing, planning, vulnerabilities, and so on. All anomalies and analytics results in Cisco Nexus Dashboard Insights can be accessed by an external system via its REST APIs or exported using Kafka, where the users can subscribe to relevant topics. Users can also choose to receive email notifications on anomalies with the option to customize which anomaly types they want to see, along with their severity and cadence.

While network monitoring, analytics, and assurance are the core functions of Nexus Dashboard Insights, it offers many other capabilities and tools to increase the efficiency of and reduce the risks in network operations. The following are the key components of Nexus Dashboard Insights:

■ **Network telemetry–based full visibility and analytics:** Nexus Dashboard Insights receives network telemetry data from the network devices. It obtains fine-grained visibility through the telemetry data, including both control-plane and data-plane operations and performance. It analyzes and learns about the baseline behavior of the network and detects anomalies in the network. The anomalies are reported to the network operations team through the Insights user interface (UI) or email notification and can be sent to other tools via programmatic methods, such as Kafka export or direct API calls.

■ **Snapshot-based network assurance through mathematical modeling:** In its 6.0 release, Nexus Dashboard Insights inherited the assurance analysis engine from the original Network Assurance Engine (NAE) application. The NAE continuously takes full snapshots of the network on a regular interval and then builds a mathematical model for each snapshot that represents the network and how it operates at a point in time. It then analyzes the network behaviors against this model. It checks the network configuration for any errors as well as examines the consistency between the network configuration and its actual operational states. Any configuration issues, any inconsistencies between the configuration and the operational states, or any incorrect behaviors of the network components will be reported as network anomalies. It ensures network configuration, policy space, connectivity, and endpoint space. The assurance functions are a comprehensive collection of automated troubleshooting processes, developed based on the deep knowledge base accumulated through years of network design, deployment, and support experience.

■ **Centralized network insights with One View:** Organizations scale out their data centers by deploying multiple data center sites that often are geographically dispersed. This creates a fragmented view of the network infrastructure and creates challenges for Day 2 operations teams, leading to slower incident detection, correlation, and resolution. Starting with the Nexus Dashboard 2.1 release, users can link their multiple Nexus Dashboard clusters together to operate their network sites from this one central point and obtain an aggregated view of the operations of all their network sites. Enabled by the "One View" capability on Nexus Dashboard, the Insights service itself can now provide its users with the centralized visibility across all the network sites on the linked Nexus Dashboards and enable the smooth navigation among the different sites on the same Insights UI.

■ **Pre-change analysis for risk-free configuration change management:** Network configuration change management has been considered an operation with risks by nature due to the network team not having a good tool to fully qualify the changes before implementing them into the product network. Pre-Change Analysis is a function originally offered by Cisco NAE to tackle this challenge by giving the network team a tool to fully test-drive their intended configuration changes. Cisco NAE is integrated into Cisco Nexus Dashboard Insights Release 6.0. Now the Insights users can take full advantage of the same pre-change verification capability to proactively validate the configuration changes against the latest snapshot of the network. This is a long-desired capability by the network operations team. Now, they can simply submit their intended changes to the Insights service, which will analyze the impacts of the changes to the network, calling out any errors or potential issues if there are any. The network team gets an opportunity to review and correct the errors and only implement the fully qualified configuration changes to the network. This pre-change analysis function removes the guesswork from network configuration change management, minimizes the risks of the change management, and thus increases the availability of the entire network.

■ **Automated continuous compliance assurance:** Most organizations have some type of compliance requirements for their networks, such as industry regulatory compliance requirements or internal requirements for security or business functions. Additionally, the network teams often have their own established best practices, standard configuration, and standardized naming conventions they would like to implement or enforce during the ongoing network operation. All these requirements can be ensured by Nexus Dashboard Insights through its compliance assurance functions. These capabilities were originally in the Cisco NAE application and now are part of the Insights service, since its 6.0 release.

The compliance assurance functions in the Insights service give the network team one more place to directly describe and submit their intents for the network, which then automatically and continuously verifies and validates the intents in the network for them. Any deviation from the intents will be captured as compliance violation anomalies and reported to the network team immediately. With the automated, continuous security and configuration compliance analysis, Nexus Dashboard Insights enables true intent-based network operation.

- **The ability to query the network like a database using natural language:** Explorer, originally from the Cisco NAE application, is now a part of Nexus Dashboard Insights, since its 6.0 release. It is a tool for the network teams to conveniently explore the entire network like a database using natural language–based queries. Explorer can answer questions such as the following:

  - Can EPG A talk to EPG B?

  - How can they talk?

  - What VRFs are deployed in my tenant space X?

  - What endpoints are attached to the leaf switch 101 port 1/1?

  This is a highly efficient way to find the objects and discover how they are associated with one another in the network.

  Network operators can easily create natural language queries to get their discovery tasks done efficiently. For example, they can quickly locate a specific object, such as a particular endpoint out of thousands of them in the entire network, or just simply get a per-device or network-wide inventory of certain network object types in the network or find out the communication relationship between different objects throughout the network that either can communicate with or are isolated from each other using past or present snapshots of the network.

  Explorer is an effective tool to assist in the troubleshooting of the network configuration, operational states, network change planning, and so on.

- **Easier and safer network software upgrading:** Starting with its 6.0 release, Nexus Dashboard Insights offers software upgrade analysis to ease and reduce the risk of a software upgrade workflow. It can assist the network team in choosing the right target software version for the upgrade. Based on the pre-upgrade analysis results, the network team can prepare for the upgrade by clearing up the identified issues or faults in the network, if any, and thus get a clear expectation of what issues will be solved by the update and be aware of whether the target version will introduce any new caveats. The post-upgrade analysis shows the network team the differences in the network state (endpoints, routes, interface status, and so on) before and after the upgrade so they can quickly tell if the network has come through the upgrade without any issues or if something is missing. The pre- and post-upgrade analysis makes the software upgrade operation easier and safer.

Cisco Nexus Dashboard Insights Licensing

Nexus Dashboard Insights is offered through the Cisco DCN Premier tier licenses and the Cisco DCN Day 2 Ops add-on license.

The Cisco Nexus Dashboard Insights licensing guidelines:

- For customers who have a Cisco DCN Essentials or Advantage license, they can acquire Cisco Nexus Dashboard Insights licenses through a Day 2 Ops bundle.

- Cisco Nexus Dashboard Insights licenses are available in subscription mode only.

- For Cisco ACI environments, the number of device licenses required is equal to the sum of the leafs. The spines do not require a device license.

- For a Cisco NX-OS/DCNM environment, device licenses are required for all nodes. The number of device licenses required is equal to the sum of the leafs, fixed spines, and/or modular spines.

- Cisco Intersight Nexus Dashboard Base application does not require additional licensing. The user is required to create an account in Cisco Intersight to use the functionality.

- Cisco Nexus Insights Cloud Connector application is included in the Cisco APIC and Cisco DCNM software operating system (OS) as a license-free offering.

- For a more detailed overview on Cisco licensing, go to cisco.com/go/licensingguide.

- Download the Cisco Nexus Dashboard Insights applications in the Cisco DC App Center.

- Try for free Cisco Nexus Dashboard Insights TAC assist feature.

- Contact your Cisco account team to learn pricing and additional details.

Key Components of Cisco Nexus Dashboard Insights

Cisco Nexus Dashboard Insights provides a direct view into the site-level anomalies (issues) that need attention, all of which are calculated by Cisco Nexus Dashboard Insights. The anomalies are consolidated into the Overview screen and sorted by category and severity. The Insights service further groups the anomalies by top nodes, timeline view, site health score, and advisories. A node inventory by roles, and corresponding health score, allows click access to the in-depth node-level visibility, which gives all details on the nodes, including trends of anomalies observed.

Cisco Nexus Dashboard Insights also allows users to create custom dashboards for any charts seen in the service:

- **Analyze Alerts:** Nexus Dashboard Insights users can interactively browse, search, and analyze the anomalies and advisory alerts generated by the service.

- **Anomalies:** Nexus Dashboard Insights can find issues around the following network operations:

  - Resource utilization.

  - Environmental issues such as power failure, memory leaks, process crashes, node reloads, CPU, and memory spikes.

- Interface and routing protocol issues such as CRC errors, DOM anomalies, interface drops, BGP issues such as lost connectivity with an existing neighbor, PIM, IGMP flaps, LLDP flaps, CDP issues, and so on. Also provides a view into microbursts with offending and victim flows.

- Flow drop with location and reason of drop, abnormal latency spikes of flows using hardware telemetry and direct hardware export, flows impacted due to events in a switch-like buffer, policer, forwarding drops, ACL or policy drops, and so on using Flow Table Events (FTE), which is another form of hardware telemetry.

- Endpoint duplicates, rapid endpoint movement, and rogue endpoints.

- Issues in the network configuration, which are detected and reported as change analysis anomalies.

- Violations to the compliance requirements for compliance assurance, which are detected and reported as compliance anomalies.

- Issues found in the network forwarding analysis and assurance, which are detected and reported as forwarding anomalies.

- Application issues as calculated by AppDynamics and Cisco Nexus Dashboard Insights (AppD Integration required).

Anomalies view consists of indication of being affected by known Cisco caveats and best practice violations at a node level.

Figure 2-1 shows the Anomalies view.

Figure 2-1 *Anomalies view*

Figure 2-2 shows the Analyze the Anomaly view.

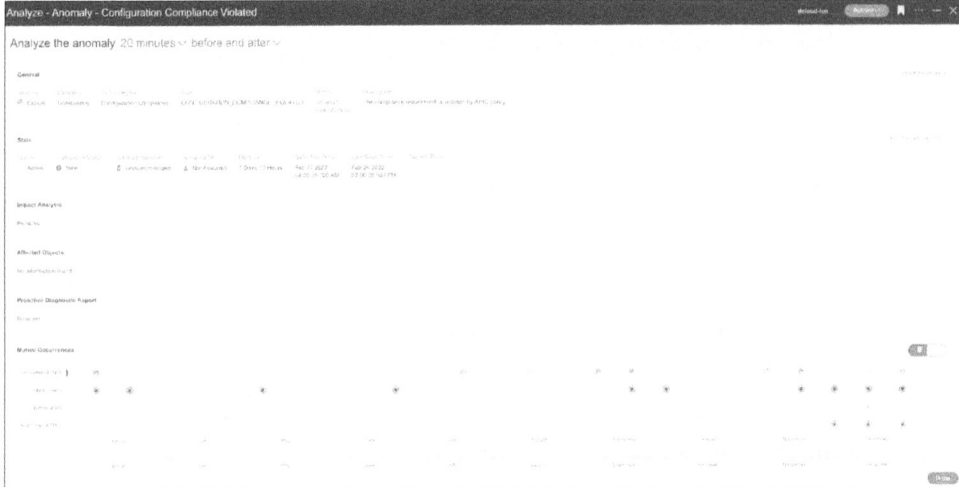

Figure 2-2 *Analyze the Anomaly view*

■ **Advisories:** Nexus Dashboard Insights can identify and generate advisory alerts to the network operations team for the following:

■ Field notices

■ Software/hardware products' end-of-life (EOL) and end-of-sales (EOS) announcements

■ PSIRTs that can potentially impact the network sites that it is monitoring

The alerts consist of the relevant impacts of the identified field notices, EOL/EOS, and PSIRTs as well as the affected devices in the network. Nexus Dashboard Insights also performs targeted bug scanning to alert the network operations team about the known defects relevant to their specific network environment based on its hardware/software versions, features enabled in the network, and network configuration. This helps the network team to carry out the remediation actions on the affected switches quickly or to form a software or hardware upgrade plan accordingly.

■ **Network Delta Analysis:** Starting with the 6.0 release, Nexus Dashboard Insights can run network delta analysis. This capability is inherited from Cisco NAE. Users of the Insights service now can select any two snapshots of the network site and ask Insights to analyze the differences between them, including configuration differences as well as differences in anomalies and advisories that reveal the differences in how the network was operating at two points in time.

Understanding the differences in the network configuration and operations is important and extremely helpful for many different scenarios. For troubleshooting a network incidence, the differences in the network configuration or operations can often help identify the cause of the issue. For performing network maintenance, such as configuration changes, software upgrade, and hardware replacement, it is helpful to check the differences in the network before and after the maintenance task. It can tell whether the network has converged or restored to how it should be after the task, whether the task has resolved the issues it is supposed to resolve, or whether it has introduced any new issues. The Delta Analysis function increases network operation efficiency for these maintenance tasks and helps reduce the mean time to resolution (MTRR) for troubleshooting.

- **Log Collector:** Nexus Dashboard Insights can assist the network team in collecting tech-support logs per node. It turns the tedious task into a simple one-step automated job. These logs can be downloaded locally and optionally uploaded to Cisco Cloud to make them available for Cisco Support when a service request (SR) is opened.

- **Connectivity Analysis:** Allows users to run a quick or full analysis for a flow within one NX-OS network site or spanning multiple NX-OS network sites in order to do the following:

  - Trace all possible forwarding paths for a given flow across source to destination endpoints

  - Identify the offending device with the issue resulting in the flow drop

  - Help narrow down the root cause of the issue, including running forwarding path checks, running software and hardware states programming consistencies through consistency checkers, and providing further details related to packet walkthrough and lookup results through packet capture

These issues are time-consuming to debug, and Connectivity Analysis provides a quick analysis of these issues in a user-driven way. Figure 2-3 shows the possible paths a flow can traverse while running thorough consistency checks.

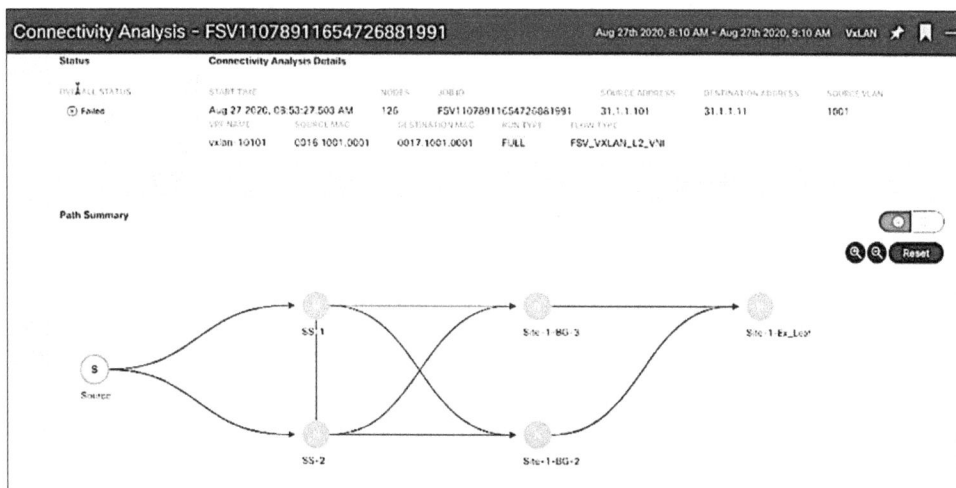

Figure 2-3 *Possible paths a flow can traverse while running through consistency checks*

Figure 2-4 shows the status of flow path consistency checks.

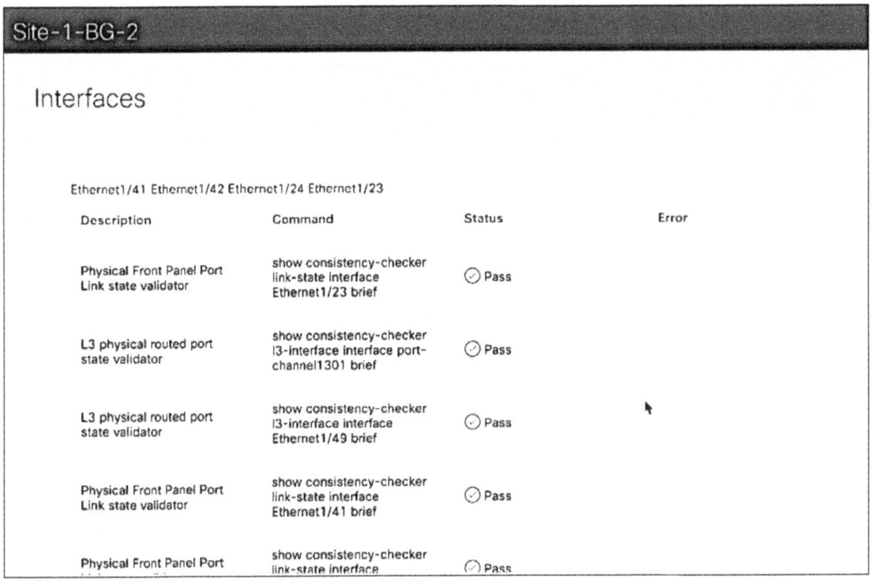

Figure 2-4   *Status of flow path consistency checks*

Browsing Cisco Nexus Dashboard Insights

All anomalies observed for any of the following data sets are rolled into the Dashboard view of the respective site to draw your attention.

Resources

It is tedious to keep track of software-verified scale per release, per resource, and what scale the hardware in your network supports. Moreover, keeping track of utilization of resources per node over time and setting static thresholds for these resources to be notified on violation do not scale for dynamically growing networks. To resolve this, Cisco Nexus Dashboard Insights baselines utilization of resources, monitors trends, and generates anomalies on abnormal usage of resources across nodes to help a user plan for capacity in their networks.

Resource utilization shows time series–based trends of capacity utilization by correlating software telemetry data collected from nodes in each site. Persistent trends help identify burdened pieces of infrastructure and plan for resizing, restructuring, and repurposing. Figure 2-5 shows resource utilization.

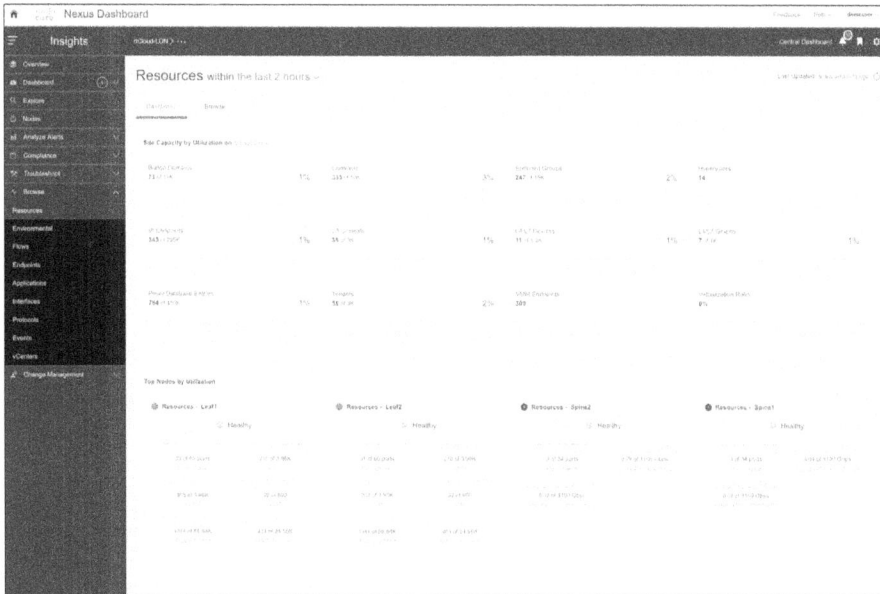

Figure 2-5 *Resource utilization*

Resource utilization categorizes capacity utilization as follows:

- **Operational resources:** Display the capacity of transient resources that are dynamic in nature and expected to change over short intervals such as routes, MAC addresses, and security TCAM (Ternary Content-Addressable Memory)

- **Configuration resources:** Display the capacity utilization of resources that are dependent on configurations such as the number of VRFs, bridge domains, VLANs, and endpoint groups (EPGs)

- **Hardware resources:** Display port and bandwidth-capacity utilization

Figure 2-6 shows capacity utilization.

Drilling down on any device shows the details of processes that are high consumers of resources. Once resource utilization crosses a 70% capacity threshold, it is color-coded yellow; beyond 80%, it is color-coded orange; beyond 90%, it is color-coded red. This proactively alerts the network operators about the specific resources that need their attention. It also helps predict anomalies based on historical trends and rates of change and forecasts resource shortages.

When it comes to policy TCAM analysis for an ACI network site, Nexus Dashboard Insights not only monitors it but also gives the network team the ability to analyze the per-contract/per-filter usage at the site or switch level. This allows the network team to easily understand which contracts are using the most TCAM (globally or at a switch level) as well as understand how much a contract is used by real traffic. This allows the network team to remove unused contracts or optimize the high TCAM consumption contracts. Figure 2-7 shows the Policy CAM Analyzer.

Figure 2-6 *Capacity utilization*

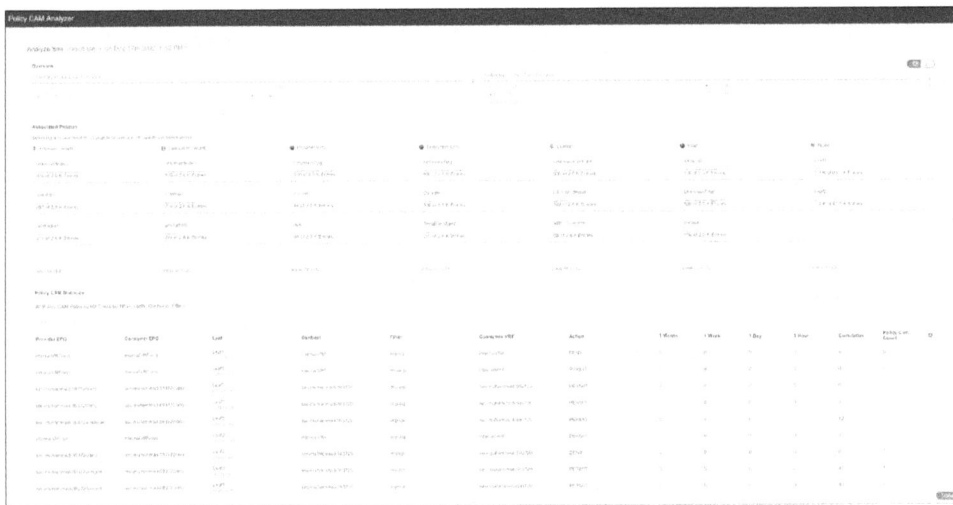

Figure 2-7 *Policy CAM Analyzer*

Environmental

Most often, environmental data is monitored using traditional applications like SNMP, CLI, and so on. Data from these applications is difficult to post-process, is device specific, is not historical in nature, and requires manual checks. Hence, monitoring environmental anomalies becomes very reactive and cumbersome. Cisco Nexus Dashboard Insights consumes environmental data using streaming software telemetry and baselines trends, and it generates anomalies every time the utilization exceeds pre-set thresholds. It enables the user to determine which process is consuming CPU or hogging memory, when storage is overfilled, when process crashes occur, and whether there are memory leaks. All this data is provided over time with historical retention, per node, to allow users to delve into specific anomalies while having full visibility.

Environmental data provides anomaly-detection capabilities in hardware components such as CPU, memory, temperature, fan speed, power, storage, and so on. As in the other screens, components exceeding thresholds and requiring the operator's attention are highlighted. Figure 2-8 shows how environmental data provides anomaly-detection capabilities.

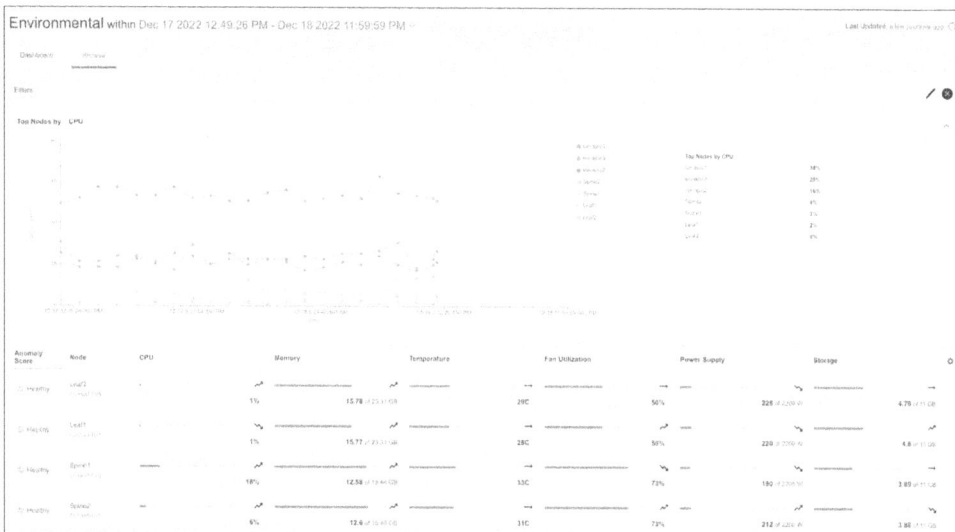

Figure 2-8   *How environmental data provides anomaly-detection capabilities*

Statistics

Statistics is all about interfaces and routing protocols. Cisco Nexus Dashboard Insights ingests data from each node in the fabric using streaming software telemetry. The data is then baselined to derive trends and identify when any of these data sets suddenly show a rapid decline, for example, in interface utilization or rapid increase in drops or CRC errors over time.

The Dashboard view presents top nodes by interface utilization and errors, thereby allowing the user to quickly identify interfaces to investigate errors.

Protocol statistics provide a view into what interfaces protocols are active (such as CDP, LLDP, LACP, BGP, PIM, IGMP, and IGMP snooping), protocol details such as neighbors, incoming and OIFs for a (*,G), (S,G) entry, along with trends of errors such as a lost connection or neighbor, OIF flaps, invalid packets, and so on.

Statistical data is also used for correlation in Cisco Nexus Dashboard Insights. For instance, if there is a CRC error, Cisco Nexus Dashboard Insights will use other data sets to find out the estimated impact (like impacted endpoints) and provide a recommendation based on other anomalies seen at that time (such as a DOM anomaly, which could potentially be causing CRC errors). Figure 2-9 shows how statistical data provides an estimated impact and recommendations.

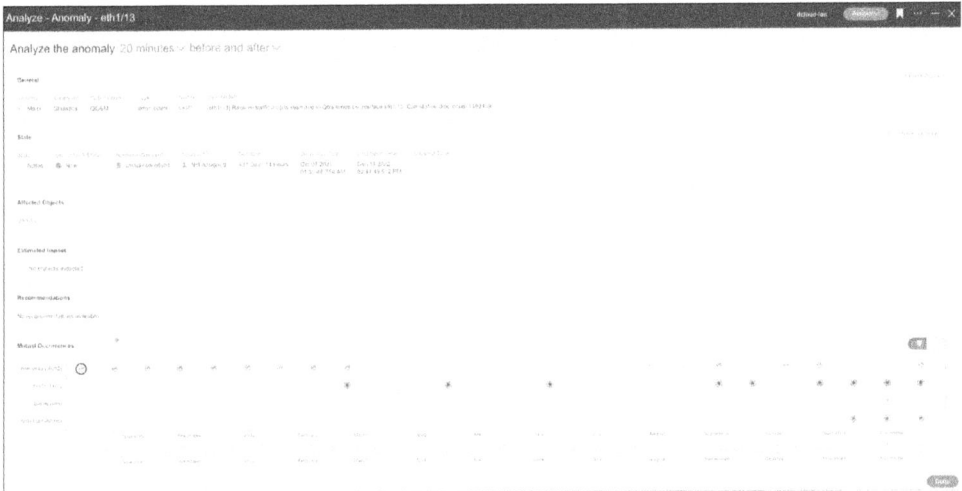

Figure 2-9 *Statistical data provides an estimated impact and recommendations*

Flows

Application problem or network problem? This is a frequently asked question in the data center world. If anything, it always begins with the network. The time to innocence and mean time to resolution become imperative as we deal with business-critical applications in the data center. The tools for network operations today often have very limited insights into data-plane counters, flows, latency, and drops.

Even if we can get the data-plane flow data from the network switches, how can the data from the individual switches be pieced together to form an end-to-end view of a flow while it is traversing the network? How can the end-to-end network latency of a flow be extracted from the flow data ? It used to be the network team that had to do all of these complex flow analysis tasks with limited tools to help them, which means a lot of man hours.

With Cisco Nexus Dashboard Insights, using Flow Telemetry, the service consumes flow records and their respective counters and then correlates this data over time to provide end-to-end flow path and latency. Cisco Nexus Dashboard Insights understands what the "normal" latency of each flow is. When the latency exceeds beyond normal, Cisco Nexus Dashboard Insights alerts the users and shows the abnormal latency increase as an anomaly on the dashboard.

The flow analytics dashboard attracts operator attention to key indicators of infrastructure data-plane health. Time-series data offers evidence of historical trends, specific patterns, and past issues and helps the operator build a case for audit, compliance, and capacity planning or infrastructure assessment. The flow analytics dashboard provides a time series–based overview with the capability to drill down on specific functions by clicking the graph.

Top Flows by Average Latency

Clicking a particular flow drills down to detailed flow data, including latency numbers, the exact path of the flow in the fabric, and the end-to-end latency. This takes away the trial-and-error and manual steps otherwise required to pinpoint latency hot spots in the infrastructure. This leads operators to focus on the root causes of the latency and remediate them. Historical trends help operators identify persistent problems and re-evaluate the infrastructure capacity.

Details of the flow, such as burstiness, help identify and remediate bandwidth issues or apply appropriate quality of service (QoS) levels. Figure 2-10 shows time series–based latency statistics.

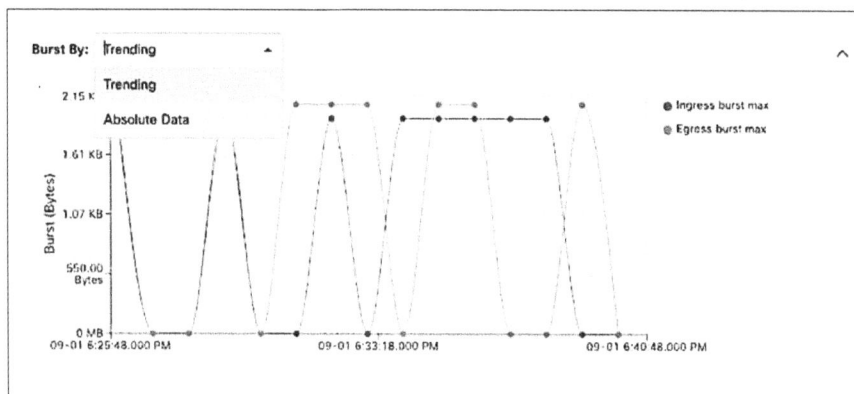

Figure 2-10 *Time series–based latency statistics*

Endpoints

It shows time series–based endpoint movement in the fabric, with endpoint details and endpoints with duplicate IPs. In virtualized data center environments, this keeps track of virtual machine (VM) movement, which is extremely useful to identify a VM's current location and its historical movements in the fabric. It provides proof points in establishing VM movements and thus aids constructively in problem solving while working with other IT teams.

Endpoint health and consistency are also monitored by Nexus Dashboard Insights:

- The Insights service quickly detects duplicated endpoints and points the user to the switch and port where the duplication is present.

- The Insights service provides built-in automation to remediate a stale endpoint situation with a single click.

Applications

With Cisco AppDynamics and Cisco Nexus Dashboard Insights integration, users get a single pane of glass for application and network statistics and anomalies. Cisco Nexus Dashboard Insights consumes data streamed from the AppDynamics controller, and in addition to showing application, tier, node health, and metrics, Cisco Nexus Dashboard Insights derives a baseline of network statistics of these applications, such as TCP Loss, Round Trip Time, Latency, Throughput, and Performance Impacting Events (PIE), and generates anomalies on threshold violations. For any AppDynamics flows, Cisco Nexus Dashboard Insights also provides an in-depth end-to-end path, latency, drops (if any), and drop reasons to help users identify if app slowness or issues are resulting from network issues. Figure 2-11 shows the Application Dashboard with all applications and respective statistics.

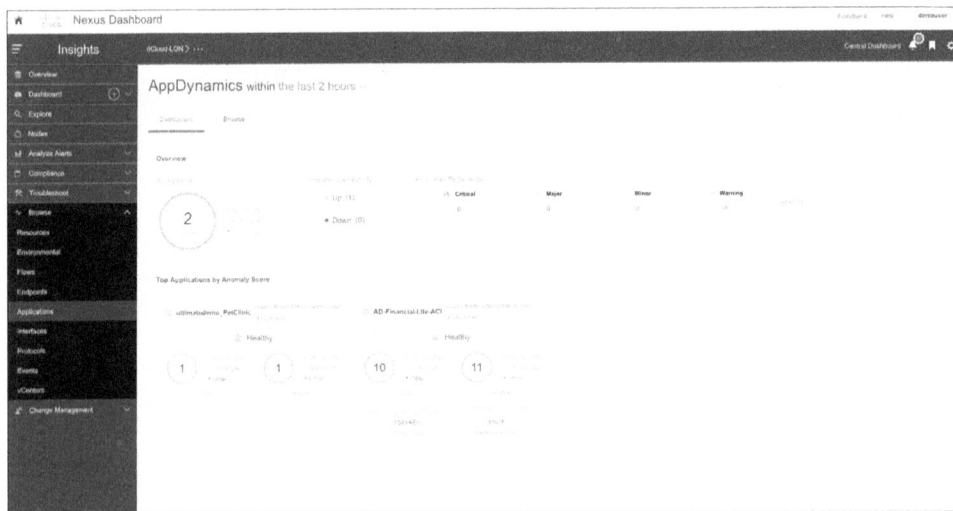

Figure 2-11 *Application Dashboard showing all applications and respective statistics*

Figure 2-12 shows application detail to view health, respective tiers, and nodes.

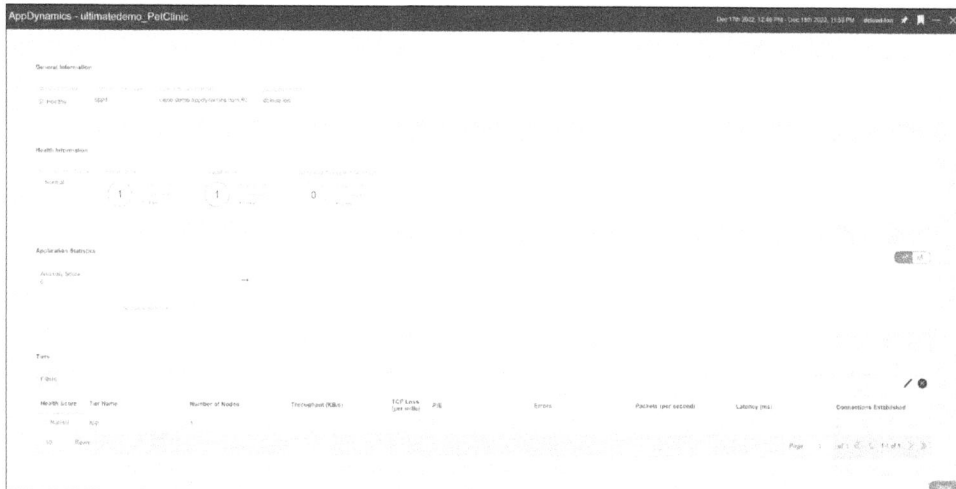

Figure 2-12   *Application detail to view health, respective tiers, and nodes*

A network link is for communication between tiers. Cisco Nexus Dashboard Insights maps links to respective flows traversing the fabric, thereby allowing users to see flow details and paths with drops, if any.

This integration is vital to blurring the lines between silos inside the organization, enabling operators to see the network from the application's point of view. The operator does not need to know which IP is associated to which application or which application flows through which nodes at any given time. Cisco Nexus Dashboard Insights provides all this information, enriches the data, and correlates it for a holistic, unified operational view.

Event Analytics

Event Analytics is tuned for control-plane events in the infrastructure. It performs the following functions:

- **Data collection:** Configuration changes and control-plane events and faults.

- **Analytics:** Artificial intelligence (AI) and machine learning (ML) algorithms determine the correlations between all changes, events, and faults.

- **Anomaly detection:** Output of AI and ML algorithms (unexpected or downtime-causing events).

The Event Analytics Dashboard displays faults, events, and audit logs in a time-series fashion. Clicking any of these points in the history displays its historical state and detailed information. Further, all these are correlated together to identify whether deletion of a configuration led to a fault. Figure 2-13 shows the Event Analytics Dashboard.

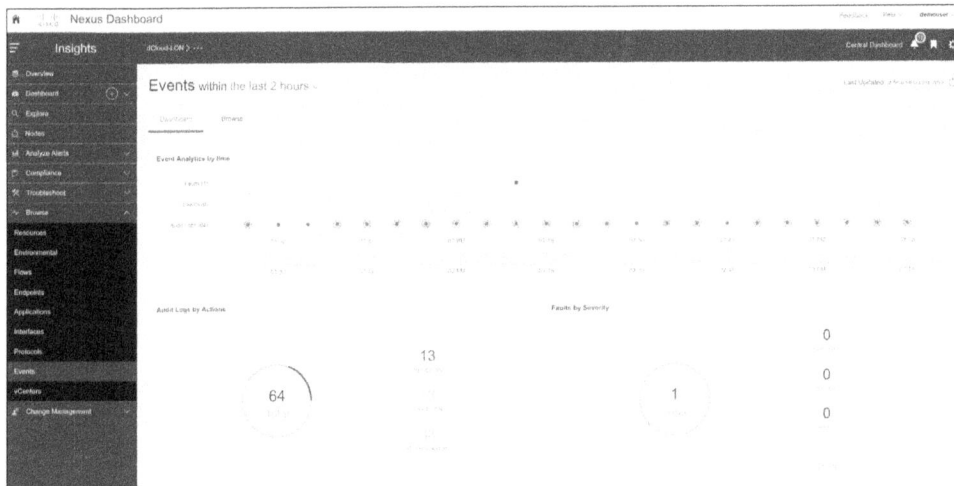

Figure 2-13 *Event Analytics Dashboard*

- **Audit logs:** Show the creation, deletion, and modifications of any object in Cisco ACI (subnet, IP address, next-hop, EPG, VRF, and so on). This is useful for identifying recent changes that may be a potential reason for unexpected behavior. It can aid in reverting changes to a stable state and helps assign accountability. The facility of the filters makes it convenient to narrow focus to specific changes by severity, action, description, object, and so on. Drilling down on the audit logs provides details for each log.

- **Events:** Show operational events in the infrastructure (for example, IP detach/attach, port attach/detach on a virtual switch, interface state changes, and so on).

- **Faults:** Are mutable, stateful, and persistent managed objects and show issues in the infrastructure (for example, invalid configurations). This function speeds up operator action toward problem rectification, thus reducing the time lost in root-cause analysis and rectification, which usually requires multiple steps, expertise, correlation of symptoms, and perhaps a bit of trial and error.

The zoom in and out function in the timeline bar helps to quickly contract or expand the timeline under investigation.

Diagnostics, Impact, Recommendation

Cisco Nexus Dashboard Insights monitors different sets of data from all nodes in the fabric and baselines the data to identify "normal" behavior. Any deviation from normal is represented as an anomaly in the service dashboard. This helps the operator spend time on resolving the issue instead of finding where in the network the issue really arose.

With the correlation algorithms that Cisco Nexus Dashboard Insights has in place, in addition to the anomaly, it can also point to an estimated impact of this anomaly, helping the user identify what is the potential impact of a problem. With the impact, the service will also generate a recommendation depending on the nature of the anomaly, thus reducing the mean time to troubleshoot and resolve.

For example, microbursts are complex to identify and cause a myriad of network issues. For applications that require reliable and low-latency networks, microbursts can pose serious issues. Since microbursts occur in a matter of microseconds, looking at a graph of overall packets per second will make the overall transmission appear smooth. Cisco Nexus Dashboard Insights detects these microbursts due to its rapid cadence of gathering data and details what flows could be impacted due to these bursts and even be causing the bursts. It makes it easier for the operator to not only detect that a burst occurred on a particular node, interface, or queue but also the flows impacted, with a recommendation for how to fix this anomaly. Figure 2-14 shows a microburst anomaly.

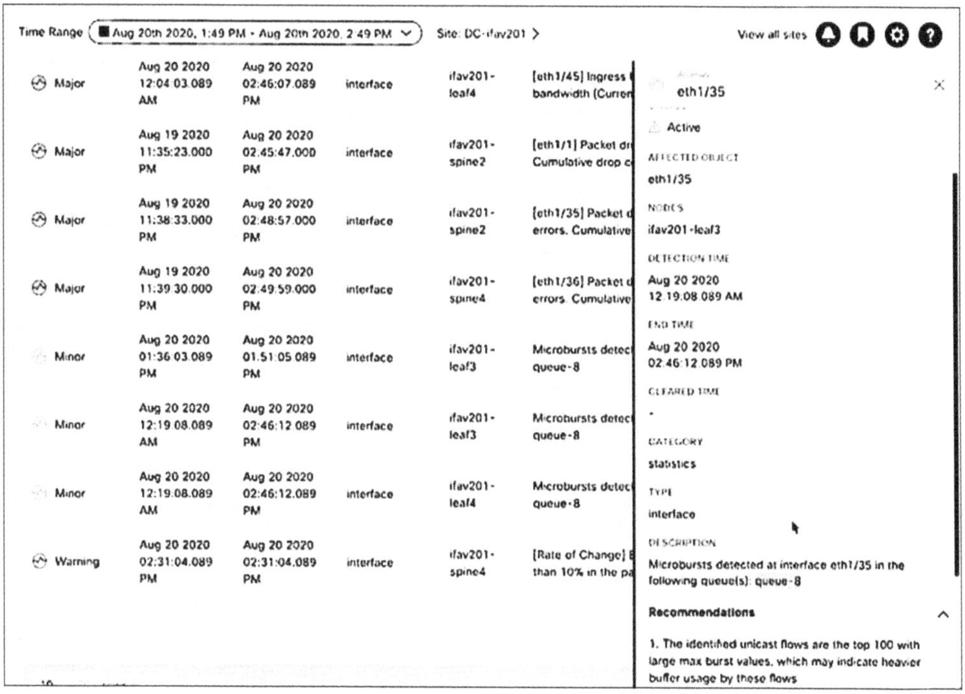

Figure 2-14   *Microburst anomaly*

Advisories

To maintain data center network availability and minimize the downtime, it is critical for network operators to ensure that their network infrastructure is built with up-to-date switch platforms and is running the right versions of software. It requires periodic and thorough audits of the entire infrastructure, which is historically a manual and time-consuming task. Cisco Nexus Dashboard Insights turns this task into an automated process, using digitized signatures to determine the vulnerability exposure of the network infrastructure at the click of a button.

Cisco Nexus Dashboard Insights scans the entire network to collect the complete information on its hardware, software versions, and active configuration. It then runs analysis against the digitalized database of known defects, PSIRTs, and field notices to identify the relevant ones that can potentially impact the particular network environment, matching on its hardware and software versions, features and topologies, and so on.

It then proactively alerts the network operators of the identified vulnerabilities and advises them on the right hardware and/or software versions for remediation. It also analyzes and advises on whether the network is running any out-of-date hardware or software based on Cisco product EOL or EOS announcement and schedule.

For any of the discovered issues, Cisco Nexus Dashboard Insights lists the impacted devices, vulnerability details, and mitigation steps (aka advisories). With the advisories, it recommends the best software version for the resolution and the upgrade path—either a single-step upgrade or through intermediate software versions. It also reveals the impact of the upgrade, either disruptive or nondisruptive, so that the operators can proactively plan for the upgrade accordingly.

With the automated scanning, network-context-aware vulnerability analysis, and actionable recommendations, the advisory function in Cisco Nexus Dashboard Insights makes it so much easier for the operation team to maintain an accurate audit of the entire network and avoid the downtime due to product defects or PSIRTs by getting proactive alerts and taking preventive remediation actions. Figure 2-15 shows an advisory for a field notice.

Firmware Update Analysis

Before an upgrade is performed, multiple validations need to be performed. Similarly, after an upgrade process, multiple checks help to determine the changes and the success of the upgrade procedure.

The Firmware Update Analysis feature suggests an upgrade path to a recommended software version and determines the potential impact of upgrading. It also helps with the pre-upgrade and post-upgrade validation checks.

Figure 2-15 *Advisory for a field notice*

The Firmware Update Analysis feature offers the following benefits:

- Assists in preparing and validating a successful upgrade of the network
- Provides visibility on the pre-upgrade checks
- Provides visibility on the post-upgrade checks and the status after the upgrade
- Minimizes the impact to the production environment
- Provides visibility as to whether the upgrade process is a single step or multiple steps
- Displays the bugs applicable to a specific firmware version

Figure 2-16 shows a firmware upgrade recommended by Cisco Nexus Dashboard Insights.

Firmware Upgrade Analysis provides a list of intermittent upgrades to get to the destination software, along with upgrade impact and release notes for each release linked directly in Cisco Nexus Dashboard Insights. Figure 2-17 shows Firmware Upgrade Analysis.

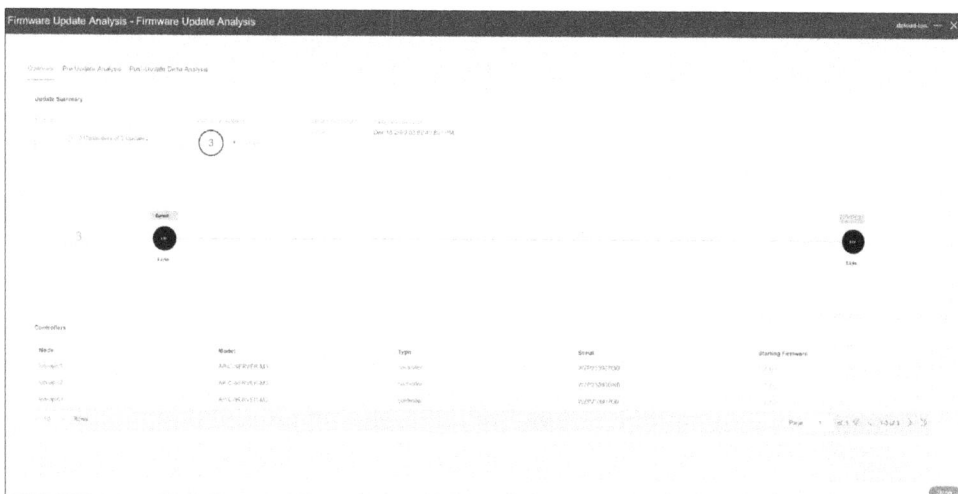

Figure 2-16 *Firmware upgrade recommended by Cisco Nexus Dashboard Insights*

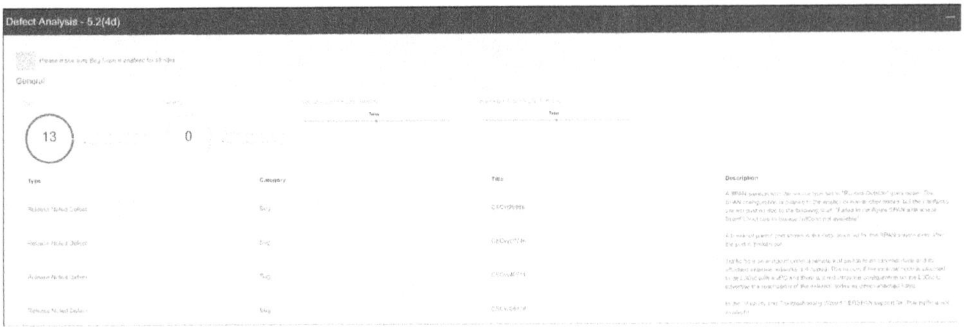

Figure 2-17   *Firmware Upgrade Analysis*

Pre-Change Analysis

You can access the Pre-Change Analysis page from the left navigation column in the Cisco Nexus Dashboard Insights GUI. Navigate to **Change Management** and select **Pre-Change Analysis**.

When you want to change a configuration for a site, this feature in Cisco Nexus Dashboard Insights allows you to model the intended changes, perform a Pre-Change Analysis against an existing base snapshot in the site, and verify if the changes generate the desired results.

After you model the changes for a Pre-Change Analysis job, you can choose Save or Save And Analyze. By choosing Save, you can save the Pre-Change Analysis job without having to start the analysis right away. You can return to the job later, edit the changes if required, and then run the analysis later. The Save option is supported only for a Pre-Change Analysis job with manual changes. If you choose Save And Analyze, the job gets scheduled and an analysis is provided.

When you choose Save And Analyze for the job, the changes are applied to the selected base snapshot, the analysis is performed, and results are generated. For every Pre-Change Analysis job listed in the table, a delta analysis is performed between the base snapshot and the newly generated snapshot. Figure 2-18 shows Pre-Change Analysis.

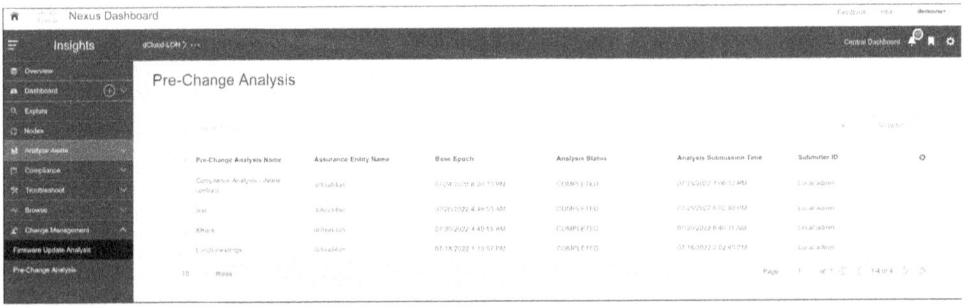

Figure 2-18   *Pre-Change Analysis*

Once the analysis starts, the status of the job will be shown as "running." During this time, the specified changes will be modeled on top of the base snapshot, and complete logical checks will be run, including Policy Analysis and Compliance. No switch software or TCAM checks will be performed.

The status of the Pre-Change Analysis job is marked "completed" when the entire analysis, including Delta Analysis, completes. The Delta Analysis is automatically triggered and the associated Pre-Change Analysis job is displayed as running during that time. The Delta Analysis is performed only on checks supported in the Pre-Change Analysis job.

In addition to multiple tenants, you can also add multiple infrastructure objects as part of a Pre-Change Analysis JSON or XML job. The Pre-Change Analysis upload path allows you to add, modify, and delete multiple objects across the policy universe. There are no additional configurations required to use this feature. Your Pre-Change Analysis job for multiple objects will run, based on the file(s) you upload.

The following file upload formats are accepted:

- A JSON or XML file with an IMDATA of size 1.

- An IMDATA that contains a single subtree of the intended changes. The root of the subtree can be the UNI or any other managed object as long as the changes are represented as a single subtree.

Use the file you had uploaded from a JSON or XML path to perform a Pre-Change Analysis. After the Pre-Change Analysis is complete, you can upload the same file to ACI to be used to make the changes.

Cisco Nexus Dashboard Insights Features and Benefits

Cisco Nexus Dashboard Insights for the data center stands out as the first comprehensive technology solution in the industry developed by Cisco for network operators to manage operations in their networks. Table 2-1 provides list of features and their benefits.

Table 2-1   *Features and Benefits*

Feature	Benefit
Multisite Support	Use a single instance of the Cisco Nexus Dashboard Insights application to monitor, maintain, and troubleshoot multiple data center sites.
Unified Application	Deploy a single tool with assurance, advisory, and troubleshooting capabilities to address your operational needs of prevention, diagnosis, and remediation.
Hybrid Site Support	Use a single instance of the application to onboard and operate Cisco ACI and DCNM multisite deployments.

Feature	Benefit
One View	With single sign-on (SSO) and role-based access control (RBAC), you can operate your multisite environment distributed across multiple Cisco Nexus Dashboard clusters from a single focal point of control.
NetFlow Collector	Maintain business continuity by having backward compatibility with legacy protocols.
One-click Remediation	Reduce MTTR with one-click automated fixes of known behaviors.
Upgrade Assist	Detect changes in configuration or operational state before and after switch upgrades and validate across 40+ checks.
Change Management	One-stop shop for information about the assurance on policy and configuration analysis changes.
Explorer	Explore associations and connectivity and understand the state of network deployment using powerful natural-language querying.
Communication Compliance	Ensure that regulatory and business communication always meets compliance.
Configuration Compliance	Ensure that naming and golden template configurations meet IT requirements for enhanced productivity.
Pre-Change Analysis	Predict the impact of the intended configuration changes for insight-driven change management.
TCAM Utilization	Manage TCAM capacity resources and security policy with advanced utilization analysis.
Delta Analysis	Comprehensive view of health drift between any two points in time, minimizing the change window.
	Comprehensive view of policy/configuration drift between two points in time, minimizing troubleshooting time.
Time Series Database	Gather evidence from past data. Peek back in time to look at a specific sequence of events and gather intelligent insights.
Flow Analytics	Use FT/FTE (Fault tree/fault tree editor) to minimize troubleshooting time through automated root-cause analysis of data-plane anomalies, such as packet drops, latency, workload movements, routing issues, ACL drops, and more.
Microburst Detection	Expose and locate invisible microbursts. Find out congestion hot spots and protect application performance.

Feature	Benefit
AppDynamics	Break operational silos between network and server teams. Gain cross-domain visibility and perform rapid troubleshooting with qualitative and quantifiable data. Know the application geography and layout with the mapping of application topology to physical topology information.
Multicast Control Plane	Use detailed statistics and state information of PIM, IGMP, and IGMP snooping protocols to monitor multicast control-plane health.
Anomaly Analysis	Compare and contrast time-synced data of multiple parameters to derive deeper understanding of issues and behaviors. Know the impacted endpoints, applications, and flows due to network anomalies.
Anomaly Assignment	Tag anomaly events to the right team member for faster resolution.
Resource Utilization	Provide efficient capacity planning to maintain top network performance. Get fabric-wide visibility of resource utilization and historical trends. Detect components exceeding capacity thresholds ahead of time. Examples are TCAM, routes, ACL entries, ports, tenants, VRFs, EPGs, and many more.
Environmental	Proactively monitor and report environmental anomalies by leveraging telemetry data from hardware sensors such as CPU, memory, disk, power supply, fan speed, and temperature.
Statistics	Use detailed data-plane statistics to diagnose, locate, and remediate issues. Monitor and use protocol anomalies and state information to remediate BGP, vPC, LACP, CDP, and LLDP problems.
Customizable Dashboards	Create custom dashboard views for your own preferred way of monitoring. Keep a close eye on parameters of your choice.
Endpoint Analytics	Locate virtual machines, bare-metal hosts, and other endpoints in the data center fabric. Use historical data to track their movements.
Topology View	Use your natural visuo-spatial ability to explore, navigate, discover, and zoom into issues. Never get lost! Visualize logical constructs such as tenant, VRF, EPG, and more on top of the physical topology. Perform rapid troubleshooting using filters to focus on problematic nodes.
Advisories	Stay up to date on new software and hardware availability. Be up to date on hardware and software end-of-sale announcements and get lead time to plan for upgrades.

Feature	Benefit
PSIRTs/Bugs	Get notified and take necessary action to stay secure and in compliance. Get instant visibility into any applicable bugs. Prevent unscheduled outages.
Cisco TAC Assist	Automate the mundane, repetitive tasks of log collection and attach them to TAC service requests (SRs). Delegate additional log collection to the TAC team, and free yourself from dull work.
Flow State Validator	Verify software and hardware programming consistency across all available traffic paths between endpoints. Track per hop information and behavior.
Kafka Messaging Support	Share Cisco Nexus Dashboard Insights' enriched, value-added output with the application ecosystem. Build synergetic workflows with third-party IT applications.
Email Notification Support	Get offline alerts about network health using the email notification facility. Pick and choose which issues you need to be alerted about.
Cisco ACI Multitier Support	Monitor the Cisco ACI multitier topology with all Cisco Nexus Dashboard Insights features and functions.
Product Usage Telemetry	Significantly improve product lifecycle management for IT teams that have deployed Cisco data center fabrics. These data and related insights proactively identify product issues, improve services and support, and activate discussions to glean additional value from new and existing features.
Offline Analysis	Import offline data logs for assurance checks.

Cisco Nexus Insights Cloud Connector

Cisco also provides a license-free version of the Cisco Nexus Insights application, called Cisco Nexus Insights Cloud Connector, that will benefit operators by collecting valuable information about the status and capabilities of Cisco data center platforms.

The Cisco Nexus Insights Cloud Connector (Cisco NI Cloud Connector) application provides customers with the benefit of faster time to remediation with Cisco Technical Assistance Center (TAC assist) functionalities, along with automatic, secure collection of tech-support logs. Cisco Nexus Insights Cloud Connector will empower IT teams to provide inventory reports of license entitlement, upcoming renewals, and proactive defect notifications, along with lifecycle management support from integrated Cisco Customer Experience (CX) programs. Figure 2-19 shows Cisco TAC Assist.

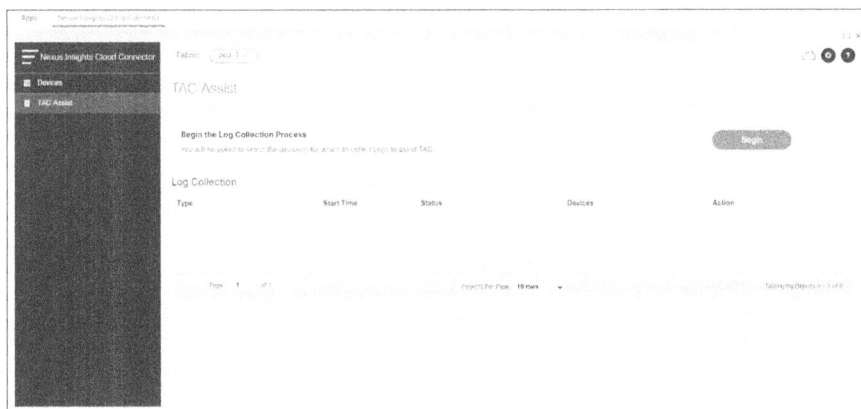

Figure 2-19 *Cisco TAC Assist*

Cisco Nexus Insights Cloud Connector is pre-packaged with Cisco data center platforms to automatically connect and transmit product usage data to Cisco. All product-usage telemetry data is transmitted to Cisco through an encrypted channel. The categories of data collected are limited to product usage. For details about the product usage telemetry information that is collected, refer to Table 2-2.

Table 2-2 *Product Usage Telemetry*

Category	Data Elements	Purpose of Collection
Cisco.com	▪ Cisco.com user ID	Identify customer account
System	▪ Controller and device information (Cisco APIC/DCNM switch/appliance serial number, type, software versions, platform ID) ▪ Operational metrics (including CPU, memory, file system, and uptime) for deployed fabric components	Identify potential device issues in customers' environments to prevent problems and improve the product
Feature usage	▪ Number of fabrics created, number of leaf nodes, spine nodes, border nodes, IP subnets, routing protocols in use, and the fabric and switch-level capacity ▪ Number of tenants/contracts/ endpoints/endpoint groups/etc. for Cisco ACI as well as access lists/hosts/VLANs/etc. for Cisco NX-OS/DCNM, in addition to virtual networks, features enabled, and feature scale	Facilitate customer adoption and customer value

Category	Data Elements	Purpose of Collection
License entitlement	■ License-entitlement information (network device type, IP address of network device, Cisco Smart Software Manager registration status, Cisco ACI and NX-OS license information, and number of days until license expires) ■ Signed EULA flag	Assist customers in tracking and maintaining license entitlement and renewals

Users can also choose to opt out of the data collection of product-usage telemetry by switching off the device connector in their specific data center platforms. For further information, refer to the Cisco Nexus Insight Cloud Connector configuration guides.

Cisco Nexus Dashboard Data Broker

Every enterprise depends on the smooth running of its business applications and the underlying infrastructure. Visibility into application traffic has traditionally been important for infrastructure operations to maintain security, resolve problems, and perform resource planning.

Now, as a result of technological advances and the ubiquity of the Internet, organizations increasingly are seeking not just visibility but real-time feedback about their business systems to more effectively engage their customers. Essentially, traffic monitoring is evolving from a tool to manage network operations to a tool for achieving smart business agility that can materially affect the revenue of the business. In addition to out-of-band traffic monitoring, migration to 40/100/400Gbps in aggregation and core network infrastructure is presenting new challenges for inline traffic monitoring at the perimeter of the network.

The following are the data broker controller modes:

■ **Centralized:** The controller is deployed on a VM, server, or bare metal outside the Test Access Point (TAP) aggregation switches. In this mode, the controller can support a multi-switch TAP aggregation topology.

■ **Embedded:** The controller is deployed on the TAP aggregation switch using a guest shell. In this mode, the controller can only be used as a single switch deployment.

■ **Nexus Dashboard:** The controller will be supported as an application on Cisco Nexus Dashboard.

■ **Cisco ACI:** The controller will be supported as an application on Cisco ACI APICs.

Using Cisco Nexus Dashboard Data Broker controller software and Cisco Nexus switches, Cisco provides a new software-defined approach for monitoring both out-of-band and inline network traffic.

Figure 2-20 illustrates the Cisco Nexus Dashboard and Nexus Dashboard Data Broker.

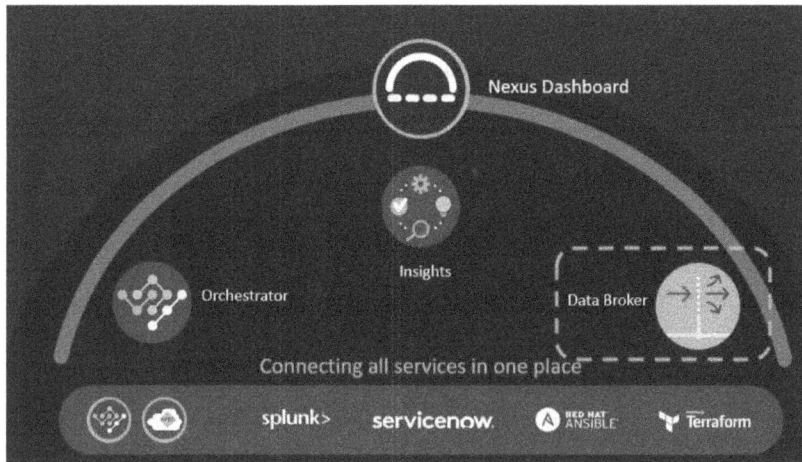

Figure 2-20 *Cisco Nexus Dashboard and Nexus Dashboard Data Broker*

Cisco Nexus Dashboard Data Broker with Cisco Nexus switches provides a software-defined, programmable solution to aggregate copies of network traffic using Switched Port Analyzer (SPAN) or network TAP for monitoring and visibility. As opposed to traditional network taps and monitoring solutions, this packet-brokering approach offers a simple, scalable, and cost-effective solution that is well-suited for customers who need to monitor higher-volume and business-critical traffic for efficient use of security, compliance, and application performance-monitoring tools.

With the flexibility to use a variety of Cisco Nexus switches and the ability to interconnect them to form a scalable topology provides the ability to aggregate traffic from multiple input TAP or SPAN ports as well as to replicate and forward traffic to multiple monitoring tools, which may be connected across different switches. Combining the use of Cisco plug-in for OpenFlow and the Cisco NX-API agent to communicate to the switches, Cisco Nexus Dashboard Data Broker provides advanced features for traffic management.

Cisco Nexus Dashboard Data Broker provides management support for multiple disjointed Cisco Nexus Data Broker networks. You can manage multiple Cisco Nexus Data Broker topologies that may be disjointed using the same application instance. For example, if you have three data centers and want to deploy an independent Cisco Nexus Data Broker solution for each data center, you can manage all three independent deployments using a single application instance by creating a logical partition (network slice) for each monitoring network.

Using Cisco Nexus 9000 platform switches, customers can build a high-density, 10/25/40/100/400Gbps visibility infrastructure. The Cisco Nexus switches form the Nexus Dashboard Data Broker (NDDB) switches, which connect to the production network to aggregate the copy traffic using TAP and SPAN methods. The aggregated traffic is filtered and redirected to tools, as per configuration.

Automated SPAN Configuration in Production Network

NetOps/SecOps teams can onboard production switches in Cisco Nexus Dashboard Data Broker and automate SPAN destination and monitoring session configurations on them. This allows administrators to manage and monitor copy traffic from source to destination from a single pane of glass. The following can be automated from the controller:

- Configuring interfaces on the production switch connected to a Data Broker switch as a SPAN destination

- Configuring SPAN sessions on the production switch using one or more source ports or VLANs

- Redirecting SPAN traffic to monitoring tools connected to the Data Broker switches

The production network can be any of the following:

- Cisco NX-OS standalone fabric

- Cisco ACI fabric

- Cisco Enterprise Network

Note   Cisco NX-API needs to be enabled on the TAP aggregation switches as a prerequisite for the controller to automate SPAN configuration.

Figure 2-21 illustrates SPAN Automation–enabled networks.

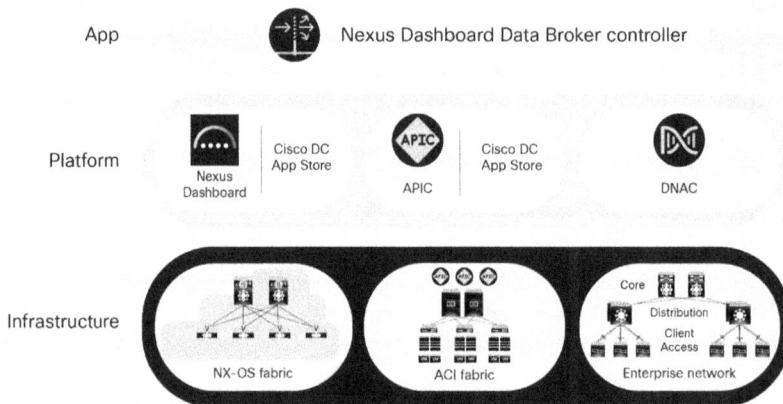

Figure 2-21   *SPAN Automation–enabled networks*

Cisco Application Centric Infrastructure (ACI) Integration

Cisco Nexus Dashboard Data Broker integrates with Cisco Application Centric Infrastructure (Cisco ACI) fabric through the Cisco Application Policy Infrastructure Controller (APIC) to push SPAN configuration on Cisco ACI leaf switches and set up SPAN sessions in Cisco ACI to monitor traffic. You can perform all these configurations through Nexus Dashboard Data Broker's web-based GUI.

This integration eliminates the need for the user to separately configure SPAN sessions or copy the function in the APIC. Data Broker supports the following functions through the web GUI and REST API:

- Setting up Cisco ACI leaf ports as SPAN sources and destinations for Access span.

- Setting up Cisco ACI EPG span by configuring Cisco Nexus Data Broker switch ports as ERSPAN tunnel destinations.

- Configuring SPAN sessions on Cisco ACI using leaf ports or EPGs as SPAN sources without logging into the APIC.

- Automatically synchronizing SPAN session information periodically with the APIC.

- Updating SPAN sessions automatically based on EPG port association changes. With this feature, the motion of the endpoint VMs on the hypervisors can be tracked for visibility.

- Redirecting SPAN traffic to monitoring tools connected to the Data Broker on Cisco Nexus switches.

The Cisco Nexus Dashboard Data Broker performs all these configurations through the APIC REST interface. Figure 2-22 illustrates Cisco Nexus Dashboard Data Broker with Cisco ACI.

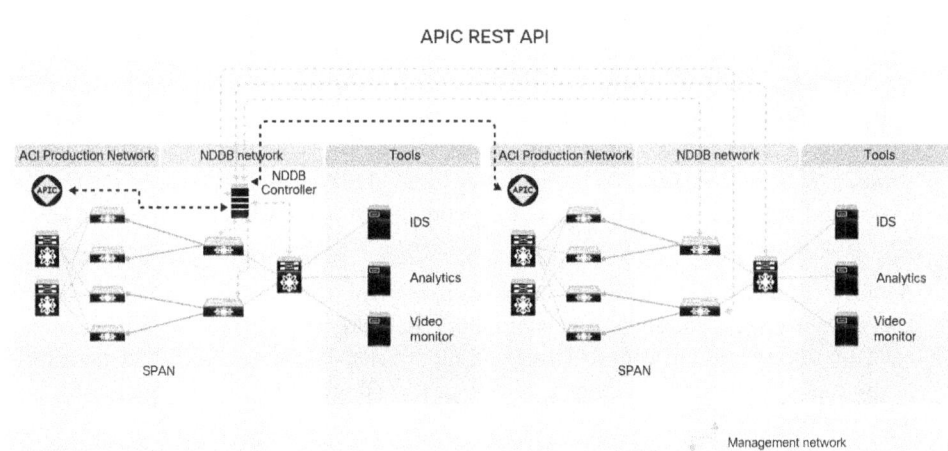

Figure 2-22   *Cisco Nexus Dashboard Data Broker with Cisco ACI*

Cisco DNA Center Integration

Nexus Dashboard Data Broker Controller can push SPAN configuration onto the access switches in an enterprise network deployment, including campus and branch locations through DNAC. In the absence of DNAC, the Nexus Dashboard Data Broker (NDDB) controller can push SPAN configuration onto the selected switches in the enterprise network by individually onboarding the switches.

Test Access Point (TAP) or Switched Port Analyzer (SPAN) can be used to copy traffic from a Cisco Catalyst switch to a Nexus Dashboard Data Broker switch. Figure 2-23 illustrates enterprise network SPAN automation.

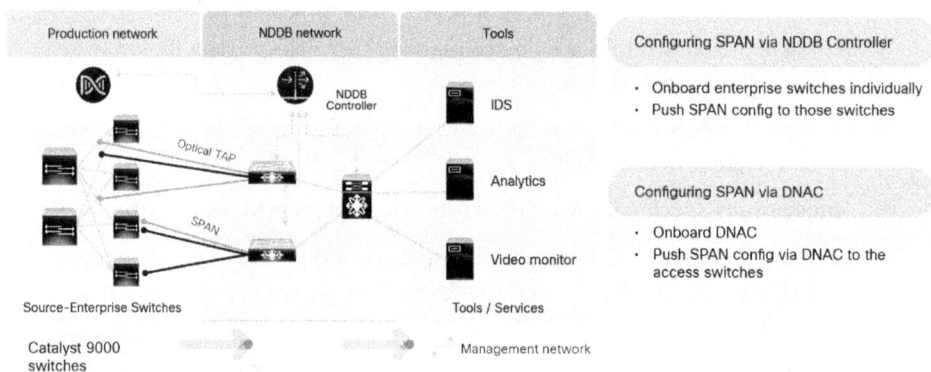

Figure 2-23   *Enterprise network SPAN automation*

Scalable Traffic Monitoring with Cisco Nexus Dashboard Data Broker Inline Option

Today, with ever-increasing volumes of traffic traversing the WAN and Internet, 10/25G bandwidth interfaces are no longer sufficient. Organizations are migrating their aggregation and core infrastructure to 40/100/200/400Gbps and higher. In addition, today's security needs demand pervasive monitoring and hence the use of multiple proactive inline security tools, such as intrusion prevention systems (IPSs), intrusion detection systems (IDSs), and other web filtering tools, at the perimeter of the network for strong and layered security.

Because of the high volume of traffic, these security tools/service nodes themselves can become bottlenecks and single points of failure. To address these concerns, customers need a solution that can adapt to increasing traffic volumes, provide flexible connections for both production infrastructure and inline tools, and provide cost-effective deployment options.

The Cisco Nexus Dashboard Data Broker Inline option allows you to insert one or more Cisco Nexus 3000 Series or 9300 platform switches in your production infrastructure to which these security tools (or service nodes) are connected.

Using the Data Broker software, you can configure redirection policies that can match specific traffic and redirect it through multiple security tools before the traffic enters or exits your data center. Cisco's Data Broker solution also automatically adapts to failure scenarios by bypassing the service nodes. It also provides the option to completely bypass all security tools for any emergency troubleshooting. Figure 2-24 illustrates inband or inline monitoring.

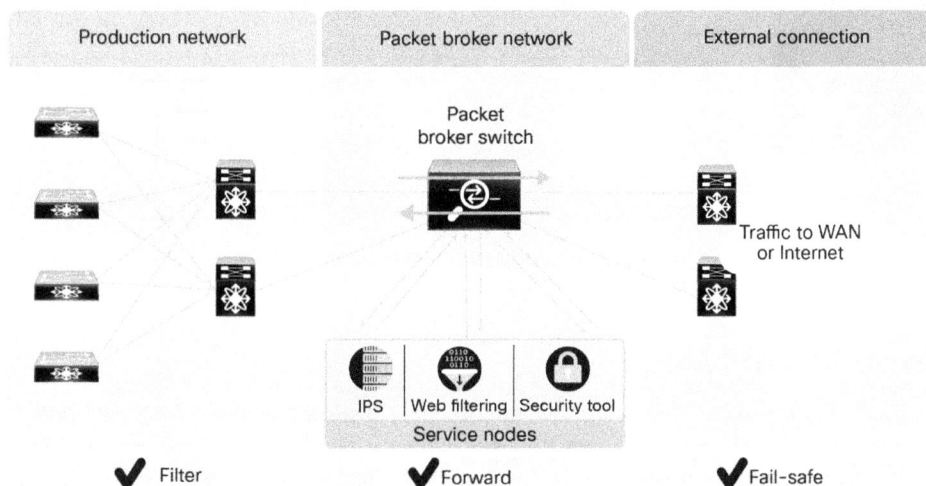

Figure 2-24   *In-band or inline monitoring*

Cisco Nexus Dashboard Data Broker Access Mechanisms

You can access the Cisco Nexus Dashboard Data Broker application through the web-based GUI or REST API. The GUI is completely redesigned with the latest and greatest GUI framework and architecture, aligned with Nexus Dashboard and Nexus Dashboard services. This redesigned GUI framework lays the foundation for further enhancements and alignment in the areas of topology and other GUI screens. Figure 2-25 shows the new GUI for Nexus Dashboard Data Broker Dashboard.

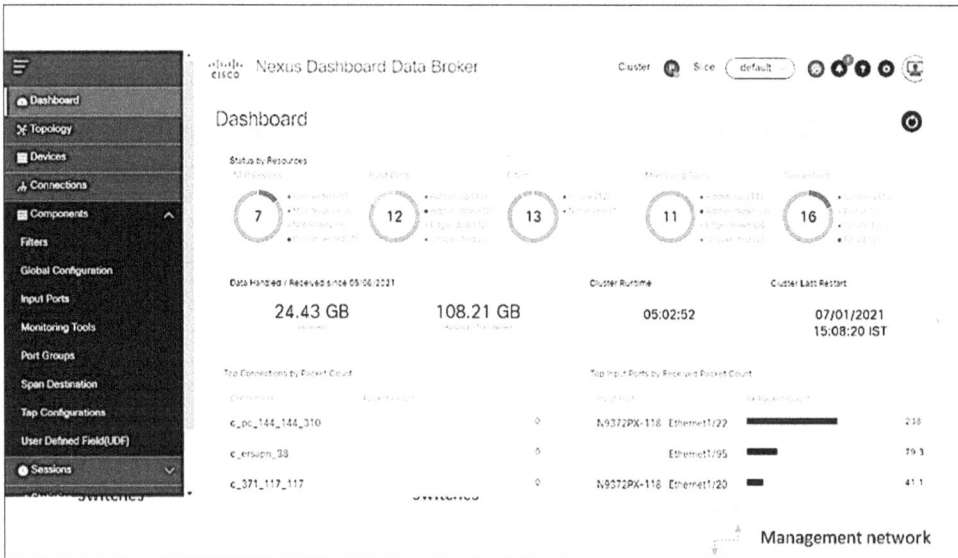

Figure 2-25   *New GUI for Nexus Dashboard Data Broker Dashboard*

Cisco Meraki MX

The Cisco Meraki MX appliances are multifunctional security and SD-WAN enterprise appliances with a wide set of capabilities to address multiple use cases—from an all-in-one device. Organizations of all sizes and across all industries rely on the MX to deliver secure connectivity to hub locations or multicloud environments, as well as application quality of experience (QoE), through advanced analytics with machine learning.

The MX is 100% cloud-managed, so installation and remote management are truly zero touch, making it ideal for distributed branches, campuses, and data center locations. Natively integrated with a comprehensive suite of secure network and assurance capabilities, the MX eliminates the need for multiple appliances. These capabilities include application-based firewalling, content filtering, web search filtering, SNORT-based intrusion detection and prevention, Cisco Advanced Malware Protection (AMP), site-to-site Auto VPN, client VPN, WAN and cellular failover, dynamic path selection, web application health, VoIP health, and more.

SD-WAN can be easily extended to deliver optimized access to resources in public and private cloud environments with virtual MX appliances (vMX). Public clouds supported with vMX include Amazon Web Services (AWS), Microsoft Azure, Google Cloud Platform, and Alibaba Cloud and private cloud support through Cisco Network Function Virtualization Infrastructure Software (NFVIS).

Cisco Enterprise Network Function Virtualization Infrastructure Software (Cisco Enterprise NFVIS) is Linux-based infrastructure software designed to help service providers and enterprises dynamically deploy virtualized network functions, such as a virtual router, firewall, and WAN acceleration, on a supported Cisco device. There is no need to add a physical device for every network function, and you can use automated provisioning and centralized management to eliminate costly truck rolls.

Cisco Enterprise NFVIS provides a Linux-based virtualization layer to the Cisco Enterprise Network Functions Virtualization (ENFV) solution. Figure 2-26 illustrates the Cisco SD-WAN extensions.

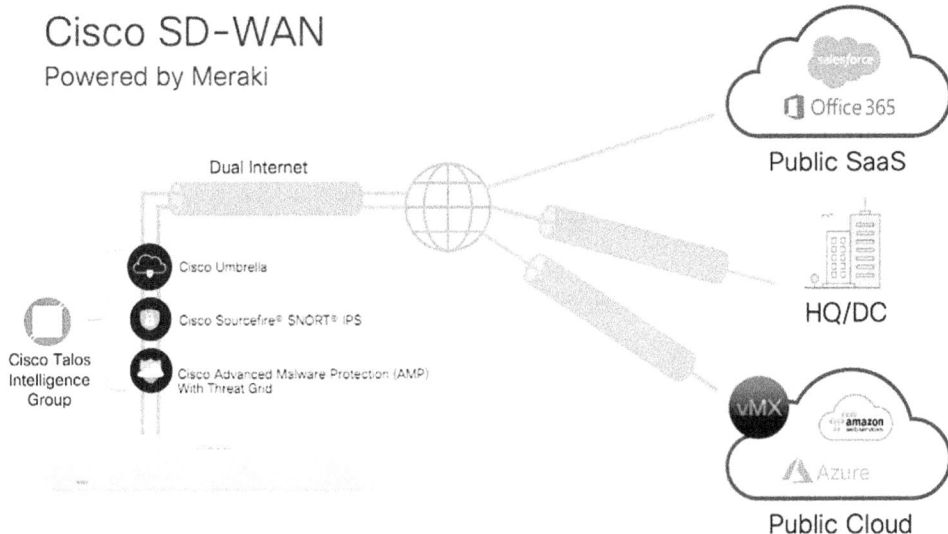

Figure 2-26   *Cisco SD-WAN extensions*

Some of the many highlights of using Meraki MX are as listed below:

- **Advanced quality of experience (QoE) analytics**

  - End-to-end health of web applications at a glance across the LAN, WAN, and application server.

  - Machine-learned smart application thresholds autonomously applied to identify true anomalies based on past behavioral patterns.

  - Monitoring of the health of all MX WAN links, including cellular, across an entire organization.

  - Detailed hop-by-hop VoIP performance analysis across all uplinks.

- **Agile on-premises and cloud security capabilities informed by Cisco Talos**

  - Next-gen Layer 7 firewall for identity-based security policies and application management.

  - Advanced Malware Protection with sandboxing; file reputation-based protection engine powered by Cisco AMP.

- Intrusion prevention with PCI-compliant IPS sensor using industry-leading SNORT signature database from Cisco.

- Granular and automatically updated category-based content filtering.

- SSL decryption/inspection, data loss prevention (DLP), cloud access security broker (CASB), SaaS tenant restrictions, granular app control, and file type control.

- **Branch gateway services**

  - Built-in DHCP, NAT, QoS, and VLAN management services.

  - Web caching accelerates frequently accessed content.

  - Load balancing combines multiple WAN links into a single high-speed interface, with policies for QoS, traffic shaping, and failover.

  - Smart connection monitoring provides automatic detection of Layer 2 and Layer 3 outages and fast failover, including the option of integrated LTE Advanced or 3G/4G modems.

- **Intelligent site-to-site VPN with Cisco SD-WAN powered by Meraki**

  - Auto VPN allows automatic VPN route generation using IKE/IKEv2/IPsec setup; runs on physical MX appliances.

  - Virtual instance in public and private clouds.

  - SD-WAN with active-active VPN, policy-based routing, dynamic VPN path selection, and support for application-layer performance profiles to ensure prioritization of application types that matter.

  - Interoperation with all IPsec VPN devices and services.

  - Automated MPLS to VPN failover within seconds of a connection failure.

  - L2TP IPsec remote client VPN included at no extra cost with support for native Windows, macOS, iPad, and Android clients.

  - Support for Cisco AnyConnect remote client VPN (AnyConnect license required).

- **Industry-leading cloud management**

  - Unified firewall, switching, wireless LAN, and mobile device management through an intuitive web-based dashboard.

  - Template-based settings scale easily from small deployments to tens of thousands of devices.

  - Role-based administration, configurable email alerts for a variety of important events, and easily auditable change logs.

  - Summary reports with user, device, and application usage details archived in the cloud.

Meraki Virtual MX Appliances for Public and Private Clouds

Virtual MX (vMX) is a virtual instance of a Meraki security and SD-WAN appliance dedicated specifically to providing the simple configuration benefits of site-to-site Auto VPN for organizations running or migrating IT services to public or private cloud environments. An Auto VPN tunnel to a vMX is like having a direct Ethernet connection to a private data center. Figure 2-27 illustrates an overview of Meraki vMX integration with cloud.

Figure 2-27   *An overview of Meraki vMX integration with cloud*

Features and Functionality of the vMX Appliance

vMX functions like a VPN concentrator and includes SD-WAN functionality like other MX devices. For public cloud environments, a vMX is added via the respective public cloud marketplace and, for private cloud environments, a vMX can be spun up on a Cisco UCS running NFVIS. Setup and management in the Meraki dashboard is just like any other MX, including the following features:

- Seamless cloud migration. You can securely connect branch sites with a physical MX appliance to resources in public cloud environments in three clicks with Auto VPN.

- Secure virtual connections. You can extend SD-WAN to public cloud environments for optimized access to business-critical resources.

- Only a Meraki license is required.

- 500Mbps of VPN throughput. vMX is available in three VPN throughput-based sizes to suit a wide range of use cases: small, medium, and large.

- Easy deployments, which support private cloud environments through the Cisco NFVIS Meraki dashboard.

Figure 2-28 illustrates Meraki vMX functioning like a VPN connector.

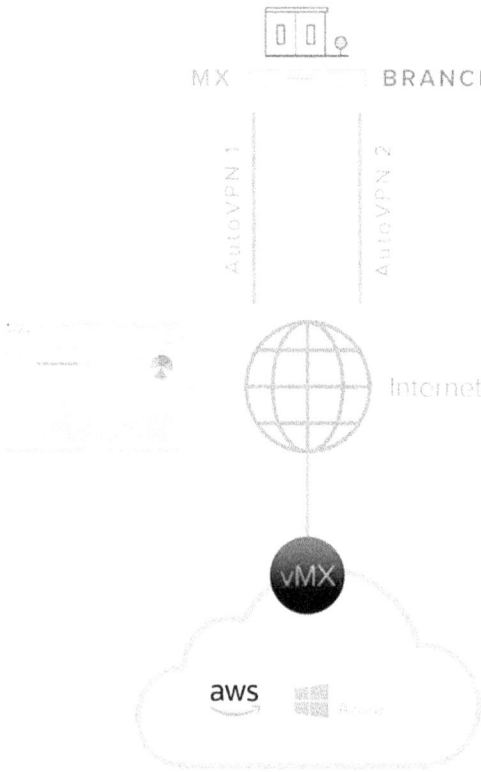

Figure 2-28   *Meraki vMX functioning like a VPN connector*

vMX Setup for Microsoft Azure

Refer to the document "vMX Setup Guide for Microsoft Azure" (see the "References/ Additional Reading" section at the end of this chapter) for a walkthrough of setting up a virtual MX (vMX) appliance in the Azure Marketplace. After completing the steps outlined in this document, you will have a virtual MX appliance running in the Azure Cloud that serves as an Auto VPN termination point for your physical MX devices.

vMX Setup for Google Cloud Platform

Refer to the document "vMX Setup Guide for Google Cloud Platform (GCP)" (see the "References/Additional Reading" section at the end of this chapter) for a walkthrough of setting up a virtual MX appliance in the Google Cloud Marketplace. After completing the steps outlined in this document, you will have a virtual MX appliance running in Google Cloud that serves as an AutoVPN termination point for your physical MX devices.

vMX Setup for Alibaba Cloud

Refer to the document "vMX Setup Guide for Alibaba Cloud" (see the "References/Additional Reading" section at the end of this chapter) for a walkthrough of setting up a virtual MX appliance in the Alibaba Cloud Marketplace. After completing the steps outlined in this document, you will have a virtual MX appliance running in Alibaba Cloud that serves as an Auto VPN termination point for physical MX devices.

Note   On November 5, 2020, the existing vMX offer on the AWS Marketplace was discontinued. For any issues that are not firmware-related, AWS will not provide support for the old vMX100 offer (as of February 3, 2021).

Summary

Network Insights builds a knowledge base by collecting software and hardware telemetry data. It has an in-depth understanding of protocols and features that run on the environment and can correlate and differentiate between expected versus unexpected behavior. It builds a relationship between behavior, symptoms, logs, and solutions and can derive root causes of the problem. A virtual assistant or an automated SME always has your back.

Network Insights detects any root-cause data-plane issues. It is the industry's first detailed end-to-end packet path with information about flow, such as 5-tuple, latency, tenant, VRF, endpoint groups, packets, drops, and more.

Network Insights provides advisories customized to the customer environment on maintenance issues that require their immediate attention so that the end user doesn't have to plow through oceans of data. You can troubleshoot across the data center with the help of connected TAC, notification of known issues, and steps toward fast remediation.

References/Additional Reading

vMX Setup Guide for Microsoft Azure:
   https://documentation.meraki.com/MX/MX_Installation_Guides/
   vMX_Setup_Guide_for_Microsoft_Azure

vMX Setup Guide for Google Cloud Platform (GCP):
   https://documentation.meraki.com/MX/MX_Installation_Guides/
   vMX_Setup_Guide_for_Google_Cloud_Platform_(GCP)

vMX Setup Guide for Alibaba Cloud:
   https://documentation.meraki.com/MX/MX_Installation_Guides/
   vMX_Setup_Guide_for_Alibaba_Cloud

Chapter 3

Cisco Data Center Solutions for Hybrid Cloud

The applications and data that run today's businesses aren't just on-premises anymore. They're spread across the entire multicloud domain, in private and public clouds and in SaaS environments. Your organization may have embraced this distributed model on purpose or arrived there by default. Either way, the hybrid cloud has a clear advantage: flexibility. You can move data and applications where they need to be, quickly and effortlessly.

Because of that flexibility, a hybrid cloud network can also be complicated to maintain. But by following the principles of simple, seamless hybrid network management, your business can harness the benefits of hybrid cloud and run more efficiently.

Cisco is making this possible—and making it easier every day. Imagine one hybrid cloud platform that provides the automation, observability, and cloud-native capabilities necessary to keep business, technology, and teams connected and moving as fast as the market demands. That's what being "cloud smart" is about.

Cisco's hybrid cloud offerings give you flexible consumption for your on-premises infrastructure so you can optimize workloads across clouds, on-premises data centers, labs, and co-location facilities for scale, performance, and agility with great value.

Cisco has a series of innovations across its portfolio of SaaS-delivered capabilities and cloud-optimized infrastructure to turn its cloud smart vision into a reality for its customers.

This chapter will cover the following solutions:

- Cisco Cloud Application Centric Infrastructure
- Cisco UCS Director
- Cisco Workload Optimization Manager
- Cisco Hyperflex-Intersight

Cisco Cloud Application Centric Infrastructure (Cisco Cloud ACI)

In today's world, enterprises are undergoing increasing pressure to innovate rapidly, to keep up with competition, and to increase IT agility to meet customer demands. To achieve these goals, businesses are choosing different infrastructure environments for deploying different types of applications. Some applications may be best suited to be hosted on the premises, whereas other applications may be best suited to be hosted in a public cloud, and yet others may benefit from hybrid deployments. In fact, hybrid cloud is becoming the new normal for many businesses.

Challenges in Hybrid Cloud Environments

In a hybrid cloud environment, it is becoming more and more challenging to maintain a homogeneous enterprise operational model, comply with corporate security policies, and gain visibility across hybrid environments.

The following are the main challenges in building and operating a hybrid cloud environment:

- Automating the creation of secure interconnects between on-premises and public clouds

- Dealing with the diverse and disjoint capabilities across on-premises private cloud and public cloud

- Multiple panes of glass to manage, monitor, and operate hybrid cloud instances

- Inconsistent security segmentation capabilities between on-premises and public clouds

- Facing the learning curve associated with operating a public cloud environment

- Inability to leverage a consistent L4–L7 services integration in hybrid cloud deployments

Cisco Cloud Application Centric Infrastructure (Cisco Cloud ACI) is a comprehensive solution for simplified operations, automated network connectivity, consistent policy management, and visibility for multiple on-premises data centers and public clouds or multicloud environments.

The solution captures business and user intents and translates them into native policy constructs for applications deployed across various cloud environments. It uses a holistic approach to enable application availability and segmentation for bare-metal, virtualized, containerized, or microservices-based applications deployed across multiple cloud domains. The common policy and operating model will drastically reduce the cost and complexity of managing hybrid and multicloud deployments. It provides a single management console to configure, monitor, and operate multiple disjointed environments spread across multiple clouds.

The Cisco Cloud ACI solution extends the successful capabilities of Cisco ACI in private clouds into public cloud environments (AWS, Microsoft Azure, and now on Google Cloud). This solution introduces Cisco Cloud APIC, which runs natively in public clouds to provide automated connectivity, policy translation, and enhanced visibility of workloads in the public cloud. This solution brings a suite of capabilities to extend your on-premises data center into true multicloud architectures, helping to drive policy and operational consistency regardless of where your applications or data reside. Figure 3-1 illustrates Cisco Cloud ACI.

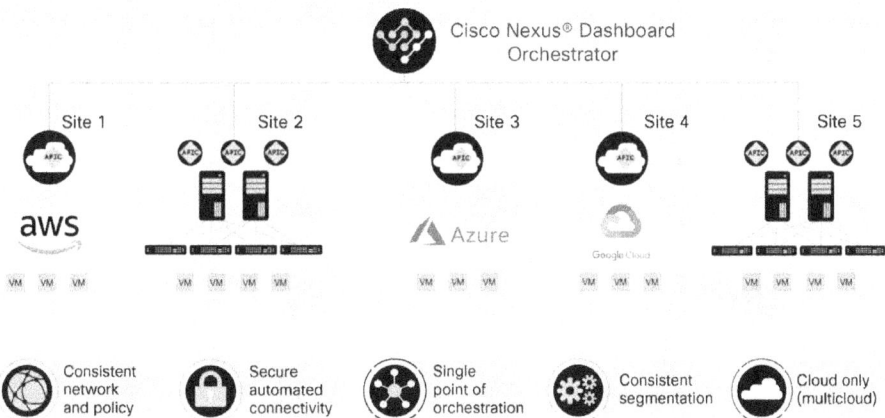

Figure 3-1   *Cisco Cloud ACI*

Cisco Nexus Dashboard offers a centralized management console that allows network operators to easily access applications needed to perform the lifecycle management of their fabric for provisioning, troubleshooting, or simply gaining deeper visibility into their network. It's a single launch point to monitor and scale across different fabric controllers, whether it is Cisco Application Policy Infrastructure Controller (APIC), Cisco Data Center Network Manager (DCNM), or Cisco Cloud APIC.

The Cisco Nexus Dashboard Orchestrator, which is hosted on the Cisco Nexus Dashboard, provides policy management, network policy configuration, and application segmentation definition and enforcement policies for multicloud deployments. Using the Cisco Nexus Dashboard Orchestrator, customers get a single view into the Cisco APIC, Cisco DCNM, and Cisco Cloud APIC policies across AWS, Microsoft Azure, and Google Cloud environments.

In an on-premises Cisco ACI data center, Cisco Application Policy Infrastructure Controller (APIC) is the single point of policy configuration and management for all the Cisco ACI switches deployed in the data center. When there is a need to seamlessly interconnect multiple Cisco ACI–powered data centers and selectively extend Cisco ACI constructs and policies across sites, Cisco Nexus Dashboard Orchestrator is the solution.

Cisco Nexus Dashboard Orchestrator can manage policies across multiple on-premises Cisco ACI data centers as well as public clouds. The policies configured from Orchestrator can be pushed to different on-premises Cisco ACI sites and cloud sites. Cisco APIC running on the premises receives this policy from Orchestrator and then renders and enforces it locally.

When extending Cisco ACI to the public cloud, a similar model applies. However, public cloud vendors do not understand Cisco ACI concepts such as endpoint groups (EPGs) and contracts. Orchestrator policies therefore need to be translated into cloud-native policy constructs. For example, contracts between Cisco ACI EPGs need to be translated into security groups on AWS first and then applied to AWS cloud instances.

This policy translation and programming of the cloud environment is performed using a new component of the Cisco Cloud ACI solution called Cisco Cloud Application Policy Infrastructure Controller (Cisco Cloud APIC or Cloud APIC).

The Cisco Cloud ACI solution ensures a common security posture across all locations for application deployments. The Cisco Cloud APIC translates ACI policies into cloud-native policy constructs, thus enabling consistent application segmentation, access control, and isolation across varied deployment models.

Cisco Cloud APIC runs natively on supported public clouds to provide automated connectivity, policy translation, and enhanced visibility of workloads in the public cloud. Cisco Cloud APIC translates all the policies received from Multi-Site Orchestrator (MSO) and programs them into cloud-native constructs such as virtual private clouds (VPCs), security groups, and security group rules.

This new solution brings a suite of capabilities to extend your on-premises data center into true hybrid cloud architectures, helping drive policy and operational consistency regardless of where your applications reside. It provides a single point of policy orchestration across hybrid environments, operational consistency, and visibility across clouds. Figure 3-2 illustrates Cisco Cloud ACI capabilities.

Figure 3-2 shows the overall high-level architecture of Cisco Cloud ACI with Cisco ACI Multi-Site Orchestrator acting as a central policy controller, managing policies across multiple on-premises Cisco ACI data centers as well as hybrid environments, with each cloud site being abstracted by its own Cloud APICs.

Consistent operations, visibility, and control for next-generation applications

Common policy abstraction, governance, and compliance

Business continuity and disaster recovery

Elasticity for resources

Multicloud workload migration

Figure 3-2 *Cisco Cloud ACI capabilities*

High-Level Architecture of Cisco Cloud ACI on AWS

An instance of MSO orchestrates multiple independent sites using a consistent policy model and provides a single pane of glass for centralized management and visibility. The sites can be either on-premises Cisco ACI fabric sites with their own site-local APIC clusters or cloud sites in AWS with Cloud APIC to manage them.

Just as with a normal Cisco ACI multisite architecture, all the sites are interconnected via a "plain" IP network. There's no need for IP multicast or Dynamic Host Configuration Protocol (DHCP) relay. You provide IP connectivity, and MSO will be responsible for setting up the intersite overlay connectivity. Figure 3-3 illustrates Cisco Cloud ACI on AWS architecture.

The following are the key building blocks of the Cisco Cloud ACI architecture:

- An on-premises Cisco ACI site running Cisco ACI software and equipped with at least one second-generation spine model (EX, FX, C, or GX)
- Cisco ACI Nexus Dashboard Orchestrator (NDO)
- Cisco Cloud APIC
- Intersite connectivity between the on-premises and cloud sites
- Network policy mapping between the Cisco ACI on-premises and cloud sites

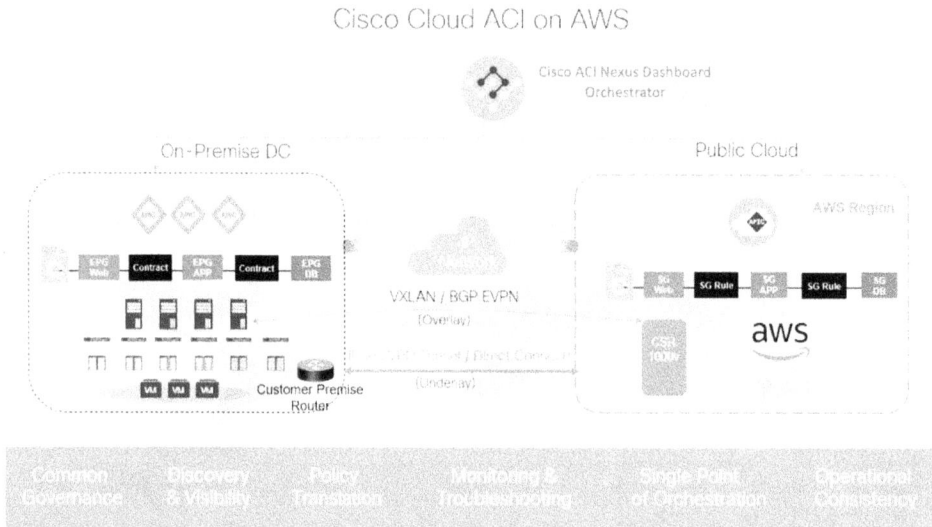

Figure 3-3 *Cisco Cloud ACI on AWS architecture*

Cisco ACI Nexus Dashboard Orchestrator

In a Cisco ACI multisite architecture, the Cisco ACI Nexus Dashboard Orchestrator (NDO) is the single pane of glass for management of all the interconnected sites. It is a centralized place to define all the intersite policies that can then be published to the individual Cisco ACI sites where the site-local APICs render them on the physical switches that build those fabrics.

With the Cisco Cloud ACI, NDO's orchestration functions expand to the cloud sites. It is responsible for site registration of both on-premises Cisco ACI data center sites and the cloud sites. It automates the creation of overlay connectivity between all the sites (on-premises and cloud). Continuing to be the central orchestrator of intersite policies, NDO publishes policies to on-premises Cisco ACI data center sites as well as pushes the same policies to cloud sites in AWS.

It is also capable of instrumenting the policy deployment among different sites by selectively distributing the policies to only the relevant sites. For instance, NDO can deploy the web front tier of an application into the cloud site in AWS while keeping its compute and database tiers in the on-premises site. Through the NDO interface, network administrators can also regulate the communication flow between the on-premises site and AWS as required by applications.

Cisco Cloud APIC on AWS

Cisco Cloud APIC is an important new solution component introduced in the architecture of Cisco Cloud ACI. It plays the equivalent of APIC for a cloud site. Like APIC for on-premises Cisco ACI sites, Cloud APIC manages network policies for the cloud site that it is running on, by using the Cisco ACI network policy model to describe the policy intent.

Cloud APIC is a software-only solution that is deployed using cloud-native instruments such as Cloud Formation templates on AWS. Network and security policies could be locally defined on the Cloud APIC for the cloud site, or they could be locally defined globally on NDO and then distributed to the Cloud APIC. While the on-premises APIC renders the intended policies onto Cisco ACI switches of the site, Cloud APIC renders the policies onto the AWS cloud network infrastructure.

It accomplishes the task by translating the Cisco ACI network policies to the AWS-native network policies and uses the AWS-native policy API to automate the provisioning of the needed AWS-native cloud resources, such as VPCs, cloud routers, security groups, and security group rules.

The key functionalities of Cloud APIC include the following:

- Providing a northbound REST interface to configure cloud deployments
- Accepting Cisco ACI Policy Model and other cloud-specific policies directly or from MSO
- Performing endpoint discovery in the cloud site
- Performing Cisco ACI Cloud Policy translation
- Configuring the cloud router's control plane
- Configuring the data-path between the Cisco ACI fabric and the cloud site

Cisco Cloud APIC is a microservices-based software deployment of APIC. Cisco Cloud APIC on AWS is deployed and runs as an Amazon Elastic Compute Cloud (Amazon EC2) instance using persistent block storage volumes in Amazon Elastic Block Store (Amazon EBS). The Amazon Machine for Cisco Cloud APIC is available at the AWS marketplace and uses a bring-your-own-license (BYOL) model.

As ACI APIC is for an on-premises ACI fabric, ACI Cloud APIC contains only policies and is not in the data-forwarding path. Any downtime of the Cloud APIC will not impact network forwarding functionality or performance in the cloud site. The Amazon EC2 instance of the Cloud APIC takes advantage of Amazon EBS built-in storage volume redundancy, high availability, and durability.

Upon a failure in the Amazon EC2 instance, it can always relaunch or restore to the previous state by rebuilding the configuration and states from persistent storage and provide seamless Cloud APIC functionalities. Therefore, for simplicity and cost-effectiveness, Cloud APIC is deployed as a single Amazon EC2 instance in the initial release of Cisco Cloud ACI on AWS. In the future, clustering of multiple virtual instances will be introduced for Cloud APIC to achieve higher scalability and instance level redundancy.

Both Cisco ACI and AWS use group-based network and security policy models. The logical network constructs of the Cisco ACI network policy model consist of tenants, bridge domains (BDs), bridge-domain subnets, endpoint groups (EPGs), and contracts. AWS uses slightly different constructs: user accounts, virtual private cloud (VPC), and security groups, plus security group rules and network access lists.

Cisco ACI classifies endpoints into EPGs and uses contracts to enforce communication policies between these EPGs. AWS uses security groups (SGs) and security group rules for classification and policy enforcement.

Cisco Cloud APIC's First Time Setup Wizard

The first time you connect to Cisco Cloud APIC UI, the First Time Setup Wizard automatically kicks off. This wizard helps you configure some of the Cisco Cloud APIC required settings, such as DNS, the TEP (Tunnel End Point) pool, the regions to be managed, and IPsec connectivity options.

At the end of the First Time Setup Wizard, Cisco Cloud APIC configures the AWS infrastructure needed to become fully operational, such as a pair of Cisco CSR 1000V Series routers. The provisioning of the AWS infrastructure is fully automated and carried out by Cisco Cloud APIC. After this step, you will be able to start deploying your Cisco ACI policy on AWS. Figure 3-4 shows the First Time Setup Wizard of Cisco Cloud APIC.

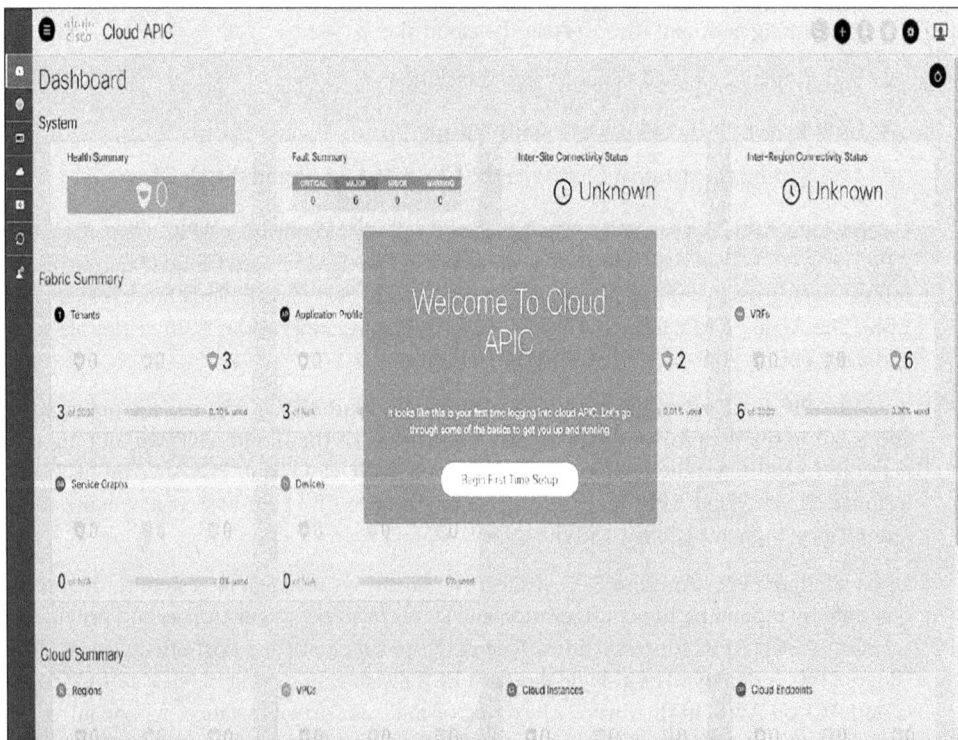

Figure 3-4   *First Time Setup Wizard of Cisco Cloud APIC*

Registering a Cisco ACI Cloud Site in NDO

Each Cisco Cloud APIC represents a Cisco ACI site. To extend policy across sites, Cisco ACI uses the Cisco ACI Nexus Dashboard Orchestrator (NDO). When you register a Cisco Cloud APIC in NDO, it will appear as a new site and will allow you to deploy existing or new schemas to AWS. NDO ensures that you specify the required site-specific options, such as subnets and EPG membership classification criteria, which are different for each site. Figure 3-5 shows how to register a Cisco ACI cloud site in NDO.

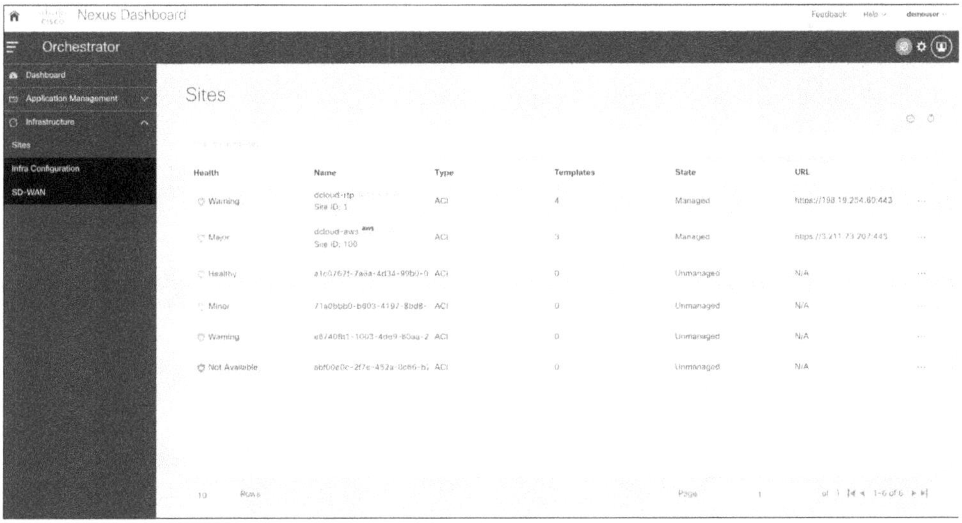

Figure 3-5   *Registering a Cisco ACI cloud site in NDO*

Cisco Cloud APIC also provides a view of the AWS-native constructs used to represent the Cisco ACI policy. This allows network administrators to gradually familiarize themselves with AWS networking constructs. Figure 3-6 shows the native cloud resources view on the Cloud APIC UI.

Deploying a Multitier Application in a Hybrid Scenario

To deploy a three-tier application, consisting of Database (DB), App, and Web tiers, across an on-premises data center and the AWS cloud using Cisco Cloud ACI integration, you will need to configure a schema on NDO that represents this policy. It should contain at least one VRF, one application profile, and three EPGs (one EPG for each tier of the application) as well as contracts between the tiers.

For example, the App and DB tiers can be deployed on the premises and the Web tier in AWS—or you can use any permutation of this set as you see fit. Figure 3-7 shows a three-tier application schema on MSO.

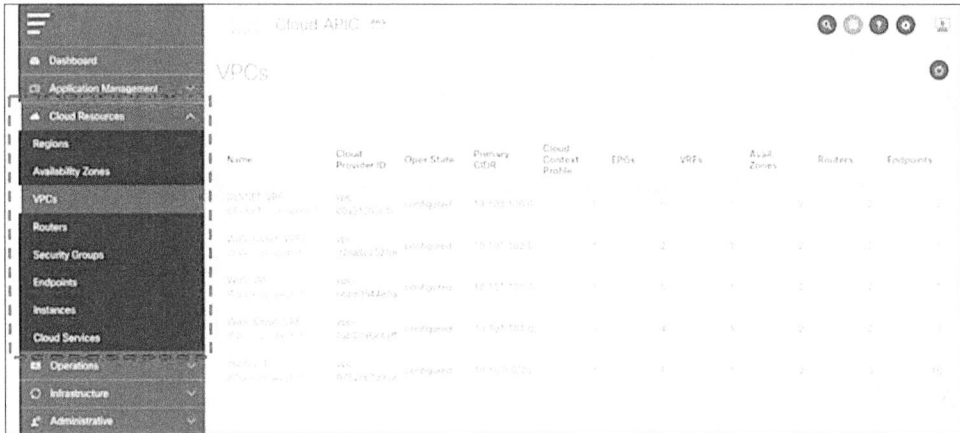

Figure 3-6   *Native cloud resources view on the Cloud APIC UI*

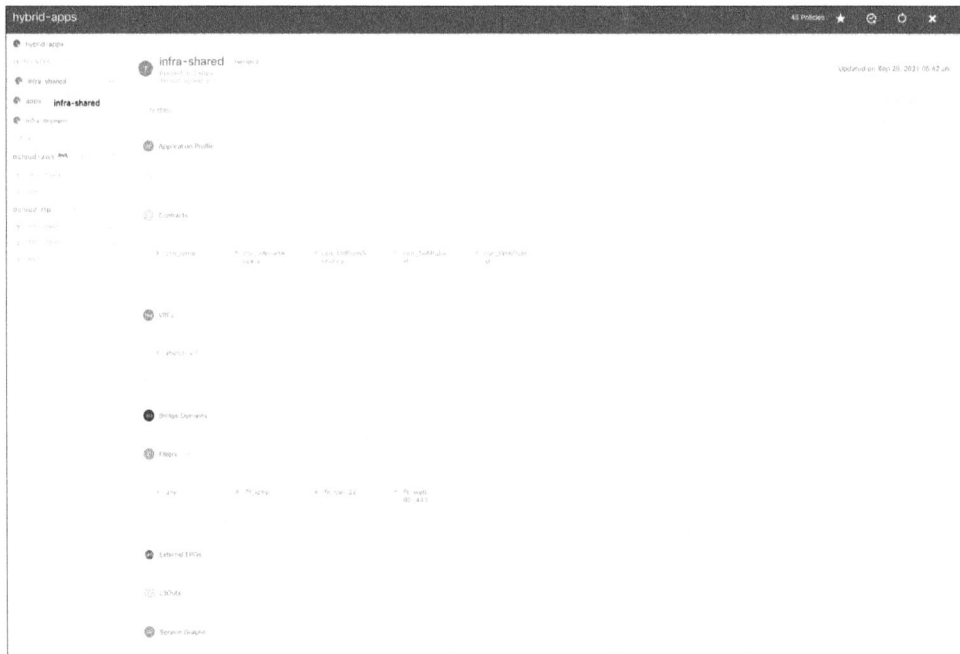

Figure 3-7   *Three-tier application schema on NDO*

The schema can then be associated with the on-premises site and the Cisco Cloud ACI site. Once the association is made, you then define the subnets to be used for the VRF on AWS. Cisco Cloud APIC model associates subnets to VRF because, in AWS, VRFs are mapped to VPCs and subnets are mapped to an availability zone (AZ) inside a VPC. Figure 3-8 illustrates how to deploy an application to on-premises and cloud sites in AWS.

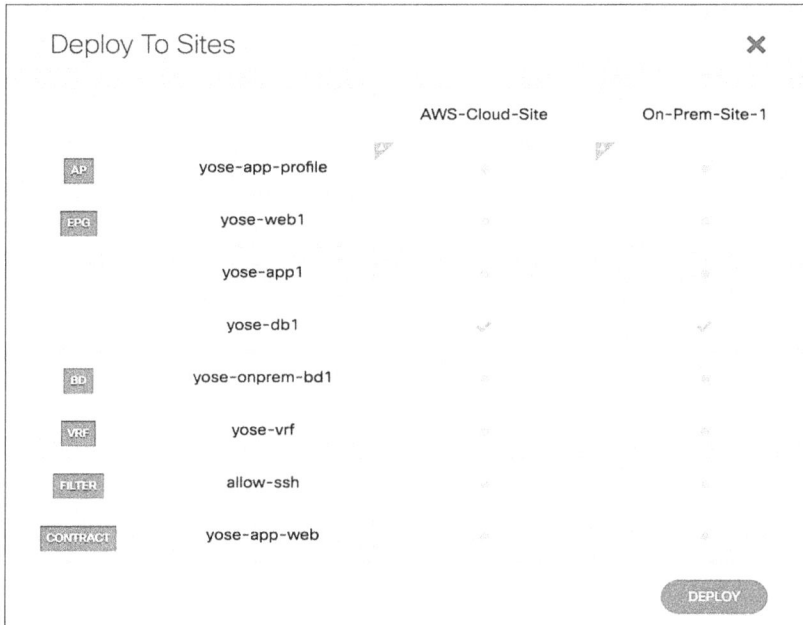

Figure 3-8 *Deploying an application to on-premises and cloud sites in AWS*

Cisco Cloud ACI ensures that the AWS cloud and on-premises ACI are configured appropriately to allow communication between the App EPG and the Web EPG residing on AWS. Figure 3-9 illustrates the three-tier application deployed across on-premises and cloud sites in AWS.

You can now deploy new Web instances on AWS to accommodate your needs.

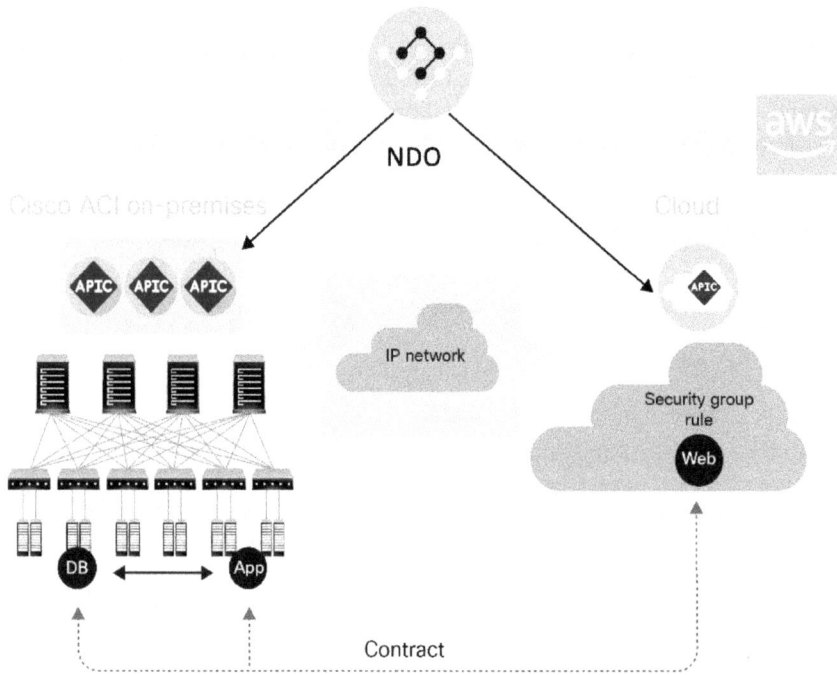

Figure 3-9   *Three-tier application deployed across on-premises and cloud sites in AWS*

Cisco UCS Director

Cisco UCS Director focuses on delivering Infrastructure as a Service (IaaS) through a highly secure, end-to-end management, orchestration, and automation solution for a wide array of Cisco and non-Cisco data center infrastructure components. Cisco UCS Director can deliver IaaS for individual components and for converged infrastructure solutions based on the Cisco Unified Computing System (Cisco UCS) and Cisco Nexus platforms.

With Cisco UCS Director, you can manage, automate, and orchestrate your physical and virtual compute, network, and storage resources. In addition, through the End User Portal, you can use those infrastructure components to deploy the desired virtual machines to support applications in cloud environments. To support this functionality, Cisco UCS Director enables you to do the following:

- Manage and support heterogeneous data centers that include compute, network, storage, and virtualization resources from multiple vendors.

- Provision physical and virtual compute, Layer 4–7 network services, and storage resources.

- Create and implement single and multitier application profiles.

■ Define application containers that describe a set of tiers that includes physical and/ or virtual compute resources, their connectivity policy, and their communication policy. You can further define those application containers with network services, such as load balancing and firewalls, across these tiers.

■ Establish secure multitenant environments so that users, whether internal to your company or external, can work only within the secure constraints of their own resource pool. With the policies and user roles that you establish, your users can view, manage, and use only the infrastructure components appropriate for their roles.

■ Automate the IT processes necessary to accomplish infrastructure provisioning and decommissioning using a role and policy-based model that limits administrator and user capabilities.

■ Implement a process-oriented approach to infrastructure orchestration that automates the processes you define using built-in workflows or customized workflows created from Cisco UCS Director task library or from tasks you create yourself.

■ Implement metering, chargeback, and showback features so your organization can be properly compensated for the IT services you provide.

Cisco UCS Director connects all the elements of the data center infrastructure, including the users and the physical and virtual infrastructures. You can provision, configure, monitor, and automate your data center management, along with Cisco UCS Director REST API or Open Automation Framework, to extend the out-of-the-box functionality. Figure 3-10 provides an overview of the Cisco UCS Director System.

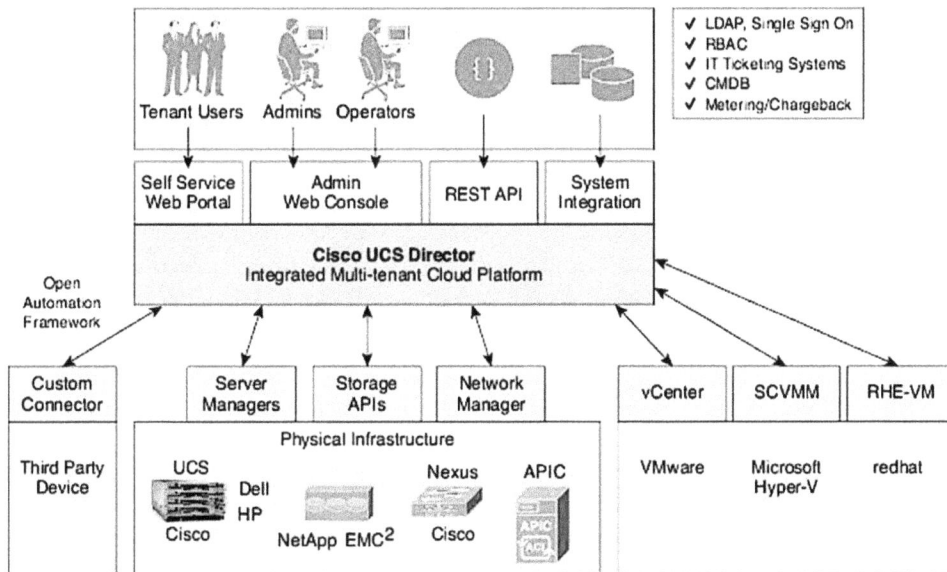

Figure 3-10   *Cisco UCS Director System Overview*

Infrastructure Configuration and Management

Cisco UCS Director extends the unification of compute, network, virtualization, and storage layers and provides comprehensive visibility into the data center infrastructure.

Cisco UCS Director can be a single appliance to manage all your infrastructure by communicating with the domain managers or domain controllers. This central management capability enables operations teams to configure, administer, manage, and monitor supported Cisco and non-Cisco physical and virtual compute, network, and storage components.

Cisco UCS Director provides out-of-the-box integration with virtual and physical components, including the following:

- Hypervisors, such as VMware vSphere, Microsoft Hyper-V, and RedHat KVM

- Compute servers and devices, such as Cisco UCS, HP, and Dell servers

- Network devices, such as Cisco Nexus and Brocade

- Storage components, such as NetApp, EMC, and IBM Storwize

- Hyperconverged storage solutions, such as VMware Virtual SAN (VSAN)

Figure 3-11 illustrates systems and hypervisors supported by UCS Director.

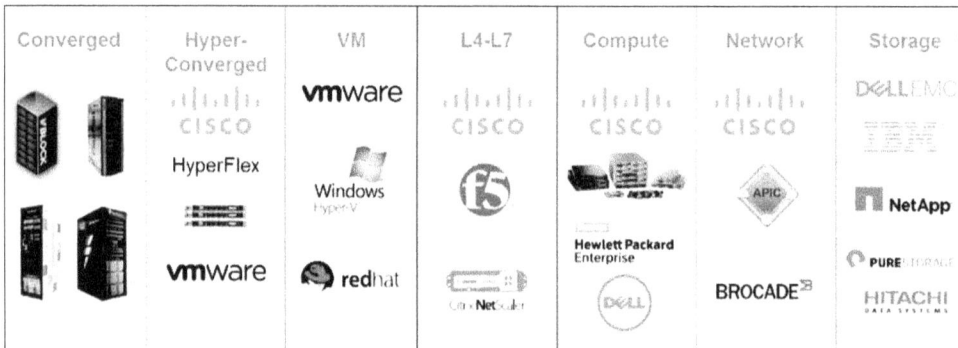

Figure 3-11 *Systems and hypervisors supported by UCS Director*

Cisco UCS Director is supported by a broad, well-established ecosystem. Third-party hardware and solution vendors support the platform using a publicly available SDK with open southbound application programming interfaces (APIs) that are downloadable. The SDK contains all of the required APIs and management functions for the third-party hardware or solution to be added into the Cisco UCS Director management model. Similarly, the northbound API is supported by the broader Cisco UCS ecosystem of DevOps and IT operations management (ITOM) tools, meaning you can transition to the cloud using existing tools as you adopt new automation and continuous delivery processes.

Cisco UCS Management Through Cisco UCS Director

Cisco UCS Director is not a replacement for Cisco UCS Manager. Rather, Cisco UCS Director uses orchestration to automate some of the steps required to configure a Cisco UCS domain. In this way, Cisco UCS Director provides a statistical analysis of the data and a converged view of each pod.

After you add a Cisco UCS domain to Cisco UCS Director as a Cisco UCS Manager account, Cisco UCS Director provides you with complete visibility into the Cisco UCS domain. In addition, you can use Cisco UCS Director to manage and configure that Cisco UCS domain.

Cisco UCS Management Tasks You Can Perform in Cisco UCS Director

You can use Cisco UCS Director to perform management, monitoring, and reporting tasks for physical and virtual devices within a Cisco UCS domain.

Configuration and Administration

You can create and configure the following Cisco UCS hardware and software components in Cisco UCS Director:

- Fabric interconnects, including ports
- Chassis, blade servers, and rack-mount servers, including auto-discovery
- I/O modules and fabric extenders (FEXes)
- Network connections
- Storage connections
- Pools
- Policies
- Service profiles

Monitoring and Reporting

You can also use Cisco UCS Director to monitor and report on your Cisco UCS domains and their components, including:

- Power consumption
- Temperature
- Server availability
- Service profile association

Table 3-1 details the UCS Director orchestration components.

Table 3-1   *UCS Director Orchestration Components*

Category	Data Elements
Task	▪ A task is the atomic unit of work in Cisco UCS Director Orchestrator. ▪ A task is a single action or operation with inputs and outputs. ▪ Cisco UCS Director has a task library containing hundreds of predefined tasks that cover most of the actions an administrator must perform using orchestration.
Workflow	▪ A workflow is a series of tasks arranged to automate a complex operation. ▪ The simplest possible workflow contains a single task, but workflows can contain any number of tasks. ▪ It allows you to automate processes of any level of complexity on your physical and virtual infrastructure.
Service Request	▪ A service request is closely related to a workflow. You create service requests by running workflows; a service request is generated every time you execute a workflow in Cisco UCS Director. ▪ A service request is a process under the control of Cisco UCS Director.
Input and Output	▪ Both tasks and workflows can have any number of input and output variables (inputs and outputs). ▪ Any task or workflow input can be either mandatory or optional. ▪ A task or workflow cannot run without all of its mandatory inputs. ▪ You define whether an input is mandatory or optional when you create the task or workflow.
Workflow Validation	▪ Orchestrator provides a mechanism for validating the flow of data from one task to the next in a workflow. ▪ Workflow validation checks the data bindings and connections between tasks.
Workflow Versioning	▪ All Orchestrator workflows have a version history. ▪ With the version history, you can revert a workflow to an earlier version or create a new version.
Approval	▪ An approval is a "gate" task that requires the intervention of a Cisco UCS Director user to allow a workflow to run to completion. ▪ This user is typically an administrator who has go-or-no-go authority over the workflow process.
Rollback	▪ Workflows can be "rolled back" to a state identical or similar to the state before the workflow was executed. ▪ You can do this, for example, to remove virtual components that were created in error.

Orchestration and Automation

Cisco UCS Director provides model-based orchestration through workflows. These workflows can include complex logic, can be imported into or exported from Cisco UCS Director, and can be configured to resume from the point of last failure. You can also include advanced orchestration features that provide agility, such as rollback of workflows, and enable you to automate the provisioning and de-provisioning of resources. This functionality is possible because Cisco UCS Director is model-aware and state-aware.

Cisco UCS Director enables you to build workflows that provide automation services and to publish those workflows and extend their services on demand. The Workflow Designer is a drag-and-drop orchestration editor that includes a large library of out-of-the-box workflow tasks and workflows.

Depending on your business needs, you can use or modify the out-of-the-box workflows and workflow tasks or you can develop your own custom workflows or workflow tasks. Custom workflow tasks can use Cloupia Script, a Java script-like programming language, REST APIs, or PowerShell cmdlets. In the workflows, you can combine your custom tasks with out-of-the-box generic tasks.

You may embed approvals inside a workflow to ensure that resources are not provisioned until they have been approved. Once built and validated, these workflows perform the same way every time, no matter who runs them or where they are run.

Infrastructure as a Service

Cisco UCS Director delivers Infrastructure as a Service (IaaS) for both virtual and physical infrastructure. With Cisco UCS Director, you can create an application container template that defines the infrastructure required for a specific application or how a customer or business unit is expected to use that application. Cisco UCS Director helps IT teams to define the rules for the business's infrastructure services:

- Either you can first onboard tenants and then define the boundaries of the physical and virtual infrastructure that they can use, or you can allow your onboarded tenants to define the infrastructure boundaries.

- Create policies, orchestration workflows, and application container templates in Cisco UCS Director that define the requirements for a specific type of application that can be used by a tenant, such as a web server, database server, or generic virtual machine (VM).

- Publish these templates as a catalog in the End User Portal.

Users can go to the End User Portal, select the catalog that meets their needs, and make a service request for that particular application or VM. Their service request triggers the appropriate orchestration workflow to allocate the required infrastructure and provision the application or VM.

If the service request requires approvals, Cisco UCS Director sends emails to the specified approver(s). Once the service request is approved, Cisco UCS Director assigns the infrastructure to those users, creating a virtual machine if necessary, and doing the base configuration, such as provisioning the operating system. You can also configure an orchestration workflow to ask questions before allowing a user to choose a catalog item. Here are some points to keep in mind:

- You can configure the workflow to ask the user what type of application they plan to run and automatically select a catalog for them based on the answers to those questions.

- The end user does not have to worry about whether to request a physical server or a VM, what kind of storage they require, or which operating system to install. Everything is predefined and prepackaged in the catalog.

For example, you can create policies, orchestration workflows, and an application container template for an SAP application that uses a minimum level of infrastructure, requires approvals from a director in the company, and has a chargeback to the department. When an end user makes a service request in the End User Portal for that catalog item, Cisco UCS Director does the following:

1. Sends an email to the director, who is the required approver.

2. When the approval is received, Cisco UCS Director creates a VM in the appropriate pod with four CPUs, 10GB of memory, and 1TB of storage.

3. Installs an operating system (OS) on the VM.

4. Notifies the end user that the VM is available for them to use.

5. Sets up the chargeback account for the cost of the VM.

With the available APIs from Cisco UCS Director, you can also script custom workflows to pre-install the SAP application in the VM after the OS is installed.

Cisco UCS Director enables you to automate a wide array of tasks and use cases across a wide variety of supported Cisco and non-Cisco hardware and software data center components, including physical infrastructure automation at the compute, network, and storage layers. A few examples of the use cases that you can automate include, but are not limited to, the following:

- VM provisioning and lifecycle management

- Network resource configuration and lifecycle management

- Storage resource configuration and lifecycle management

- Tenant onboarding and infrastructure configuration

- Application infrastructure provisioning

- Self-service catalogs and VM provisioning

- Bare-metal server provisioning, including installation of an operating system

For each of the processes that you decide to automate with orchestration workflows, you can choose to implement the processes in any of the following ways:

■ Use the out-of-the-box workflows provided with Cisco UCS Director.

■ Modify the out-of-the-box workflows with one or more of the tasks provided with Cisco UCS Director.

■ Create your own custom tasks and use them to customize the out-of-the-box workflows.

■ Create your own custom workflows with custom tasks and the out-of-the-box tasks.

Beginning with version 6.6, Cisco UCS Director can be claimed as a managed device in Intersight, so usage data, license usage, and so on can be collected. UCS Director administrators can update UCS Director southbound connectors that are used to communicate with supported devices, including networking and storage platforms, during a maintenance window for rapid delivery of new features and functionality. This will enable users to leverage endpoint capabilities and APIs faster through UCS Director by enabling the update of device libraries. Figure 3-12 illustrates Cisco UCS Director Intersight integration.

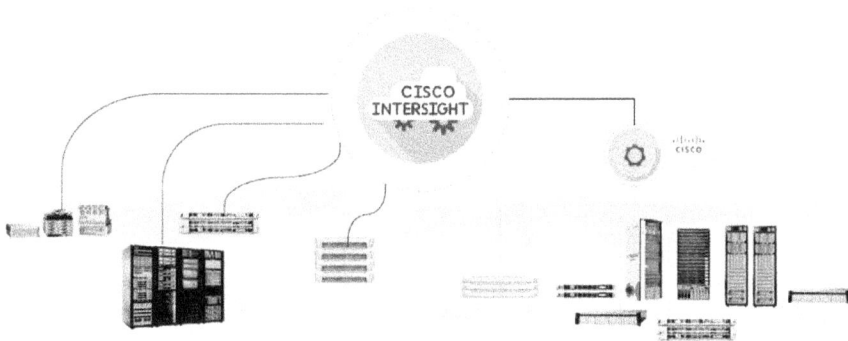

Figure 3-12   *Cisco UCS Director Intersight integration*

The benefits of SaaS and CI/CD (continuous integration/continuous delivery) can be achieved by claiming on-premises UCS Director instances in Intersight. Once these are claimed, the traditional on-premises software is transformed into a secure hybrid SaaS setup that delivers ongoing new capabilities:

■ Automatic downloads of software enhancements upgrades, bug fixes, and updates for the following:

  ■ UCS Director Base Platform Pack

  ■ System Update Manager

  ■ Infrastructure specific Connector Packs (EMC storage, F5 load balancers, RedHat KVM)

■ Enhanced problem resolution with Cisco Support through Intersight

■ Proactive notifications and streamlined "one-click" diagnostics collection

Figure 3-13 illustrates Cisco UCS Director Intersight integration benefits.

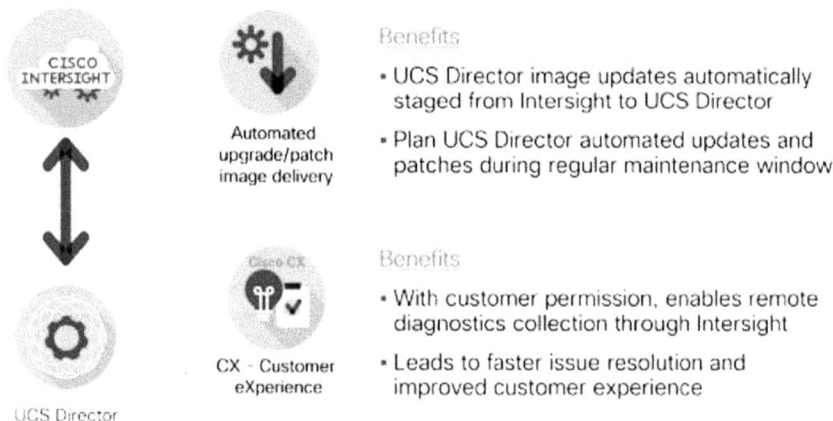

Figure 3-13 *Cisco UCS Director Intersight integration benefits*

UCS Director–specific dashboard widgets can be added to provide useful summary information for the following:

■ Instance summary

■ Service status summary

■ Last backup status

■ Trends for last 10 backups

Figure 3-14 shows the UCS Director dashboard widgets in Intersight.

It is possible for an Intersight workflow to call a UCSD workflow, if desired, which can allow an organization to gradually migrate to Intersight as the primary orchestrator. However, the UCS Director and Intersight workflows are not compatible, and they cannot be directly imported from UCS Director into Intersight.

With Cisco ACI, you can create application infrastructure containers that contain the appropriate network services as well as support infrastructure components for each respective application. Figure 3-15 illustrates UCS Director integration with ACI.

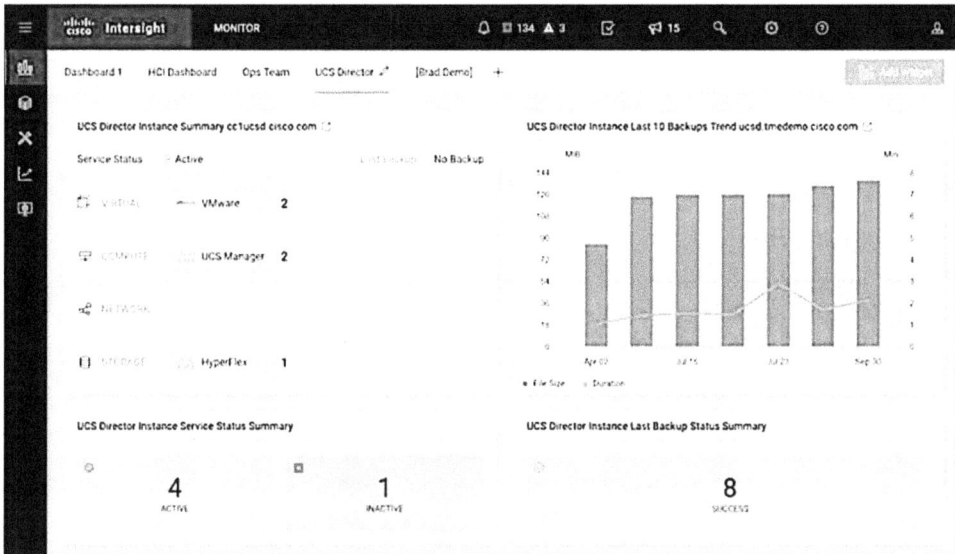

Figure 3-14 *UCS Director dashboard widgets in Intersight*

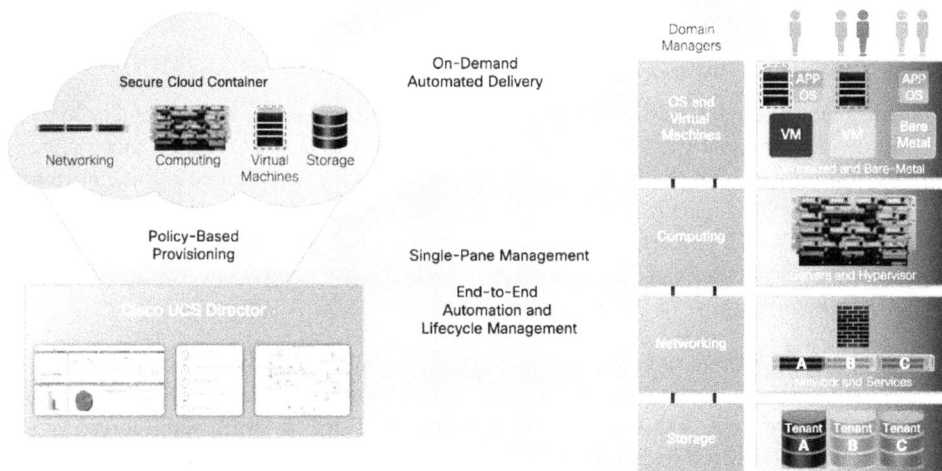

Figure 3-15 *UCS Director integration with ACI*

The following are the business benefits of Cisco UCS Director and Cisco ACI integration:

- Cisco UCS Director and Cisco ACI integrate through native tasks and prebuilt workflows.

- This integration supports IaaS with three main features:

  - Secure multitenancy

  - Rapid application deployment

  - Self-service portal

Secure Multitenancy

The integrated solution provides consistent delivery of infrastructure components that are ready to be consumed by clients in a secured fashion. Here are some key points concerning secure multitenancy:

- The solution optimizes resource sharing capabilities and provides secure isolation of clients without compromising quality of service (QoS) in a shared environment.

- To provide IaaS, secure multitenancy reserves resources for exclusive use and securely isolates them from other clients.

- Cisco ACI supports multitenancy by using Virtual Extensible LAN (VXLAN) tunnels internally within the fabric, inherently isolating tenant and application traffic.

- Cisco UCS Director manages the resource pools assigned to each container. Only Cisco supports secure multitenancy that incorporates both physical and virtual resources.

Rapid Application Deployment

The combination of Cisco UCS Director and Cisco ACI enhances your capability to rapidly deploy application infrastructure for you and your clients. With the increasing demands of new applications and the elastic nature of cloud environments, administrators need to be able to quickly design and build application profiles and publish them for use by clients. Cisco UCS Director, in conjunction with Cisco ACI, gives you the ability to quickly meet the needs of your clients. Here are some key points concerning rapid application deployment:

- Cisco UCS Director interacts with Cisco ACI to automatically implement the networking services that support applications. In Cisco UCS Director, you can specify a range of Layer 4 through Layer 7 networking services between application layers that are deployed with a zero-touch automated configuration model.

  - You can dynamically place workloads based on current network conditions so that service levels are maintained at the appropriate level for the applications being supported by the client.

■ You can use resource groups to establish tiers of resources based on application requirements, including computing, networking, and storage resources, with varying levels of performance. For example, a bronze level of service might be used for developers and include resources such as thin-provisioned storage and virtualized computing resources. In contrast, a gold level of service might be used for production environments and include thick-provisioned storage and bare-metal servers for performance without compromise.

■ After your resources and services are deployed, you can monitor your application infrastructure with real-time health scores, dynamically reconfigure your network if necessary to meet your performance goals, and obtain resource consumption information that can be used for charging clients.

■ Cisco UCS Director in conjunction with Cisco ACI also provides complete application infrastructure lifecycle management, returning resources to their respective free pools and eliminating stranded resources.

Self-Service Portal

After you have defined or adopted a set of application profiles, you can make them available to clients in a service catalog visible in the self-service portal. Your clients can log in to Cisco UCS Director's self-service portal, view the service catalog published by your organization, and order the infrastructure as desired.

The application profiles you define can be parameterized so that clients can provide attributes during the ordering process to customize infrastructure to meet specific needs.

For example, clients can be allowed to specify the number of servers deployed in various application infrastructure tiers or the amount of storage allocated to each database server. After your clients have placed their orders, they can monitor the status of application infrastructure orders, view the progress of application infrastructure deployment, and perform lifecycle management tasks.

Cisco Workload Optimization Manager

Data centers and applications are getting more complex and distributed. The result is a dizzying array of monitoring, orchestration, and management solutions that has not been able to ensure workload performance. In addition, applications are becoming more distributed and complex as enterprises build them on containers and microservices in multicloud environments. The ability to continuously deliver application performance while minimizing costs is critical. It enables development teams to innovate and run applications efficiently. It ensures that end users and customers have great digital experiences. It drives revenue. However, workload management is now so complex that it is moving beyond human capabilities.

Cisco Workload Optimization Manager (CWOM) is a real-time decision engine that drives continuous health in the IT environment. Its intelligent software constantly analyzes workload consumption, costs, and compliance constraints. It ensures application performance by giving workloads the resources they need, when they need them. Figure 3-16 illustrates today's workload management.

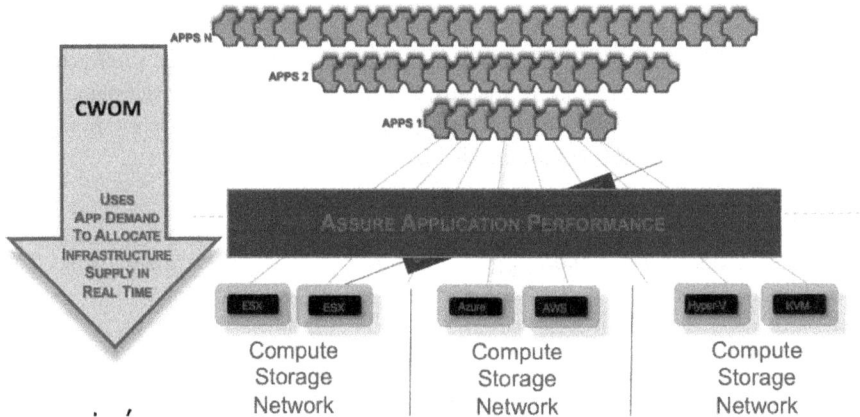

Figure 3-16   *Today's workload management*

Cisco Workload Optimization Manager is an easy-to-install, agentless technology that detects relationships and dependencies between the components in your environment, from applications through the infrastructure layers. Within one hour of deployment, Cisco Workload Optimization Manager delivers a global topological mapping of your environment (local and remote, and across private and public clouds) and the interdependent relationships within the environment, mapping each layer of the full infrastructure stack to application demand. Figure 3-17 illustrates closed-loop infrastructure optimization using CWOM.

Cisco Workload Optimization Manager provides specific real-time actions that ensure workloads get the resources they need when they need them, enabling continuous placement, resizing, and capacity decisions that can be automated, driving continuous health in the environment. Once Cisco Workload Optimization Manager is deployed, you connect to your browser of choice, add the license key, and select your targets. After you have selected your targets, you then add IP addresses, usernames, and password credentials. Targets include hypervisors, cloud platforms, applications, storage, network, and more. Cisco Workload Optimization Manager uses these targets to discover your environment and determine the specific actions that will drive continuous health in your environment.

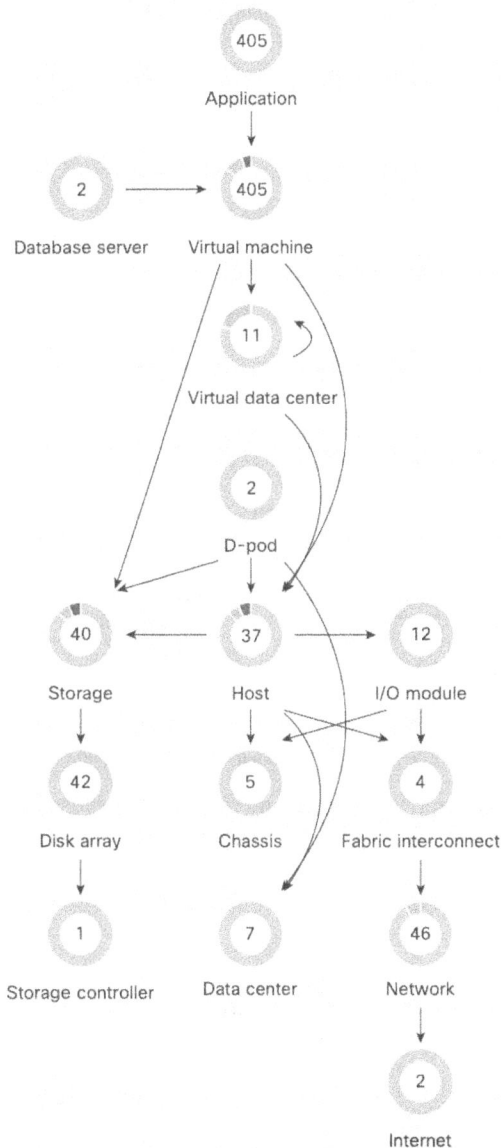

Figure 3-17 *Closed-loop infrastructure optimization using CWOM*

Create More Effective Teams

Cisco Workload Optimization Manager enables your application and IT team to ensure application performance on virtual machine or container platforms without the need for IT involvement. Integration with ServiceNow workflows enables agility and speed without relinquishing control. Your teams have the freedom to create application environments quickly and efficiently, so your IT staff can focus on strategic business initiatives. Cisco Workload Optimization Manager application resource management works with the industry's top platforms, including VMware vSphere, OpenStack, Citrix XenServer, and Microsoft Hyper-V hypervisors as well as Kubernetes, RedHat OpenShift, and Cloud Foundry, to create self-managing and optimized container environments that can do the following:

■ Minimize human intervention

■ Enable automated scheduling of pods to ensure performance

■ Provide intelligent cluster scaling to reduce outages

■ Ensure full-stack control to unite DevOps teams and infrastructure

Optimize Your Multicloud Environment

Cisco Workload Optimization Manager can ensure application performance across your data centers and into public clouds. The software does the following:

■ Automates workload placement, scaling, and capacity to ensure performance while maximizing efficiency

■ Quickly models what-if scenarios based on the real-time environment to accurately forecast capacity needs

■ Continuously ensures performance for VMware Horizon virtual desktop users

■ Tracks, reports, and views trends for compute, storage, and database consumption metrics, such as CPU, memory, IOPs, latency, and database transaction unit (DTU), across regions and zones

Optimize Public Cloud Costs

Performance cost optimization takes into account your Microsoft Azure and Amazon Web Services (AWS) subscriptions to better utilize these resources in the following ways:

■ Scale down AWS instances or Azure virtual machines, storage tiers, and database tiers, reducing costs without impacting performance

■ Understand advanced reserved instance (RI) calculations to both purchase new RIs (coverage) and efficiently use existing RIs (utilization)

■ Identify ghost and unattached storage instances

■ Suspend or terminate unused instances

■ Project actual cost of workloads by calculating compute, licensing (OS), IP address, and storage costs

■ Aggregate monthly bills across services, regions, accounts, specific workloads, and lines of business

Optimize Hyperconverged Workloads

Cisco Workload Optimization Manager works with many third-party solutions to ensure your applications get the resources they need. However, its deep integration with the entire Cisco environment greatly enhances your Cisco deployments to optimize your data centers. It helps you safely maximize cloud elasticity in Cisco UCS server environments and Cisco Hyperflex systems to gain better performance and efficiency. With Cisco Tetration network awareness, you can confidently re-platform to application architectures that have increased network complexity. Cisco Cloud Center can help you intelligently deploy new workloads anywhere, anytime. Cisco Workload Optimization Manager optimizes initial cloud placement for performance, cost, and compliance. Figure 3-18 illustrates CWOM meeting changing demands.

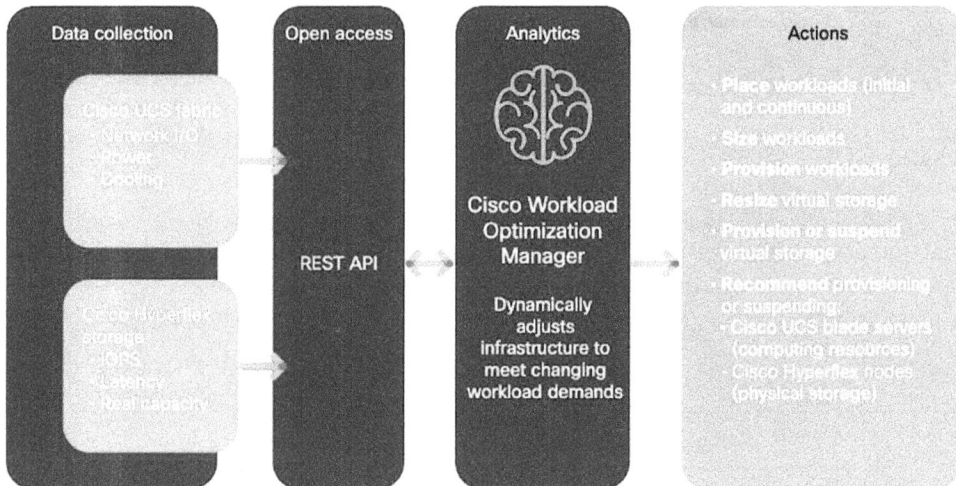

Figure 3-18   *CWOM meeting changing demands*

Ensure Application Performance

Application awareness with AppDynamics metrics complements Cisco Workload Optimization Manager and enables you to do the following:

- Continuously ensure application performance and eliminate application performance risk due to infrastructure

- Show your IT organization's value to the business when infrastructure-resource decisions are directly tied to the performance of business-critical applications

- Bridge the application-infrastructure gap with full-stack control that elevates teams and provides a common understanding of application dependencies

■ Accelerate and de-risk application migration with a holistic understanding of application topology, resource utilization, and the data center stack

Figure 3-19 illustrates CWOM meeting AppDynamics.

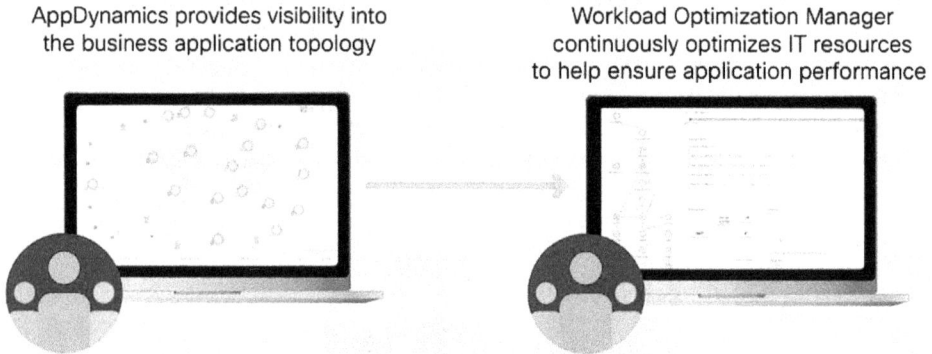

AppDynamics provides visibility into
the business application topology

Workload Optimization Manager
continuously optimizes IT resources
to help ensure application performance

Figure 3-19   *CWOM meeting AppDynamics*

Cisco AppDynamics and Cisco Workload Optimization Manager provide complete visibility and insight into application and infrastructure interdependencies and business performance. The result is application-aware IT infrastructure that is continuously resourced to deliver business objectives. Figure 3-20 illustrates the CWOM and AppDynamics benefits.

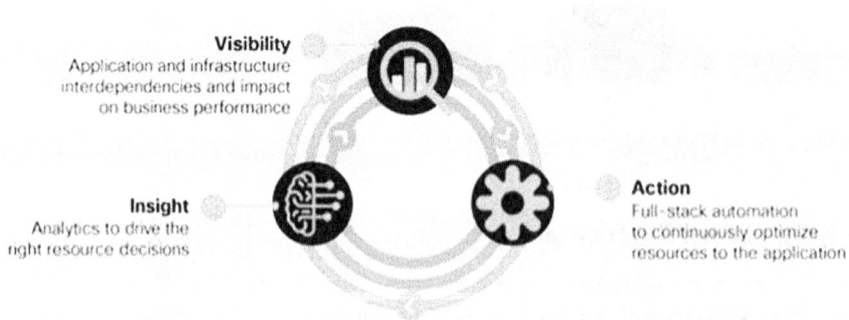

Visibility
Application and infrastructure
interdependencies and impact
on business performance

Action
Full-stack automation
to continuously optimize
resources to the application

Insight
Analytics to drive the
right resource decisions

Figure 3-20   *CWOM and AppDynamics benefits*

Cisco Workload Optimization Main Features

Workload Optimization Manager continuously analyzes workload consumption, costs, and compliance constraints and automatically allocates resources in real time. It helps ensure performance by giving workloads the resources they need, when they need them. When fully automated, the self-managing platform promotes a continuous state of health in the environment by making placement, scaling, and capacity decisions in real time. It empowers data center and cloud operators to focus on innovation—on bringing new products and services to market that promote digital transformation.

Target Integration

A target is a service that performs management in your virtual environment. Workload Optimization Manager uses targets to monitor workloads and to perform actions in your environment. The target configuration specifies the ports that Workload Optimization Manager uses to connect with these services. You must install Workload Optimization Manager on a network that has access to the specific services you want to set up as targets. For each target, Workload Optimization Manager communicates with the service through the management protocol that it exposes: the Representational State Transfer (REST) API, Storage Management Initiative Specification (SMI-S), XML, or some other management transport mechanism. Workload Optimization Manager uses this communication to discover the managed entities, monitor resource utilization, and perform actions.

Use the steps that follow to configure target integration:

Step 1.   In the New User interface, click **Try It Now**. Another login page will open.

Step 2.   Enter a username and password to log in.

Figure 3-21 shows the CWOM login page.

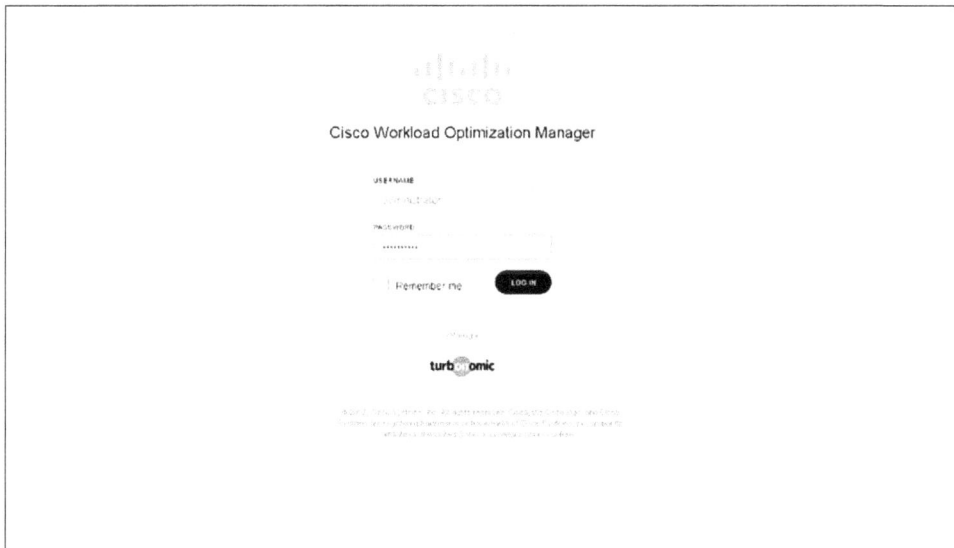

Figure 3-21   *CWOM login page*

Step 3.   Click **Settings** and select **Target Configuration** (see Figure 3-22).

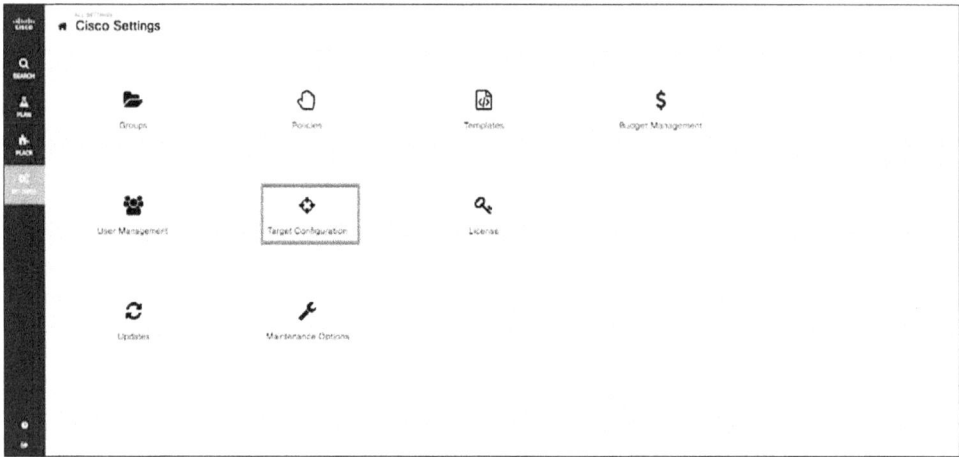

Figure 3-22   *CWOM Target Configuration*

You are now ready to add targets.

View Your Global Environment

When you log in to Workload Optimization Manager after setup, the Home page is the first view you see. By default, the Home page gives you a global view of your environment. From the Home page, you can do the following:

- Use the Supply Chain Navigator to set the Home page focus and see details about your environment.

- Display an overview of your environment's supply chain.

- Display an overview and details about the entities in your environment.

- Navigate to other areas of Workload Optimization Manager, including:

  - **Search:** Set the session scope.

  - **Plan:** Plan deployments and model what-if scenarios.

  - **Place:** Place a consumer on a different provider.

  - **Settings:** Configure Workload Optimization Manager.

- Whenever you are in a Workload Optimization Manager session, you can always click the **Cisco Home** icon to return to the Home page.

Figure 3-23 illustrates CWOM Global Environment view.

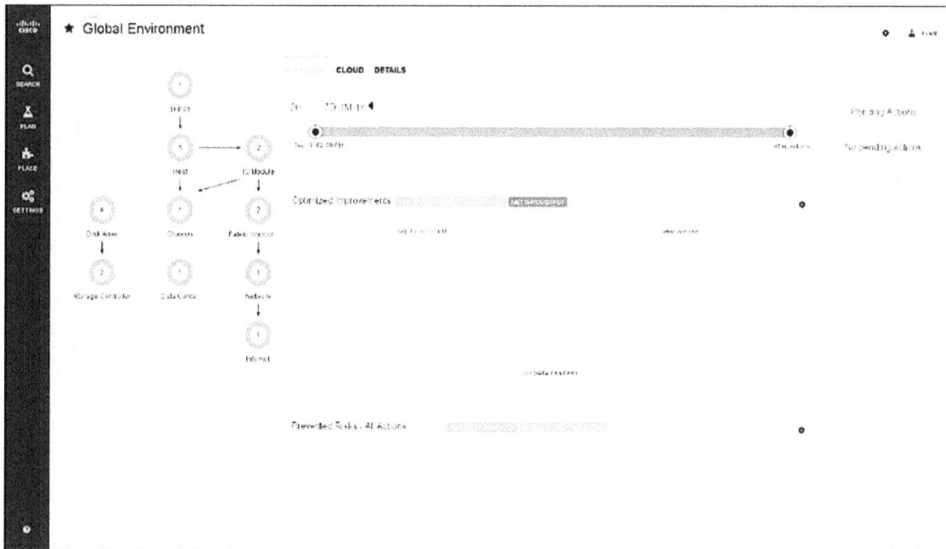

Figure 3-23 *CWOM Global Environment view*

Automate Actions

The visibility into the entities that exist in your environment and the relationships among them underlies Workload Optimization Manager's core value: real-time decision automation in the data center and cloud. To make the right placement, scaling, and capacity decisions, the platform needs to understand the entire environment. Workload Optimization Manager models your environment as a market of buyers and sellers linked together in a supply chain. This supply chain represents the flow of resources—from the data center, through the physical tiers of your environment, to the virtual tier, and to the cloud. By managing relationships between these buyers and sellers, Workload Optimization Manager provides closed-loop management of resources—from the data center through to the application. You see the supply chain and use detail across entities, and the platform sees what needs to be done to achieve continuous health in the environment.

Workload Optimization Manager actions can be implemented manually (with a mouse click) by an operator, on command (for example, based on a change management process), or automatically as events arise. Users can define the level of automation by action type and at multiple levels of detail; for example, you can automate actions for individual virtual machines, for a cluster, or for a data center.

To configure the level of automation for actions, use the steps that follow.

Step 1.   In the **Home** menu, select **Actions**.

Step 2.   Click to check the box for the entity for which you want to automate the action (for example, select a virtual machine).

Step 3.   Click **Configure Automation**.

Figure 3-24 illustrates CWOM automation.

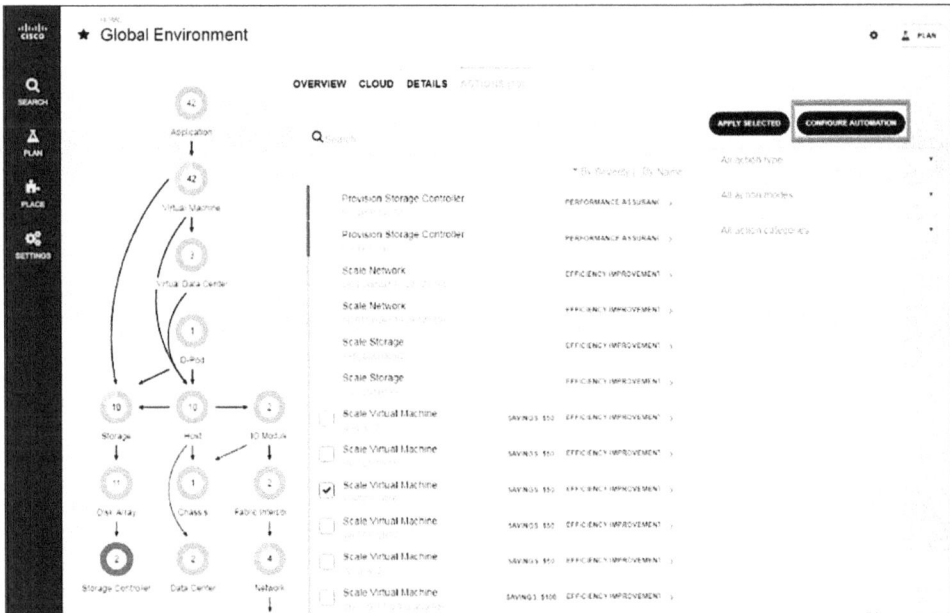

Figure 3-24   *CWOM automation*

Step 4.   On the **Setup Automation** screen, open the **Action Type** menu and choose a type. Workload Optimization Manager performs many general types of actions, such as the following:

- **Provision:** Add resource capacity, usually by adding an entity.

- **Decommission:** Stop, suspend, or remove an entity.

- **Place:** Place a consumer on a different provider.

- **Right size:** Change the allocation of resources for an entity.

Step 5.   Choose the scope and the action execution level.

Figure 3-25 shows CWOM automation execution.

Step 6.   Click **Save**.

Plan for the Future

Workload Optimization Manager can simulate certain scenarios in the environment before the changes are implemented. It uses the same underlying common data model (the supply chain market) for both real-time performance assurance and simulation. This unique capability helps ensure that simulations can be performed seamlessly in the environment and that real-time workload resource demands and infrastructure resource availability are taken into account. Table 3-2 details the plan types in Cisco Workload Optimization Manager.

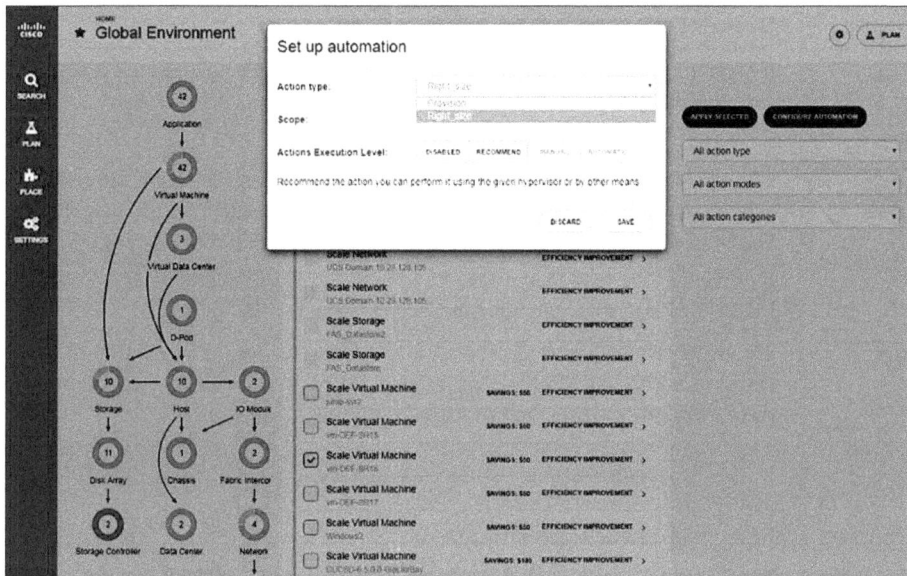

Figure 3-25 *CWOM automation execution*

Table 3-2 *Plan Types in Cisco Workload Optimization Manager*

Plan Type	Description
+ Add Workload	Adding a workload increases the demands that you place on your environment's infrastructure. You can set up a plan to add a new workload based on individual virtual machines or groups of virtual machines in your environment, or based on templates.
⇄ Workload Migration	You can choose groups of workloads to migrate to a public cloud. Workload Optimization Manager chooses the appropriate cloud templates to support the virtual machines in your cloud account, and it chooses the best regions to host these virtual machines. The plan shows two results: migration to templates that match your current virtual machine resources, and migration to the smallest templates that can ensure performance of your applications without overprovisioning your cloud virtual machines. The plan shows the costs you would see in your cloud account for both sets of results.
☁ Migrate to Public Cloud	Simulate migration to the public cloud to see whether you have enough resources to move your workload from one provider group to another. For example, assume that you want to decommission one data center and move its entire workload to a different data center. Does the target data center have enough physical resources to support the workload you plan to move? Where should that workload be placed? Use this plan to calculate the effect such a change would have on your overall infrastructure.

Plan Type	Description
Decommission Hosts	If your environment includes underutilized hardware, you can use a plan to see whether you can decommission hosts or storage.
Hardware Refresh	Choose hosts or storage that you want to replace with different hardware. For example, assume that you are planning to upgrade the hosts in a cluster. How many hosts do you need to deploy and still ensure the performance of your applications? Create templates to represent the upgraded hosts and let the plan figure out how many hosts you really need.
`</>` Custom	The other plan types get you started on the setup for certain common types of scenarios. With a custom plan, you skip directly to the plan configuration and set up whatever type of scenario you want.

Set Policies and Service Level Agreements

Typically, in data center environments, tiers of resources are made available for various groups. By creating policies to match applications to the appropriate resources, organizations can help ensure that lower-tier applications are not using very costly resources. Workload Optimization provides the capability to create and customize policies, enabling you to set the way that Workload Optimization Manager analyzes resource allocation, displays resource status, and displays or performs actions. Figure 3-26 shows the CWOM settings detailed in the following list:

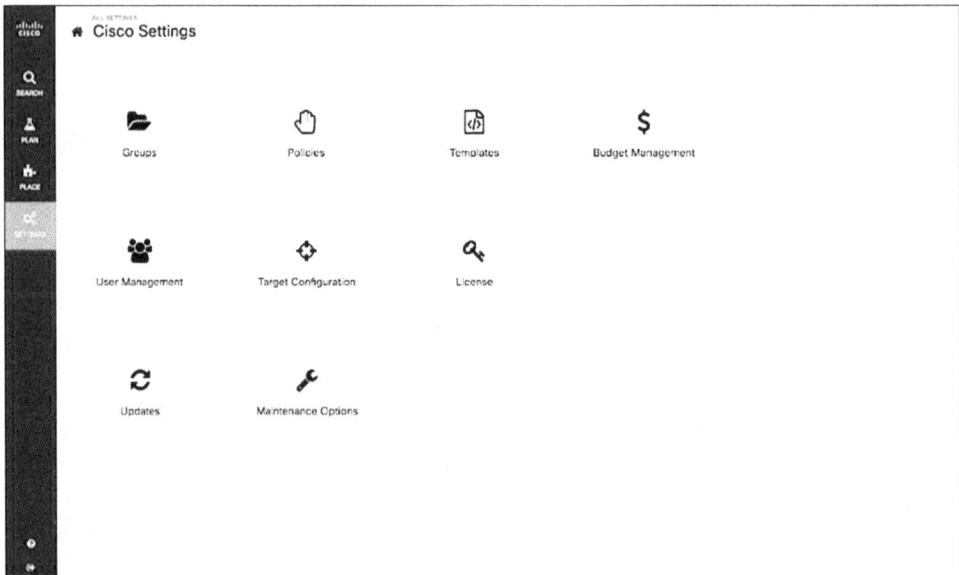

Figure 3-26 *CWOM settings*

- **Groups:** Groups assemble collections of resources for Workload Optimization Manager to monitor and manage.

- **User Management:** As an administrator, you can specify accounts that grant specific users access to Workload Optimization Manager.

- **Budget Management:** A budget group specifies the monthly expenditure you want to devote to keeping your workload on the public cloud.

- **Updates:** You can check Cisco Workload Optimization Manager version details and the availability of more recent versions.

- **Maintenance Options:** You can configure HTTP proxy, export state, configuration files, and logging levels.

- **Templates:** You can view a variety of templates, including virtual machine, Cisco UCS, and public cloud templates.

- **License:** You can view the total number of host licenses, license features in use, and license expiration dates.

Cisco Intersight Workload Optimizer

Cisco Intersight Workload Optimizer is another consumption model for CWOM. Cisco Intersight Workload Optimizer offers the same capabilities as today's CWOM on-premises offering in a SaaS model. Customers interested in workload optimization capabilities can purchase the CWOM standalone version and, if they choose, can transition to the SaaS-based Intersight Workload Optimizer offering.

Cisco Intersight Workload Optimizer is available as an option with Cisco Intersight. It extends the capabilities of Cisco Intersight with multidomain visibility across the full stack of applications and infrastructure, from on-premises to the cloud. The Cisco Intersight Workload Optimizer analytics engine matches real-time workload demand to the underlying infrastructure supply. The supply includes public cloud, virtual machines, containers, third-party hardware, and Cisco infrastructure resources.

The optimization functionality is engineered for limitless scale and true SaaS multi-tenancy. It is architected to enable scaling to support the entirety of Cisco's UCS and Hyperflex portfolio and third-party systems. Finally, it is a singular platform with common credentials, common accounting, and a common user experience.

Cisco Intersight Workload Optimizer, when combined with AppDynamics, correlates business, application-performance, and infrastructure metrics to provide full-stack visibility and common data for a single source of truth. Cisco Intersight Workload Optimizer applies machine intelligence to drive automation of physical and virtual resources. It dynamically optimizes the infrastructure in a cost-effective manner while ensuring the user experience. This enables a top-to-bottom closed-loop system—all the way from the business logic, across a hybrid cloud, to DIMMs on a server or links on a network.

Cisco Hyperflex – Intersight

The "new normal" is causing most IT departments to work remotely. Even when organizations determine they are ready to resume admitting staff onsite, IT operations are going to look different. You still need the ability to manage and support your infrastructure remotely, and you'll want a simple, convenient, and secure way to do that. Cisco has been on the forefront of empowering teams to work from anywhere, through innovative systems management and support capabilities designed to meet the needs of more than 14,000 Cisco data center customers—a number that is rapidly growing.

A cloud-based management platform provides unified access to applications and to infrastructure monitoring, configuration, and orchestration, which helps reduce IT management complexity and unify the deployment and management of many edge devices. Cisco Intersight is a Software as a Service (SaaS) hybrid cloud operations platform that delivers intelligent automation, observability, and optimization to customers for traditional and cloud-native applications and infrastructure. It supports Cisco Unified Computing System (Cisco UCS) and Cisco Hyperflex hyperconverged infrastructure, other Intersight-connected devices, third-party Intersight-connected devices, cloud platforms and services, and other integration endpoints. Because it's a SaaS-delivered platform, Intersight functionality increases and expands with weekly releases. Figure 3-27 shows the Cisco Intersight login page.

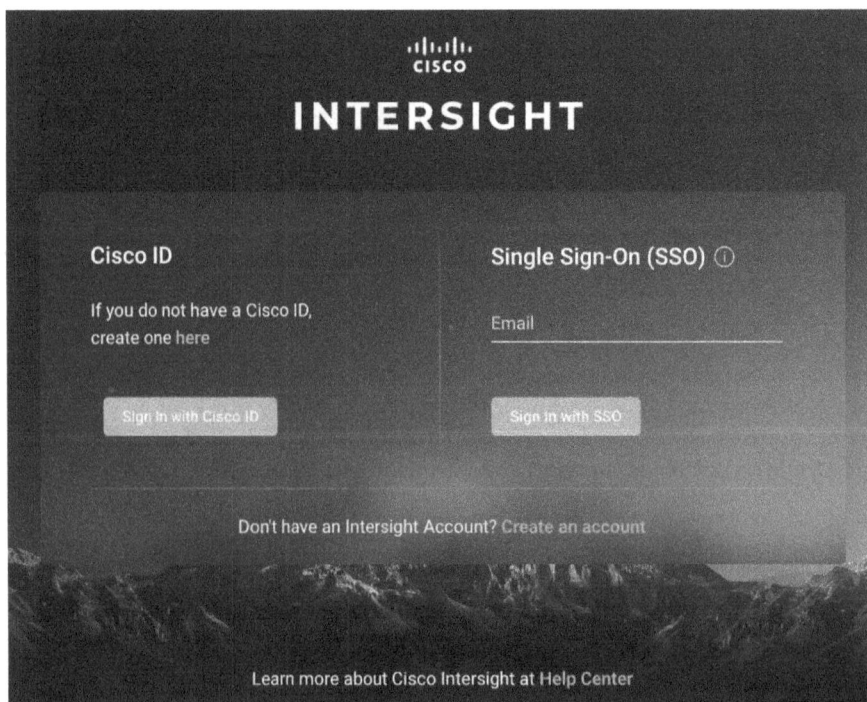

Figure 3-27 *Cisco Intersight login page*

With Intersight, you get all the benefits of SaaS delivery and full lifecycle management of distributed infrastructure and workloads across data centers, remote sites, branch offices, and edge environments. This empowers you to analyze, update, fix, and automate your environment in ways not previously possible. As a result, your organization can achieve significant total cost of ownership (TCO) savings and deliver applications faster in support of new business initiatives.

For Cisco infrastructure, the Intersight platform works in conjunction with Cisco UCS Manager, Cisco Integrated Management Controller (IMC), and Cisco Hyperflex Connect. In addition, Intersight integrates with third-party storage, cloud services, virtualization, and container platforms. You can simply associate a model-based configuration to provision servers and associated storage and fabric automatically, regardless of form factor. Using profiles, IT staff can consistently align policy, server personality, and workloads. These policies can be created once and used to simplify server deployments, resulting in improved productivity and compliance as well as lower risk of failures due to inconsistent configuration. In addition, Cisco provides integrations to third-party operations tools, starting with ServiceNow, to allow customers to use their existing solutions more efficiently. Figure 3-28 illustrates Cisco Intersight Management as a Service (MaaS).

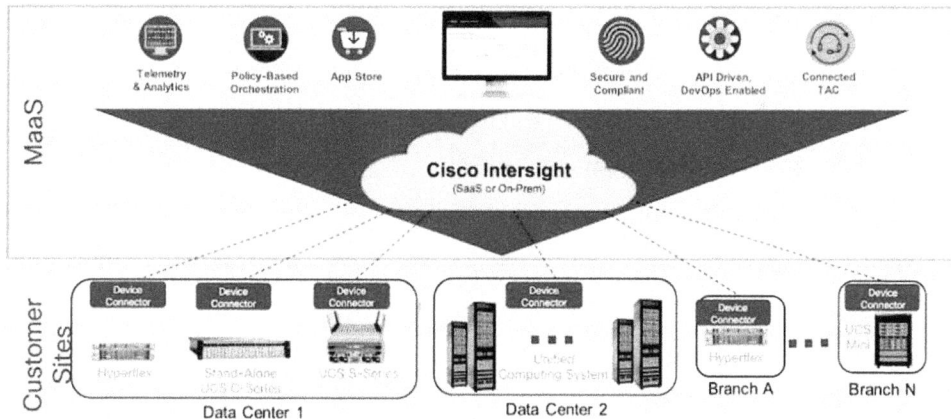

Figure 3-28   *Cisco Intersight MaaS*

Deployment Options

Cisco Intersight is a SaaS-delivered cloud operations platform with the flexibility of advanced deployment options. You can take advantage of new features as they become available from Cisco without the challenges and complexity of maintaining your management tools. The majority of Cisco users enjoy the benefits of SaaS; however, if you have data locality or security needs for managing systems that may not fully meet a SaaS management model, you can leverage the Cisco Intersight Virtual Appliance software on your premises to connect your servers through Intersight.com.

Alternatively, the Cisco Intersight Private Virtual Appliance provides an easy way to deploy a VMware Open Virtual Appliance (OVA), which can be configured, deployed, and run off-premises. The Private Virtual Appliance allows you to still take advantage of much of the SaaS functionality without connectivity back to Intersight.com. Both the Intersight Virtual Appliance and Private Virtual Appliance provide advantages over conventional on-premises management tools.

Benefits of Using Cisco Intersight

The following list and Figure 3-29 explain some of the benefits of Cisco Intersight Customer:

- Reduces complexity and manual effort to deploy, maintain, and upgrade Cisco Intersight–connected devices

- Delivers proactive support and Return Materials Authorizations (RMAs) through tight integration with Cisco Technical Assistance Center (TAC)

- Shifts the burden of building, maintaining, and securing your management environment to Cisco

- Learns and evolves to deliver greater capabilities and improved insights to help you proactively manage your environment

- Is fully programmable and can be integrated with third-party systems and tools

- Can add workload optimization and Kubernetes services seamlessly

- Has a choice of deployment options

Customer Benefits: Greater Simplicity

Unified Management
Single pane of glass, consistent operations model and experience for managing all systems and solutions

Enhanced Support Experience
Hosted platform allows Cisco to address issues platform-wide and experience extends into TAC-supported platforms

SaaS/Subscription
Hosted management will free customers from care/feeding of management tools and eliminate upgrade dependencies

Programmability
End-to-end programmability with native API, SDKs and popular DevOps toolsets will enable customers to consume natively

Recommendation Engine
Embedded recommendation platform with insights sourced from across Cisco installed base and tailored to each customer

No-Impact Transition
IMC/UCSM/HX embedded connector will allow customers to start consuming benefits without forklift upgrade

Figure 3-29   *Cisco Intersight Customer benefits*

Figure 3-30 illustrates Cisco Intersight seamless scalability.

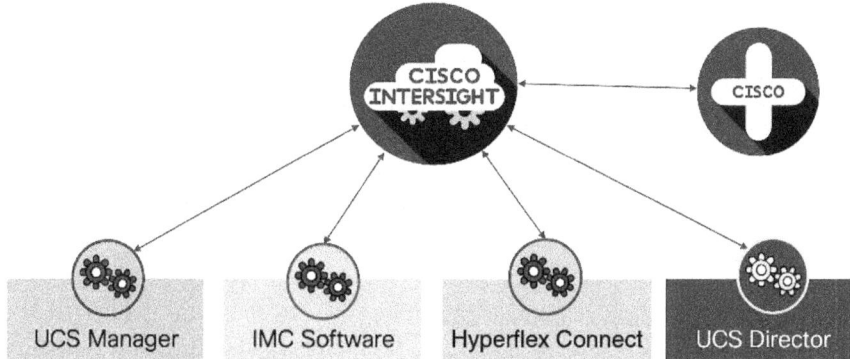

Figure 3-30   *Cisco Intersight seamless scalability*

Figure 3-31 illustrates Cisco Intersight Device Connector.

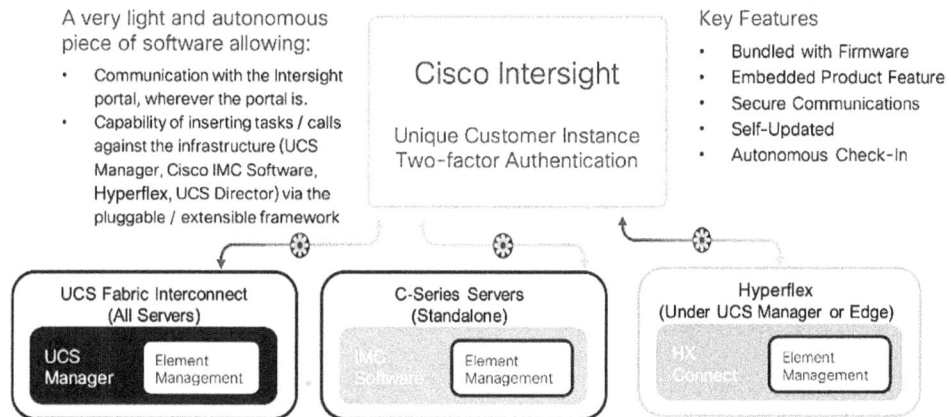

Figure 3-31   *Cisco Intersight Device Connector*

Hyperconverged Infrastructure (HCI): Hyperflex

Hyperflex is Cisco's hyperconverged infrastructure (HCI) platform. Hyperflex systems combine software-defined storage and data services software with Cisco UCS (Unified Computing System), a converged infrastructure system that integrates computing, networking, and storage resources to increase efficiency and enable centralized management.

Cisco Hyperflex systems with Intel Xeon Scalable processors deliver hyperconvergence with power and simplicity for any application, anywhere. Engineered with Cisco UCS technology and managed through the Cisco Intersight cloud operations platform, Cisco Hyperflex systems can power your applications and data anywhere, optimize operations from your core data center to the edge and into public clouds, and increase agility by accelerating DevOps practices.

In today's world, this adaptable platform acts as your on-premises and edge infrastructure that complements and integrates with the workloads you deploy into public clouds. Tight integration with Cisco Intersight cloud operations platform enables full lifecycle management of your workloads wherever you want to deploy them—locally, at the edge, and into the cloud. With management hosted in the cloud, you have access to unlimited deployment locations and scale.

Cisco Hyperflex systems help you bridge the gap by providing the IT capabilities you need to thrive in an always-on world:

- **App-centric platform:** You can deliver any app, to any location, at any scale, both predictably and securely. Cisco's infrastructure provides cloud-like resource delivery that complements what you get from the cloud, so you can differentiate your services from the competition.

- **Cloud operations platform:** A cloud operating model helps you manage distributed operations at scale—from physical and virtual infrastructure deployment to workload placement and resource optimization based on real-time analysis of application performance. With true IT as a Service, your business can deliver more applications in more locations.

- **Adaptable infrastructure:** An open, futureproof infrastructure supports your applications. A hyperconverged application platform is optimized to deliver cloud-native apps as microservices. Traditional application hosting supports both VMware vSphere and Microsoft Windows Server Hyper-V virtual machines. Together, these capabilities support the DevOps processes your teams are embracing and open the door to more growth opportunities.

Figure 3-32 illustrates Cisco Hyperflex systems supporting the data center core, cloud, and edge.

Cisco UCS provides a single point of connectivity and hardware management that integrates Cisco Hyperflex nodes into a single unified cluster. The system is self-aware and self-integrating so that when a new component is attached, it is automatically incorporated into the cluster. Rather than requiring you to configure each element in the system manually through a variety of element managers, every aspect of a node's personality, configuration, and connectivity is set through management software. You can choose the combination of CPU, flash memory, graphics acceleration, and disk storage resources you need to deliver an optimal infrastructure for your applications. Also, incremental scalability allows you to start small and scale up and out as your needs grow. Figure 3-33 illustrates Cisco Hyperflex systems architecture.

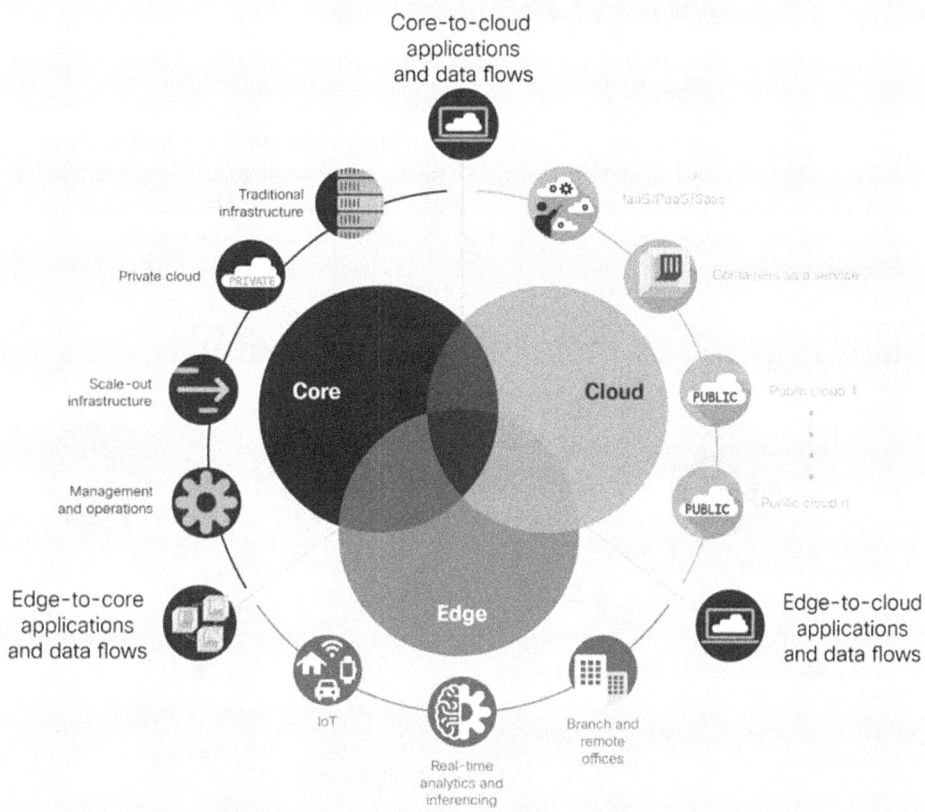

Figure 3-32   *Cisco Hyperflex systems supporting the data center core, cloud, and edge*

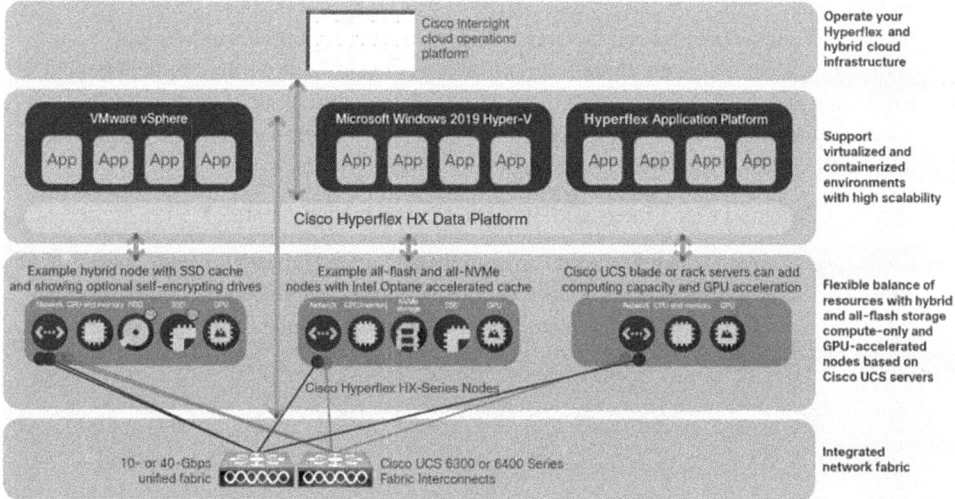

Figure 3-33   *Cisco Hyperflex systems' architecture*

Deploying Hyperflex Anywhere with Intersight

With Intersight, you can deploy and manage all your Hyperflex clusters from anywhere. The new Hyperflex Installer makes it easy to deploy clusters automatically.

The new Hyperflex Installer for Intersight is consumed as a service, eliminating the need for an on-premises infrastructure, along with the lengthy download and setup of a static virtual installer appliance. The intuitive wizard includes reusable policies for rapid and consistent deployment. Figure 3-34 compares Cisco Hyperflex on-prem installer and Intersight.

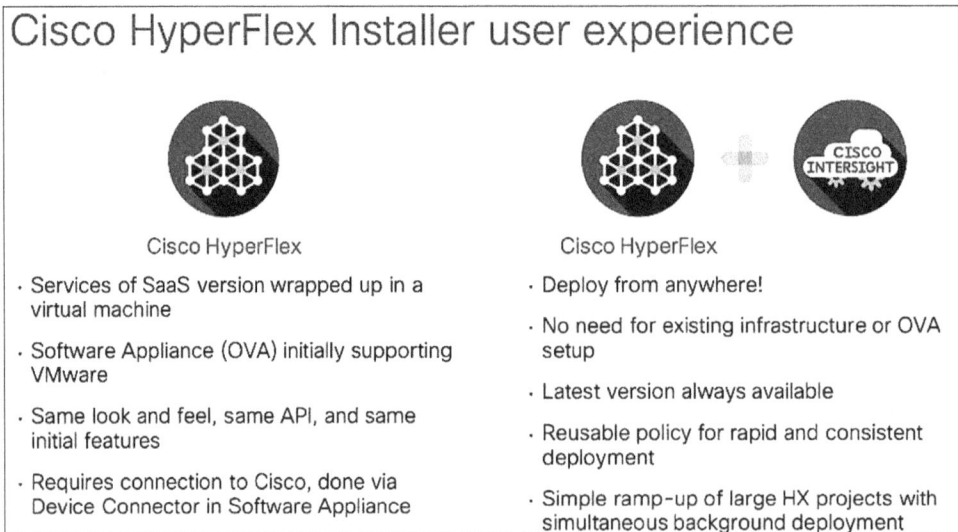

Figure 3-34 *Cisco Hyperflex on-prem installer versus Intersight*

Hyperflex cluster profiles can be cloned and then executed on-demand for fast and easy scaling. There are three levels of built-in validation to ensure the deployment runs smoothly from start to finish. Intersight is always up to date, securing the latest features and improvements to the platform automatically without any user intervention. Figure 3-35 shows Cisco Intersight Hyperflex cluster profiles.

Figure 3-36 shows Cisco Intersight Hyperflex policy management.

Once deployment is complete, you can seamlessly launch Hyperflex Connect in context from Intersight to drill down for more detailed monitoring and analysis. All these capabilities are available in Cisco Intersight Base, so they are included for free with every Hyperflex cluster!

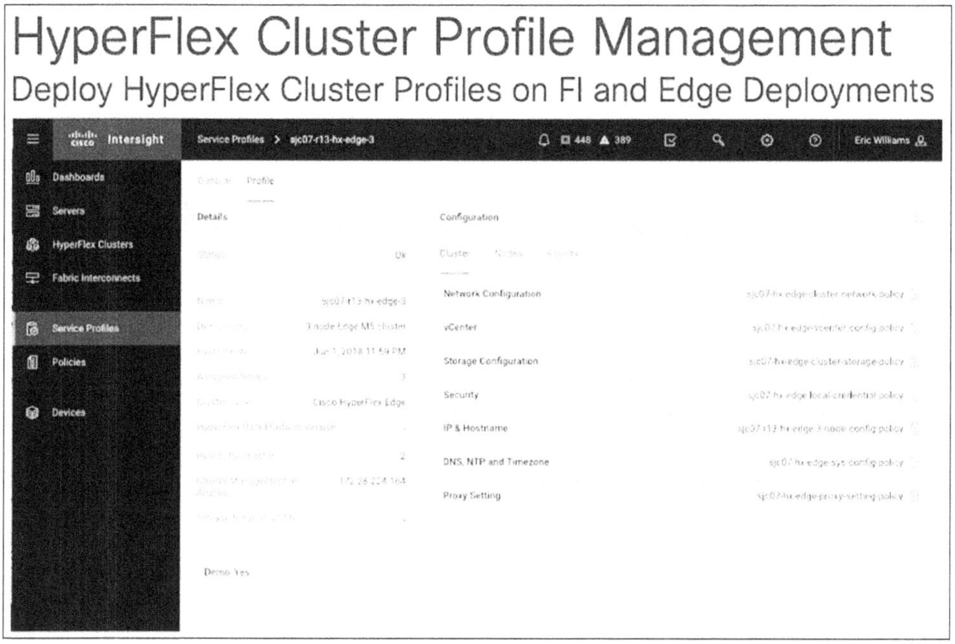

HyperFlex Cluster Profile Management
Deploy HyperFlex Cluster Profiles on FI and Edge Deployments

Figure 3-35 *Cisco Intersight Hyperflex cluster profiles*

HyperFlex Policy Management
Share Policies Across FI and Edge Deployments

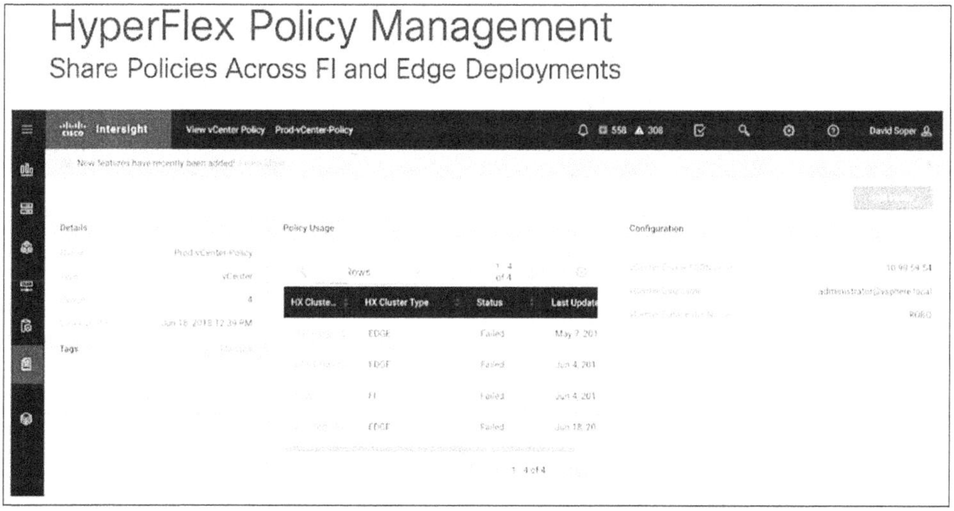

Figure 3-36 *Cisco Intersight Hyperflex policy management*

A major pain point for traditional hyperconverged infrastructure (HCI) offerings is how to deploy at scale. In the old operational model, HCI appliances are typically shipped to a staging site, partially checked and configured, boxed up, shipped to the final site, and then installed by skilled IT administrators who help set up the solution on site. Figure 3-37 shows some of the benefits of Cisco Intersight Hyperflex.

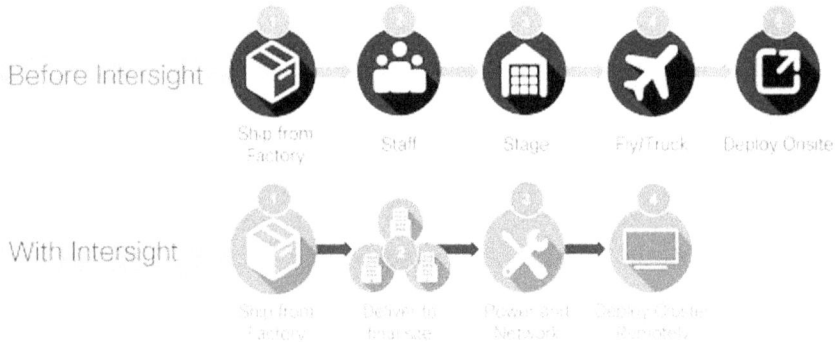

Figure 3-37   *Cisco Intersight Hyperflex benefits*

With Intersight, this model is completely transformed. The Hyperflex appliances can be shipped directly to the final site, bypassing the expensive and complex staging process. The gear is racked, connected to power and the network, and then all appliances automatically connect to Intersight and are securely claimed. The rest of the deployment can now be completed by the centralized IT staff. It is all done remotely and from anywhere. To top it all off, the Hyperflex Installer for Intersight can run multiple deployment jobs in parallel, enabling quick ramp-up of even the largest HCI projects.

Cisco can now deliver deployment and lifecycle management benefits at scale as well as deliver this remotely from the cloud. In addition to this, Hyperflex Edge and Intersight also allows ROBO and edge customers to do the following:

■ Meet aggressive cost envelopes for infrastructure deployment at scale for edge and branch locations

■ Deploy clusters as small as two nodes and up to four nodes—a form factor that fits the needs of edge sites

■ Drive data resiliency without the expense (through industry-leading innovations around an invisible cloud-based witness resident in Intersight)

■ Simplify operations through centralized lifecycle management and actionable intelligence from Intersight

Figure 3-38 illustrates Cisco Intersight Innovations for Hyperflex.

· Intersight Innovations

- · Invisible arbitrator service (two-node clusters)
- · Lights-out, multisite deployment in parallel
- · Rapid cluster profile creation with REST API
- · Upgrade logic decoupled from platform, following true CI/CD model
- · Connected TAC enables quick case resolution

· Invisible Arbitrator Service

- · No third site for a witness required
- · No upgrades, patches, or backups, ever
- · No scale limitations

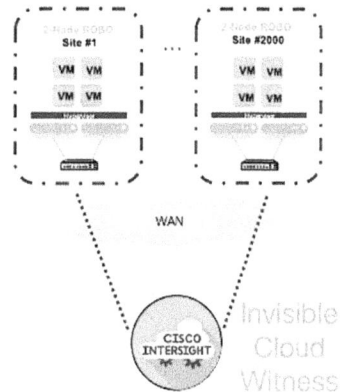

Figure 3-38   *Cisco Intersight Innovations for Hyperflex*

Cisco Intersight Workload Engine at a Glance

Cisco Intersight Workload Engine (IWE) is a next-generation private cloud architecture for modern cloud-native workloads. With Cisco IWE, customers no longer need to cobble together open source distributions, excessive virtualization licenses, multiple management panes, and disparate hardware to support their enterprise service applications on the premises. The seamless integration of Cisco Intersight, Intersight Workload Engine, Intersight Kubernetes Service, and Hyperflex Data Platform (HXDP) eliminates the complexity and risk associated with integration at different layers of the infrastructure and application. This makes the cloud-native journey for enterprise applications faster, more predictable, and more cost-effective. Customers also get full stack support SLAs from Cisco's industry-leading Technical Assistance Center (TAC) teams.

The Intersight Workload Engine provides the software infrastructure to run Intersight Kubernetes Service either virtualized or on bare-metal servers in a Cisco Hyperflex cluster. The result is a ready-to-consume Kubernetes Containers as a service (CaaS) platform that balances the need for increased application release velocity with the traditional IT needs for reduced cost and complexity. It is a fully integrated solution that supports every infrastructure layer needed to support modern microservices-based applications— from the physical layer to the software stack. Figure 3-39 illustrates Cisco IWE full stack integration.

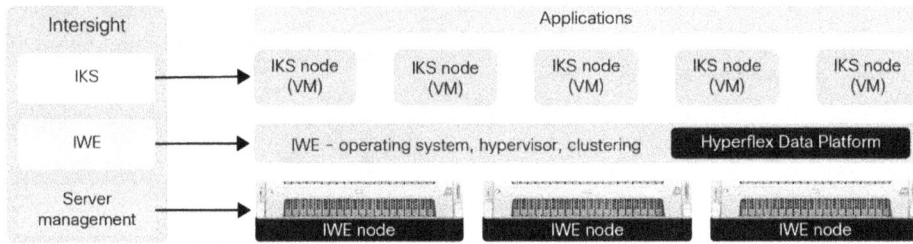

Figure 3-39   *Cisco IWE full stack integration*

Benefits

The Intersight Workload Engine (IWE) is used to create and operate a cluster of UCS servers. The IWE OS is installed and runs on those servers, and IWE contains all the software needed to operate the IWE cluster, including the operating system, hypervisor, clustering software, and storage software. The following list explains some of the benefits of using IWE:

- **Simplify operations:** Address any application workload with an all-in-one integrated platform, including hypervisor, operating system, Kubernetes clustering, and storage.

- **Unify VM and container management:** Manage clusters from the cloud using one control point for upgrades, capacity expansion, repairs, and security with Cisco Intersight Cloud Operations Platform.

- **Reduce costs:** Utilize infrastructure efficiently with a purpose-built hypervisor without adding the cost of third-party virtualization solutions.

- **Intersight Kubernetes Service integration:** Automate balancing and optimization according to Kubernetes best practices.

- **Full-stack cloud management:** Simplify Day 2 upgrades and enable faster resolution of issues with full stack visibility.

Key Features

The IWE management UI and equivalent APIs are used to deploy and manage your cluster, including cluster lifecycle tasks such as upgrades, expansion, repair, security patching, and software or firmware upgrades. Your app or DevOps teams can use your IWE clusters to run the Cisco Intersight Kubernetes Service (IKS) and manage Kubernetes clusters. The following list mentions some features of IWE:

- Fully automated installer integrated in Cisco Intersight

- Operating system software maintained in Cisco Intersight repositories and automatically deployed on Intersight Workload Engine nodes

- Hypervisor with support for features like VM scheduling, VM migration, and CPU oversubscription

- Clustering software deployed with multiple control nodes to deliver system resiliency

- Automatically configured resilient network connectivity and segmented virtual networking for separation of system, user, and storage traffic

- Persistent enterprise storage based on Cisco Hyperflex deployed within Intersight Workload Engine nodes

- Unified Intersight management, including inventory viewing, monitoring, and alerting at the node, storage, and VM levels

- Connected TAC and secure access shells for cluster administration and support

- Node maintenance mode to allow for the replacement of defective node components

Summary

Application innovation is at the heart of the digital economy. A new era of apps is redefining what data centers are and need to be capable of supporting. Today, the data center is no longer a fixed place. It exists wherever data is created, processed, and used. "Enterprises should be able to deploy applications based on the needs of their business, not the limitations of their technology," according to Roland Acra, senior vice president and general manager of the Data Center Business Group at Cisco. "Customers want to deploy applications and manage data across a range of diverse platforms, from on-premises to cloud-based. That is why we are taking the 'center' out of the data center. Today, Cisco is helping our customers expand their reach into every cloud, every data center, and every branch."

ACI Anywhere and Hyperflex Anywhere are the major innovations that remove data center boundaries.

With Cisco Workload Optimization Manager, data center operators can deliver differentiated performance while making the best use of the environment. When used in combination with Cisco UCS Manager and Cisco UCS Director, it can help organizations achieve elastic computing with cloud economics. Full automation can empower data center operators to focus on innovation: to deliver new products and services that enable the digitization of their organization and provide competitive advantage for their business.

References/Additional Reading

https://www.cisco.com/c/dam/en/us/solutions/collateral/data-center-virtualization/unified-computing/cwom-setup.pdf

Chapter 4

Application, Analytics, and Workload Performance Management with AppDynamics

Monitor, correlate, analyze, and act on application and business performance data in real time with AppDynamics.

This chapter covers the following topics:

- What is AppDynamics?

- Application Monitoring

- End User Monitoring

- Database Visibility

- Infrastructure Visibility

- Analytics

- Monitoring Cloud Applications

- Cloud monitoring using AppDynamics Cloud

What Is AppDynamics?

Cisco AppDynamics is an Application Performance Management (APM) solution that enhances application performance and visibility in the multicloud world. Cisco AppDynamics can help your organization make critical, strategic decisions. It uses artificial intelligence (AI) to solve application problems and prevent them from occurring in the future, and it enhances the visibility into your IT architecture.

Note This book will not cover deployment of AppDynamics. It will only focus on key concepts and fundamentals of AppDynamics without going into configuration details.

AppDynamics Concepts

The AppDynamics APM platform enables management and monitoring of your application delivery ecosystem, ranging from mobile/browser client network requests to backend databases/servers and more. This global view across your application landscape allows you to quickly navigate through the distributed application into the call graphs and exception reports generated on individual hosts.

User Interface

AppDynamics provides a tenant to collect, store, analyze, and baseline the performance data collected by agents as well as a user interface (UI) to view and manage the information. You access the AppDynamics Tenant UI through a URL that uses your account name. Each tenant has a distinct set of users, reporting agents, and application-monitoring configurations.

AppDynamics can host one or more accounts, where each account represents one tenant. The AppDynamics cloud-based Software as a Service (SaaS) deployment is a multi-tenant environment that allows you to access multiple tenants independently.

Note   What Is a Tenant?

Each AppDynamics customer account is a tenant of the AppDynamics cloud-based SaaS platform. AppDynamics can host one or more accounts, where each account represents one tenant. The tenant collects, stores, analyzes, and baselines performance data collected by agents. The SaaS deployment is a multi-tenant environment that allows you to access multiple tenants independently. You can manage users through the Tenant UI. Once everything is set up, you can add user accounts, allowing other users to access the UI and configure AppDynamics.

Application Performance Monitoring

At the tier level, AppDynamics provides a view of the runtime operation of your code via an AppDynamics app server agent. The agent detects calls to a service entry point at the tier and follows the execution path for the call through the call stack. It sends data about usage metrics, code exceptions, exit calls to backend systems, and error conditions to your tenant. Figure 4-1 illustrates application performance monitoring in AppDynamics.

Most application environments contain more than one application server. They may contain distributed, interconnected servers and processes that participate in fulfilling a given user request. In this context, AppDynamics tracks transactions across distributed, heterogeneous services.

Figure 4-1 *Application performance monitoring*

Infrastructure Visibility with Database Visibility

For greater visibility into your application delivery environment, you can add AppDynamics Database Visibility to the deployment. App agents provide information about calls to backend databases, including errors and call counts. The Database Visibility module extends your visibility into the workings of the database server itself by providing you with information about query execution and performance with an agentless profile.

AppDynamics Infrastructure Visibility contributes to your view of the data center by adding valuable information on the performance of the machines and networks in your environment. Figure 4-2 illustrates Infrastructure Visibility with Database Visibility in AppDynamics.

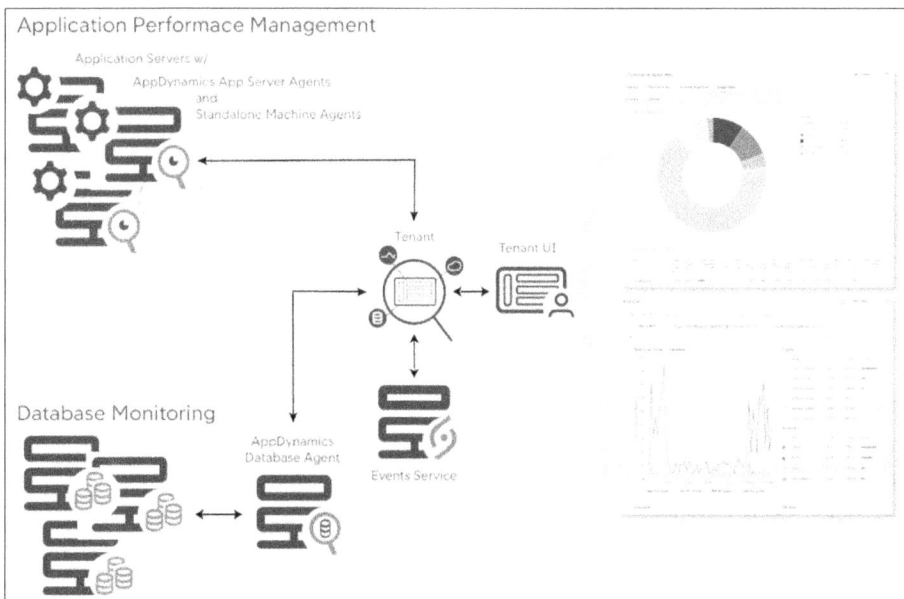

Figure 4-2 *Infrastructure Visibility with Database Visibility*

In this deployment, the database agent collects information from the database servers and sends it to the tenant, which persists some of that information in the Events Service. Database Analytics features may use the Events Service, which is the document storage component of the platform that AppDynamics has optimized for searching and storing high volumes of information.

Note   A database agent is a standalone Java program that collects performance metrics about your database instances and database servers. You can view these performance metrics in the Metric Browser of the AppDynamics Controller UI.

End User Monitoring for Client Experience

While server-side monitoring provides insight into the end user's experience with application performance and suggests performance improvements to the server, end-user monitoring extends those insights from the initial client request to the client device response. AppDynamics End User Monitoring (EUM) allows you to collect the information about where your requests are coming from, what devices/channels your users are using, and your code performance once deployed on your users' devices. Additionally, AppDynamics provides you with the visibility you need to investigate mobile crashes by displaying stack traces and other contextual data at the time of the crash and tying that to the business transaction data from the server.

Business iQ and Analytics for Business Impact

How does the overall performance of your application environment affect your business? Business iQ, powered by AppDynamics Analytics, helps you understand how the performance of your application environment and end-user applications ties to the business data of the transactions. It lets you sort, order, and understand the data that composes the business transactions. It also enables you to drill into the varieties of log data that your environment generates. See Using Analytics Data (https://docs.appdynamics.com/appd/21.x/21.3/en/analytics/using-analytics-data) for information about how to install and use AppDynamics Analytics.

Use Metrics

A *metric* is a particular class of measurement, state, or event in the monitored environment. Many defaults relate to the overall performance of the application or business transaction, such as request load, average response time, and error rate. Others describe the state of the server infrastructure, such as percentage CPU busy and percentage of memory used.

Agents register the metrics they detect with the tenant. They then report measurements or occurrences of the metrics (depending on the nature of the metric) to the tenant at regular intervals. You can view metrics using the Metric Browser in the Tenant UI.

An information point is a particular type of metric that enables you to report on how your business (as opposed to your application) is performing. For example, you could set up an information point to total the revenue from the purchase on your website of a specific product or set of products. You can also use information points to report on how your code is performing; for example, how many times a specific method is called and how long it is taking to execute.

You can create extensions that use the machine agent to report custom metrics that you define. These metrics are baselined and reported in the tenant, just like the built-in AppDynamics metrics. As an alternative to using the Tenant UI, you can access metrics programmatically with the AppDynamics APIs.

Baselines and Thresholds

The AppDynamics platform uses both self-learned baselines and configurable thresholds to help identify application issues. A complex, distributed application has many performance metrics, and each metric is important in one or more contexts. In such environments, it is difficult to do the following:

- Determine the values or ranges that are normal for a particular metric.
- Set meaningful thresholds on which to base and receive relevant alerts.
- Determine what is a "normal" metric when the application or infrastructure undergoes change.

For these reasons, anomaly detection based on dynamic baselines or thresholds is one of the essential features of the AppDynamics platform.

The AppDynamics platform automatically calculates dynamic baselines for your metrics, defining what is "normal" for each metric based on actual usage. Then the platform uses these baselines to identify subsequent metrics whose values fall outside this normal range. Static thresholds that are tedious to set up and, in rapidly changing application environments, error-prone are no longer needed.

You can create health rules with conditions that use baselines, allowing you to trigger alerts or kick off other types of remedial actions when performance problems are occurring or may be about to happen. See Alert and Respond (https://docs.appdynamics.com/appd/21.x/21.3/en/appdynamics-essentials/alert-and-respond) and Health Rules (https://docs.appdynamics.com/appd/21.x/21.3/en/appdynamics-essentials/alert-and-respond/health-rules) and Dynamic Baselines (https://docs.appdynamics.com/appd/21.x/21.3/en/application-monitoring/business-transactions/business-transaction-performance/dynamic-baselines).

AppDynamics thresholds help you to maintain service level agreements (SLAs) and ensure optimum performance levels for your system by detecting slow, very slow, and stalled transactions. Thresholds provide a flexible way to associate the right business context with a slow request to isolate the root cause.

Health Rules, Policies, and Actions

AppDynamics uses dynamic baselining to establish what is considered normal behavior for your application automatically. Then you can set up health rules against those standard baselines (or use other health indicators) to track non-optimal conditions. A health rule might be, for example, to create a critical event when the average response time is four times slower than the baseline.

Policies that allow you to connect such problematic events (such as the health rule critical event) with actions that can trigger alerts/remedial behavior address the system's issues long before your users will be affected.

AppDynamics supplies default health rules. You can customize the default health rules and create new rules specific to your environment.

The out-of-the-box health rules test business transaction performance as follows:

- **Business Transaction response time is much higher than normal:** Defines a critical condition as the combination of an average response time higher than the default baseline by three standard deviations and a load greater than 50 calls per minute. This rule defines a warning condition as the combination of an average response time higher than the default baseline by two standard deviations and a load greater than 100 calls per minute.

- **Business Transaction error rate is much higher than normal:** Defines a critical condition as the combination of an error rate greater than the default baseline by three standard deviations and an error rate higher than ten errors per minute and a load greater than 50 calls per minute. This rule defines a warning condition as the combination of an error rate greater than the default baseline by two standard deviations and an error rate greater than five errors per minute and a load greater than 50 calls per minute.

Infrastructure Monitoring

While Business Transaction performance is typically the focus of a performance monitoring strategy, monitoring infrastructure performance can add insight into underlying factors about performance. AppDynamics can alert you of the problem at the Business Transaction and infrastructure levels.

AppDynamics provides preconfigured application infrastructure metrics and default health rules to enable you to discover and correct infrastructure problems. You can also configure additional persistent metrics to implement a monitoring strategy specific to your business needs and application architecture.

In addition to health rules, you can view infrastructure metrics in the Metric Browser. In this context, the Correlation Analysis and Scalability Analysis graphs are useful to understand how infrastructure metrics can correlate or relate to Business Transaction performance.

Integrate and Extend AppDynamics

AppDynamics provides many ways for you to extend AppDynamics Pro and integrate metrics with other systems. The AppDynamics Exchange contains many extensions that you can download, and if you cannot find what you need, you can develop your own.

AppDynamics extensions are available in the following categories:

- Monitoring extensions add metrics to the existing set of metrics that AppDynamics agents collect and report to the tenant. These can include metrics that you obtain from other monitoring systems. They can also include metrics that your system extracts from services that are not instrumented by AppDynamics, such as databases, LDAP servers, web servers, and C programs. To write specific monitoring extensions, see Extensions and Custom Metrics (https://docs.appdynamics.com/appd/21.x/21.3/en/infrastructure-visibility/machine-agent/extensions-and-custom-metrics).

- Alerting extensions let you integrate AppDynamics with external alerting or ticketing systems and create custom notification actions. To learn how to write specialized custom notifications, see Build a Custom Action (https://docs.appdynamics.com/appd/21.x/21.3/en/appdynamics-essentials/alert-and-respond/actions/custom-actions/build-a-custom-action). Also, see Email Templates (https://docs.appdynamics.com/appd/21.x/21.3/en/appdynamics-essentials/alert-and-respond/actions/notification-actions/email-templates) and HTTP Request Actions and Templates(https://docs.appdynamics.com/appd/21.x/21.3/en/appdynamics-essentials/alert-and-respond/actions/http-request-actions-and-templates).

- Performance-testing extensions consist of performance-testing extensions.

- Built-in integration extensions are bundled into the AppDynamics platform and only need to be enabled or configured. These include the following:

  - Integrate AppDynamics with Splunk (https://docs.appdynamics.com/appd/21.x/21.3/en/extend-appdynamics/integration-modules/integrate-appdynamics-with-splunk)

  - Integrate AppDynamics with DB CAM (https://docs.appdynamics.com/appd/21.x/21.3/en/extend-appdynamics/integration-modules/integrate-appdynamics-with-db-cam)

In the next section, we will cover deployment models and how to plan an AppDynamics installation.

Deployment Planning Guide

This section describes the best practice and guidelines for deploying the AppDynamics Application Performance Management (APM) platform.

Once you install the necessary agents, AppDynamics automatically builds an environment of the chosen applications.

The tenant performs the following functions:

- Monitors your application workload

- Uses machine learning to determine what is normal for your environment

- Applies sensible defaults for detecting abnormal activity and application errors

You can start using AppDynamics dashboards, flow maps, and monitoring tools in the Tenant UI immediately without instrumentation and configuration. Later, you can customize the configuration for your specific environment and requirements.

Deployment Models

An AppDynamics deployment uses installed agents to collect data from a monitored environment. The AppDynamics UI provides the access to view, understand, and analyze the data.

The AppDynamics SaaS deployment is a cloud-based solution that enables real-time visibility into the health and performance of your instrumented environment, with significantly reduced cost and maintenance. A SaaS deployment provides these benefits:

- No need to install the tenant.

- AppDynamics manages the server-side components of the AppDynamics platform, including its installation and upgrades.

- Lower total costs, guaranteed availability, data security, significantly reduced maintenance, and automatic upgrades.

Installation Overview

Before you install the platform, review the requirements for the components you plan to install and prepare the host machines. The requirements vary based on the components you deploy and the size of your deployment.

For the Controller and Events Service, you first need to install the AppDynamics Enterprise Console. You then use the application to deploy the Controller and Events Service. Note that the Events Service can be deployed as a single node or a cluster. The Enterprise Console is not only the installer for the Controller and Events Service; it can manage the entire lifecycle of new or existing AppDynamics Platforms and components.

You cannot use the Enterprise Console to perform the End User Monitoring (EUM) Server installation. Instead, you must use a package installer that supports interactive GUI or console modes, or you can use a silent response file installation.

Platform Components and Tools

An on-premises AppDynamics platform installation consists of several, separately installed and configured components. These include the Controller, MySQL database, Events Service, and optionally the EUM Server.

The AppDynamics Enterprise Console is a GUI- and command-line-based application that can manage the installation, configuration, and administration of the Controller and Events Service.

For the EUM Server, you must continue to use the package installer to deploy the EUM Cloud.

After you install the platform, you can configure and manage different components with component-specific scripts. Based on how you deploy the platform, you might use a combination of the Enterprise Console and package installers to install and manage the various components of the platform.

On-Premises Deployment Architecture

Figure 4-3 depicts the components of a complete on-premises AppDynamics APM platform deployment. It shows how the components interact to fulfill application, database, infrastructure, end-user monitoring, and more.

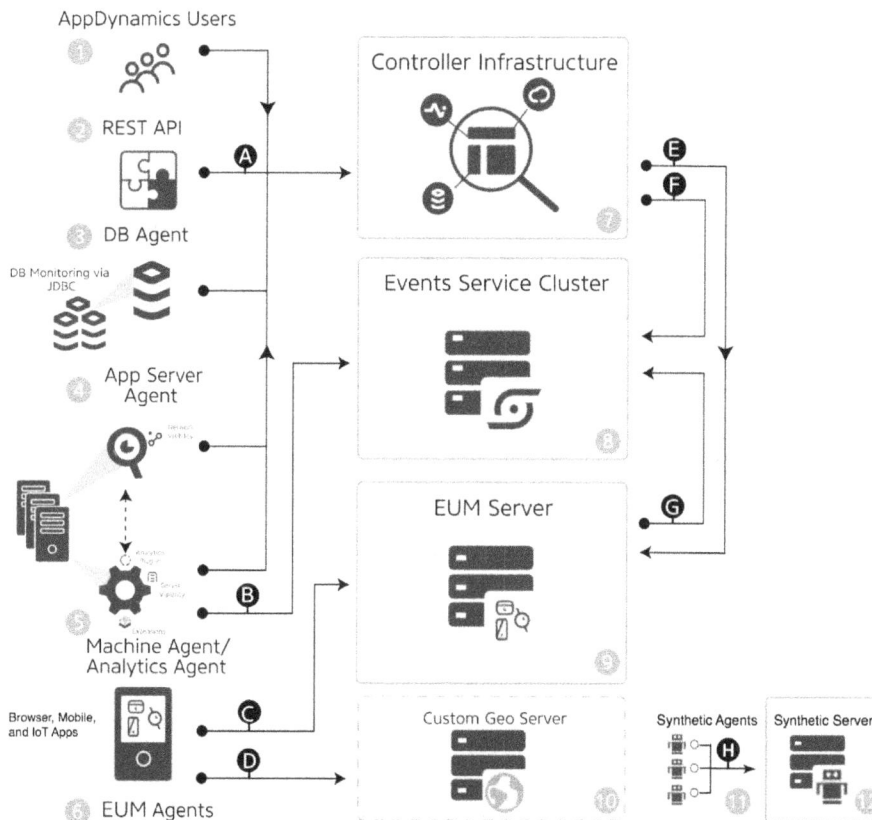

Figure 4-3   *Components of a complete on-premises AppDynamics APM platform deployment*

Depending on the scale of your deployment, your requirements, and the products you are using, your own deployment is likely to consist of a subset of the components shown in the diagram.

Platform Components

Table 4-1 describes how the components work together in the AppDynamics platform.

Table 4-1   *Platform Components*

Product Feature	Components Involved
Application Performance Management	App Server Agents attach to monitored applications and send data to the Controller via connection Ⓐ.
Server Visibility	Machine Agents reside on monitored servers and report data to the Controller via connection Ⓐ.
Application Analytics	The Analytics Dynamic Service (formerly called the Analytics plug-in) on the App Server Agent communicates with a local Analytics Agent instance. One or more Analytics Agents in a deployment send data to the Events Service via connection Ⓑ. The Analytics Agent is bundled with the Machine Agent but can be installed and run individually as well.
Database Visibility	The Database Agent connects by JDBC to monitored databases. The agent sends data to the Controller (via connection), which uses the Events Service to store certain types of data.
End User Monitoring (EUM)	For an on-premises EUM installation, you configure a connection to the web and mobile real user-monitoring agents to the on-premises EUM Server via connection Ⓒ. The EUM Server sends data to the Events Service cluster via connection Ⓖ. The optional Custom EUM Geo Server stores EUM Geo Resolution data taken via connection Ⓓ. The optional Synthetic Server receives synthetic job requests from the Controller that are then fetched from the Synthetic Services via connection Ⓗ.

Platform Connections

Table 4-2 lists and describes the traffic flow between AppDynamics platform components.

Table 4-2 *Platform Connections*

Connection	Source	Destination	Traffic	Protocol	Default Port(s)
Ⓐ	⊙ AppDynamics users through the web GUI, ⊚ REST API, ⊚ Database Agent, ⊙ Application Server Agent, and ⊙ Machine and Analytics Agents	⊚ Controller	APM/Database Metrics	HTTP / HTTPS	8090 / 8181
Ⓑ	⊙ Analytics Agent	⊙ Events Service Cluster	Log and Transaction Analytics Event Data	HTTP	9080
Ⓒ	⊙ Real User Monitoring (RUM) Agents	⊙ End User Monitoring (EUM) Server	EUM Beacon Data	HTTP / HTTPS	7001 / 7002
Ⓓ	⊙ Real User Monitoring (RUM) Agents	⊙ Custom EUM Geo Server	EUM Geo Resolution Mapping Data	HTTP / HTTPS	80 / 443
Ⓔ	⊚ Controller	⊙ EUM Server	EUM Metric Data	HTTP / HTTPS	7001 / 7002 (demo mode only)
Ⓕ	⊚ Controller	⊙ Events Service Cluster	Events Service API Store / Events Service API Store Admin	HTTP(S) / HTTP(S)	9080 / 9081
Ⓖ	⊙ EUM Server	⊙ Events Service Cluster	Events Service API Store (EUM Event Data) / Events Service API Store Admin (EUM Event Data)	HTTP(S) / HTTP(S)	9080 / 9081
Ⓗ	⊙ Synthetic Agents Synthetic	⊙ Synthetic Server	Synthetic Measurement Data	HTTP / HTTPS	10101 / 10102

Note AppDynamics End User Monitoring (EUM) gives you visibility into the performance of your application from the viewpoint of the end user.

Data Storage Location

Data is stored in the following locations:

- APM configuration and metric data is stored in the on-premises Controller MySQL database.

- EUM event data is stored in the Events Service.

- Transaction and log analytics data is stored in the Events Service.

- EUM Geo Resolution data is stored in the on-premises GeoServer.

- EUM Synthetic data is stored in the on-premises Synthetic Server.

SaaS Deployment Architecture

In this scenario, all AppDynamics services run as SaaS, and agents are configured to talk to the public SaaS endpoints. For EUM, by default, we resolve end-user locations using public geographic databases.

Although not strictly required, we recommend using a reverse proxy such as NGINX or Apache for all server-side components.

Note Components must be licensed separately.

Figure 4-4 illustrates a SaaS AppDynamics deployment architecture.

Figure 4-5 illustrates the connections, datastores, and key for the SaaS deployment architecture.

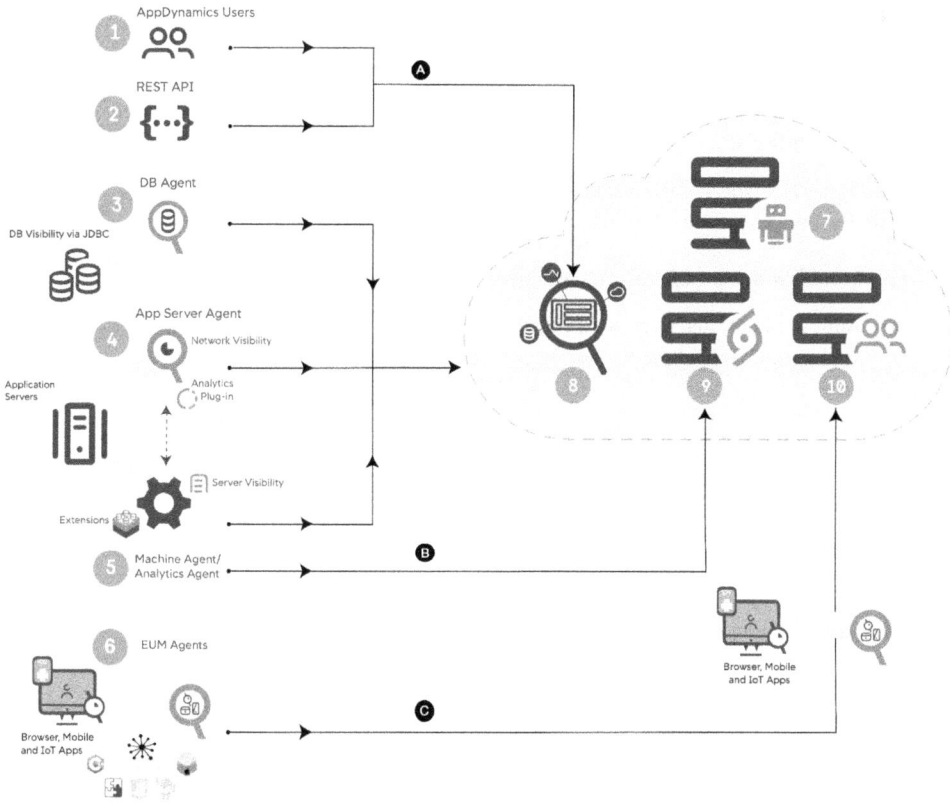

Figure 4-4   *SaaS AppDynamics deployment architecture*

Connections

A Traffic: APM/Database Metrics
Protocol: HTTP(S)
Default Ports: 443
Public Endpoint: <customer>.saas.appdynamics.com

C Traffic: EUM Beacon Data
Protocol: HTTP(S)
Default Ports: 80/443
Public Endpoint: col.eum-appdynamics.com

B Traffic: Log/ Transaction Analytics Event Data
Protocol: HTTPS
Default Ports: 443
Public Endpoint: analytics.api.appdynamics.com

Data Stores

APM Configuration and Metrics:
Controller Database (MySQL) + Data Aggregation Service (HBase) [🔵]

EUM Configuration and Metrics:
Controller Database (MySQL) + Data Aggregation Service (HBase) [🔵]

EUM Events: Events Service: SaaS [🔵]

Transaction/Log Analytics: SaaS [🔵]

Key

1 GUI users via web browser

2 Applications using the AppDynamics REST APIs

3 Database Agent

4 APM Agents (Java, .NET, Node.js, PHP, Python, Serverless APM for AWS Lamda, Apache, Web Server, C/C++ SDK, Go Language, IBM Integration Bus) with Analytics Plug-in and Network Visibility

5 Machine Agents (with Analytics Agent, Server Visibility, and/or AppDynamics Extensions)

6 Browser and Mobile RUM Agents for web/mobile/and iOT applications

SaaS Hosted

7 EUM Synthetic Monitoring Service

8 Controller Service

9 Events Service

10 EUM Real User Monitoring Service

Figure 4-5   *Understanding SaaS deployment architecture*

In the next sections, we review the various monitoring capabilities in AppDynamics.

Application Monitoring

AppDynamics Application Performance Monitoring (APM), a component of the AppDynamics platform, provides end-to-end visibility into the performance of your applications.

AppDynamics works with popular programming languages such as Java, .NET, Node.js, PHP, Python, C/C++, and more, enabling you to do the following:

- Troubleshoot problems such as slow response times and application errors.

- Automatically discover an application's topology and how components in the application environment work together to fulfill key business transactions for its users.

- Measure end-to-end business transaction performance, along with the health of individual application and infrastructure nodes.

- Receive alerts based on custom or built-in health rules, including rules against dynamic performance baselines that alert you to issues in the context of business transactions.

- Analyze your applications at the code execution level using snapshots.

Overview of Application Monitoring

After you understand the basics of AppDynamics, you can learn how AppDynamics models application environments. The model serves as the framework around which AppDynamics organizes and presents performance information.

A typical application environment consists of the following different components, which interact in a variety of ways to fulfill requests from the application's users:

- Web applications served from an application server

- Databases or other datastores

- Remote services such as message queues and caches

AppDynamics app agents automatically discover the most common application frameworks and services. Using built-in application detection and configuration settings, agents collect application data and metrics to build flow maps.

A flow map visually represents the components of your application to help you understand how data flows among the application components. For example, the business transaction flow map for a simple e-commerce application shows data flowing between web services, message queues, and databases. Figure 4-6 shows the Business Transaction flow map.

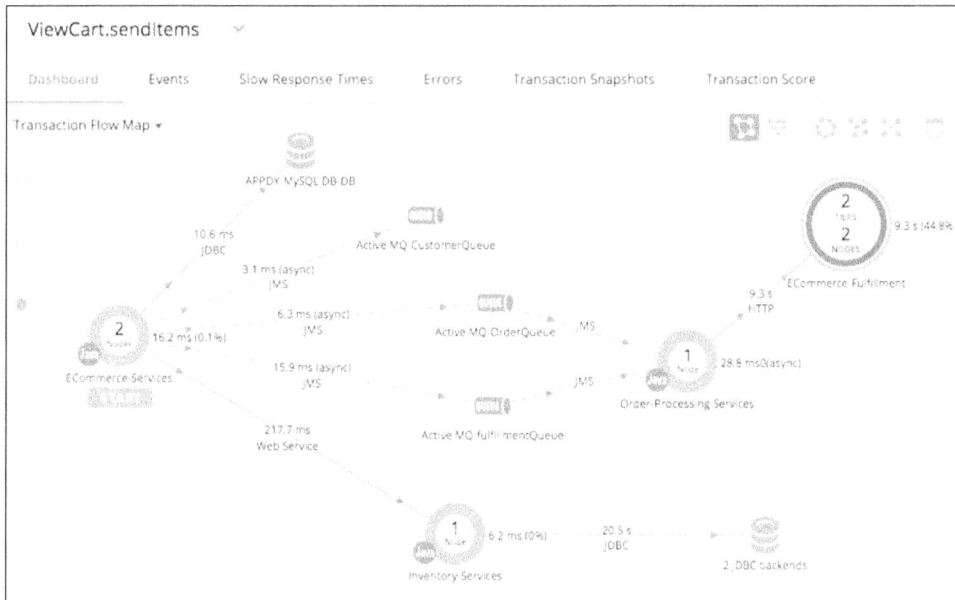

Figure 4-6 *Business Transaction flow map*

Automatic detection lets you start exploring AppDynamics features quickly. As your understanding of AppDynamics matures and you identify areas unique to your environment, you can refine your application model.

Business Transactions

In the AppDynamics model, a *business transaction* represents the data processing flow for a request, most often a user request. In real-world terms, many different components in your application may interact to provide services to fulfill the following types of requests:

- In an e-commerce application, a user logging in, searching for items or adding items to a cart

- In a content portal, a user requesting content such as sports, business, or entertainment news

- In a stock trading application, operations such as receiving a stock quote, buying a stock, and selling a stock

AppDynamics app agents discover requests to your application as entry points to a business transaction. Similar requests, such as user login, are treated as multiple instances of the same business transaction. The agents tag the request data and trace the request path as it passes from web servers to databases and other infrastructure components.

AppDynamics collects performance metrics for each tier that processes the business transaction.

Because AppDynamics orients performance monitoring around business transactions, you can focus on the performance of your application components from the user perspective. You can quickly identify whether a component is readily available or if it is having performance issues. For instance, you can check whether users are able to log in, check out, and view their data. You can see response times for users as well as the causes of problems when they occur.

Business Applications

A *business application* is the top-level container in the AppDynamics model. A business application contains a set of related services and business transactions.

In a small AppDynamics deployment, only a single business application may be needed to model the environment. In larger deployments, you may choose to divide the model of the environment into several business applications.

The best way to organize business applications for you depends on your environment. A leading consideration for most cases, however, is to organize business applications in a way that reflects work teams in your organization, since role-based access controls in the Controller UI are oriented by business application.

Nodes

A *node* in the AppDynamics model corresponds to a monitored server or Java virtual machine (JVM) in the application environment. A node is the smallest unit of the modeled environment. Depending on the agent type, a node may correspond to an individual application server, JVM, CLR (Common Language Runtime), PHP application, or Apache Web server.

Each node identifies itself in the AppDynamics model. When you configure the agent, you specify the name of the node, tier, and business application under which the agent reports data to the Controller.

Tiers

A *tier* is a unit in the AppDynamics model composed of a grouping of one or more nodes. How you organize tiers depends on the conceptual model of your environment.

Often, a tier is used to group of a set of identical, redundant servers. But that is not strictly required. You can group any set of nodes, identical or not, for which you want performance metrics to be treated as a unit into a single tier.

The single restriction is that all nodes in a single tier must be the same type. That is, a tier cannot have mixed types of agents, such as both .NET and Java nodes.

The traffic in a business application flows between tiers, as indicated by lines on the flow map, which are annotated with performance metrics.

In the AppDynamics model, there is no interaction among nodes within a single tier. Also, an application agent node cannot belong to more than one tier.

Entities

An *entity* is any object that AppDynamics monitors, such as an application, tier, node, or even a business transaction. Entities typically have associated metrics, events, and a health status.

Historical and Live Entity Data

The Controller has an entity liveness module that tracks the "live" or "historical" status of the four entity types—application, tier, node, and business transaction—for 365+ days.

- **Historical:** Oldest time (a year before the latest Controller restart) to the latest Controller restart time
- **Live:** Latest Controller restart time until the current time

Anchor Metrics for Entities

The entities have special metrics called *anchor metrics* that are used to determine the liveness of the entity. Table 4-3 lists the anchor metrics for each of the entities.

Table 4-3   *Anchor Metrics for Entities*

Entity	Anchor Metric
Application	Agent | App | Availability
Tier	Agent | App | Availability
Node	Agent | App | Availability
Business transactions (BTs)	BTM | BTs | BT: %d | Component: %d | Calls per Minute

Liveness Status

The liveness of an entity affects the associated entities, as the liveness is rolled up the hierarchy. If the entity type in Table 4-4 is live, you can determine the liveness of the associated entities in the right column.

Table 4-4   *Liveness Status*

Live Entity	Liveness Status
Application	An app is alive if any tiers in this app are alive.
Tier	A tier is alive if any nodes in this tier are alive.
Node	Any metrics from the particular node.
Business transactions (BTs)	BT metrics, Calls per Minute.

How the Controller Displays Live Entities

Based on entity liveness status of the selected time range, the Controller determines whether to count and display entities in these places:

- Flow map.

- Tier and Node list pages. This is also determined by the Performance Data checkboxes. See Live Entity Data in Flowmaps (https://docs.appdynamics.com/appd/21.x/21.3/en/application-monitoring/business-applications/flow-maps).

- Metric tree of the Metric Browser.

- Custom dashboards.

- AppDynamics REST APIs related to topology such as the Application Model API.

Backends

A *backend* is a component that is not instrumented by an AppDynamics agent but one that participates in the processing of a business transaction instance. A backend may be a web server, database, message queue, or another type of service.

The agent recognizes calls to these services from instrumented code (called *exit calls*). If the service is not instrumented and cannot continue the transaction context of the call, the agent determines that the service is a backend component. The agent picks up the transaction context at the response at the backend and continues to follow the context of the transaction from there.

Performance information is available for the backend call. For detailed transaction analysis for the leg of a transaction processed by the backend, you need to instrument the database, web service, or other application.

Integration with Other AppDynamics Modules

This section describes how other AppDynamics APM platform products work with Application Monitoring to provide complete, full visibility on application health and user experience.

Application Monitoring and Infrastructure Visibility

Infrastructure Visibility provides end-to-end visibility into the hardware and networks on which your applications run. You can use Infrastructure Visibility to identify and trouble-shoot problems that affect application performance such as server failures, JVM crashes, and hardware resource utilization.

You use the Machine Agent to collect basic hardware metrics. One Machine Agent license is included with each App Agent license that you purchase. You can deploy this Machine Agent only on the same machine where the App Agent is installed. The follow-ing functionality is provided by the Machine Agent:

- Basic hardware metrics from the server OS (for example, %CPU and memory utiliza-tion, disk and network I/O).

- Custom metrics passed to the Controller by extensions.

- Run remediation scripts to automate your runbook procedures. You can option-ally configure the remediation action to require human approval before the script is started.

- Run JVM Crash Guard to monitor JVM crashes and optionally run remediation scripts.

If you have a Server Visibility license, the Machine Agent provides this additional functionality:

- Extended hardware metrics such as machine availability, disk/CPU/virtual memory utilization, and process page faults.

- Monitor application nodes that run inside Docker containers and identify container issues that impact application performance.

- Tier Metric Correlator, which enables you to identify load and performance anoma-lies across all nodes in a tier.

- Monitor internal or external HTTP and HTTPS services.

- Group servers together so that health rules can be applied to specific server groups.

- Define alerts that trigger when certain conditions are met or exceeded based on monitored server hardware metrics.

Network Visibility monitors traffic flows, network packets, TCP connections, and TCP ports. Network Agents leverage the APM intelligence of App Server Agents to identify the TCP connections used by each application. Network Visibility includes the following functionality:

- Detailed metrics about dropped/retransmitted packets, TCP window sizes (Limited / Zero), connection setup/teardown issues, high round-trip times, and other performance-impacting issues

- Network Dashboard that highlights network key performance indicators (KPIs) for tiers, nodes, and network links

- Right-click dashboards for tiers, nodes, and network links that enable quick drill-downs from transaction outliers to network root causes

- Automatic mapping of TCP connections with application flows

- Automatic detection of intermediate load balancers that split TCP connections

- Diagnostic mode for collecting advanced diagnostic information for individual connections

Application Monitoring and Browser Real User Monitoring

When you add End User Monitoring to Application Performance Management, you can correlate business transaction performance to the user experience for those transactions.

If app server agents run on the applications that serve your browser applications, you can further configure the app server agents to inject the JavaScript Agent into the code that runs on the browser. You can access the settings to configure injection in the Applications Configuration page.

Application Monitoring and Database Visibility

In Application Monitoring, a database called by an instrumented node is considered a remote service. You can get a significant amount of information on the interaction between the application node and database, but not from the database server perspective. When using Database Visibility with Application Monitoring, you can drill down to detailed database performance information directly from application flow maps.

Application Monitoring and Analytics

For those times when tracing application code does not provide enough clues to track down the cause of a problem, AppDynamics provides visibility into the transaction logs that can be correlated to specific business transaction requests. Log correlation visibility requires a license for both Transaction Analytics and Log Analytics.

Application Security Monitoring

AppDynamics with Cisco Secure Application reduces the risk of security exposure without compromising the delivery speed for an APM-managed application. Normally, the traditional vulnerability scanning occurs before the application is launched to production and then continues a monthly or quarterly cadence. As soon as the app is deployed to production, new security gaps and zero-day exploits make the application vulnerable despite pre-production testing. Cisco Secure Application enables continuous vulnerability assessment and protection by scanning code execution to prevent possible exploits.

Note   Cisco Secure Application is available for the SaaS environment only.

Cisco Secure Application enables the following:

- The IT Operations team responsible for performance monitoring to gain real-time access to all security events

- Application security (AppSec) developers and application developers to gain insights into violations of best practices and to collaborate on a solution without friction

- AppSec and DevOps to add security into the existing automation, which benefits the DevSecOps environment

- Businesses to operate at a faster pace with a lower risk profile due to constant run-time protection, real-time remediation, and security automation

To monitor the application security, you must enable the security for the application using the Cisco Secure Application dashboard. Use the **Security Events** widget on the **AppDynamics Application dashboard** to navigate to the **Cisco Secure Application dashboard.** To view the Security Events widget within AppDynamics Performance Monitoring (APM), enable your SaaS account with the subscription license for Secure Application.

Supported APM Agents

The Cisco Secure Application features are built into these AppDynamics APM Agents:

- Java Agent
- .NET Agent

Cisco Secure Application Components

Cisco Secure Application uses the combination of the supported APM Agent, Controller, and Cisco Secure Application dashboard to monitor the security of the applications. The following list explains what each does:

- **APM Agent:** The Cisco Secure Application library is bundled with the Java and .NET Agents. The agent communicates with the Cisco Secure Application service within the Controller, which is maintained in the cloud.

- **AppDynamics Controller:** The Cisco Secure Application service is maintained in the cloud by AppDynamics. The APM Agent sends data to the service within the Controller. The service analyzes the data to protect against different types of attacks and vulnerabilities and then the service provides the analysis to the dashboard.

It uses external feeds along with internal data to analyze the behavior of the application. It analyzes the CVEs (Common Vulnerabilities and Exposures) against a curated vulnerability feed. The service can detect:

- A vulnerability when it is enabled in the policy and when the associated behavior and the library used are considered vulnerable.

- An attack when it is enabled in the policy and abnormal behavior is detected.

- **Cisco Secure Application dashboard:** A graphical representation of all the analyzed data. You can view this dashboard based on the role defined in the AppDynamics Controller. The data is updated on the dashboard when the service within the Controller sends the analyzed data to the dashboard.

Cisco Secure Application Architecture

Figure 4-7 illustrates the high-level architecture of Cisco Secure Application.

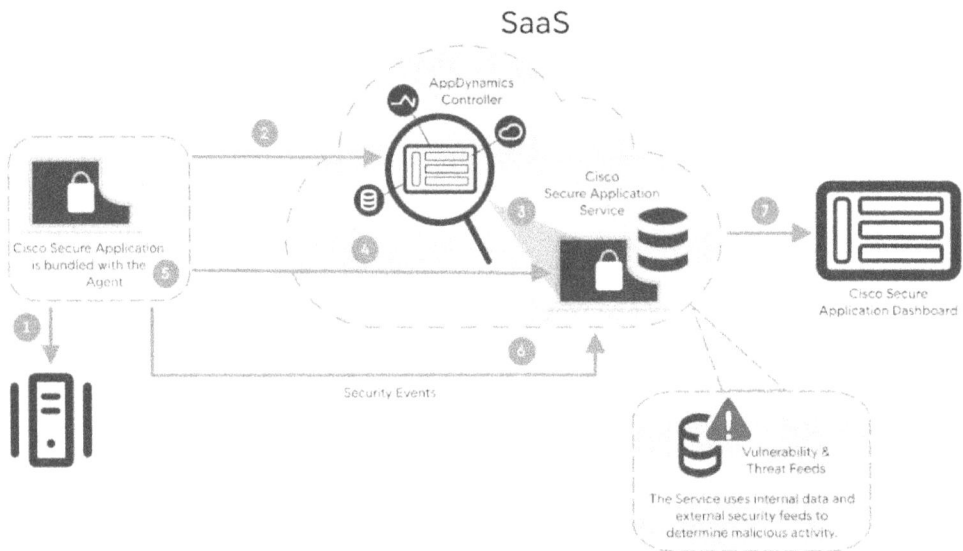

Figure 4-7 *High-level architecture of Cisco Secure Application*

Note   The APM Agent (Java Agent) communicates to the Cisco Secure Application service through the AppDynamics Controller.

The high-level architecture works as follows:

- You install the supported APM Agent and then add the Cisco Secure Application license.

- The APM-managed application runs and the APM Agent retrieves the data to send to the Controller.

- The Cisco Secure Application service retrieves the application, tiers, and nodes data from the Controller.

- The APM Agent communicates with the Cisco Secure Application service to check if the security is enabled for the application.

- If the security is enabled, the agent downloads the configuration along with the policies from the Cisco Secure Application service.

- Based on the configured policies, the agent sends the security events to the Cisco Secure Application service.

- The service collects all the data, analyzes the application behavior, and then provides the analyzed data to the Cisco Secure Application dashboard.

Monitor Application Security Using Cisco Secure Application

Cisco Secure Application offers a real-time dashboard that provides visibility into the security health of your applications. This dashboard is available when an application is registered with an APM Agent and has the appropriate licensing. The agent sends the security events to Cisco Secure Application through the Controller.

The Security Events widget on the AppDynamics Application dashboard provides high-level information about the security of a registered application. This widget displays the number of critical, warning, and normal security events. To view the details of security for the selected application on Cisco Secure Application, click the **Security Events** widget. Figure 4-8 illustrates the AppDynamics Application flow map.

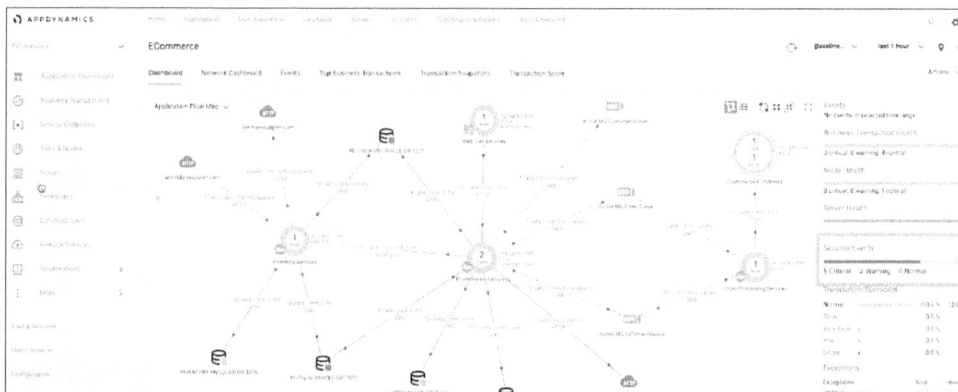

Figure 4-8   *AppDynamics Application flow map*

Select Scope for the Dashboard

Cisco Secure Application dashboard provides a filter to select the required application and tier scope that is applied across all views within this dashboard, except for Policies. By default, the application scope is the selected application on the AppDynamics dashboard prior to navigating to Cisco Secure Application.

Perform the following steps to view the data on the dashboard for a specific application:

Step 1.   Click the filter icon *application name/tier name* on the top right corner of the dashboard.

Step 2.   In the Applications tab, search for the specific application.

Step 3.   Select the application.

Step 4.   (Optional) In the Tiers tab, search for the required tier.

　　　　　　 If you do not select any specific tier, data is displayed for all the tiers.

Step 5.   Click **Apply Changes**.

Figure 4-9 shows an example of the application/tier filter.

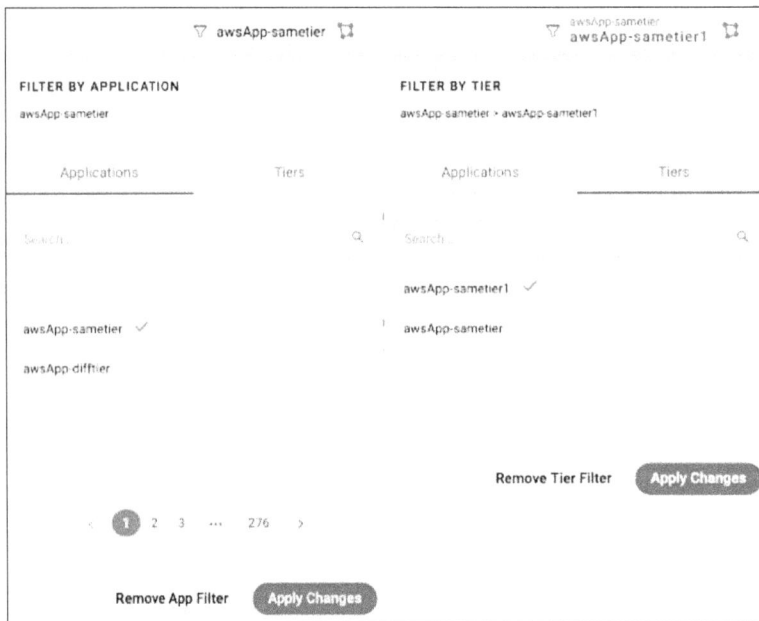

Figure 4-9   *Application/ Tier Filter*

To return to the default view of all applications, click *application name/ tier name >* Applications > Remove App Filter. Similarly, click *application name/ tier name >* Tiers > Remove Tier Filter to return to the default view of all tiers.

Navigate to AppDynamics Application or Tier Flow Map

To navigate from the Cisco Secure Application dashboard to the AppDynamics flow map, click the **flow map icon** at the top-right corner of the Cisco Secure Application dashboard. The flow map icon is associated with the selected scope for the Cisco Secure Application dashboard.

For example, in Figure 4-10, the tier scope is **awsApp-sametier1**. You can click the flow map icon to launch the awsApp-sametier1 flow map on the AppDynamics dashboard.

Figure 4-10 illustrates how to navigate to the AppDynamics dashboard.

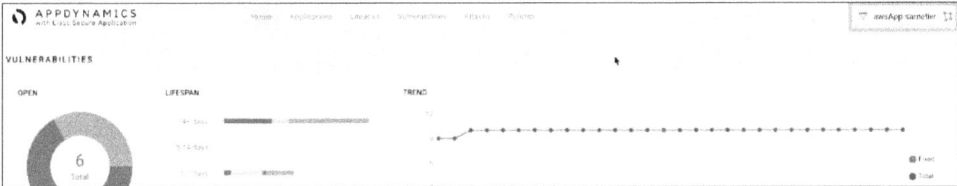

Figure 4-10   *Navigating to the AppDynamics dashboard*

Figure 4-11 shows the AppDynamics dashboard.

Figure 4-11   *AppDynamics dashboard*

View Data Using Search Filter

The Cisco Secure Application provides a search filter on various pages in the dashboard. This filter helps in getting the required data quickly. The search filter allows you to search based on the selected category. For example, in Figure 4-12, these are the categories:

- Vulnerability
- Severity
- Affected Services/Tiers
- Status

Figure 4-12 shows an example of the Vulnerability search filter.

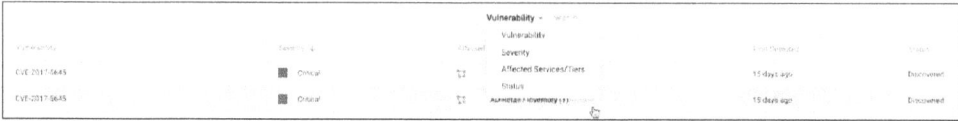

Figure 4-12 *Vulnerability search filter*

You can select the required search category from the drop-down list and then click the **Search** field to view the list of values corresponding to the category. You can also find the required value as you type.

If you do not require an exact match, you can enter the required generic value in the Search field. For example, consider that you want to search for all applications that start with a specific prefix, AD. You can select the search category as Application and enter AD in the Search field.

Note You can search using one or all the categories, but each category can have a single search value. A category is disabled when you specify a search value for that category, but you can continue to select another available category and specify its search value. These search values act as filters. You can remove the search values to remove the search filter.

Cisco Secure Application provides a real-time dashboard that displays these pages:

- **Home:** This page provides an overview of attacks and vulnerabilities of monitored applications.

- **Applications:** This page provides the details of monitored nodes that are registered with Cisco Secure Application for the managed applications.

- **Libraries:** This page provides details of the existing libraries that require remediation.

- **Vulnerabilities:** This page provides information about all discovered vulnerabilities.

- **Attacks:** This page provides information about all detected attacks.

- **Policies:** This page allows you to create or customize the policies for vulnerabilities and attacks.

End User Monitoring

AppDynamics End User Monitoring (EUM) provides end-to-end visibility on the performance of your web and mobile applications. EUM helps you troubleshoot problems such as slow web responses, Ajax errors, mobile network requests, and IoT application errors. EUM provides metrics on application performance and user activity, such as:

- How server performance impacts your web, mobile, and device performance

- How third-party APIs impact your web, mobile, and device performance

- Where your heaviest loads originate

- How your users connect to and navigate your application

Overview of End User Monitoring

AppDynamics EUM gives you visibility into the performance of your application from the viewpoint of the end user.

Whereas Application Performance Monitoring (APM) measures user interaction starting at the web server or application server entry point, EUM extends that visibility all the way to the web browser, mobile, or IoT application. As a result, EUM reveals the impact the network and browser rendering times have on the user experience of your application.

Figure 4-13 provides an overview of the different components, deployment models (SaaS/on-premises), and the Controller UI as seen by AppDynamics end users. The SaaS deployment employs services (Controller Service, Events Service, EUM Service, EUM Synthetic Monitoring Service) to collect, store, and process data, whereas the on-premises deployment requires customers to install discrete components such as the Controller and servers (Events Server, EUM Server, and so on) that run processes to collect, store, and process data.

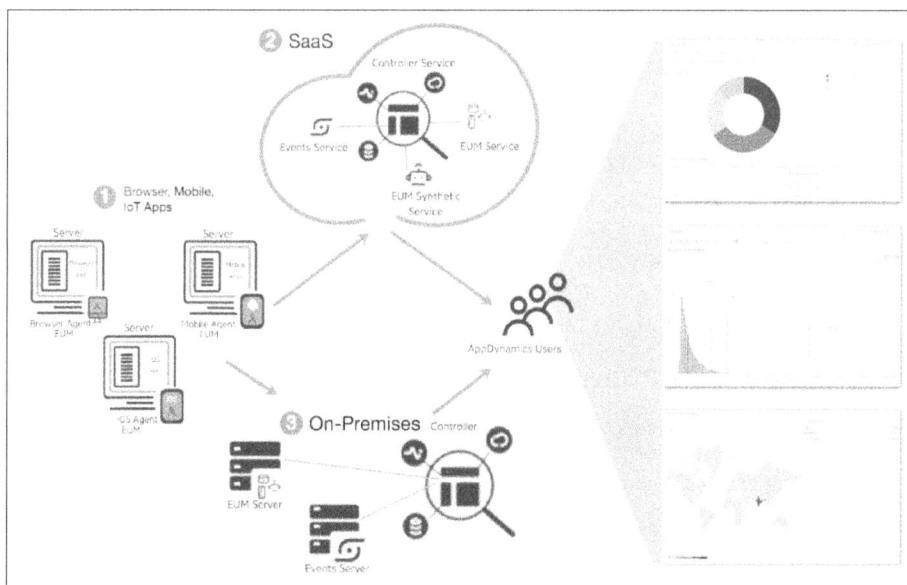

Figure 4-13 *Overview of End User Monitoring*

AppDynamics users can go to the AppDynamics Controller UI to view and analyze RUM metrics as snapshots, pages, Ajax requests, sessions, network requests, or in the form of charts and graphs. Table 4-5 provides details of the components and their description used in End User Monitoring.

Table 4-5   *Overview of End User Monitoring*

Step	Description	Component(s)
①	The Browser, Mobile, and IoT Agents run in web/mobile/IoT applications, collect metrics, and then transmit that data to either a SaaS or an on-premises deployment of AppDynamics.	Browser/Mobile/IoT Apps EUM Agents
②	The AppDynamics SaaS Cloud, consisting of the components listed to the right, stores, processes, and analyzes data and then delivers RUM metrics to the Controller UI.	**Controller Service:** stores data and metadata, makes calls to the EUM Server for raw data and the Events Service for analytic data. **Events Service:** Stores short-term RUM data (such as sessions, network requests, snapshots) for heavier analysis. **EUM Service:** Verifies, aggregates, and packages raw browser/mobile app metrics. **EUM Synthetic Monitoring Service:** Schedules and executes Browser Synthetic jobs and returns session data to the Controller.
③	The on-premises deployment of AppDynamics has most of the same components and data as the SaaS model. In this model, DevOps installs and administers their own Controller, Events Service, and EUM Server. The EUM Synthetic Monitoring Service and sessions data, however, are not available in the on-premises deployment.	Controller Events Server EUM Server

Understand End User Activity

Using EUM, you can determine the following:

- Where geographically your heaviest application load is originated.

- Where geographically your slowest end-user response times occur.

- How performance varies by the following:

- Location

- Client type, device, browser and browser version, and network connection for web requests

- Application and application version, operating system version, device, and carrier for mobile requests

- What your slowest web/Ajax requests are, and where the problem may lie.

- What your slowest mobile and IoT network requests are, and where the problem may lie.

- How application server performance impacts the performance of your web and mobile traffic.

- Whether your mobile or IoT applications are experiencing errors or crashes and the root cause of the issues. For example, for mobile applications, EUM provides stack traces and event trails for the crash or error, helping you troubleshoot and optimize mobile applications.

View EUM Data

The performance information generated by EUM is distinct from the application monitoring data generated by app server agents.

EUM data appears in various locations in the Controller UI, including in the User Experience dashboard, Metric Browser, and AppDynamics Analytics pages.

When linked to application business transactions, EUM data gives you a complete view of your end users' experience—from the client request, through to the application environment, and back to the client as the user response.

You can view EUM performance data in the Controller UI in the User Experience tab. From there, you can access information specific to browser applications, mobile applications, or connected devices (IoT applications).

On-Premises EUM Deployments

By default, EUM is configured to use an AppDynamics-hosted component called the EUM Cloud. For a fully on-premises installation, the EUM Server provides the functionality of the EUM Cloud.

Some functionality for EUM depends on the AppDynamics Platform Events Service. In a SaaS environment, this is managed by AppDynamics, but it is also possible to use this functionality in an on-premises form.

If you are adding EUM to an existing on-premises Controller installation, you should evaluate your current configuration's ability to handle the additional load imposed by EUM.

Access the SaaS EUM Server

The SaaS EUM Server consists of the following components. Each component may have different endpoints, depending on the region of your Controller.

- **EUM Services:** The Mobile Agents, JavaScript Agent, and IoT SDKs send data to the EUM Services. The Controller fetches data from the EUM Server.

- **Events Service:** The EUM Server sends analytics data to the Events Service. The Controller also queries the Events Service.

- **Synthetic Services:** The Synthetic Private Agent and Synthetic Hosted Agent send data to the Synthetic Services.

If your SaaS or on-prem deployment requires access to any of these components on the Internet, make sure the URLs given in SaaS domains and IP ranges are accessible from your network.

How EUM Works with Other AppDynamics Products

This section describes how other App iQ Platform products work with EUM to provide complete, full visibility on application health and user experience.

EUM and Application Performance Monitoring

Using APM with EUM provides you with greater insight into how the performance of your business application affects the end-user experience. To integrate APM with EUM, you correlate business transactions with browser snapshots. This enables you to trace bad user experiences to issues with your backends such as an unresponsive web service, bad database query, or slow server response.

You can also use the app server agents running on business applications that serve your browser applications to inject a JavaScript Agent into the code that runs on the browser. This obviates the need to manually inject the JavaScript Agent.

Note   You must assign unique names to EUM applications and business applications. For example, if you created a business application called "E-Commerce," you cannot create a browser, mobile, or IoT application with that same name, and vice versa.

EUM and Application Analytics

AppDynamics Application Analytics enables you to use the powerful AppDynamics Query Language (ADQL) to analyze different types of EUM data through complex queries. The Analytics components are based on the Events Service, which is also the source of data for Browser Analyze, Crash Analyze, Network Requests Analyze, and all IoT data. Analytics requires a license separate from the EUM licenses, except for IoT Monitoring.

Experience Journey Map

Experience Journey Map provides real-time insights into business and application performance, visualizing key user journeys and the correlation between performance and traffic. This perspective unifies all application stakeholders: application owners, developers, and IT operations.

Experience Journey Map visualizes the following:

- Performance metrics for each step in a user journey

- Top incoming and outgoing traffic data for each step

- Drop-off rates

To use Experience Journey Map, you need the following:

- SaaS: Controller >= 20.6.0

- On-premises: Controller >= 20.7.0

- EUM Peak license (RUM Peak, Browser RUM Peak, or Mobile RUM Peak)

- Instrumented browser or mobile application

To access Experience Journey Map, follow these steps:

Step 1.   Under the User Experience tab, go to a browser or mobile app.

Step 2.   In the left application panel, click **Experience Journey Map**.

Experience Journey Map UI

The following sections provide an overview of the Experience Journey Map UI. In the Controller, click on the **Legend** for key terms.

Experience Journey Map Dashboard

The Experience Journey Map dashboard displays the top user journeys, or the most trafficked parts of an app. The default time frame is set to one hour, but you can adjust the time, and the dashboard automatically updates the user journeys and data for that time frame. Figure 4-14 shows an example of a Browser Application Journey Map.

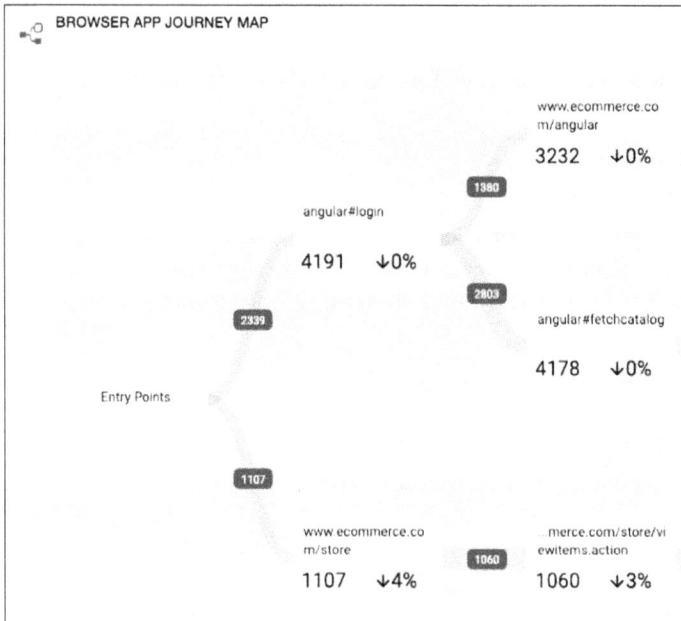

Figure 4-14   *Browser Application Journey Map*

End User Events

Each step in an Experience Journey Map user journey is visualized by end-user events (browser pages, iOS views, or Android activities). Experience Journey Map displays the user journeys with the most traffic.

Click an end user event to see the following information:

- Total user visits (all incoming traffic) to an end-user event page/view/activity

- Where users are "journeying" through your app

- How each user journey is performing over time

- When users drop off your app

Figure 4-15 shows an example of the End User Event (Browser).

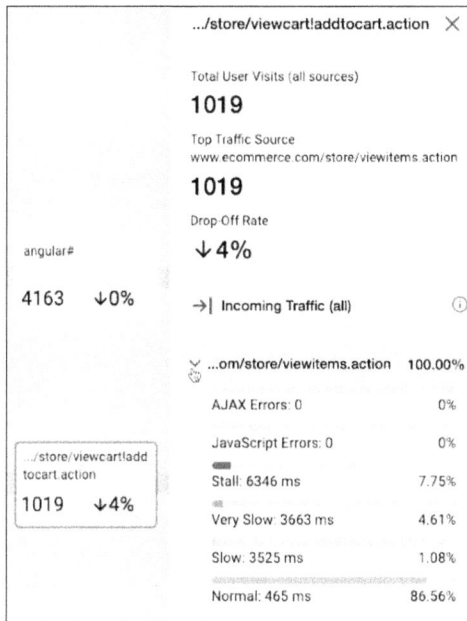

Figure 4-15   *End User Event (Browser)*

Traffic Segments

A traffic segment connects two end-user events in a journey and contains data about what users experience in that journey. If the journey exceeds health performance metrics, a health status icon will appear on the traffic segment with more details on the user impact of poor performance.

Click a traffic segment to see the following information:

- Number of users who journeyed from one end-user event to the next
- Performance metrics for users within a journey
- Option to analyze individual browser or mobile sessions within a journey

Figure 4-16 shows an example of Traffic Segment (Browser).

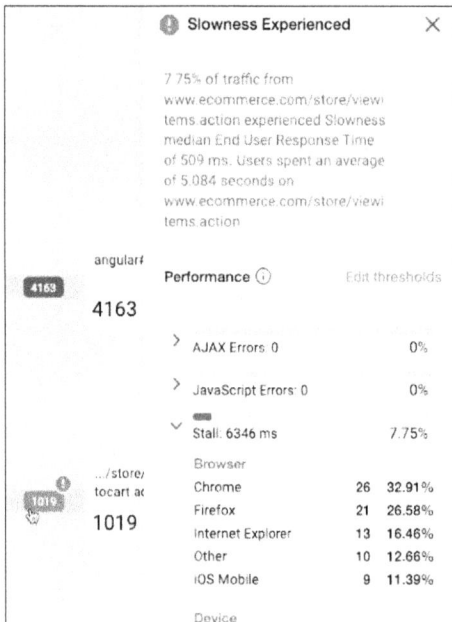

Figure 4-16   *Traffic Segment (Browser)*

Refresh Loops

A refresh loop is a type of traffic segment and contains data for users who refresh an end-user event.

Click a refresh loop to see the following information:

- How many users needed to hit Refresh because of poor app performance
- Insights into what causes poor app performance
- Location and hardware of users impacted by poor app performance

Figure 4-17 shows an example of Refresh Loop (Browser).

Figure 4-17   *Refresh Loop (Browser)*

Browser Monitoring

In this section, we will look at Browser Monitoring and options available to track application performance. AppDynamics offers two products to monitor browser applications:

- **Browser Real User Monitoring (Browser RUM):** Monitors how your web application is performing, using real user data to analyze application performance and user experience

- **Browser Synthetic Monitoring:** Analyzes application availability and performance, using scheduled testing to analyze website availability

Overview of the Controller UI for Browser Monitoring

Browser RUM and Browser Synthetic Monitoring share two dashboards: Browser App Dashboard and Resource Performance Dashboard. Figure 4-18 shows an example of Browser Monitoring.

Figure 4-18   *Browser Monitoring*

Browser App Dashboard

The Browser App Dashboard provides a high-level understanding of your application's overall performance. When you first navigate to a browser application, you are defaulted to the Browser App Dashboard's Overview tab. The Overview tab contains widgets for both browser and synthetic data.

Overview Tab

The Overview tab displays a set of configurable widgets. The default widgets contain multiple graphs and lists featuring common high-level indicators of application performance. Figure 4-19 shows an example of a Browser Application Dashboard.

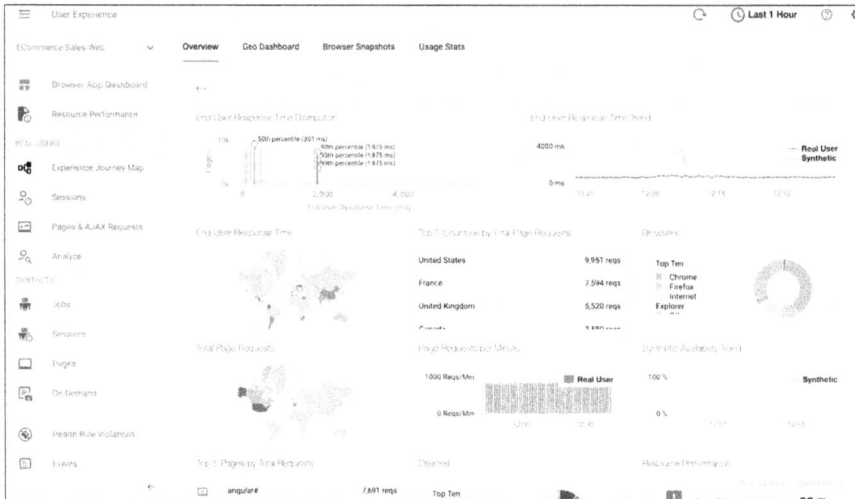

Figure 4-19 *Browser Application Dashboard*

Geo Tab

The Geo tab displays key performance metrics by geographic location based on page loads. If you are using Browser Synthetic Monitoring for an application, you can view either "real user" or "synthetic" data using the View drop-down.

The metrics displayed throughout the dashboard are for the region currently selected on the map or in the grid. For example, on the map, if you click France, the widgets and trend graphs update to display data for France. Figure 4-20 shows an example of a Geo Dashboard.

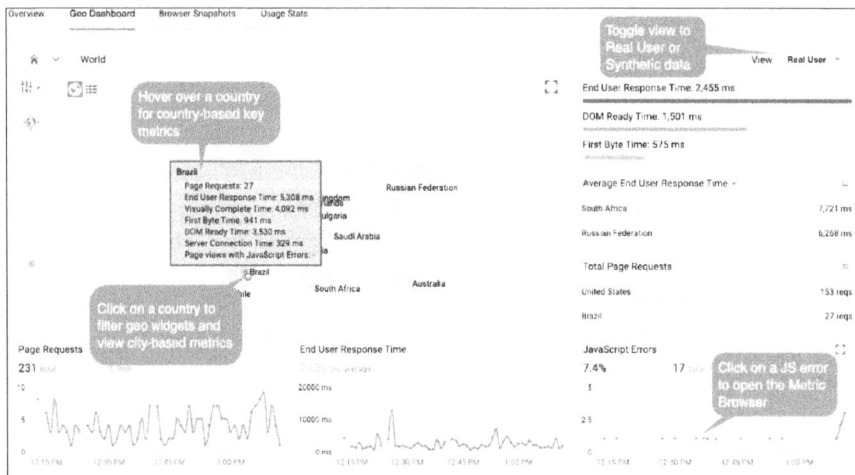

Figure 4-20 *Geo Dashboard*

Resource Performance Dashboard

The Resource Performance Dashboard provides a high-level understanding of how your resources affect the performance of your browser application. You can use this dashboard to pinpoint resource-related performance issues affecting the user experience, such as the following:

- A prioritized list of resource performance issues generated by comparing their performance against thresholds.

- Changes in the number of resources.

- Large resources (images, JavaScript, CSS, and so on).

- Size increase of resources impacting performance. For example, a page banner might be replaced with an uncompressed image, thus slowing down the page load.

- Slow CDNs.

- Resources that haven't been compressed.

- Comparison of real user and synthetic resource performance.

Overview of the Resource Performance Dashboard UI

Once you navigate to a browser application, the Resource Performance Dashboard is located on the left-side panel. Figure 4-21 shows the Resource Performance Dashboard.

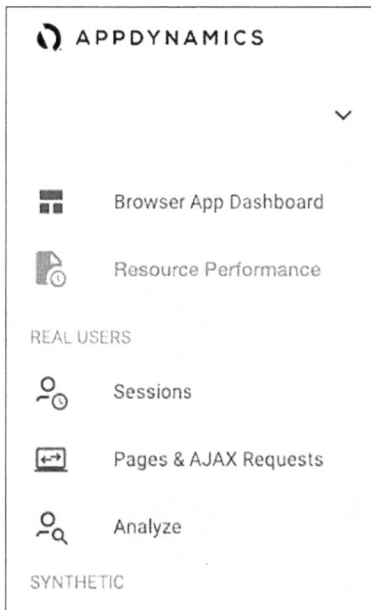

Figure 4-21   *Resource Performance Dashboard*

Overview Tab

The Overview tab displays widgets providing high-level indicators of resource performance over a specified time period. The dashboard can be filtered to real user or synthetic data. The widgets only show a small number of resources, but you can click **See More** to view up to 100 resources per widget. Figure 4-22 shows Overview under Resource Performance.

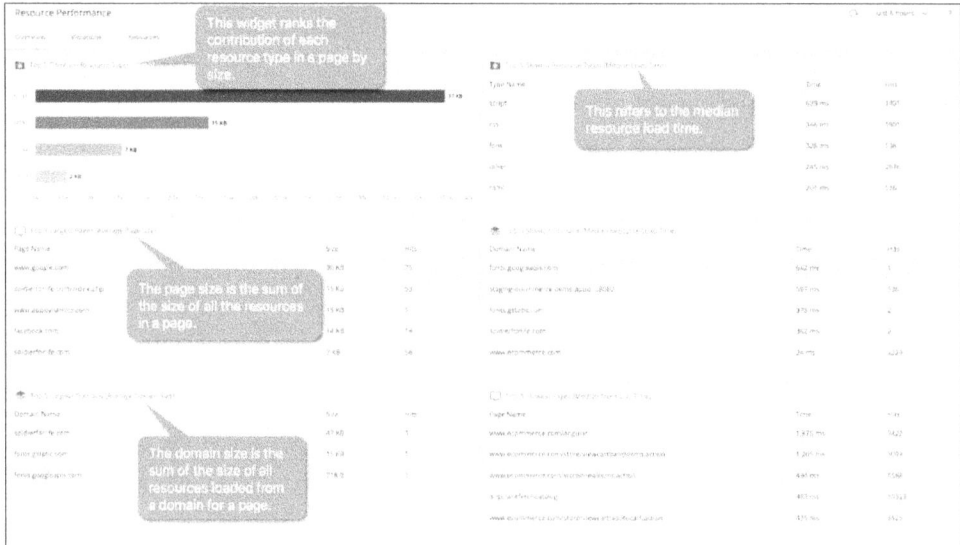

Figure 4-22 *Overview tab*

Violations Tab

The Violations tab shows a list of pages, resource types, and domain or resource violations that have exceeded performance thresholds. You can use the Violations tab not to only find problematic resources but also to become aware of sudden changes that negatively impacted the performance of a resource. Clicking a specific violation leads to the Resources tab, and the data is filtered with that violation for further diagnostics. The configured violation rules are evaluated every 10 minutes for the last 30 minutes. Figure 4-23 shows Violations under Resource Performance.

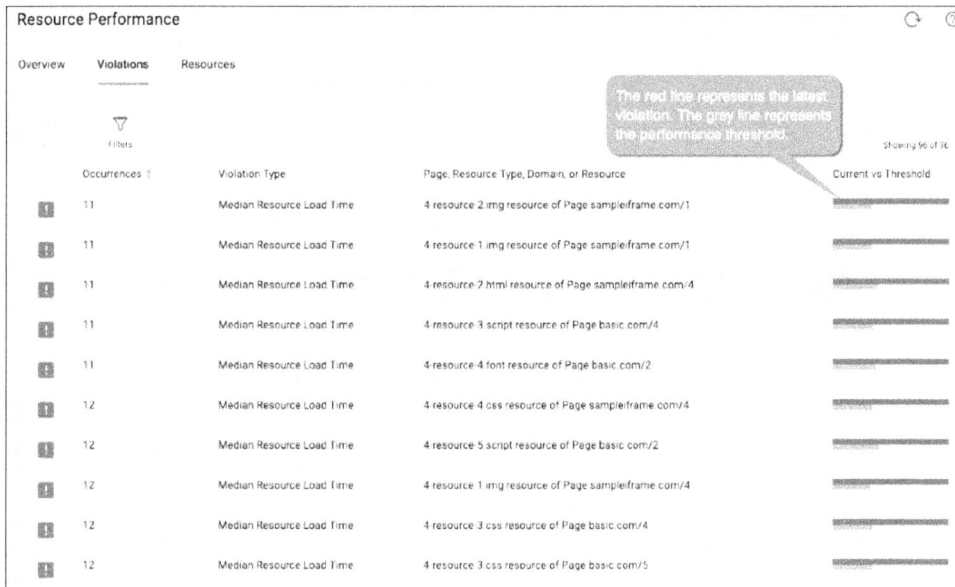

Figure 4-23 *Violations tab*

The supported violation types include the following:

- Median Domain Load Time
- Average Domain Size
- Average Page Size
- Median Resource Load Time
- Average Resource Size
- Median Resource Type Load Time
- Average Resource Type Size

Resources Tab

You can use the Resources tab to diagnose a problematic resource. You can also add criteria as a filter to the widgets. All use cases to troubleshoot a resource lead to the Resources tab, where you can learn more about an individual resource's impact on an application. Figure 4-24 illustrates Resource under Resource Performance.

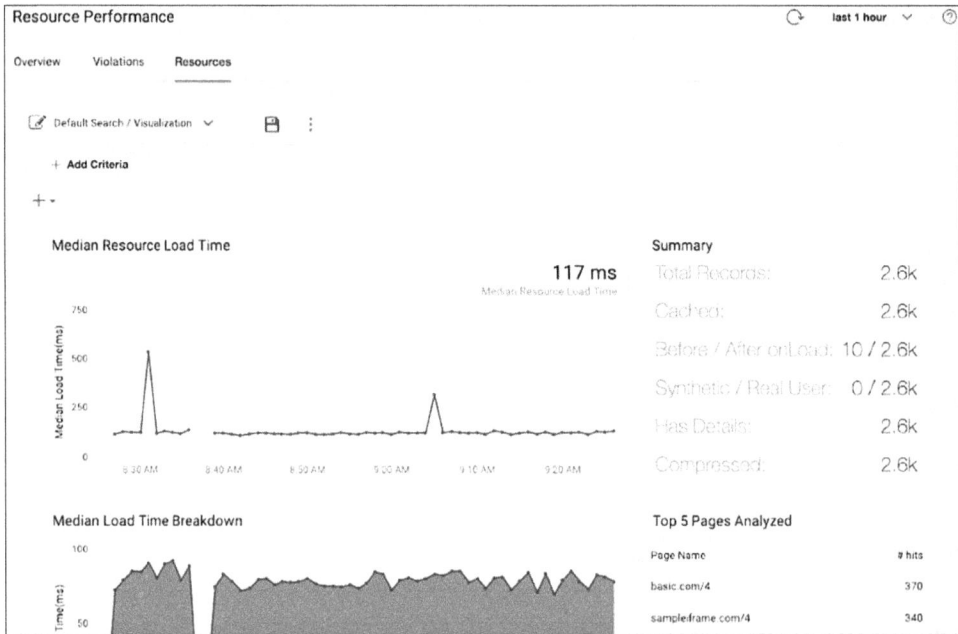

Figure 4-24   *Resources tab*

Additional Resource Performance Data Information

For the Resource Performance Dashboard to be effective, it is highly recommended that you set the Timing-Allow-Origin HTTP header in all of your CORS (Cross-Origin Resource Sharing) domains to enable access to resource timing information. Without this header, the JavaScript Agent cannot capture the resource size, and, of the supported Resource Timing Metrics, only the resource load time can be calculated.

IoT Monitoring

AppDynamics IoT Monitoring enables you to track and understand the transactions of your IoT applications. Because IoT devices are diverse, both in terms of the platforms they use and their business functions, AppDynamics has developed a REST API in addition to language SDKs to provide the maximum flexibility for reporting IoT data. This API can be used from any device that supports HTTPS and is connected to the Internet.

IoT Monitoring requires application developers to instrument their code. To make this process easier, AppDynamics has developed C/C++ and Java SDKs so that developers using the platforms supporting these languages can leverage the features of the SDK instead of using the REST API.

The IoT SDKs ➊ use the REST APIs to report IoT data to the EUM Server ➋, where the data is aggregated and made available to the AppDynamics Controller and the Events Service ➌, as shown in Figure 4-25.

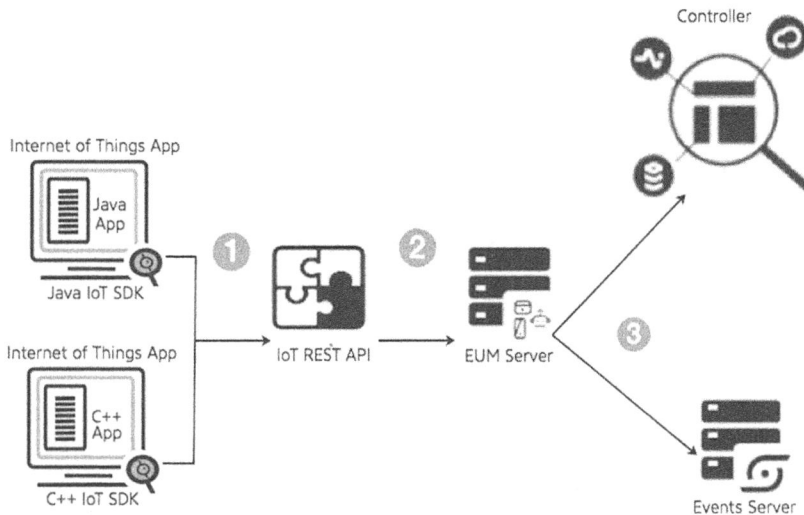

Figure 4-25   *IoT Monitoring architecture diagram*

Mobile Real User Monitoring

Mobile Real User Monitoring (Mobile RUM) allows you to understand your native (iOS, Android) and hybrid (Xamarin, Cordova-based, React Native, Flutter) mobile applications as your end users actually use them.

Mobile RUM provides you with visibility into the functioning of the application itself and the application's interactions with the network it uses and any server-side applications it may talk to.

Database Visibility

Database Visibility in AppDynamics provides end-to-end visibility on the performance of your database, helps you troubleshoot problems such as slow response times and excessive load, and provides metrics on database activities such as the following:

- SQL statements or stored procedures that are consuming most of the system resources

- Statistics on procedures, SQL statements, and SQL query plans

- Time spent on fetching, sorting, or waiting on a lock

- Activity from the previous day, week, or month

Once Database Visibility is available, you can create collectors that run on the Database Agent to monitor any of the supported databases or operating systems included in Table 4-6 and Table 4-7.

Table 4-6 *Supported Database and Versions*

Database	Supported Through Amazon RDS	Version
Apache Cassandra		>= 3.11.4
Datastax Enterprise (DSE) Cassandra		>= 6.7.3
Couchbase		>=4.5
IBM DB2 LUW		9.x, 10.x, 11.x
MongoDB, MongoDB cluster		>=2.6
MySQL	Yes	All versions, including MySQL Version 8.0, Percona, MariaDB, and Aurora
Microsoft SQL Server	Yes	2005, 2008, 2012, 2014, 2016, 2017, 2019, and SQL Azure
Microsoft SQL Server on Linux		SQL Server on Linux is currently available as a public preview and is not recommended for production use. Database Visibility works well with this preview release, but monitoring results may vary until a stable version of SQL Server on Linux is available.
Oracle, Oracle RAC	Yes	10g (>= 10.2), 11g, 12c, 18c, and 19c
PostgreSQL	Yes	All the versions, including Azure Database for PostgreSQL and Aurora
Sybase ASE		>=15
Sybase IQ		All versions

Table 4-7 *Supported Operating Systems and Versions*

Operating System	Version
Windows	64-bit
Linux	32-bit and 64-bit
Solaris	All versions
AIX	>=6.1
Amazon RDS	All versions

Infrastructure Visibility

AppDynamics Infrastructure Visibility provides end-to-end visibility into the performance of the hardware running your applications. You can use Infrastructure Visibility to identify and troubleshoot problems that can affect application performance such as server failures, JVM crashes, and network packet loss.

Infrastructure Visibility provides the following metrics:

- CPU busy/idle times, disk and partition reads/writes, and network interface utilization (Machine Agents)

- Packet loss, round-trip times, connection setup/tear down errors, TCP window size issues, and retransmission timeouts (Network Visibility, additional license required)

- Disk/CPU/memory utilization, process, and machine availability (Server Visibility, additional license required)

Overview of Infrastructure Visibility

You can determine the root cause of application issues by looking at application, network, server, and machine metrics that measure infrastructure utilization. For example, the following infrastructure issues may slow down your application:

- Too much time spent in garbage collection of temporary objects (application metric)

- Packet loss between two nodes that results in retransmissions and slow calls (network metric)

- Inefficient processes that result in high CPU utilization (server metric)

- Excessively high rates of reads/writes on a specific disk or partition (hardware metric)

Infrastructure Visibility enables you to isolate, identify, and troubleshoot these types of issues. Infrastructure Visibility is based on a Machine Agent that runs with an App Server Agent on the same machine. These two agents provide multi-layer monitoring, as follows:

1. The App Server Agent collects metrics about applications and identifies applications, tiers, and nodes with slow transactions, stalled transactions, and other application-performance issues.

2. The Network Agent monitors the network packets sent and received on each node and identifies lost/retransmitted packets, TCP bottlenecks, high round-trip times, and other network issues.

3. The Machine Agent collects metrics at two levels:

   - Server Visibility metrics for local processes, services, and resource utilization.

   - Basic machine metrics for disks, memory, CPU, and network interfaces.

This multilayer monitoring enables you to determine possible correlations between application issues and service, process, hardware, network, or other issues on the machine. Figure 4-26 illustrates the Agent Monitoring Metrics.

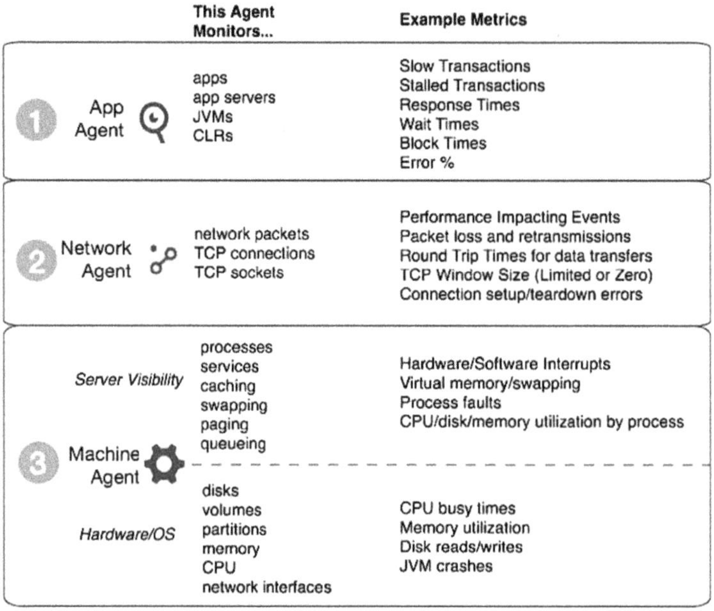

Figure 4-26   *Agent Monitoring Metrics*

Network Visibility

Network Visibility monitors traffic flows, network packets, TCP connections, and TCP ports. Network Agents leverage the APM intelligence of App Server Agents to identify the TCP connections used by each application. Network Visibility includes the following items:

■ Detailed metrics about dropped/retransmitted packets, TCP window sizes (Limited/Zero), connection setup/tear down issues, high round-trip times, and other performance-impacting issues

■ Network Dashboard that highlights network KPIs for tiers, nodes, and network links

■ Right-click dashboards for tiers, nodes, and network links that enable quick drill-downs from transaction outliers to network root causes

■ Automatic mapping of TCP connections with application flows

■ Automatic detection of intermediate load balancers that split TCP connections

■ Diagnostic mode for collecting advanced diagnostic information for individual connections

Network Visibility extends the application intelligence of AppDynamics APM down the stack from the application to the network. With "app-only" visibility, it can be easy to mistakenly blame (or not blame) the network when an application issue arises. Network Visibility can help reduce or eliminate the guesswork involved in identifying root causes. Network Agents and App Agents, working together, automate the work of mapping TCP connections to the application flows that use them. Network Agents can identify intermediate load balancers (which often split TCP connections) and correlate the connections on either side of these devices. Figure 4-27 illustrates the agent-based Network Visibility approach.

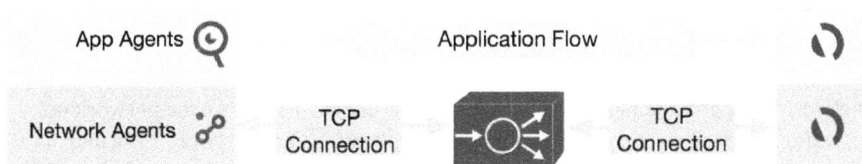

Figure 4-27   *Agent-based Network Visibility approach*

The agent-based approach of Network Visibility provides these advantages over standard approaches to network monitoring:

- More cost-efficient than using network monitoring appliances, which often view traffic from a few central locations

- Especially useful for distributed environments and multitier applications that span multiple network segments

- Works in cloud and hybrid networks, unlike most network-monitoring solutions

Drill Down to the Root Cause

If network issues are affecting your application, Network Visibility can help you determine the cause:

- You see a spike in transaction outliers in the Application Dashboard. Are network issues to blame?

- Switch over to the Network Dashboard. Each tier, node, and link show network KPIs that measure the network health of that element. Use baselining to highlight network elements with KPIs outside the baseline.

- To diagnose a tier, node, or network link, right-click and select **View Metrics.** In the right-click dashboard, look for network metrics with spikes that correlate with the spikes in your transaction outliers. This often provides direction to the network root cause.

■ If a network element requires more in-depth troubleshooting, configure the relevant Network Agents to collect metrics on the individual Connections used by that element. You can then do the following:

■ Click a node or link and view KPIs for the Connections used by the relevant nodes.

■ Right-click a Connection and view detailed metrics in a right-click dashboard or in the Metric Browser.

Network Visibility Metrics

Network Visibility collects and displays these metric types:

■ Network KPIs provide high-level, at-a-glance measures of whether the network is affecting the performance of the monitored application. The Network flow map shows KPIs for each tier, node, and link.

■ The PIE (Performance Impacting Events) metric enables you to see immediately if there are any such events on a connected client, server, or network link.

Figure 4-28 shows an example of a PIE metric.

Figure 4-28   *PIE metric*

■ If the KPI metrics indicate an issue with a specific element, you can view additional metrics for that element to identify root causes. Right-click an element and select **View Metrics.** The metrics and charts in the right-click dashboard are all designed to answer the question, Are there any bottlenecks on this element that are affecting my applications?

Figure 4-29 shows an example of a KPI metric.

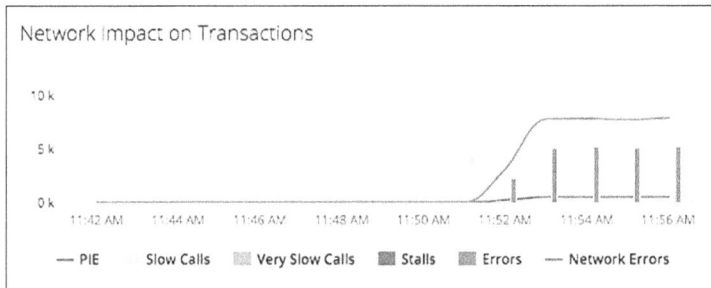

Figure 4-29 *KPI metric*

- To perform in-depth analysis, you can view detailed TCP Flow metrics in the Metric Browser.

- You can view node metrics to evaluate the health of TCP sockets and network interfaces.

Network Agents can also monitor multiple nodes that are associated with the same IP address because they run on the same physical or virtual server. The agent monitors each node individually and calculates network metrics for each node. These metrics are based on the ingress/egress traffic for each individual node, not aggregate traffic for the IP address of the host on which the node is running. Figure 4-30 illustrates an example of Network Visibility for multiple app nodes.

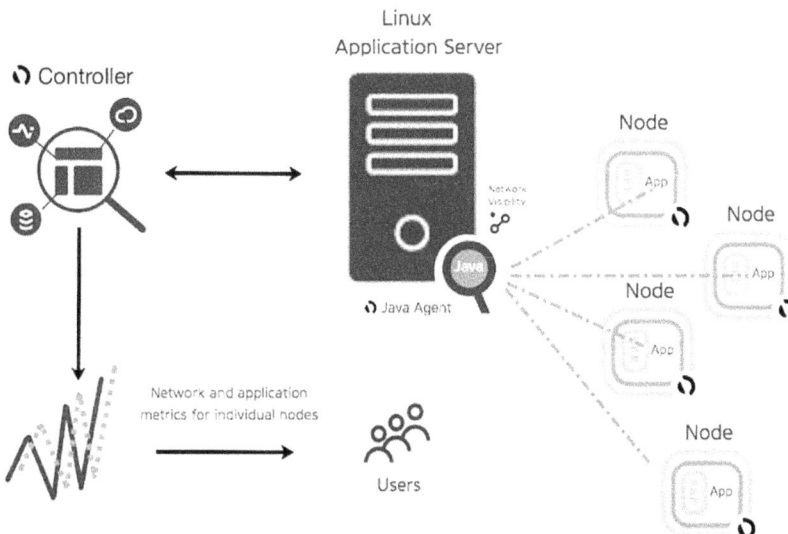

Figure 4-30 *Network Visibility for multiple app nodes*

Server Visibility

Server Visibility monitors local processes, services, and resource utilization. You can use these metrics to identify time windows when problematic application performance correlates with problematic server performance on one or more nodes.

Server Visibility is an add-on module to the Machine Agent. With Server Visibility enabled, the Machine Agent provides the following functionality:

- Extended hardware metrics such as machine availability, disk/CPU/virtual-memory utilization, and process page faults

- Monitor application nodes that run inside Docker containers and identify container issues that impact application performance

- The Tier Metric Correlator, which enables you to identify load and performance anomalies across all nodes in a tier

- Import and define server tags used to query, filter, and compare related servers using custom metadata

- Monitor internal or external HTTP and HTTPS services

- Support for grouping servers so you can apply health rules to specific server groups

- Support for defining alerts that trigger when certain conditions are met or exceeded based on monitored server hardware metrics

Using the Server Visibility UI

The Server Visibility user interface uses many of the same mechanisms that are common to the various panels of the Controller UI, as shown in Figure 4-31.

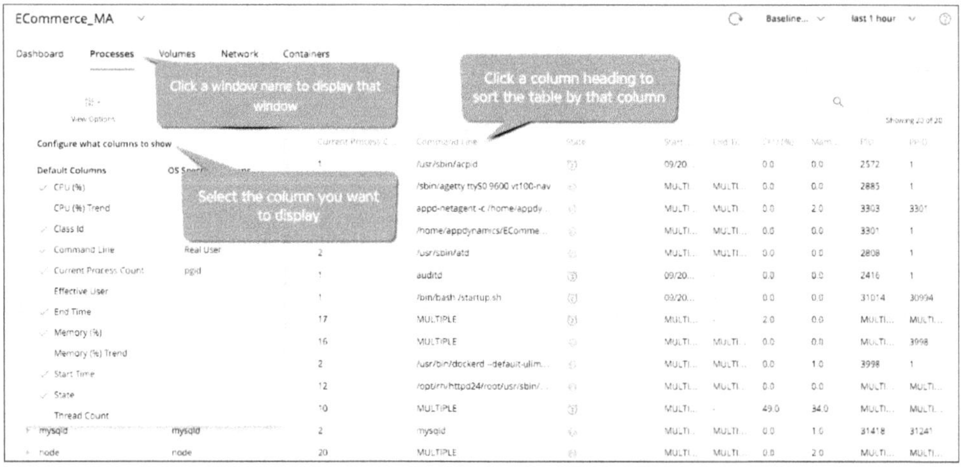

Figure 4-31 *Server Visibility UI*

Basic Machine Metrics

The Machine Agent collects basic hardware metrics from the server's OS and provides the following functionality:

- Basic hardware metrics from the server's OS, such as CPU and memory utilization, throughput on network interfaces, and disk and network I/O.

- Support for creating extensions to generate custom metrics.

- Support for running remediation scripts to automate your runbook procedures. You can optionally configure the remediation action to require human approval before starting the script.

- JVM Crash Guard for monitoring JVM crashes and optionally running remediation scripts.

Java and .NET Infrastructure Monitoring

Infrastructure Visibility uses different agents to monitor Java and .NET environments:

- The Java Agent collects metrics for business applications and JVMs. The Machine Agent collects Server Visibility and hardware/OS metrics.

- The .NET Agent collects metrics for business applications and instrumented CLRs. The .NET Agent includes a .NET Machine Agent that collects IIS and hardware/OS metrics. The Machine Agent collects Server Visibility metrics.

Figure 4-32 illustrates Java and .NET Monitoring metrics.

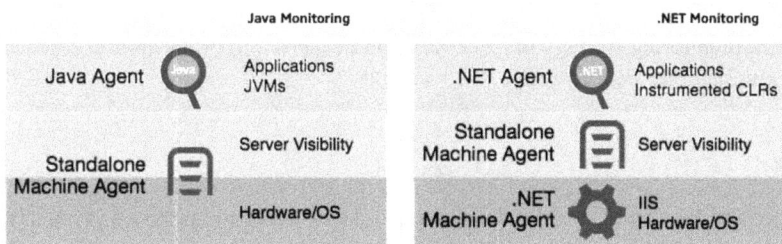

Figure 4-32 *Java and .NET Monitoring metrics*

Infrastructure Visibility Strategies

You can use these strategies to locate infrastructure issues that affect application performance:

- Use transaction snapshots to correlate infrastructure metrics for the specific node so that you can identify the root cause of slow or stalled transactions.

- Use the Tier Metric Correlator, which enables you to identify load and performance anomalies in a tier composed of a cluster of nodes running on containers or servers.

- Configure health rules on metrics such as garbage collection time, connection pool contention, and CPU usage to catch issues early in the cycle before any impact on your business transactions.

- Use infrastructure rules, policies, and alerts:

  - Define policies that trigger actions (such send an email, start diagnostics, or perform a thread dump) when infrastructure metrics report a critical level.

  - Configure alerts for JVM and CLR crashes using JVM Crash Guard and the .NET Machine Agent, respectively.

  - Configure the agent to run scripts in response to critical events (for example, restart an application or JVM in response to a crash).

- Use metric correlation:

  - The Network Dashboard includes right-click dashboards for tiers, nodes, and network links. Use these dashboards to find correlations between application issues and network root causes.

  - One example workflow is to open the Node Dashboard for a mission-critical server with a machine agent installed and then cross-compare data in the following tabs:

    - JVM (application performance)

    - JMX (server performance)

    - Server (hardware resource consumption)

With the right monitoring strategy in place, you can be alerted to problems and fix them before user transactions are affected.

Analytics

Analytics extracts the data, generates baselines and dashboards, and provides perspective beyond traditional APM by enabling real-time analysis of business performance correlated with your application performance.

You can use Analytics with the APM, Browser RUM, Mobile RUM, and Browser Synthetic Monitoring product modules for the following:

- Transaction Analytics

- Log Analytics

- Browser Analytics

- Mobile Analytics

- Browser Synthetic Analytics

- Connected Devices Analytics

Overview of Analytics

Analytics is built on the AppDynamics APM platform, which includes the Events Service, the unstructured document store for the platform.

Analytics can answer business-oriented questions such as the following:

- How many users experienced failed checkout transactions in the last 24 hours?

- How much revenue was lost because of these failures?

- How is the lost revenue distributed across different product categories?

- What is your revenue for the day for a geographical region?

- What was the revenue impact, by product category, associated with the two marketing campaigns we ran last week?

Analytics Home Page

The Analytics Home page consolidates data from the transaction, browser, and mobile events. The Home page automatically generates Transaction and End User Monitoring Summary panels through queries that aggregate data into widgets.

Note   To view the different widgets on the Home page, you need the appropriate licenses and access.

You can access the AppDynamics Home page by clicking the **Home** icon on the left navigation pane in **Analytics**. You can either use the left navigation pane or click **Home** on the right pane to navigate to the **Analytics** modules (Searches, Metrics, Business Journeys, Experience Levels, Alert & Respond, and Configuration).

Figure 4-33 shows the Analytics Home view.

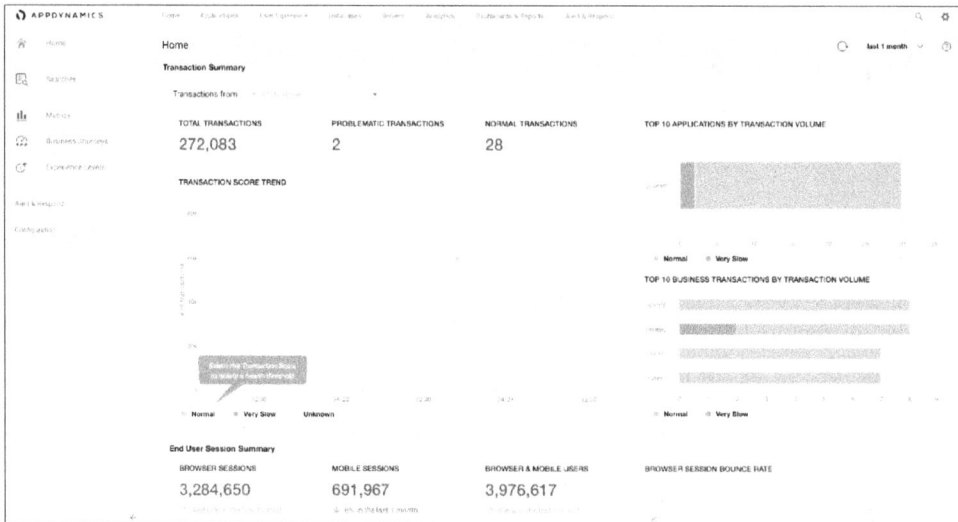

Figure 4-33   *Analytics Home view*

Monitoring Cloud Applications

In cloud environments, services and components are added and removed continuously. AppDynamics provides robust support for monitoring applications in these dynamic environments.

Docker

In simple terms, the Docker platform is all about making it easier to create, deploy, and run applications by using containers. Containers let developers package up an application with all the necessary parts, such as libraries and other elements it is dependent on, and then ship it all out as one package. By keeping an app and associated elements within the container, developers can be sure that the apps will run on any Linux machine no matter what kind of customized settings that machine might have, or how it might differ from the machine that was used for writing and testing the code. This is helpful for developers because it makes it easier to work on the app throughout its lifecycle.

Docker is kind of like a virtual machine, but instead of creating a whole virtual operating system (OS), it lets applications take advantage of the same Linux kernel as the system they're running on. That way, the app only has to be shipped with things that aren't already on the host computer instead of a whole new OS. This means that apps are much smaller and perform significantly better than apps that are system-dependent.

AppDynamics Docker monitoring offers container monitoring for dynamic, fast-moving microservice architectures, as covered in the following section.

Monitor Containers with Docker Visibility

Use the Machine Agent to monitor application nodes running inside Docker containers and to identify container issues that impact application performance. By viewing and comparing APM metrics with the underlying container and server/machine metrics, you can easily answer the question, Is my application problem purely an application problem, or is the root cause in the container or the server?

Note   Container monitoring requires a Server Visibility license (>=4.3.3) for both the Controller and the Machine Agent.

You should deploy the Machine Agent inside a Docker container. The Machine Agent collects metrics for Docker containers on the same host, and it collects server and machine metrics for the host itself. The Controller shows all monitored containers for each host as well as the container and host IDs for each container.

In the BRIDGE networking mode, the containers take on the container ID as the host name. If networking is in host mode, the containers take on the node name of the host ID. This means every container on that node has the same host ID. In this case, you need to use the unique host ID settings. When you're using Docker Visibility, if the unique host ID setting is not configured to use container ID in host network mode, the Machine Agent automatically registers the container using the container ID as the host ID. If you have an older version of the Controller or Machine Agent, AppDynamics recommends that you upgrade to Machine Agent version 20.7 or later.

With Controller version 20.11.0 or later:

- If the Machine Agent is 20.7.0 or later, the Machine Agent automatically registers the container using the container ID as the host ID. No further action is needed.

- If the Machine Agent is 20.6.0 or earlier and is configured incorrectly, the Controller rejects the misconfigured containers registration.

By default, the Machine Agent only monitors containers that have a running APM Agent. You can change this by setting the sim.docker.monitorAPMContainersOnly property on the Controller.

Note   To deploy a Machine Agent on a host outside a Docker container, create a symbolic link (**ln -s / /hostroot**) on the host. This symbolic link enables the Machine Agent to collect host metrics with Docker container metrics. When you deploy a Machine Agent inside a Docker container for monitoring, the symbolic link is automatically created when the volume mounts. To grant more restrictive permissions, enter this command to create symbolic links: **ln -s /proc /hostroot/proc; ln -s /sys /hostroot/sys; ln -s /etc /hostroot/ etc**. You can make these links read-only because the AppDynamics Agent does not need write privileges to these directories.

Figure 4-34 illustrates how to deploy container monitoring, as detailed in the following list:

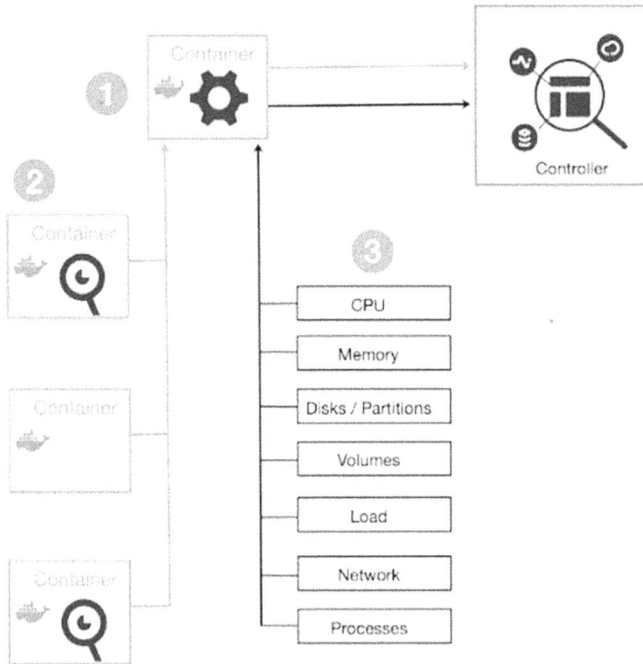

Figure 4-34   *How to deploy container monitoring*

- Install the Machine Agent ⓵ in a standalone container. The Machine Agent collects hardware metrics for each monitored container, as well as Machine and Server metrics for the host ⓷, and forwards the metrics to the Controller.

- The Machine Agent can monitor all containers that are running on that host, subject to established limits, and will report runtime metrics and metadata for every container. Additionally, if any of the containers have an APM Agent installed ⓶, the Machine Agent also correlates the container metadata and runtime metrics with the associated APM Node.

Enable Container Monitoring

Follow these steps to enable Container Monitoring:

Step 1.   On the Controller, log in to the Administration Console and verify that **sim. docker.enabled** is set to **true**.

Step 2.   On the Agent, enable Server Visibility and Docker Visibility.

Container Monitoring Setup

The quickest and easiest way to run the Machine Agent with Container Monitoring enabled is to use one of the official images from the Docker Store (https://store. docker.com/images/appdynamics). These images are produced by AppDynamics, based on certified base images from the Docker Community, and can either be run directly or used as base images for your own application containers. For full details of how to download and run containers based on these official images, see the documentation posted on the Docker Store. To build your own base images, the full source code for building these images is posted to GitHub. You can use this as a pattern for your own builds (https://github.com/Appdynamics/appdynamics-docker-images).

For the Machine Agent to monitor containers running on the server, configure these settings:

- **Server Visibility Enabled:** Enable Server Visibility

- **Docker Enabled:** Enable Docker Visibility

- **Volume Mounts:** Specify one of the following:

  - Volume mounts to allow read-only access to the underlying file system (/proc, /etc and /sys). This allows the Server Agent to collect host-level metrics for containers running on the server.

  - The UNIX domain socket on which the Docker daemon is configured to listen for API calls.

View Container Details

Follow these steps to view container metadata and metrics in the Controller:

Step 1. In the Applications Dashboard, go to Containers to see all monitored containers used by the application.

Figure 4-35 shows an example of the Applications Dashboard.

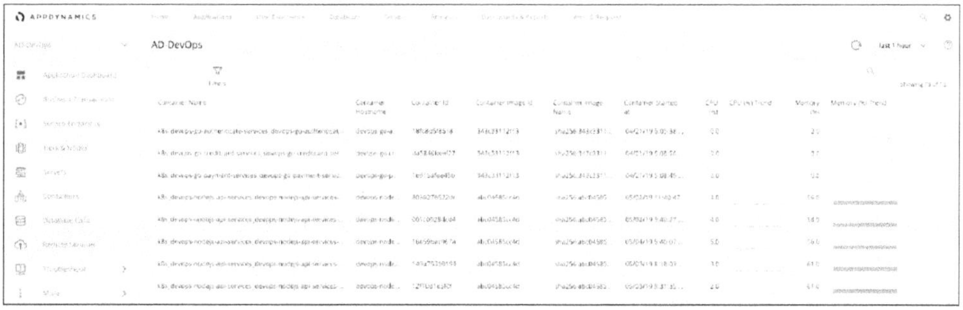

Figure 4-35 *Applications Dashboard*

Step 2.   In the Servers Dashboard, go to Containers to see all monitored containers on that host.

Figure 4-36 shows the Servers Dashboard.

Figure 4-36   *Servers Dashboard*

Step 3.   To open the Container Dashboard, right-click the container name and choose **View Details**.

Figure 4-37 shows the Container Dashboard.

Figure 4-37   *Container Dashboard*

The Container Details view contains the following tabs, which provide an overview of the health and resource usage for the container:

- **Overview:** Container metadata, tags (name-value pairs derived from Docker/Kubernetes) and AWS tags where applicable, and single chart views for CPU, memory, network, and disk usage.

- **CPU:** CPU Usage and Throttled Time metrics.

- **Memory:** Memory Usage and Memory Fault metrics.

Step 4. The Node Dashboard also includes a Container tab for the container in which that node is running. Figure 4-38 illustrates the Container tab.

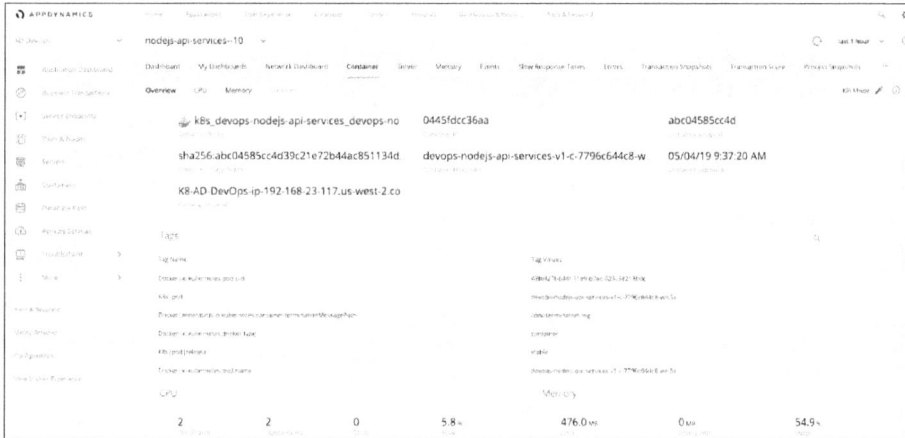

Figure 4-38 *Container tab*

View Container Metrics Using the Metric Browser

To view time-series metric data for containers, double-click one of the container metric graphs (CPU, Memory, Network, or Disk) to open the Metric Browser with the displayed metric selected. The Metric Browser tree displays the full set of metrics available for that container, and you can add these to the Metric Browser display by double-clicking the metric you wish to select. Figure 4-39 shows an example of Container Metrics.

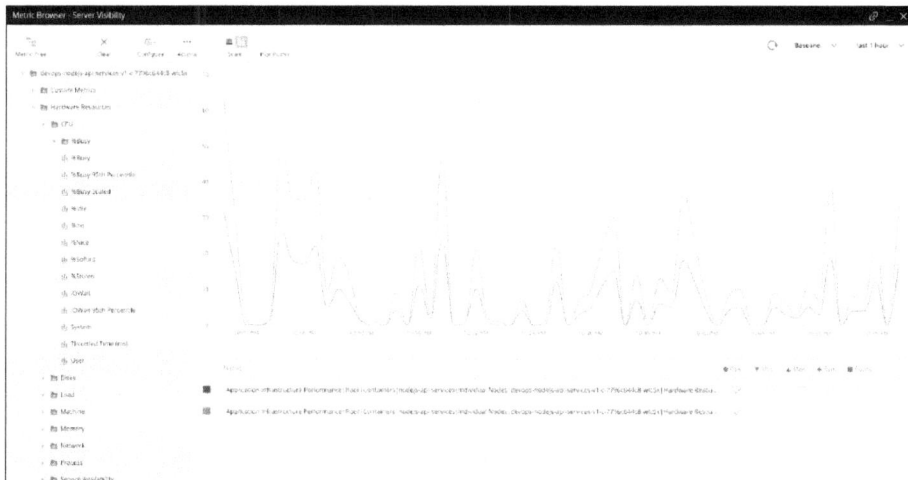

Figure 4-39 *Container Metrics*

Kubernetes

Kubernetes is a container-orchestration platform for automating deployment, scaling, and operations of applications running inside the containers across clusters of hosts. Open-sourced by Google in 2014, Kubernetes was built based on the search giant's own experience with running containers in production. It's now under the aegis of the Cloud Native Computing Foundation (CNCF), which reports that Kubernetes is the most popular container management tool among large enterprises, used by 83% of respondents in a recent CNCF survey (https://www.cncf.io/wp-content/uploads/2020/11/CNCF_Survey_Report_2020.pdf). And in case you're wondering, the name "Kubernetes" is Greek for "helmsman" or "pilot."

Kubernetes Monitoring with AppDynamics gives organizations visibility into application and business performance, providing insights into containerized applications, Kubernetes clusters, Docker containers, and underlying infrastructure metrics.

Using Docker Visibility with Kubernetes

With AppDynamics, you can gain real-time visibility into your containerized applications deployed to Kubernetes. Kubernetes is an open source container-orchestration platform for automating deployment, scaling, and management of applications running in containers.

With Container Visibility, you can enhance container-level metrics and gain visibility into CPU, packet visibility, memory, and network utilization. These metrics can then be baselined and have health rules associated along with detailed resource usage statistics about your APM-monitored container applications. By viewing and comparing APM metrics, with the underlying container and server metrics, you quickly receive deep insights into the performance of your containerized applications, along with potential impediments in your infrastructure stack. For example, specific metrics can help you identify both "bandwidth-hogging" applications and container-level network errors.

Container Visibility allows you to monitor containerized applications running inside Kubernetes pods and to identify container issues that impact application performance. The agent is deployed as a Kubernetes DaemonSet in every node of a Kubernetes cluster. Deploying the Machine Agent as a DaemonSet ensures that every Kubernetes worker node runs the Machine Agent and that the agent collects critical resource metrics from both the node host and the associated Docker containers.

Container Visibility with Kubernetes

Deploy the Machine Agent in Docker-enabled mode. For more information and details on how to configure and run the Machine Agent using Docker, see Configuring Docker

Visibility (https://docs.appdynamics.com/appd/21.x/21.3/en/infrastructure-visibility/
monitor-containers-with-docker-visibility/configure-docker-visibility). The Machine
Agent will then do the following:

- Identify the containers managed by Kubernetes.

- Determine if these containers contain App Server Agents.

- Correlate containers with App Server Agents with the APM nodes for that
  application.

Figure 4-40 illustrates the following deployment scenario for Container Visibility in
Kubernetes:

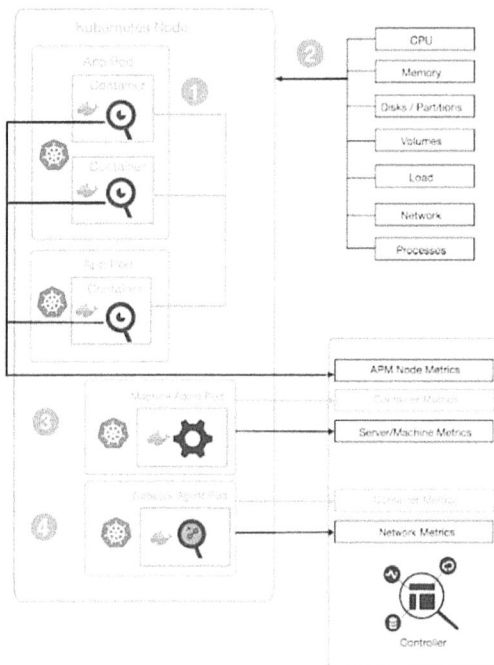

Figure 4-40   *Container Visibility in Kubernetes*

- Install the Machine Agent container ① as a DaemonSet on each Kubernetes node.

- If you wish to collect APM metrics from any container in a pod, install the correct
  APM Agent ② in the container before deploying the pod.

- The Machine Agent collects resource usage metrics for each monitored container ③,
  as well as Machine and Server metrics for the host, and then forwards the metrics to
  the Controller.

■ (Optional) Install the Network Agent ④ as a DaemonSet on the node you want to monitor. The Network Agent collects the metrics for all network connections between application components being monitored and sends the metrics to the Controller.

Container Visibility with Kubernetes requires the following:

■ The Machine Agent must run as a DaemonSet on every Kubernetes node that you wish to monitor.

■ Each node to be monitored must have a Server Visibility license.

■ Docker Visibility must be enabled on the Machine Agent.

■ Both App Server Agents and Machine Agents are registered by the same account and are using the same Controller.

■ If you have multiple App Server agents running in the same pod, register the container ID as the host ID on both the App Server Agent and the Machine Agent.

Enable Container Visibility

Update the Controller to 4.4.3 or higher if you have not already done so. To enable Kubernetes visibility in your environment, edit the following parameters:

■ Controller

■ **sim.machines.tags.k8s.enabled:** The value defaults to **true**. The global tag's **enabled** flag has priority over this.

■ **sim.machines.tags.k8s.pollingInterval:** The value defaults to one minute. The minimum value you can set for the polling interval is 30 seconds.

■ Machine Agent

■ **k8sTagsEnabled:** The value defaults to **true** and is specified in the ServerMonitoring.yml file.

Continue with Using Docker Visibility with Red Hat OpenShift. You can use the example DaemonSet, the sample Docker image for Machine Agent, and the sample Docker start script to quickly set up the Standalone Machine Agent. You can find it here: https://docs.appdynamics.com/appd/21.x/21.3/en/infrastructure-visibility/monitor-containers-with-docker-visibility/use-docker-visibility-with-red-hat-openshift.

Register the Container ID as the Host ID

Install an App Server Agent in each container in a Kubernetes pod to collect application metrics. If multiple App Server Agents are running in the same pod (in the RedHat OpenShift platform, for example), you must register the container ID as the unique host

ID on both the App Server Agent and the Machine Agent to collect container-specific metrics from the pod. Kubernetes pods can contain multiple containers, and they share the same host ID. The Machine Agent cannot identify different containers running in a pod unless each container ID is registered as the host ID.

To register the container ID as the host ID, follow these steps:

Step 1.   Get the container ID from the cgroup:

```
cat /proc/self/cgroup | awk -F '/' '{print $NF}'  | head -n 1
```

Step 2.   Register the App Server Agents:

```
-Dappdynamics.agent.uniqueHostId=$(sed -rn '1s#.*/##;
1s/(.{12}).*/\1/p' /proc/self/cgroup)
```

Note   For OpenShift, run the following command:
```
-Dappdynamics.agent.uniqueHostId=$(sed -rn '1s#.*/##; 1s/docker-
(.{12}).*/\1/p' /proc/self/cgroup)
```

Step 3.   Register the Machine Agent:

```
-Dappdynamics.docker.container.containerIdAsHostId.
enabled=true
```

Instrument Applications with Kubernetes

There are several approaches to instrumenting applications deployed with Kubernetes, and which one you choose will depend on your particular requirements and DevOps processes. In order to monitor an application container with AppDynamics, an APM Agent must be included in that container. This can be done in a number of ways:

- Using an appropriate base image that has the APM agent pre-installed

- Loading the agent dynamically as part of the container startup

- Loading the agent and dynamically attaching to a running process (where the language runtime supports it)

The third option is usually applicable only to Java-based applications since the JVM supports Dynamic Attach, which is a standard feature of the AppDynamics Java APM Agent. For the other options, it is common practice to make use of standard Kubernetes features such as Init Containers, ConfigMaps, and Secrets.

Deploy the Machine Agent on Kubernetes

AppDynamics Machine Agent can be deployed in a single container image, without the need for an init container. By default, the Machine Agent is deployed to the cluster as a DaemonSet to distribute each agent instance evenly across all cluster nodes. Where required, the DaemonSet can be configured with node affinity rules or node anti-affinity rules to ensure that it is deployed to a desired set of nodes and not across the entire cluster.

In order to harvest pod metadata, the service account used to deploy the machine agent must have the cluster-reader role in OpenShift. The "cluster-reader" role is also required for the Kubernetes extensions to the machine agent. The following CLI command is an example of assigning the cluster-reader role to the appd service account in OpenShift:

```BASH
# assigning cluster-reader role in OpenShift oc adm policy
add-cluster-role-to-user cluster-reader -z appd-account
```

If you are working with a vanilla Kubernetes distribution, it may not have a pre-built cluster role similar to cluster-reader in OpenShift.

Resource Limits

Consider the following resource limits for applications and the Machine Agent when deploying the AppDynamics Machine Agent on Kubernetes:

- The main application being monitored should have resource limits defined. Provide 2% padding for CPU and add up to 100MB of memory.

- To support up to 500 containers, the Machine Agent can be configured with the following resource requests and limits: Mem = 400M, CPU = "0.1" and limits: Mem = 600M, CPU = "0.2".

Note AppDynamics provides a Kubernetes Snapshot Extension for monitoring the health of the Kubernetes cluster. When deploying this extension, it is important to keep in mind that only a single version of the extension should be deployed to the cluster. Do not include it in the DaemonSet to avoid duplicates and potential cluster overload. Instead, consider deploying the instance of the Machine Agent with the extension as a separate deployment with one replica in addition to the DaemonSet for Server Visibility. The machine agent SIM and Docker can be disabled in this case, and the memory request can be dropped to 250M.

ClusterRole Configuration

Refer to the sample role definition shown in Figures 4-41a and 4-41b. It provides a wide read access to various Kubernetes resources. These permissions are more than sufficient to enable Kubernetes extensions to the Machine Agent as well as the pod metadata collection. The role is called "appd-cluster-reader," but you can obviously name it as needed. The cluster role definition outlines various api groups that will be available for members of this role. For each api group, we define a list of resources that will be accessed and the access method. Because we only need to retrieve information from these api endpoints, we only need the read-only access, expressed by "get," "list," and "watch" verbs.

```
1   kind: ClusterRole
2   apiVersion: rbac.authorization.k8s.io/v1
3   metadata:
4     name: appd-cluster-reader
5   rules:
6   - nonResourceURLs:
7       - '*'
8     verbs:
9       - get
10  - apiGroups: ["batch"]
11    resources:
12      - "jobs"
13    verbs: ["get", "list", "watch"]
14  - apiGroups: ["extensions"]
15    resources:
16      - daemonsets
17      - daemonsets/status
18      - deployments
19      - deployments/scale
20      - deployments/status
21      - horizontalpodautoscalers
22      - horizontalpodautoscalers/status
23      - ingresses
24      - ingresses/status
25      - jobs
26      - jobs/status
27      - networkpolicies
28      - podsecuritypolicies
29      - replicasets
30      - replicasets/scale
31      - replicasets/status
32      - replicationcontrollers
33      - replicationcontrollers/scale
34      - storageclasses
35      - thirdpartyresources
36    verbs: ["get", "list", "watch"]
37  - apiGroups: [""]
38    resources:
39      - bindings
40      - componentstatuses
41      - configmaps
42      - endpoints
43      - events
44      - limitranges
45      - namespaces
46      - namespaces/status
47      - nodes
48      - nodes/status
49      - persistentvolumeclaims
50      - persistentvolumeclaims/status
51      - persistentvolumes
52      - persistentvolumes/status
53      - pods
54      - pods/binding
55      - pods/eviction
56      - pods/log
57      - pods/status
58      - podtemplates
```

Figure 4-41a *Sample ClusterRole*

```
59      - replicationcontrollers
60      - replicationcontrollers/scale
61      - replicationcontrollers/status
62      - resourcequotas
63      - resourcequotas/status
64      - securitycontextconstraints
65      - serviceaccounts
66      - services
67      - services/status
68    verbs: ["get", "list", "watch"]
69  - apiGroups:
70    - apps
71    resources:
72      - controllerrevisions
73      - daemonsets
74      - daemonsets/status
75      - deployments
76      - deployments/scale
77      - deployments/status
78      - replicasets
79      - replicasets/scale
80      - replicasets/status
81      - statefulsets
82      - statefulsets/scale
83      - statefulsets/status
84    verbs:
85      - get
86      - list
87      - watch
88  - apiGroups:
89    - apiextensions.k8s.io
90    resources:
91      - customresourcedefinitions
92      - customresourcedefinitions/status
93    verbs:
94      - get
95      - list
96      - watch
97  - apiGroups:
98    - apiregistration.k8s.io
99    resources:
100      - apiservices
101      - apiservices/status
102    verbs:
103      - get
104      - list
105      - watch
106  - apiGroups:
107    - events.k8s.io
108    resources:
109      - events
110    verbs:
111      - get
112      - list
113      - watch
```

Figure 4-41b   *Sample ClusterRole*

Once the role is defined, you will need to create cluster role bindings to associate the role with a service account. Refer to the example of a ClusterRoleBinding spec in Figure 4-42, which makes the appd-cluster-reader service account a member of the appd-cluster-reader-role in project "myproject." Note that the naming is purely coincidental. The names of the service account and the cluster role do not have to match.

```
1   kind: ClusterRoleBinding
2   apiVersion: rbac.authorization.k8s.io/v1
3   metadata:
4     name: cluster-reader-role-binding
5   subjects:
6   - kind: ServiceAccount
7     name: appd-cluster-reader
8     namespace: myproject
9   roleRef:
10    kind: ClusterRole
11    name: appd-cluster-reader
12    apiGroup: rbac.authorization.k8s.io
```

Figure 4-42   *Sample ClusterRoleBinding*

Network Visibility with Kubernetes

You can use Network Visibility to monitor applications running on Kubernetes. Network Visibility isolates an application's network issues from its application issues. It monitors an application's network interactions and reports key performance metrics in the context of application performance monitoring.

To monitor the communication between pods and between nodes, the agent opens up a TCP port in each node for app containers to communicate with the Network DaemonSet container using a REST API. The agent is deployed as a DaemonSet in each node that has host mode enabled. Follow the steps covered next to create a Docker image for the DaemonSet and configure the agent.

Figure 4-43 illustrates a sample network setup between pods and nodes.

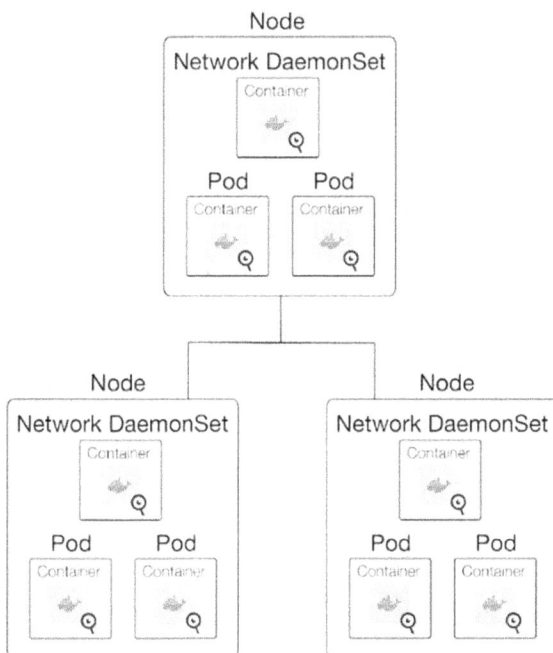

Figure 4-43 *Sample Network setup between pods and nodes*

Note   Make sure you have at least one pod with a Java Agent (version 4.4 or higher) deployed to the same cluster as the Network Agent.

Also, ensure that TCP port 3892 is not already used by the node. Port 3892 will be used by the application pods to communicate with the DaemonSet.

Creating a Docker Image

To deploy Network Visibility with Kubernetes, you must first create a Docker image for the Network Visibility DaemonSet and push the image to your Docker Trusted Registry.

Step 1.   Use the sample Dockerfile shown in Figure 4-44 in a text file and save the file.

Figure 4-44 shows the sample code to create a Docker image.

```
1   FROM centos:centos7
2
3   RUN yum update -y && yum install -y \
4       net-tools \
5       tcpdump \
6       curl  \
7       unzip   \
8       sysvinit-tools \
9       iproute2 \
10      openssh-clients
11
12  WORKDIR /netviz-agent
13
14  ARG NETVIZ_ZIP_PKG
15
16  # copy NetViz agent contents
17  ADD ${NETVIZ_ZIP_PKG} .
18
19  # run the agent install script
20  RUN unzip *.zip && ./install.sh \
21      && sed -i -e "s|enable_netlib = 1|enable_netlib = 0|g" ./conf/agent_config.lua \
22      && sed -i -e "s|WEBSERVICE_IP=.*|WEBSERVICE_IP=\"0.0.0.0\"|g" ./conf/agent_config.lua
23  # default command to run for the agent
24  CMD  ./bin/appd-netagent -c ./conf -l ./logs -r ./run
```

Figure 4-44   *Sample code to create a Docker image*

Step 2.   Navigate to the directory where you saved the Dockerfile. Build the Docker image by running the following command:

```
$ docker build --build-arg NETVIZ_ZIP_PKG=/path/to/netviz-
agent-pkg.zip -t appd-netviz .
```

Step 3.   Push the Docker image to your Docker Trusted Registry.

Configuring Network Visibility with Kubernetes

Step 1.   Use the configuration shown in Figure 4-45 in a YAML file. This configuration file is used for deploying the Network Visibility agent.

Figure 4-45 illustrates the sample code for deploying the Network Visibility Agent.

Step 2.   In the configuration file, update these fields:

a. image (under containers): The file path to the DaemonSet image in your Docker Trusted Registry

b. name (under imagePullSecrets): The key for your Docker Trusted Registry

```
 1  apiVersion: apps/v1 # for versions before 1.9.0 use apps/v1beta2
 2  kind: DaemonSet
 3  metadata:
 4    name: appd-netviz-agent
 5  spec:
 6    selector:
 7      matchLabels:
 8        name: appd-netviz-agent
 9    template:
10      metadata:
11        name: appd-netviz-agent
12        labels:
13          name: appd-netviz-agent
14      spec:
15        hostIPC: true
16        hostNetwork: true
17        containers:
18        - name: appd-netviz-agent
19          image: path/to/your/Docker/image # docker registry image
20          resources:
21            requests:
22              memory: "250Mi"
23              cpu: "0.5"
24            limits:
25              memory: "2Gi"
26              cpu: "1"
27          securityContext:
28            capabilities:
29              add: ["NET_ADMIN", "NET_RAW"]
30          ports:
31          - containerPort: 3892
32            hostPort: 3892
33        imagePullSecrets:
34        - name: your-registry-key # add the registery key, kubectl create secret ...
```

Figure 4-45   *Sample code for deploying the Network Visibility Agent*

Step 3.   Deploy the Network Visibility Agent for Kubernetes by running the following command:

```
$ kubectl apply -f MyConfigFile.yaml
```

Configuring Network Visibility to Monitor Application Pods

After installing Network Visibility for Kubernetes, you'll need to correlate Network Visibility with a Java Agent. This allows you to map network metrics to application flows. To do this, deploy at least one pod with a Java Agent (version 4.4 or higher) to the same cluster as the Network Agent.

Step 1.   Open the application's deployment configuration YAML file with Kubernetes in a text editor and set the APPDYNAMICS_NETVIZ_AGENT_HOST and APPDYNAMICS_NETVIZ_AGENT_PORT values, as shown in Figure 4-46.

```
1  - name: APPDYNAMICS_NETVIZ_AGENT_HOST
2    valueFrom:
3      fieldRef:
4        fieldPath: status.hostIP
5  - name: APPDYNAMICS_NETVIZ_AGENT_PORT
6    value: 3892
```

Figure 4-46   *Sample Code for the Host and Port values*

Step 2.   In the Controller UI, enable socket instrumentation so that you can map network metrics to application flows.

There are more examples for Kubernetes monitoring using Docker Visibility with Red Hat OpenShift and Kubernetes in the cloud on EKS, AKS, and GKE, which can be referenced as a part of online documentation and webinars. Examples are:

https://docs.appdynamics.com/appd/21.x/21.3/en/infrastructure-visibility/monitor-containers-with-docker-visibility/use-docker-visibility-with-red-hat-openshift

https://aws.amazon.com/kubernetes/

https://cloud.google.com/kubernetes-engine/docs

Cloud Monitoring with AppDynamics Cloud

AppDynamics Cloud is a Software as a Service (SaaS) product that offers cloud-native and full-stack observability for large, managed Kubernetes deployments on public clouds (Amazon Web Services and Microsoft Azure). It provides real-time observability across your entire technology stack—applications, software-defined compute, storage, services, network, and other infrastructure—through the collection and correlation of metrics, events, logs, and traces (MELT).

Figure 4-47 provides a high-level overview of how AppDynamics Cloud works.

Figure 4-47   *High-level view of how AppDynamics Cloud works*

The AppDynamics Cloud user interface includes a Relationships map, Interactions map, and Properties panel. Correlating application metrics and interactions to the cloud infrastructure in a unified view, AppDynamics Cloud enables you to do the following:

- Automatically discover service instances associated with a cloud platform account and ingest relevant cloud platform metrics and metadata.

- Get insights on the impact of cloud provider services on application performance.

- Compare key performance metadata and visualize data flow based on application entities and interactions.

- Drill down to the cloud infrastructure layer to understand how two application service topologies intersect.

- View your application infrastructure data, service, and business transactions in one application landscape. Determine what infrastructure exists and where it is located.

AppDynamics Cloud visualizes and correlates metrics, events, logs, and traces (MELT) data so you can identify, triage, and troubleshoot problems and analyze performance issues. Additional features include the following:

- Observability for cloud-native architectures at scale

- Correlated full-stack context across domains and data types

- OpenTelemetry-based extensibility

Cloud Infrastructure Monitoring

To get started with monitoring cloud infrastructure, you must configure one or more Cloud Connections. A Cloud Connection is associated with a cloud account or subscription and enables AppDynamics Cloud to pull metrics for the services associated with the account or subscription. The supported services that AppDynamics Cloud can monitor depend on the target cloud platform, with AWS and Azure as the two supported cloud platforms.

AWS Cloud Infrastructure Observability

AppDynamics Cloud provides end-to-end visibility into the performance of the infrastructure running your applications. This solution, along with the OpenTelemetry-instrumented applications, provides full-stack observability and simplifies deployment.

The Cloud Monitoring solution does the following:

- Ingests data from cloud services automatically. For example, Amazon CloudWatch provides metrics for a better understanding of your resource availability and utilization.

  ■ Enables you to manage alerts based on infrastructure metrics and monitors the cloud service's health and performance.

Here are some of the cloud services you can observe:

  ■ AWS Application, Classic, and Network Load Balancers

  ■ Hosts

    ■ Amazon Elastic Compute Cloud

    ■ AppDynamics Hosts

  ■ AWS Databases

    ■ Amazon Relational Database Service (RDS)

  ■ AWS Storage

    ■ Amazon Elastic Block Storage

Azure Cloud Infrastructure Observability

AppDynamics Cloud provides end-to-end visibility into the performance of the infrastructure running your applications. This solution, along with the OpenTelemetry-instrumented applications, provides full-stack observability and simplifies deployment.

The Cloud Monitoring solution for Azure does the following:

  ■ Collects data from Azure monitor without using agents (that is, agentless monitoring)

  ■ Correlates the data to underlying infrastructure and business applications

  ■ Baselines performances and alerts customers when there are deviations

AppDynamics Cloud enables you to observe Azure virtual machines, including Azure virtual machine scale sets (VMSSs).

Summary

This chapter has covered a lot of information around the AppDynamics monitoring features, including Application Monitoring, End User Monitoring, Database Visibility, Infrastructure Visibility, and Monitoring Cloud Applications. It also provided basic information on App Dynamics Cloud and its ability to provide observability into the AWS and Azure Cloud infrastructures. There is a lot more to cover in AppDynamics, but what was covered in this chapter should help you being to understanding AppDynamics and how it helps in a hybrid cloud environment with its unique monitoring capabilities.

References/Additional Reading

https://docs.appdynamics.com/appd-cloud/en/what-s-new

https://docs.appdynamics.com/appd-cloud/en/about-appdynamics-cloud

https://docs.appdynamics.com/appd/21.x/21.3/en/infrastructure-visibility/monitor-containers-with-docker-visibility/use-docker-visibility-with-red-hat-openshift

https://docs.appdynamics.com/appd/21.x/21.3/en/infrastructure-visibility/monitor-kubernetes-with-the-cluster-agent

Chapter 5

Management

Cisco has been working for over three years to bring the industry-leading Application Resource Management (ARM) capability to Cisco customers. It started with Cisco Workload Optimization Manager (CWOM). CWOM is powered by Turbonomic, and it enables Cisco customers to continuously resource applications to perform at the lowest cost while adhering to policies irrespective of where the application is hosted (that is, on the premises or in the cloud, containers, or VMs). In January 2020, Cisco announced Intersight Workload Optimizer (IWO), which is the integration of CWOM and Intersight. With IWO, application and infrastructure teams can now speak the same language to ensure that applications are automatically and continuously resourced to perform.

Alongside the Intersight Workload Optimizer, Cisco offers Intersight Kubernetes Service (IKS), which is a fully curated, lightweight container management platform for delivering multicloud production-grade upstream Kubernetes. It simplifies the process of provisioning, securing, scaling, and managing virtualized Kubernetes clusters by providing end-to-end automation, including the integration of networking, load balancers, native dashboards, and storage provider interfaces.

This chapter will cover the following topics:

- IT challenges and workload management solutions
- Intersight Workload Optimization Manager
- Cisco Container Platform
- Cisco Intersight Kubernetes Service

IT Challenges and Workload Management Solutions

Managing application resources in a dynamic, hybrid cloud world is increasingly complex, and IT teams are struggling. With application components running on the premises and in public clouds, end users can suffer outages or experience slow application performance because IT teams simply lack visibility to see how things are connected and how to manage their dynamic environment at scale.

With more people accessing your business through a digital experience, application performance is more critical than ever. Managing workload placement and resources across your ever-changing IT environment is a complex, time-consuming task that has big implications on user experience and costs.

Cisco Intersight Workload Optimizer (CWOM) discovers how all the parts of your hybrid world are connected and then automates these day-to-day operations for you. Supporting more than 50 common platforms and public clouds, it provides real-time, full-stack visibility across your applications and infrastructure. Now you can harness the power of data to continuously monitor supply and demand, match workloads and resources in the most efficient way, and ensure that governance rules are always enforced. The result? Better application performance, reduced cost, faster troubleshooting, and more peace of mind.

Business Impact

Unchecked complexity can result in the following:

- **Underutilized on-premises infrastructure:** To ensure application performance, IT teams often allocate resources modeled to peak-load estimates and/or set conservative utilization limits.

- **Public cloud overprovisioning and cost overruns:** When planning and placing workloads in public clouds, IT teams routinely overprovision computing instance sizes as a hedge to ensure application performance.

- **Wasted time:** IT teams end up chasing alerts and meeting in war rooms to unravel problems instead of supporting innovation.

Figure 5-1 illustrates why managing hybrid cloud resources to ensure application performance and control costs is a complex problem.

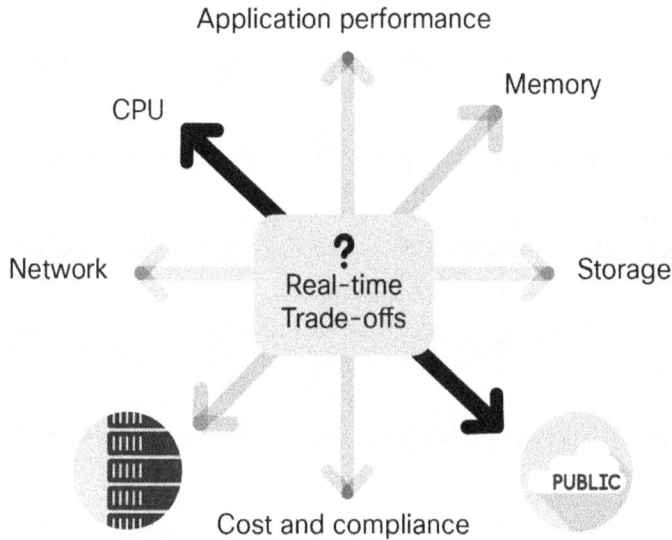

Figure 5-1   *Hybrid cloud resources for ensuring performance and cost*

The following are some of the challenges of workload management in a hybrid cloud:

- Siloed teams with different toolsets managing different layers of the stack and multiple types of resources

- Flying blind without a unified view of the complex interdependencies between layers of infrastructure and applications across on-premises and public cloud environments

- Separating the signal from the noise and prioritizing the constant flow of alerts coming from separate tools

- Lack of visibility into underutilized capacity in public clouds and cost overruns from unmanaged spikes in utilization

To deal with all this complexity, the only choice is to automate resource management and workload placement operations. But how? To optimize effectively, you need a way to collect and track streams of telemetry data from dozens, hundreds, perhaps thousands of sources. You need a way to correlate and continuously analyze all of this data to understand how everything fits together and what's important, as well as how to decide what to do from moment to moment as things continue to change. New tooling is required to connect all the dots and give you the insight you need to stay ahead of demand, stay ahead of problems, and respond to new projects with confidence. What if you could create a unified view of your environment and continuously ensure that applications get the resources they need to perform, all while increasing efficiency and lowering costs?

Cisco Intersight Workload Optimizer

Cisco Intersight Workload Optimizer is a real-time decision engine that ensures the health of applications across your on-premises and public cloud environments while lowering costs. The intelligent software continuously analyzes workload demand, resource consumption, resource costs, and policy constraints to determine an optimal balance. Cisco IWO is an artificial intelligence for IT operations (AIOps) toolset that makes recommendations for operators and can trigger workload placement and resource allocations in your data center and the public cloud, thus fully automating real-time optimization.

With Cisco IWO, infrastructure and operations teams are armed with visibility, insights, and actions that ensure service level agreements (SLAs) are met while improving the bottom line. Also, application and DevOps teams get comprehensive situational awareness so they can deliver high-performing and continuously available applications.

Benefits of using Cisco Intersight Workload Optimizer:

■ Radically simplify application resource management with a single tool that dynamically optimizes resources in real time to ensure application performance.

■ Continuously optimize critical IT resources, resulting in more efficient use of existing infrastructure and lower operational costs on the premises and in the cloud.

■ Take the guesswork out of planning for the future with the ability to quickly model what-if scenarios based on the real-time environment.

Figure 5-2 illustrates how IWO ensures application performance with continuous visibility, deep insights, and informed actions.

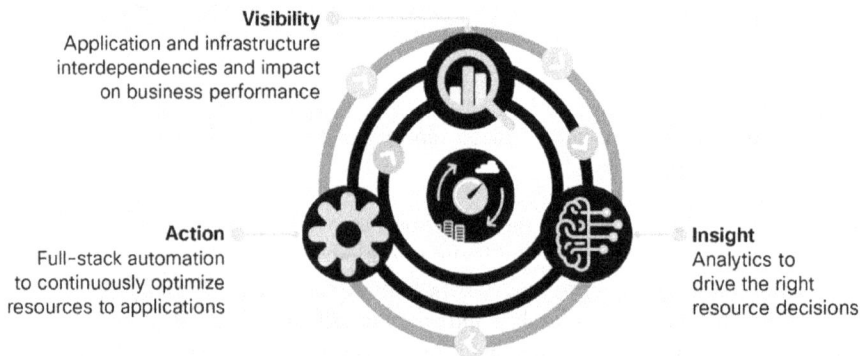

Figure 5-2 *Application performance with continuous visibility, deep insights, and informed actions*

CWOM-to-IWO Migration

In June 2019, Turbonomic and CWOM became inaugural members of the Integration Partner Program (IPP), which takes the technology partnership to another level by helping joint customers maximize the value of their AppDynamics and CWOM investment. The extended integration and partnership delivers on the vision of AIOps, where software is making dynamic resourcing decisions and automating actions to ensure that applications are always performing, enabling positive business outcomes and improved user experiences. Organizations across the world are investing heavily in developing new applications and innovating faster to deliver better, more simplified user experiences. The partnership and the combination of AppDynamics and CWOM ensure that applications are architected and written well and are continuously resourced for performance.

As a full-stack, real-time decision engine, Intersight Workload Optimizer revolutionizes how teams manage application resources across their multicloud landscape, significantly simplifying operations. It delivers unprecedented levels of visibility, insights, and automated actions, as customers look to prevent application performance issues.

Figure 5-3 provides a very high-level view of IWO application management.

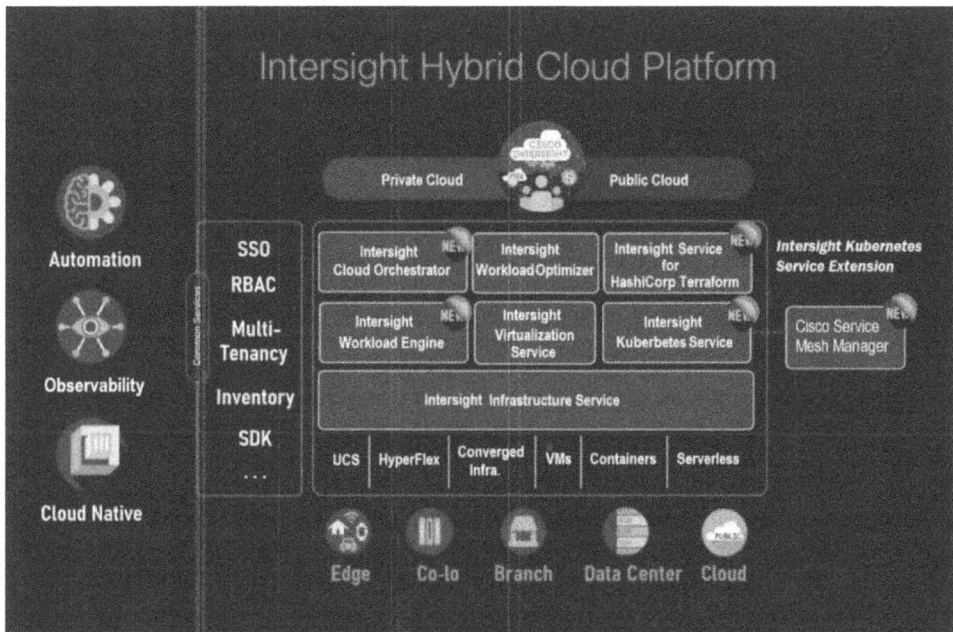

Figure 5-3 *Very high-level view of IWO application management*

Simply put, IWO provides the following customer benefits:

■ It bridges the gap between application and IT teams to ensure application performance.

■ It eliminates application resourcing as a source of application delay, meaning applications can perform and continuously deliver services.

■ It helps IT departments stop overspending and delivers a modern application hosting platform to end users.

■ It enables high-value application and IT teams to focus on strategy and innovation without jeopardizing applications.

IWO expands Intersight capabilities. All in one place, Intersight customers can manage the health of the infrastructure and how well that infrastructure is utilized to ensure application performance. Additionally, Intersight customers can monitor and manage application resources on third-party infrastructure, public cloud, and container environments.

Optimize Hybrid Cloud Infrastructure with IWO

Application resource management is a top-down, application-driven approach that continuously analyzes applications' resource needs and generates fully automatable actions to ensure applications always get what they need to perform. It runs 24/7/365 and scales with the largest, most complex environments.

To perform application resource management, Intersight Workload Optimizer represents your environment holistically as a supply chain of resource buyers and sellers, all working together to meet application demand. By empowering buyers (VMs, instances, containers, and services) with a budget to seek the resources that applications need to perform and empowering sellers to price their available resources (CPU, memory, storage, network) based on utilization in real time, IWO keeps your environment within the desired state, with operating conditions that achieve the following conflicting goals at the same time:

■ **Ensured application performance:** Prevent bottlenecks, upsize containers/VMs, prioritize workload, and reduce storage latency

■ **Efficient use of resources:** Consolidate workloads to reduce infrastructure usage to the minimum, downsize containers, prevent sprawl, and use the most economical cloud offerings

IWO is a containerized, microservices-architected application running in a Kubernetes environment (or within a VM) on your network or a public cloud VPC (Virtual Private Cloud). You assign services running on your network to be IWO targets. IWO discovers the entities (physical devices, virtual components, and software components) that each target manages and then performs analysis, anticipates risks to performance or efficiency, and recommends actions you can take to avoid problems before they occur.

Intelligent, proactive workload optimization simplifies and automates operations. With many tools, the focus is on monitoring and alerting users after a problem has occurred. Cisco IWO is a proactive tool that is designed to avoid application performance issues in the first place. It continuously analyzes workload performance, costs, and compliance rules and makes recommendations on what specific actions to take to avoid issues before they happen, thus radically simplifying and improving day-to-day operations.

While some tools provide visibility into applications or visibility into an individual tier of physical or virtual infrastructure, Cisco IWO bridges all these layers with a single tool. It creates a dynamic dependency graph that visualizes the connections between application elements and infrastructure throughout the layers of the stack, all the way down to component resources within servers, networking, and storage. Figure 5-4 shows how Cisco IWO analyzes telemetry data across your hybrid cloud environment to optimize resources and reduce cost.

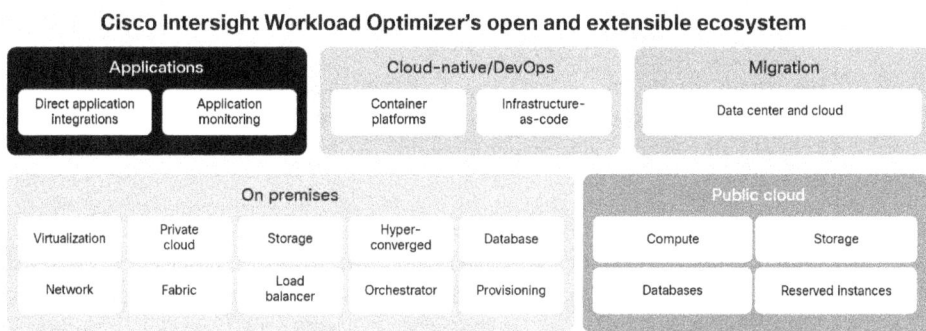

Cisco Intersight Workload Optimizer's open and extensible ecosystem

Applications		Cloud-native/DevOps		Migration
Direct application integrations	Application monitoring	Container platforms	Infrastructure-as-code	Data center and cloud

On premises					Public cloud	
Virtualization	Private cloud	Storage	Hyper-converged	Database	Compute	Storage
Network	Fabric	Load balancer	Orchestrator	Provisioning	Databases	Reserved Instances

Figure 5-4 *Cisco IWO analyzes telemetry data across your hybrid cloud environment to optimize resources and reduce cost*

Cisco IWO can optimize workloads in any infrastructure, any environment, and any cloud, and it works with the industry's top platforms, including VMware vSphere, Microsoft Hyper-V, Citrix XenServer, and OpenStack. It automatically manages compute, storage, and network resources across these platforms, both on the premises and in the cloud. It analyzes telemetry data from a broad ecosystem of data center and cloud technologies, with agentless support for over 50 targets across a range of hypervisors, compute platforms (including Cisco UCS and HyperFlex), container platforms, public clouds, and more. Cisco IWO correlates these telemetry sources into a holistic view to deliver intelligent recommendations and trigger actions, including where to place workloads and how to size and scale resources.

Cisco Intersight is a cloud operations platform that delivers intelligent visualization, optimization, and orchestration for applications and infrastructure across public cloud and on-premises environments. It provides an essential control point for customers to get more value from hybrid cloud investments.

The Cisco IWO service extends these capabilities with hybrid cloud application resource management and support for a broad third-party ecosystem. With this powerful solution, you can have confidence that your applications have continuous access to the IT resources they need to perform, at the lowest cost, whether they reside on the premises or in a public cloud.

The combination of Cisco IWO and AppDynamics can break down siloes between IT teams. This integration provides a single source of truth for application and infrastructure teams to work together more effectively, avoiding finger pointing and late-night war rooms.

AppDynamics discovers and maps your business application topology and how it uses IT resources. Cisco IWO correlates this data with your infrastructure stacks to create a dynamic dependency graph of your hybrid IT environment. It analyzes supply and demand and drives workload placement and resource allocation actions in your IT environment to help ensure that application components get the computing, storage, and network resources they need. Together, these intelligent tools replace sizing guesswork with real-time analytics and modeling so that you know how much infrastructure is needed to allow your applications and business to keep pace with demand.

If you have workloads running on the premises and in public clouds, your IT teams need to make complex, on-going decisions about where to locate workloads and how to size resources in order to ensure performance and minimize cost.

Figuring out what workloads should run where is nearly impossible if you lack clear visibility into available resources and associated costs. And for workloads that run in the cloud, how do you determine what cloud instance or tier is the best fit at the lowest cost? Cloud costs can become volatile, and you can get lost in a myriad of sizing, placement, and pricing decisions that can have very expensive consequences. Cisco IWO can help in the following ways:

- Manage resource allocation and workload placement in all your infrastructure environments, giving you full-stack visibility in a single pane of glass for supply and demand across your combined on-premises and cloud estate.

- Optimize cloud costs with automated selection of instances, reserved instances (RIs), relational databases, and storage tiers based on workload consumption and optimal costs.

- Dynamically scale, delete, and purchase the right cloud resources to ensure performance at the lowest cost.

- Extend on-premises resources by continuously optimizing workload placement and cutting overprovisioning based on utilization trends.

- De-risk migrations to and from the cloud with a data-driven scenario modeling engine.

In increasingly competitive markets, more organizations are adopting containerized deployment options to deliver business-differentiating applications quickly. Kubernetes has become the de facto standard for container orchestration and helps to build, deliver, and scale applications faster. For IT teams, Kubernetes has introduced new layers of complexity with interdependencies and fluctuating demand that make it nearly impossible to effectively manage modern IT at scale.

Cisco IWO simplifies Kubernetes deployments and optimizes performance and cost in real time for on-going operations in the following ways:

■ **Container rightsizing:** Scale container limits/requests up or down based on application demand.

■ **Pod "move"/rescheduling:** Reschedule pods while maintaining service availability to avoid resource fragmentation and/or contention on the node.

■ **Cluster scaling:** When Cisco IWO sees that pods have too little (or too much) capacity in a cluster, it will give the recommendation to spin up another node (or to suspend nodes).

■ **Container planning:** Model what-if scenarios based on your real-time environment. With a few clicks, you can determine how much headroom you have in your clusters or simulate adding or removing Kubernetes pods.

How Intersight Workload Optimizer Works

To keep your infrastructure in the desired state, IWO performs application resource management. This is an ongoing process that solves the problem of ensuring application performance while simultaneously achieving the most efficient use of resources and respecting environment constraints to comply to business rules. This is not a simple problem to solve. Application resource management has to consider many different resources and how they are used in relation to each other, in addition to numerous control points for each resource. As you grow your infrastructure, the factors for each decision increase exponentially. On top of that, the environment is constantly changing—to stay in the desired state, you are constantly trying to hit a moving target. To perform application resource management, IWO models the environment as a market made up of buyers and sellers. These buyers and sellers make up a supply chain that represents tiers of entities in your inventory. This supply chain represents the flow of resources from the data center, through the physical tiers of your environment, into the virtual tier and out to the cloud. By managing relationships between these buyers and sellers, IWO provides closed-loop management of resources, from the data center through to the application.

IWO uses virtual currency to give a budget to buyers and assign cost to resources. This virtual currency assigns value across all tiers of your environment, making it possible to compare the cost of application transactions with the cost of space on a disk or physical space in a data center. The price that a seller charges for a resource changes according to the seller's supply. As demand increases, prices increase. As prices change, buyers and sellers react. Buyers are free to look for other sellers that offer a better price, and sellers can duplicate themselves (open new storefronts) to meet increasing demand. IWO uses its Economic Scheduling Engine to analyze the market and make these decisions. The effect is an invisible hand that dynamically guides your IT infrastructure to the optimal use of resources. To get the most out of IWO, you should understand how it models your environment, the kind of analysis it performs, and the desired state it works to achieve. Figure 5-5 illustrates the desired state graph for infrastructure management.

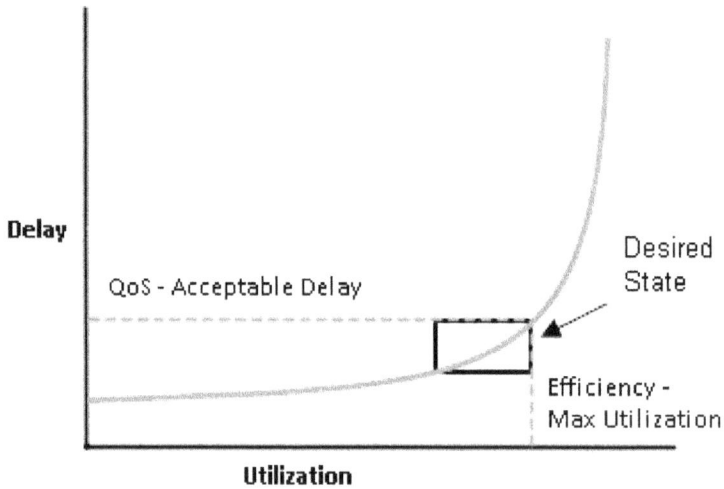

Figure 5-5   *Desired state graph for infrastructure management*

The goal of application resource management is to ensure performance while maintaining efficient use of resources. When performance and efficiency are both maintained, the environment is in the desired state. You can measure performance as a function of delay, where zero delay gives the ideal quality of service (QoS) for a given service. Efficient use of resources is a function of utilization, where 100% utilization of a resource is the ideal for the most efficient utilization.

If you plot delay and utilization, the result is a curve that shows a correlation between utilization and delay. Up to a point, as you increase utilization, the increase in delay is slight. There comes a point on the curve where a slight increase in utilization results in an unacceptable increase in delay. On the other hand, there is a point in the curve where a reduction in utilization doesn't yield a meaningful increase in QoS. The desired state lies within these points on the curve.

You could set a threshold to post an alert whenever the upper limit is crossed. In that case, you would never react to a problem until delay has already become unacceptable. To avoid that late reaction, you could set the threshold to post an alert before the upper limit is crossed. In that case, you guarantee QoS at the cost of over-provisioning—you increase operating costs and never achieve efficient utilization.

Instead of responding after a threshold is crossed, IWO analyzes the operating conditions and constantly recommends actions to keep the entire environment within the desired state. If you execute these actions (or let IWO execute them for you), the environment will maintain operating conditions that ensure performance for your customers, while ensuring the lowest possible cost thanks to efficient utilization of your resources.

Understanding the Market and Virtual Currency

To perform application resource management, IWO models the environment as a market and then uses market analysis to manage resource supply and demand. For example, bottlenecks form when local workload demand exceeds the local capacity—in other words, when demand exceeds supply. By modeling the environment as a market, IWO can use economic solutions to efficiently redistribute the demand or increase the supply.

IWO uses two sets of abstraction to model the environment:

- **Modeling the physical and virtual IT stack as a service supply chain**: The supply chain models your environment as a set of managed entities. These include applications, VMs, hosts, storage, containers, availability zones (cloud), and data centers. Every entity is a buyer, a seller, or both. A host machine buys physical space, power, and cooling from a data center. The host sells resources such as CPU cycles and memory to VMs. In turn, VMs buy host services and then sell their resources (VMem and VCPU) to containers, which then sell resources to applications.

- **Using virtual currency to represent delay or QoS degradation, and to manage the supply and demand of services along the modeled supply chain**: The system uses virtual currency to value these buy/sell transactions. Each managed entity has a running budget. The entity adds to its budget by providing resources to consumers, and the entity draws from its budget to pay for the resources it consumes. The price of a resource is driven by its utilization—the more demand for a resource, the higher its price.

Figure 5-6 illustrates the IWO abstraction model.

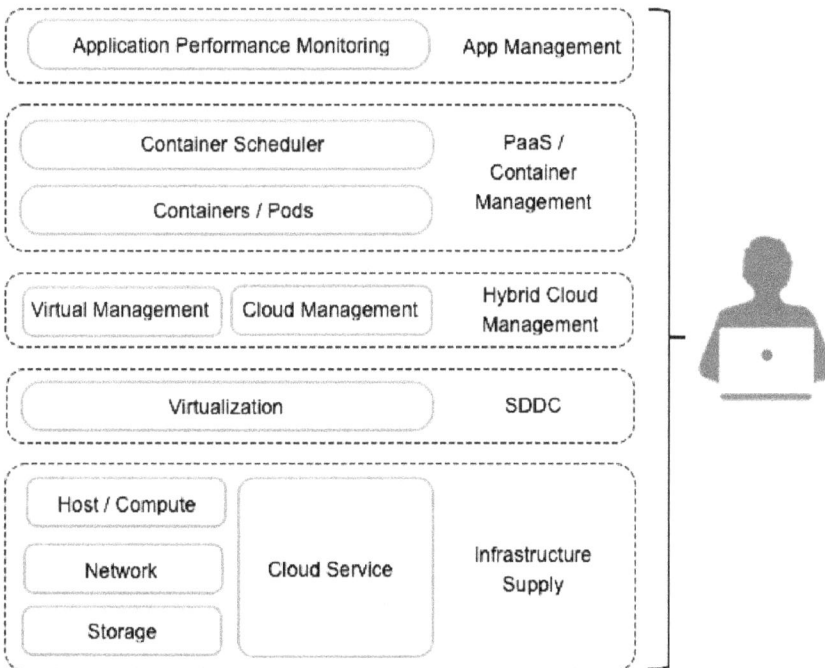

Figure 5-6 *IWO abstraction model*

These abstractions open the whole spectrum of the environment to a single mode of analysis—market analysis. Resources and services can be priced to reflect changes in supply and demand, and pricing can drive resource allocation decisions. For example, a bottleneck (excess demand over supply) results in rising prices for the given resource. Applications competing for the same resource can lower their costs by shifting their workloads to other resource suppliers. As a result, utilization for that resource evens out across the environment and the bottleneck is resolved.

Risk Index

Intersight Workload Optimizer tracks prices for resources in terms of the Risk Index (RI). The higher this index for a resource, the more heavily the resource is utilized, the greater the delay for consumers of that resource, and the greater the risk to your QoS. IWO constantly works to keep the RI within acceptable bounds.

You can think of the RI as the cost for a resource, and IWO works to keep the cost at a competitive level. This is not simply a matter of responding to threshold conditions. IWO analyzes the full range of buyer/seller relationships, and each buyer constantly seeks out the most economical transaction available.

This last point is crucial to understanding IWO. The virtual environment is dynamic, with constant changes to workload that correspond with the varying requests your customers make of your applications and services. By examining each buyer/seller relationship, IWO arrives at the optimal workload distribution for the current state of the environment. In this way, it constantly drives your environment toward the desired state.

Understanding Intersight Workload Optimizer Supply Chain

Intersight Workload Optimizer models your environment as a market of buyers and sellers. It discovers different types of entities in your environment via the targets you have added, and it then maps these entities to the supply chain to manage the workloads they support. For example, for a hypervisor target, IWO discovers VMs, the hosts and datastores that provide resources to the VMs, and the applications that use VM resources. For a Kubernetes target, it discovers services, namespaces, containers, container pods, and nodes. The entities in your environment form a chain of supply and demand, where some entities provide resources while others consume the supplied resources. IWO stitches these entities together, for example, by connecting the discovered Kubernetes nodes with the discovered VMs in vCenter.

Supply Chain Terminology

Cisco introduces specific terms to express IT resources and utilization in relation to supply and demand. The terms shown in Table 5-1 are largely intuitive, but you should understand how they relate to the issues and activities that are common for IT management.

Table 5-1   *The Supply Chain Terminologies Used in IWO*

Term	Definition
Commodity	This is the basic building block of IWO supply and demand. All the resources that IWO monitors are commodities. For example, the CPU capacity and memory that a host can provide are commodities. IWO can also represent clusters and segments as commodities. When the user interface (UI) shows "commodities," it's showing the resources a service provides. When the interface shows "commodities bought," it's showing what that service consumes.
Composed of	This refers to the resources or commodities that make up the given service. For example, in the UI you might see that a certain VM is *composed of* commodities, such as one or more physical CPUs, an Ethernet interface, and physical memory. Contrast "composed of" with "consumes," where consumption refers to the commodities the VM has bought. Also contrast "composed of" with the commodities a service offers for sale. A host might include four CPUs in its composition, but it offers CPU cycles as a single commodity.
Consumes	This refers to the services and commodities a service has bought. A service *consumes* other commodities. For example, a VM consumes the commodities offered by a host, and an application consumes commodities from one or more VMs. In the UI, you can explore the services that provide the commodities the current service consumes.
Entity	This refers to a buyer or seller in the market. For example, a VM or a datastores is an entity.
Environment	This refers to the totality of data center, network, host, storage, VM, and application resources that you are monitoring.
Inventory	This is the list of all entities in your environment.
Risk Index	This is a measure of the risk to quality of service (QoS) that a consumer will experience. The higher the Risk Index (RI) on a provider, the more risk to QoS for any consumer of that provider's services. For example, a host provides resources to one or more VMs. The higher the RI on the provider, the more likely that the VMs will experience QoS degradation. In most cases, for optimal operation, the RI on a provider should not go into double digits.

Working with Intersight Workload Optimizer

The public cloud provides compute, storage, and other resources on demand. By adding an AWS Billing Target (AWS) or Microsoft Enterprise Agreement (Azure) to use custom pricing and discover reserved instances, you enable IWO to use that richer pricing information to calculate workload size and RI coverage for your Azure environment. You can run all of your infrastructure on a public cloud, or you can set up a hybrid environment where you burst workload to the public cloud as needed. IWO can analyze the performance of applications running on the public cloud and then provision more instances as demand requires. For a hybrid environment, IWO can provision copies of your application VMs on the public cloud to satisfy spikes in demand, and as demand falls off, it can suspend those VMs if they're no longer needed. With public cloud targets, you can use IWO to perform the following tasks:

- Scale VMs and databases

- Change storage tiers

- Purchase VM reservations

- Locate the most efficient workload placement within the hybrid environment while ensuring performance

- Detect unused storage volumes

Claiming AWS Targets

For IWO to manage an AWS account, you provide the credentials via the Access Key that you use to access that account. (For information about getting an Access Key for an AWS account, see the Amazon Web Services documentation.)

To add an AWS target, specify the following:

- **Custom Target Name:** The display name that will be used to identify the target in the Target List. This is for display in the UI only; it does not need to match any internal name.

- **Access Key:** Provide the Access Key for the account you want to manage.

- **Access Key Secret:** Provide the Access Key Secret for the account you want to manage.

Claiming Azure Targets

Microsoft Azure is Microsoft's infrastructure platform for the public cloud. You gain access to this infrastructure through a service principal target. To specify an Azure target, you provide the credentials for the subscription and IWO discovers the resources available to you through that service principal. Through Azure service principal targets, IWO automatically discovers the subscriptions to which the service principal has been granted access in the Azure portal. This, in turn, creates a derived target for each subscription that inherits the authorization provided by the service principal (for example, contributor). You cannot directly modify a derived target, but IWO validates the target and discovers its inventory as it does with any other target.

To claim an Azure service principal target, you must meet the following requirements:

- Set up your Azure service principal subscription to grant IWO the access it needs. To set up the Azure subscription, you must access the Administrator or Co-Administrator Azure Portal (portal.azure.com). Note that this access is only required for the initial setup. IWO does not require this access for regular operation.

- Claim the target with the credentials that result from the subscription setup (Tenant ID, Client ID, and so on).

- Azure Resource Manager Intersight Workload Optimizer requires the Azure Resource Manager deployment and management service. This provides the management layer that IWO uses to discover and manage entities in your Azure environment.

Cisco Container Platform

Setting up, deploying, and managing multiple containers for multiple micro-sized services gets tedious—and difficult to manage across multiple public and private clouds. IT Ops has wound up doing much of this extra work, which makes it difficult for them to stay on top of the countless other tasks they're already charged with performing. If containers are going to truly be useful at scale, we have to find a way to make them easier to manage.

The following are the requirements in managing container environments:

- The ability to easily manage multiple clusters

- Simple installation and maintenance

- Networking and security consistency

- Seamless application deployment, both on the premises and in public clouds

- Persistent storage

That's where Cisco Container Platform (CCP) comes in, which is a fully curated, lightweight container management platform for production-grade environments, powered by Kubernetes, and delivered with Cisco enterprise-class support. It reduces the complexity of configuring, deploying, securing, scaling, and managing containers via automation, coupled with Cisco's best practices for security and networking. CCP is built with an open architecture using open source components, so you're not locked in to any single vendor. It works across both on-premises and public cloud environments. And because it's optimized with Cisco HyperFlex, this preconfigured, integrated solution sets up in minutes.

The following are the benefits of CCP:

- **Reduced risk:** CCP is a full-stack solution built and tested on Cisco HyperFlex and ACI Networking, with Cisco providing automated updates and enterprise-class support for the entire stack. CCP is built to handle production workloads.

- **Greater efficiency:** CCP provides your IT Ops team with a turnkey, preconfigured solution that automates repetitive tasks and removes pressure on them to update people, processes, and skill sets in-house. It provides developers with flexibility and speed to be innovative and respond to market requirements more quickly.

- **Remarkable flexibility:** CCP gives you choices when it comes to deployment—from hyperconverged infrastructure to VMs and bare metal. Also, because it's based on open source components, you're free from vendor lock-in.

Figure 5-7 provides a holistic overview of CCP.

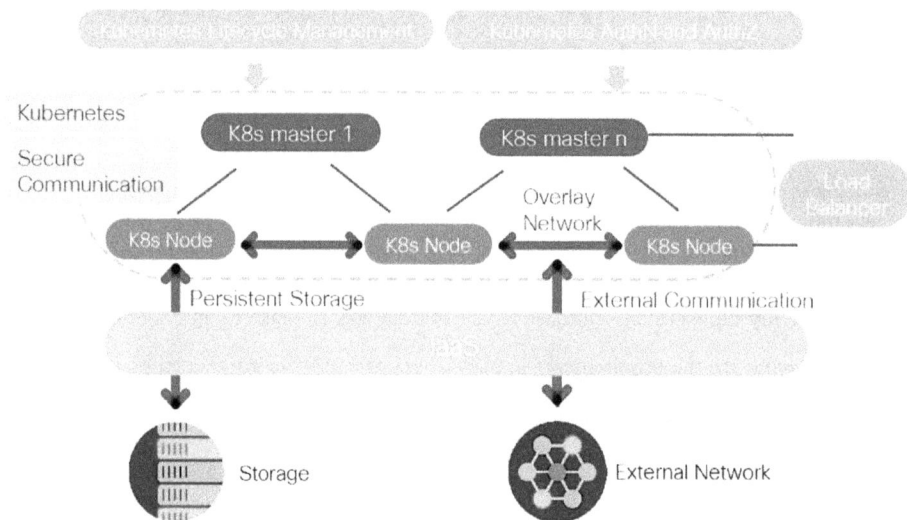

Figure 5-7   *Holistic overview of CCP*

Cisco Container Platform ushers all of the tangible benefits of container orchestration into the technology domain of the enterprise. Based on upstream Kubernetes, CCP presents a UI for self-service deployment and management of container clusters. These clusters consume private cloud resources based on established authentication profiles, which can be bound to existing RBAC models. The advantage to disparate organizational teams is the flexibility to consistently and efficiently deploy clusters into IaaS resources, a feat not easily accomplished and scaled when utilizing script-based frameworks. Teams can discriminately manage their cluster resources, including responding to conditions requiring a scale-out or scale-in event, without fear of disrupting another team's assets.

CCP boasts an innately open architecture composed of well-established open source components—a framework embraced by DevOps teams aiming their innovation toward cloud-neutral work streams.

CCP deploys easily into an existing infrastructure, whether it be of a virtual or bare-metal nature, to become the turnkey container management platform in the enterprise. CCP incorporates ubiquitous monitoring and policy-based security and provides essential services such as load balancing and logging. The platform can provide applications an extension into network management, application performance monitoring, analytics, and logging. CCP offers an API layer that is compatible with Google Cloud Platform and Google Kubernetes Engine, so transitioning applications potentially from the private cloud to the public cloud fits perfectly into orchestration schemes. The case could be made for containerized workloads residing in the private cloud on CCP to consume services brokered by Google Cloud Platform, and vice versa. For environments with a Cisco Application Centric Infrastructure (ACI), Contiv, a CCP component, will secure the containers in a logical policy-based context. Those environments with Cisco HyperFlex (HX) can leverage the inherent benefits provided by HX storage and provide persistent volumes to the containers in the form of FlexVolumes. CCP normalizes the operational experience of managing a Kubernetes environment by providing a curated production quality solution integrated with best-of-breed open source projects. Figure 5-8 illustrates the CCP feature set.

Cisco Container Platform Feature Set

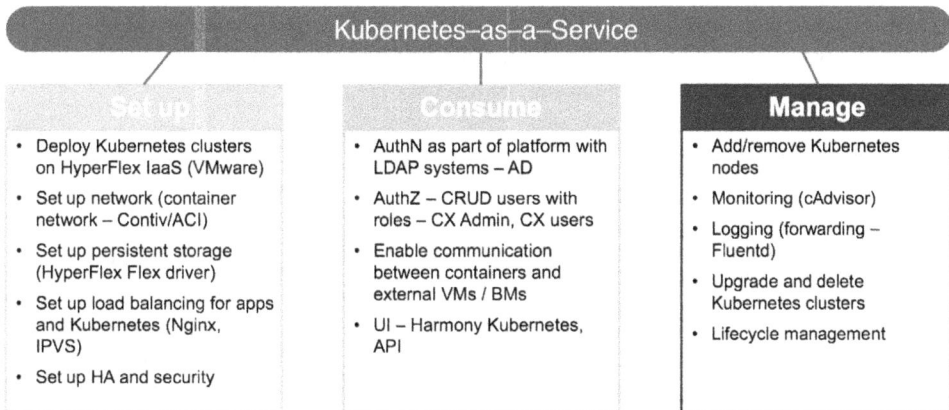

Figure 5-8 *CCP feature set*

The following are some CCP use cases:

- **Simple GUI-driven menu system to deploy clusters:** You don't have to know the technical details of Kubernetes to deploy a cluster. Just fill in the questions, and CCP will do the work.

■ **The ability to deploy Kubernetes clusters in air-gapped sites:** CCP tenant images contain all the necessary binaries and don't need Internet access to function.

■ **Choice of networking solutions:** Use Cisco's ACI plug-in, an industry standard Calico network, or if scaling is your priority, choose Contiv with VPP. All work seamlessly with CCP.

■ **Automated monthly updates:** Bug fixes, feature enhancements, and CVE remedies are pushed automatically every month—not only for Kubernetes, but also for the underlying operating system (OS).

■ **Built-in visibility and monitoring:** CCP lets you see what's going on inside clusters to stay on top of usage patterns and address potential problems before they negatively impact the business.

■ **Preconfigured persistent volume storage:** Dynamic provisioning using HyperFlex storage as the default. No additional drivers need to be installed. Just set it and forget it.

■ **Deploy EKS clusters using CCP control plane:** CCP allows you to use a single pane of glass for deploying on-premises and Amazon clusters, plus it leverages Amazon Authentication for both.

■ **Pre-integrated Istio:** It's ready to deploy and use without additional administration.

Cisco Container Platform Architecture Overview

At the bottom of the stack is Level 1, the Networking layer, which can consist of Nexus switches, Application Policy Infrastructure Controllers (APICs), and Fabric Interconnects (FIs).

Level 2 is the Compute layer, which consists of HyperFlex, UCS, or third-party servers that provide virtualized compute resources through VMware and distributed storage resources.

Level 3 is the Hypervisor layer, which is implemented using HyperFlex or VMware.

Level 4 consists of the CCP control plane and data plane (or tenant clusters). In Figure 5-9, the left side shows the CCP control plane, which runs on four control-plane VMs, and the right side shows the tenant clusters. These tenant clusters are preconfigured to support persistent volumes using the vSphere Cloud Provider and Container Storage Interface (CSI) plug-in. Figure 5-9 provides an overview of the CCP architecture.

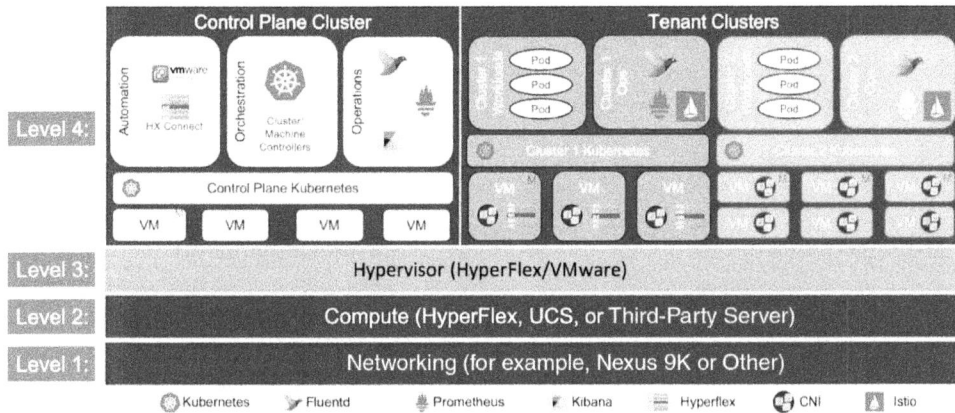

Figure 5-9 *Container Platform Architecture Overview*

Components of Cisco Container Platform

Table 5-2 lists the components of CCP.

Table 5-2 *Components of CCP*

Function	Component
Operating System	Ubuntu
Orchestration	Kubernetes
IaaS	vSphere
Infrastructure	HyperFlex, UCS
Container Network Interface (CNI)	ACI, Contiv, Calico
SDN	ACI
Container Storage	HyperFlex Container Storage Interface (CSI) plug-in
Load Balancing	NGINX, Envoy
Service Mesh	Istio, Envoy
Monitoring	Prometheus, Grafana
Logging	Elasticsearch, Fluentd, and Kibana (EFK) stack
Container Runtime	Docker CE

Sample Deployment Topology

This section describes a sample deployment topology of the CCP and illustrates the network topology requirements at a conceptual level.

In this case, it is expected that the vSphere-based cluster is set up, provisioned, and fully functional for virtualization and virtual machine (VM) functionality before any installation of CCP. You can refer to the standard VMware documentation for details on vSphere installation. Figure 5-10 provides an example of a vSphere cluster on which CCP is to be deployed.

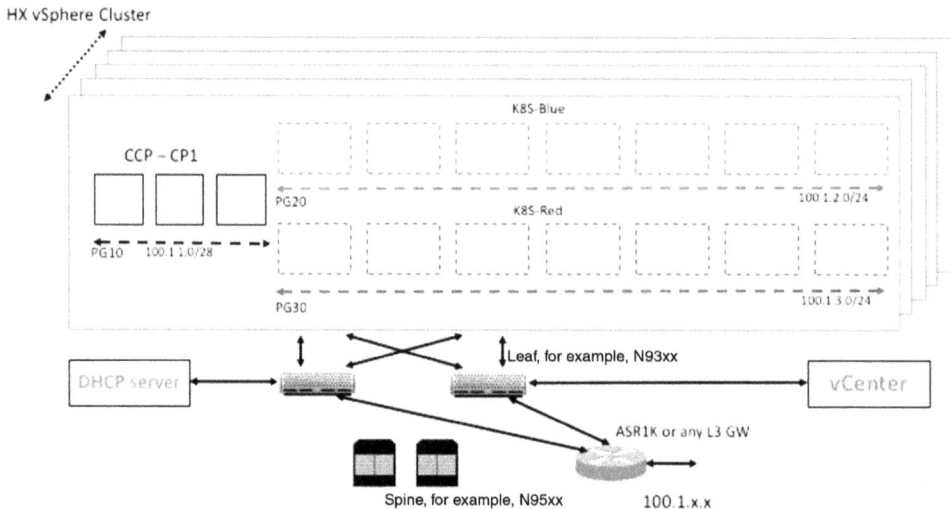

Figure 5-10   *vSphere cluster on which CCP is to be deployed*

Once the vSphere cluster is ready to provision VMs, the admin then provisions one or more VMware port groups (for example, PG10, PG20, and PG30 in the figure) on which virtual machines will subsequently be provisioned as container cluster nodes. Basic L2 switching with VMware vswitch functionality can be used to implement these port groups. IP subnets should be set aside for use on these port groups, and the VLANs used to implement these port groups should be terminated on an external L3 gateway (such as the ASR1K shown in the figure). The control-plane cluster and tenant-plane Kubernetes clusters of CCP can then be provisioned on these port groups.

All provisioned Kubernetes clusters may choose to use a single shared port group, or separate port groups may be provisioned (one per Kubernetes cluster), depending on the isolation needs of the deployment. Layer 3 network isolation may be used between these different port groups as long as the following conditions are met:

- There is L3 IP address connectivity among the port group that is used for the control-plane cluster and the tenant cluster port groups

- The IP address of the vCenter server is accessible from the control-plane cluster

- A DHCP server is provisioned for assigning IP addresses to the installer and upgrade VMs, and it must be accessible from the control-plane port group cluster of the cluster

The simplest functional topology would be to use a single shared port group for all clusters with a single IP subnet to be used to assign IP addresses for all container cluster VMs. This IP subnet can be used to assign one IP per cluster VM and up to four virtual IP addresses per Kubernetes cluster, but would not be used to assign individual Kubernetes pod IP addresses. Hence, a reasonable capacity planning estimate for the size of this IP subnet is as follows:

(The expected total number of container cluster VMs across all clusters) + 3 × (the total number of expected Kubernetes clusters)

Administering Clusters on vSphere

You can create, upgrade, modify, or delete vSphere on-premises Kubernetes clusters using the CCP web interface. CCP supports v2 and v3 clusters on vSphere. The v2 clusters use a single master node for their control plane, whereas the v3 clusters can use one or three master nodes for their control plane. The multimaster approach of v3 clusters is the preferred cluster type, as this approach ensures high availability for the control plane. The following steps show you how to administer clusters on vSphere:

Step 1.   In the left pane, click **Clusters** and then click the **vSphere** tab.

Step 2.   Click **NEW CLUSTER**.

Step 3.   In the **BASIC INFORMATION** screen:

a. From the **INFRASTRUCTURE PROVIDER** drop-down list, choose the provider related to your Kubernetes cluster.

For more information, see **Adding vSphere Provider Profile**.

b. In the **KUBERNETES CLUSTER NAME** field, enter a name for your Kubernetes tenant cluster.

c. In the **DESCRIPTION** field, enter a description for your cluster.

d. In the **KUBERNETES VERSION** drop-down list, choose the version of Kubernetes that you want to use for creating the cluster.

e. If you are using ACI, specify the ACI profile.

For more information, see **Adding ACI Profile**.

f. Click **NEXT**.

Step 4.   In the **PROVIDER SETTINGS** screen:

a. From the **DATA CENTER** drop-down list, choose the data center that you want to use.

b. From the **CLUSTERS** drop-down list, choose a cluster.

Note   Ensure that DRS and HA are enabled on the cluster that you choose. For more information on enabling DRS and HA on clusters, see *Cisco Container Platform Installation Guide*.

      c. From the **DATASTORE** drop-down list, choose a datastore.

Note   Ensure that the datastore is accessible to the hosts in the cluster.

      d. From the **VM TEMPLATE** drop-down list, choose a VM template.

      e. From the **NETWORK** drop-down list, choose a network.

Note   Ensure that you select a subnet with an adequate number of free IP addresses. For more information, see **Managing Networks**. The selected network must have access to vCenter.

      For v2 clusters that use HyperFlex systems:

- The selected network must have access to the HypexFlex Connect server to support HyperFlex Storage Provisioners.

- For HyperFlex Local Network, select **k8-priv-iscsivm-network** to enable HyperFlex Storage Provisioners.

      f. From the **RESOURCE POOL** drop-down list, choose a resource pool.

      g. Click **NEXT**.

Step 5.   In the **NODE CONFIGURATION** screen:

      a. From the **GPU TYPE** drop-down list, choose a GPU type.

Note   GPU configuration applies only if you have GPUs in your HyperFlex cluster.

      b. For v3 clusters, under **MASTER**, choose the number of master nodes as well as their VCPU and memory configurations.

Note   You may skip this step for v2 clusters. You can configure the number of master nodes only for v3 clusters.

      c. Under **WORKER**, choose the number of worker nodes as well as their VCPU and memory configurations.

d. In the **SSH USER** field, enter the SSH username.

e. In the **SSH KEY** field, enter the SSH public key that you want to use for creating the cluster.

Note   Ensure that you use the Ed25519 or ECDSA format for the public key. Because RSA and DSA are less-secure formats, Cisco prevents the use of these formats.

f. In the **ROUTABLE CIDR** field, enter the IP addresses for the pod subnet in the CIDR notation.

g. From the **SUBNET** drop-down list, choose the subnet that you want to use for this cluster.

h. In the **POD CIDR** field, enter the IP addresses for the pod subnet in the CIDR notation.

i. In the **DOCKER HTTP PROXY** field, enter a proxy for the Docker.

j. In the **DOCKER HTTPS PROXY** field, enter an HTTPS proxy for the Docker.

k. In the **DOCKER BRIDGE IP** field, enter a valid CIDR to override the default Docker bridge.

Note   If you want to install the HX-CSI add-on, ensure that you set the CIDR network prefix of the **DOCKER BRIDGE IP** field to **/24.**

l. Under **DOCKER NO PROXY**, click **ADD NO PROXY** and then specify a comma-separated list of hosts that you want to exclude from proxying.

m. In the **VM USERNAME** field, enter the VM username that you want to use as the login for the VM.

n. Under **NTP POOLS**, click **ADD POOL** to add a pool.

o. Under **NTP SERVERS**, click **ADD SERVER** to add an NTP server.

p. Under **ROOT CA REGISTRIES**, click **ADD REGISTRY** to add a root CA certificate to allow tenant clusters to securely connect to additional services.

q. Under **INSECURE REGISTRIES**, click **ADD REGISTRY** to add Docker registries created with unsigned certificates.

r. For v2 clusters, under **ISTIO**, use the toggle button to enable or disable Istio.

s. Click **NEXT**.

Step 6.   For v2 clusters, to integrate Harbor with CCP:

Note   Harbor is currently not available for v3 clusters.

        a. In the **Harbor Registry** screen, click the toggle button to enable Harbor.

        b. In the **PASSWORD** field, enter a password for the Harbor server administrator.

        c. In the **REGISTRY** field, enter the size of the registry in gigabits.

        d. Click NEXT.

Step 7.   In the **Summary** screen, verify the configuration and then click **FINISH**.

Administering Amazon EKS Clusters Using CCP Control Plane

Before you begin, make sure you have done the following:

- Added your Amazon provider profile.
- Added the required AMI files to your account.
- Created an AWS IAM role for the CCP usage to create AWS EKS clusters.

Here is the procedure for administering Amazon EKS clusters using the CCP control plane:

Step 1.   In the left pane, click **Clusters** and then click the **AWS** tab.

Step 2.   Click **NEW CLUSTER**.

Step 3.   In the **Basic Information** screen, enter the following information:

        a. From the **INFRASTUCTURE PROVIDER** drop-down list, choose the provider related to the appropriate Amazon account.

        b. From the **AWS REGION** drop-down list, choose an appropriate AWS region.

Note   Not all regions support EKS. Ensure that you select a supported region. Currently, CCP supports the ap-northeast-1, ap-northeast-2, ap-southeast-1, ap-southeast-2, eu-central-1, eu-north-1, eu-west-1, eu-west-2, eu-west-3, us-east-1, us-east-2, and us-west-2 regions.

        c. In the **KUBERNETES CLUSTER NAME** field, enter a name for your cluster.

        d. Click NEXT.

Step 4.   In the **Node Configuration** screen, specify the following information:

    a. From the **INSTANCE TYPE** drop-down list, choose an instance type for your cluster.

    b. From the **MACHINE IMAGE** drop-down list, choose an appropriate CCP Amazon Machine Image (AMI) file.

    c. In the **WORKER COUNT** field, enter an appropriate number of worker nodes.

    d. In the **SSH PUBLIC KEY** drop-down field, choose an appropriate authentication key.

    This field is optional. It is needed if you want to ssh to the worker nodes for troubleshooting purposes. Ensure that you use the Ed25519 or ECDSA format for the public key.

Note   Because RSA and DSA are less-secure formats, Cisco prevents the use of these formats.

    e. In the **IAM ACCESS ROLE ARN** field, enter the Amazon Resource Name (ARN) information.

Note   By default, the AWS credentials specified at the time of Amazon EKS cluster creation (that is, the credentials configured in the Infrastructure Provider) are mapped to the Kubernetes cluster-admin ClusterRole. A default ClusterRoleBinding binds the credentials to the system:masters group, thereby granting superuser access to the holders of the IAM identity. The **IAM ACCESS ROLE ARN** field allows you to specify the ARN of an additional AWS IAM role or IAM user who is also granted administrative control of the cluster.

    f. Click **NEXT**.

Step 5.   In the **VPC Configuration** screen, specify the following information:

    a. In the **SUBNET CIDR** field, enter a value of the overall subnet CIDR for your cluster.

    b. In the **PUBLIC SUBNET CIDR** field, enter values for your cluster on separate lines.

    c. In the **PRIVATE SUBNET CIDR** field, enter values for your cluster on separate lines.

Step 6.   In the **Summary** screen, review the cluster information and then click FINISH.

Cluster creation can take up to 20 minutes. You can monitor the cluster creation status on the **Clusters** screen.

Note   If you receive the "Could not get token: AccessDenied" error message, this indicates that the AWS account is not a trusted entity for the Role ARN.

Licensing and Updates

You need to configure Cisco Smart Software Licensing on the Cisco Smart Software Manager (Cisco SSM) to easily procure, deploy, and manage licenses for your CCP instance. The number of licenses required depends on the number of VMs necessary for your deployment scenario.

Cisco SSM enables you to manage your Cisco Smart Software Licenses from one centralized website. With Cisco SSM, you can organize and view your licenses in groups called "virtual accounts." You can also use Cisco SSM to transfer the licenses between virtual accounts, as needed.

You can access Cisco SSM from the Cisco Software Central home page, under the Smart Licensing area. CCP is initially available for a 90-day evaluation period, after which you need to register the product.

Connected Model

In a connected deployment model, the license usage information is directly sent over the Internet or through an HTTP proxy server to Cisco SSM.

For a higher degree of security, you can opt to use a partially connected deployment model, where the license usage information is sent from CCP to a locally installed VM-based satellite server (Cisco SSM satellite). Cisco SSM satellite synchronizes with Cisco SSM on a daily basis.

Registering CCP Using a Registration Token

You need to register your CCP instance with Cisco SSM or Cisco SSM satellite before the 90-day evaluation period expires. The following is the procedure for registering CCP using a registration token, and Figure 5-11 shows the workflow for this procedure.

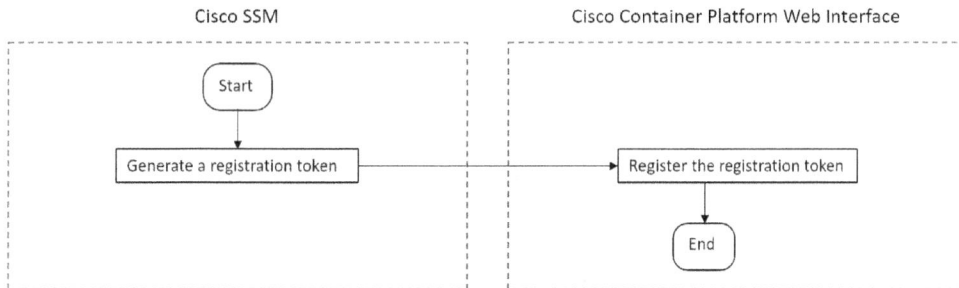

Figure 5-11   *Registering CCP using a registration token*

Step 1.   Perform these steps on Cisco SSM or Cisco SSM satellite to generate a registration token:

   a. Go to **Inventory >** *Choose Your Virtual Account* **> General** and then click **New Token.**

   b. If you want to enable higher levels of encryption for the products registered using the registration token, check the **Allow Export-Controlled functionality on the products registered with this token** check box.

Note   This option is available only if you are compliant with the Export-Controlled functionality.

   c. Download or copy the token.

Step 2.   Perform these steps in the CCP web interface to register the registration token and complete the license registration process:

   a. In the left pane, click **Licensing.**

   b. In the license notification, click **Register.**

   The Smart Software Licensing Product Registration dialog box appears.

   c. In the **Product Instance Registration Token** field, enter, copy and paste, or upload the registration token that you generated in Step 1.

   d. Click **REGISTER** to complete the registration process.

Upgrading Cisco Container Platform

Upgrading CCP and upgrading tenant clusters are independent operations. You must upgrade CCP to allow tenant clusters to upgrade. Specifically, tenant clusters cannot be upgraded to a higher version than the control plane. For example, if the control plane is at version 1.10, the tenant cluster cannot be upgraded to the 1.11 version.

Upgrading CCP is a three-step process:

You can update the size of a single IP address pool during an upgrade. However, we recommend that you plan ahead for the free IP address requirement by ensuring that the free IP addresses are available in the control-plane cluster prior to the upgrade.

If you are upgrading from a CCP version, you must do the following:

■ Ensure that at least five IP addresses are available (3.1.x or earlier).

■ Ensure that at least three IP addresses are available (3.2 or later).

■ Upgrade the CCP tenant base VM.

■ Deploy/upgrade the VM.

■ Upgrade the CCP control plane.

To get the latest step-by-step upgrade procedure, you can refer to the CCP upgrade guide.

Cisco Intersight Kubernetes Service

Cisco Intersight Kubernetes Service (IKS) effectively expands CCP's functionality to benefit from Intersight's native infrastructure management capabilities, further simplifying building and managing Kubernetes environments. IKS is a SaaS offering, taking away the hassle of installing, hosting, and managing a container management solution. For organizations with specific requirements, it also offers two additional deployment options (with a virtual appliance). So, let's take a look at how IKS can make our lives easier. Figure 5-12 provides an overview of Intersight Cloud management.

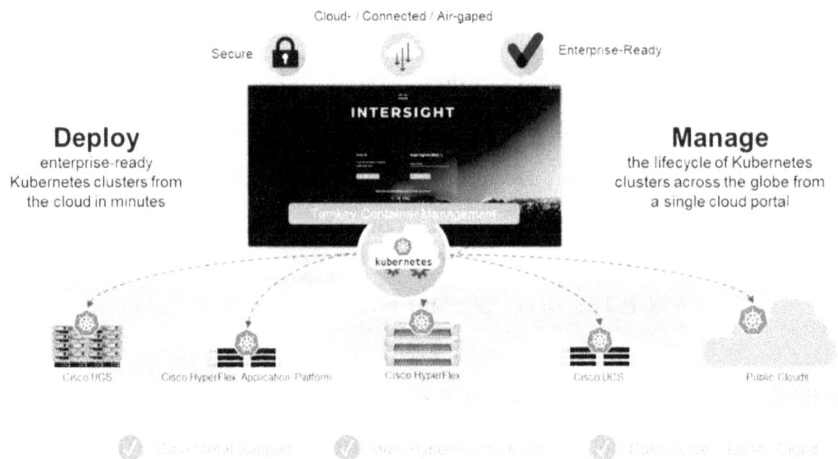

Figure 5-12 *Intersight Cloud management*

Benefits of IKS

The following are the benefits of using IKS:

- Simplify Kubernetes Day 0 to Day N operations and increase application agility with a turnkey SaaS platform that makes it easy to deploy and manage clusters across data centers, the edge, and public clouds.

- Reduce risk, lower cost, improve governance, and take multicloud control on a security-hardened platform, with enhanced availability, native integrations with AWS, Azure, and Google Cloud, and end-to-end industry-leading Cisco TAC support.

- Get more value from your investments with a flexible, extensible Kubernetes platform that supports multiple delivery options, hypervisors, storage, and bare-metal configurations.

- Automate and simplify with self-service built-in add-ons and optimizations such as AI/ML frameworks, service mesh, networking, monitoring, logging, and persistent object storage.

Common Use Case

A good example comes from the retail sector: an IT admin needs to quickly create and configure hundreds of edge locations for the company's retail branches to perform AI/ML processing and a few core ones in privately owned or co-located data centers. The reason it makes sense for processing or storing large chunks of data at the edge is the cost of shipping the data back to the core DC or to a public cloud (and latency to a certain extent).

Creating those Kubernetes clusters would require firmware upgrades as well as OS and hypervisor installations before the IT admin can even get to the container layer. With Cisco Intersight providing a comprehensive, common orchestration and management layer—from server and fabric management to hyperconverged infrastructure management to Kubernetes—creating a container environment from scratch can be literally done with just a few clicks. Figure 5-13 illustrates a high-level architecture of IKS.

IT admins can use either the IKS GUI or its APIs, or they can integrate with an Infrastructure as Code plan (such as HashiCorp's Terraform) to quickly deploy a Kubernetes environment on a variety of platforms—VMware ESXi hypervisors or Cisco HyperFlex—thus enabling significant savings and efficiency without the need of virtualization.

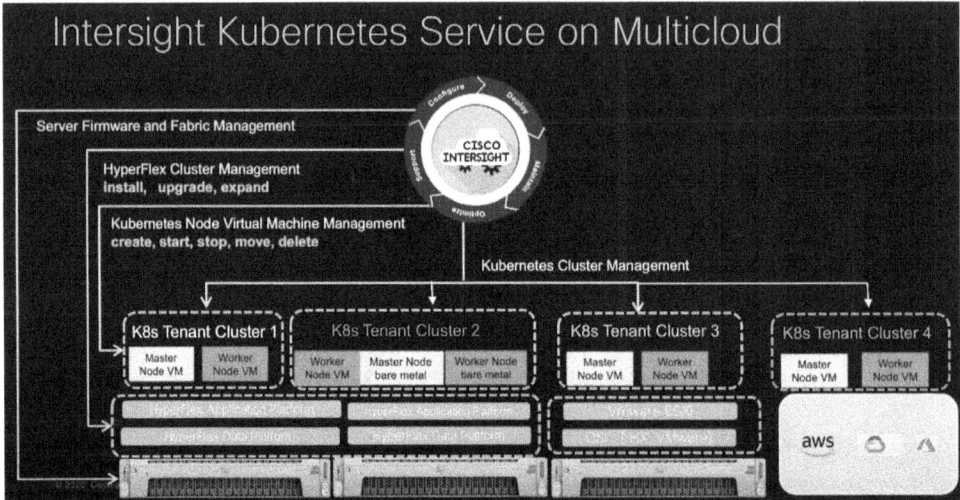

Figure 5-13   *Architecture of IKS*

Deploying Consistent, Production-Grade Kubernetes Anywhere

Few open source projects have been as widely and rapidly adopted as Kubernetes (K8s), the de facto container orchestration platform. With Kubernetes, development teams can deploy, manage, and scale their containerized applications with ease, making innovations more accessible to their continuous delivery pipelines. However, Kubernetes comes with operational challenges, because it requires time and technical expertise to install and configure. Multiple open source packages need to be combined on top of a heterogeneous infrastructure, across on-premises data centers, edge locations, and, of course, public clouds. Installing Kubernetes and the different software components required, creating clusters, configuring storage, networking, and security, optimizing for AI/ML, and other manual tasks can slow down the pace of development and can result in teams spending hours debugging. In addition, maintaining all these moving parts (for example, upgrading, updating, and patching critical security bugs) requires ongoing significant human capital investment.

The solution? Cisco Intersight Kubernetes Service (IKS), a turnkey SaaS solution for managing consistent, production-grade Kubernetes anywhere.

How It Works

Cisco Intersight Kubernetes Service (IKS) is a fully curated, lightweight container management platform for delivering multicloud, production-grade, upstream Kubernetes. Part of the modular SaaS Cisco Intersight offerings (with an air-gapped on-premises option also available), IKS simplifies the process of provisioning, securing, scaling, and managing virtualized or bare-metal Kubernetes clusters by providing end-to-end automation, including the integration of networking, load balancers, native dashboards, and storage provider interfaces. It also works with all the popular public cloud–managed K8s offerings, integrating with common identity access with AWS Elastic Kubernetes Service (EKS), Azure Kubernetes Service (AKS) and Google Cloud Google Kubernetes Engine (GKE). IKS is ideal for AI/ML development and data scientists looking for delivering GPU-enabled clusters, and Kubeflow support with a few clicks. It also offers enhanced availability features, such as multimaster (tenant) and self-healing (operator model).

IKS is easy to install in minutes and can be deployed on top of VMware ESXi hypervisors, Cisco HyperFlex Application Platform (HXAP) hypervisors, and/or directly on Cisco HyperFlex Application Platform bare-metal servers, enabling significant savings and efficiency without the need of virtualization. In addition, with HXAP leveraging container-native virtualization capabilities, you can run virtual machines (VMs), VM-based containers, and bare-metal containers on the same platform! Cisco Intersight also offers native integrations with Cisco HyperFlex (HX) for enterprise-class storage capabilities (for example, persistent volume claims and public cloud-like object storage) and Cisco Application Centric Infrastructure (Cisco ACI) for networking, in addition to the industry- standard Container Storage Interface and Container Network Interface (for example, Calico).

Intersight Kubernetes Service integrates seamlessly with the other Cisco Intersight SaaS offerings to deliver a powerful, comprehensive cloud operations platform to easily and quickly deploy, optimize, and lifecycle-manage end-to-end infrastructure, workloads, and applications. Figure 5-14 illustrates the benefits of IKS.

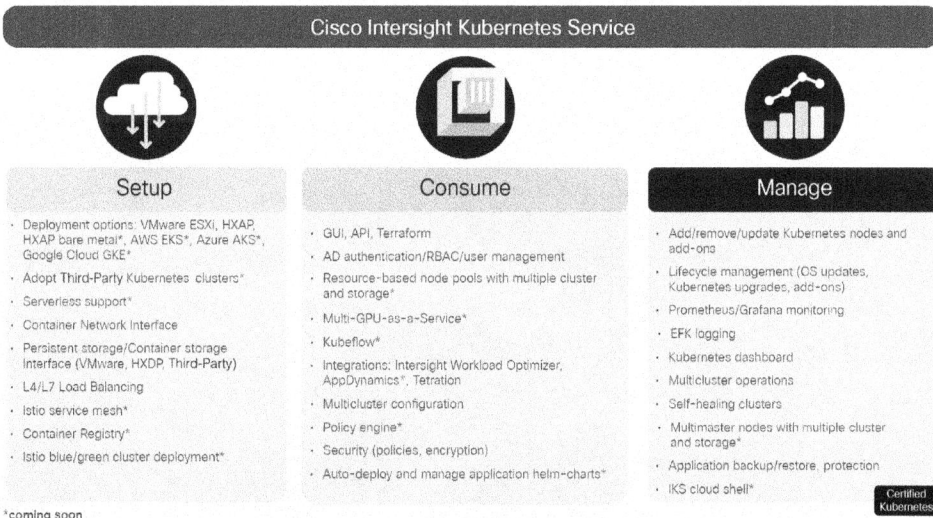

Figure 5-14   *Benefits of IKS*

IKS Release Model

IKS software follows a continuous-delivery release model that delivers features and maintenance releases. This approach enables Cisco to introduce stable and feature-rich software releases in a reliable and frequent manner that aligns with Kubernetes supported releases.

Intersight Kubernetes Service Release and Support Model:

- The IKS team supports releases from N-1 versions of Kubernetes. The team will not fully support/make available IKS versions older than N-1.

- IKS follows a fix-forward model that requires release upgrades to fix issues. Release patches are not necessary with this model.

- Tenant images are versioned according to which version of Kubernetes they contain.

Deploy Kubernetes from Intersight

The Intersight policies allow simplified deployments, as they abstract the configuration into reusable templates. The following sections outline the steps involved in deploying Kubernetes from Intersight.

Step 1: Configure Policies

All policies are created under the **Configure > Polices & Configure > Pools** section on Intersight. You can see the path of the policy at the top of each of the following figures.

1. The IP Pool will be used for IP addresses on your Control and Worker nodes virtual machines, when launched on the ESXi host. Figure 5-15 illustrates the IPv4 Pool details for policy configuration.

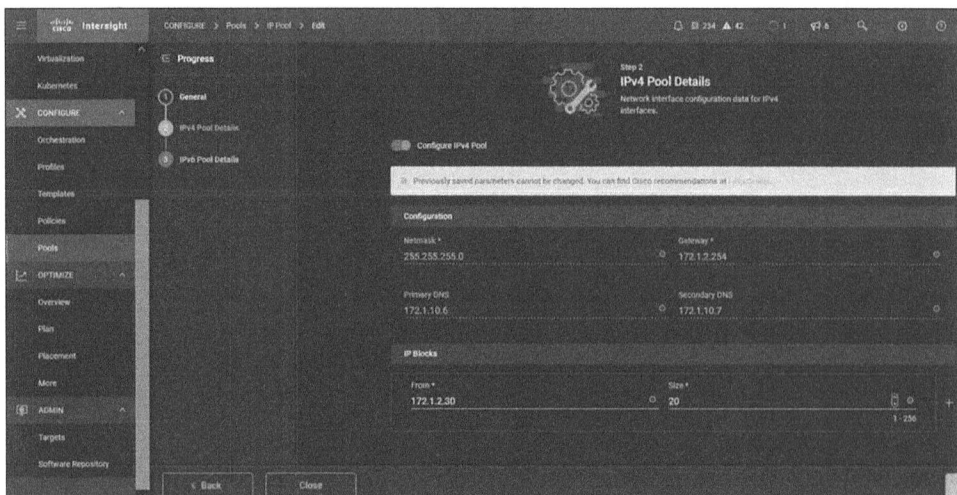

Figure 5-15 *IPv4 Pool details for policy configuration*

2. The Pod and Services Network CIDR is defined for internal networking within the Kubernetes cluster. Figure 5-16 illustrates the CIDR network to be used for the pods and services.

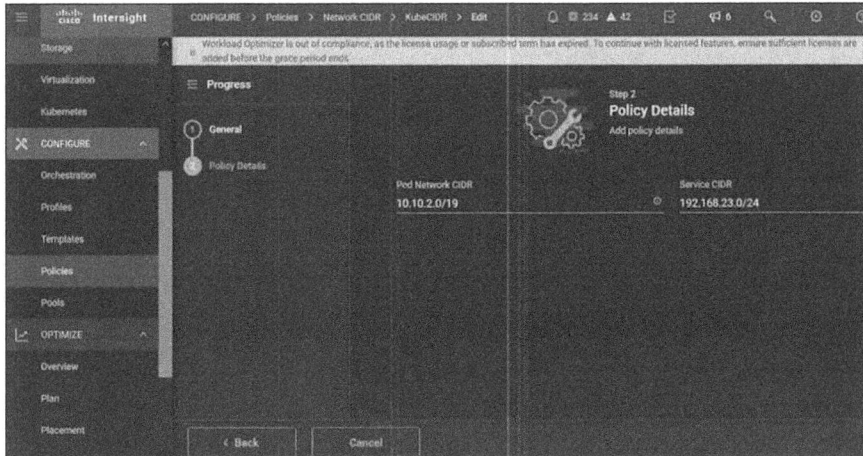

Figure 5-16   *CIDR network to be used for the pods and services*

3. The DNS and NTP configuration policy defines your NTP and DNS configuration (see Figure 5-17).

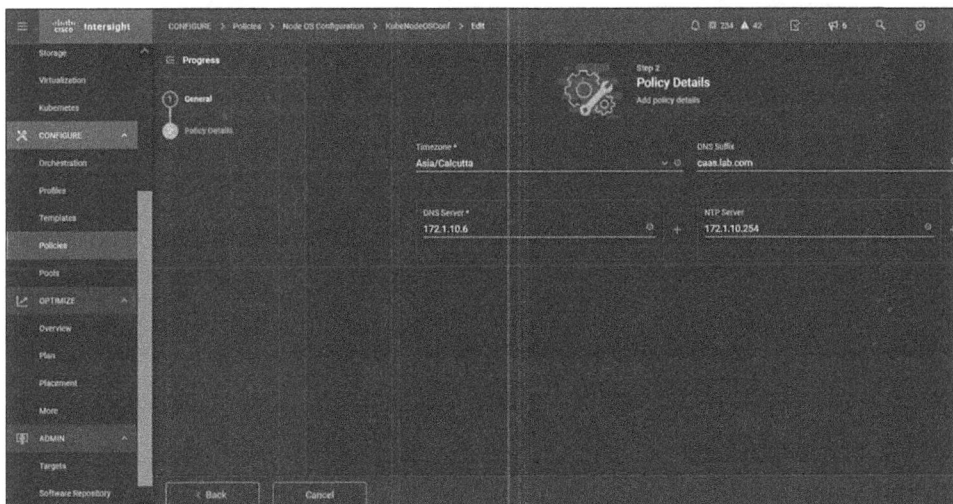

Figure 5-17   *DNS and NTP configuration policy*

4. You can define the proxy configuration policy for your Docker container runtime. Figure 5-18 illustrates this policy.

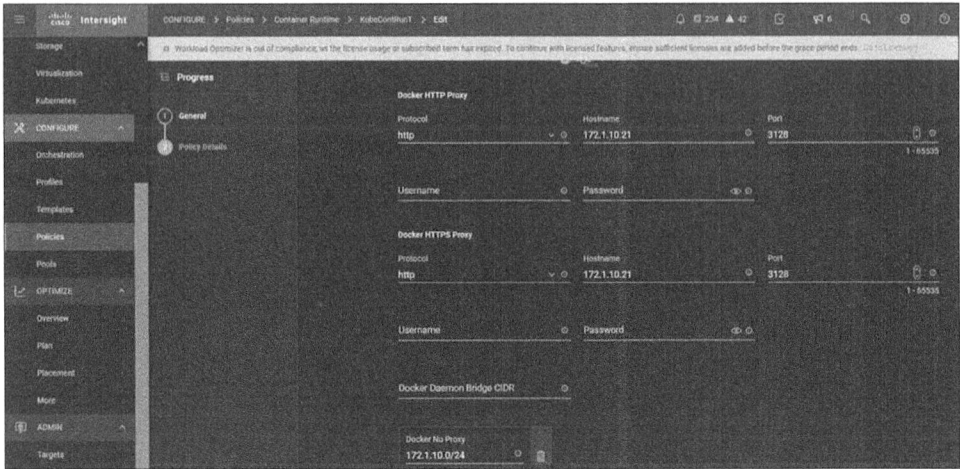

Figure 5-18 *Policy for configuring a proxy for Docker*

5. In the master and worker node VM policy, you define the configuration needed on the virtual machines deployed as Master and Worker nodes (see Figure 5-19).

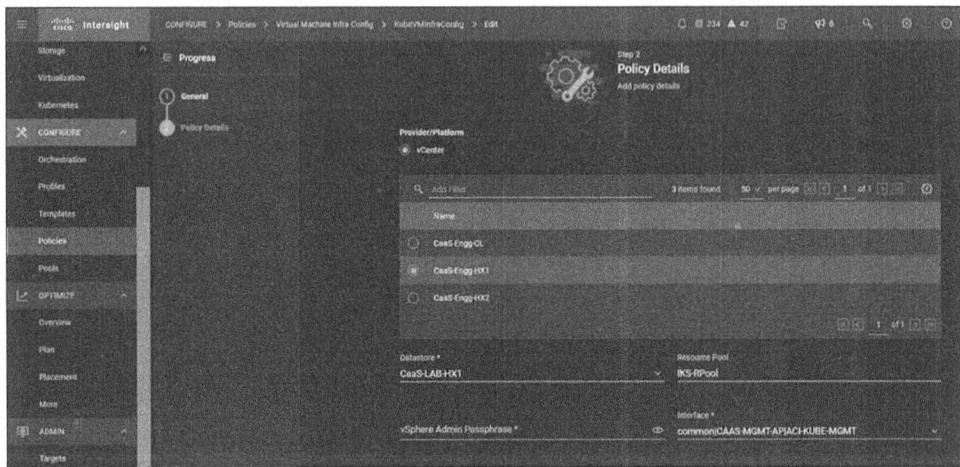

Figure 5-19 *Master and worker node VM policy*

Step 2: Configure Profile

Once we have created the preceding policies, you would then bind them into a profile that you can then deploy.

Deploying the configuration using policies and profiles abstracts the configuration layer so that it can be repeatedly deployed quickly.

1. You can copy this profile and create a new one with modifications on the underlying policies within minutes, to one or more Kubernetes clusters, in a fraction of the time needed for the manual process. Figure 5-20 illustrates the name and tag configuration in the profile.

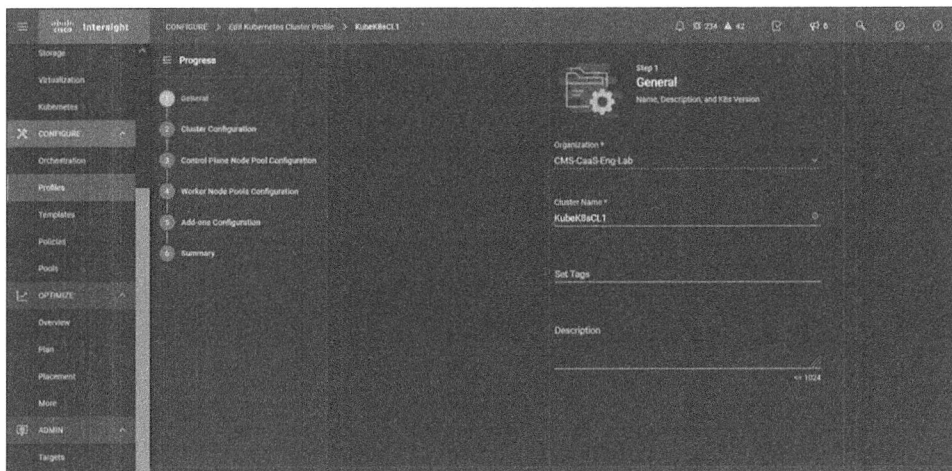

Figure 5-20 *Name and tag configuration in the profile*

2. Set the Pool, Node OS, and Network CIDR policies. You also need to configure a user ID and SSH key (public). Its corresponding private key would be used to ssh into the Master and Worker nodes. Figure 5-21 illustrates the created policies being referred to in the profile.

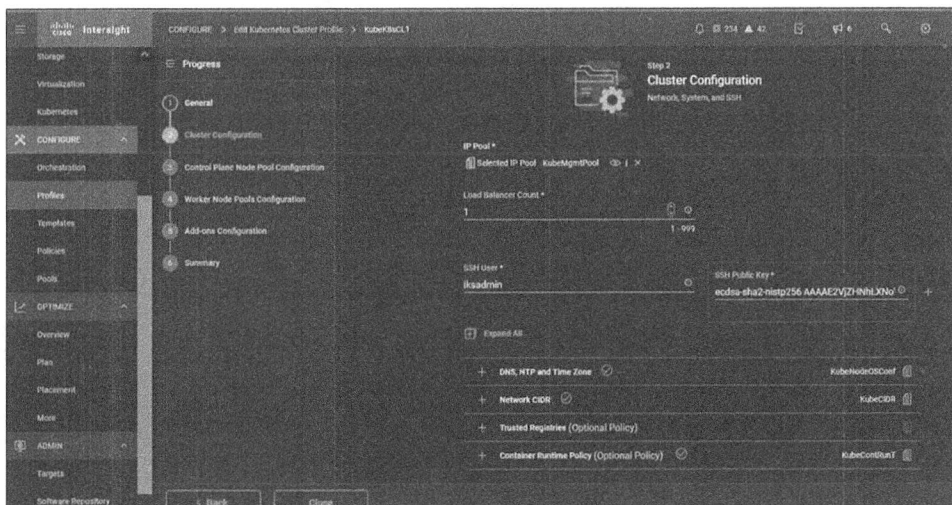

Figure 5-21 *Created policies being referred to in the profile*

3. Configure the control plane. You can define how many Master nodes you would need on the control plane. Figure 5-22 illustrates the K8s cluster configuration and number of Master nodes.

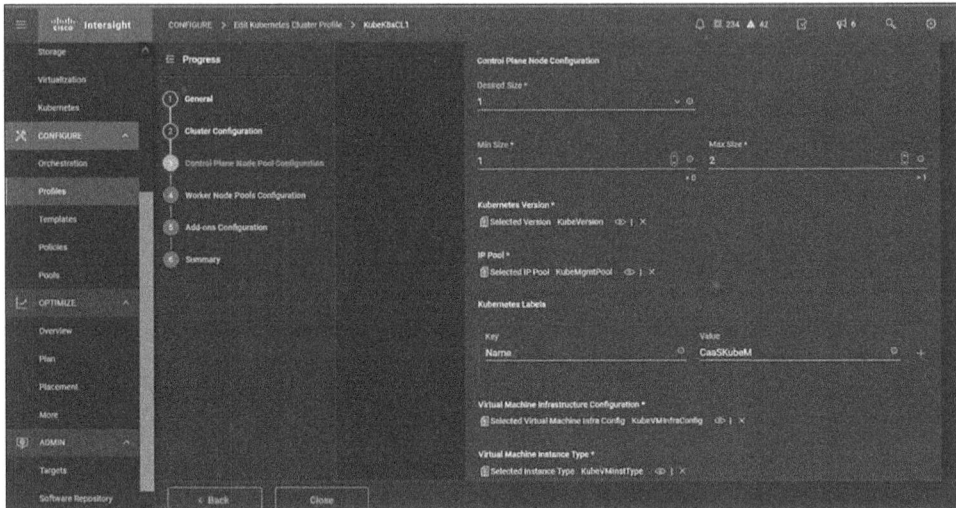

Figure 5-22   *Cluster configuration and number of Master nodes*

4. Configure the Worker nodes. Depending on the application requirements, you can scale up or scale down your Worker nodes. Figure 5-23 illustrates the K8s cluster configuration and number of Worker nodes.

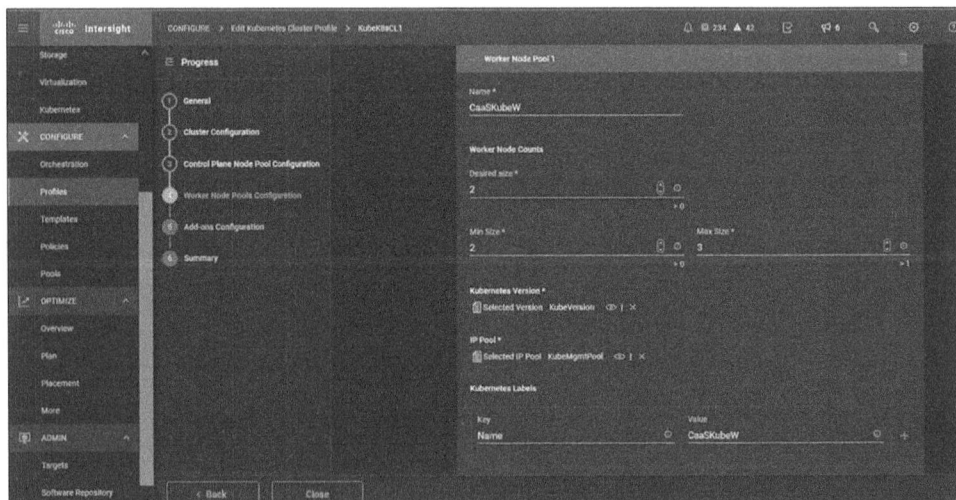

Figure 5-23   *Cluster configuration and number of Worker nodes*

5. Configure add-ons. As of now, you can automatically deploy Kubernetes Dashboard and Graffana with Prometheus monitoring. In the future, you can add more add-ons, which you can automatically deploy using IKS. Figure 5-24 illustrates the K8s cluster add-ons configuration.

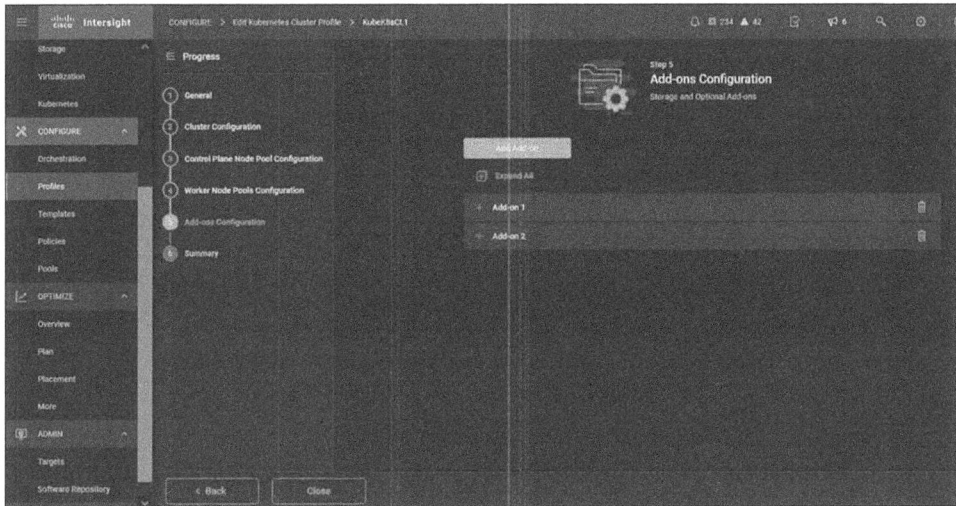

Figure 5-24   *Cluster add-ons configuration*

6. Check the **Summary** and click **Deploy**.

Figure 5-25 illustrates the K8s cluster **Summary and Deployment** screen.

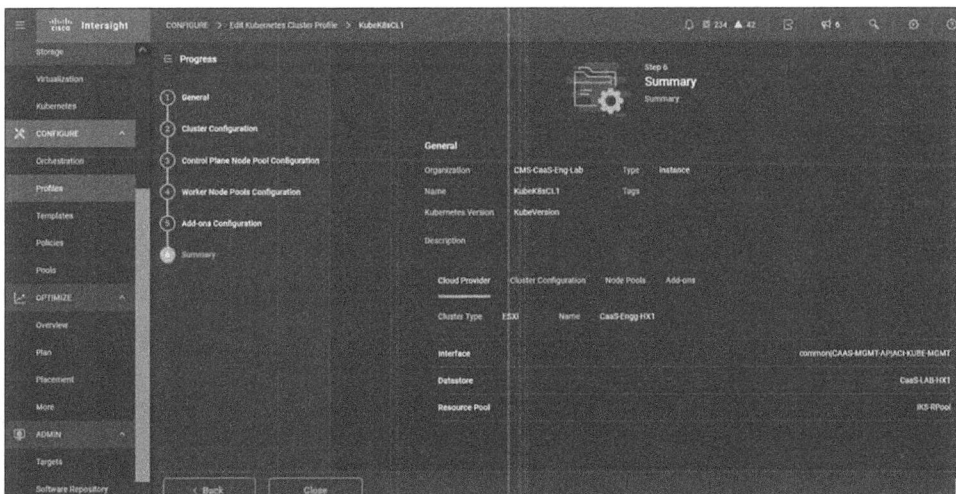

Figure 5-25   *Cluster Summary and Deployment screen*

Summary

Containers are the latest—and arguably one of the most powerful—technologies to emerge over the past few years to change the way we develop, deploy, and manage applications. The days of the massive software release are quickly becoming a thing of the past. In their place are continuous development and upgrade cycles that are allowing a lot more innovation and quicker time to market, with a lot less disruption—for customers and IT organizations alike.

With these new Cisco solutions, you can deploy, monitor, optimize, and auto-scale your applications.

References/Additional Reading

cisco.com/c/en/us/products/collateral/cloud-systems-management/intersight-workload-optimizer/solution-overview-c22-744342.html

https://www.cisco.com/c/en/us/support/docs/cloud-systems-management/intersight/217640-configure-deployment-of-kubernetes-clust.html

https://blogs.cisco.com/cloud/ciscocontainerplatform

https://www.cisco.com/c/dam/global/en_uk/products/cloud-systems-management/pdfs/cisco-container-platform-at-a-glance.pdf

https://blogs.cisco.com/cloud/saas-based-kubernetes-lifecycle-management-an-introduction-to-intersight-kubernetes-service?ccid=cc001268

https://www.cisco.com/c/en/us/products/collateral/cloud-systems-management/intersight/at-a-glance-c45-744332.html

https://www.cisco.com/c/en/us/support/docs/cloud-systems-management/intersight/217640-configure-deployment-of-kubernetes-clust.html

Chapter 6

Cisco Cloud Webex Application

Collaboration is a key component of any IT solution, and Cisco Webex provides an ideal platform for staying connected and collaborating with individuals, teams, and meetings to move projects forward faster. In this chapter, we are going to cover the Cisco Webex application, which provides new and advanced features in instant messaging and presence, voice and video communication, business-to-business communication, Public Switched Telephone Network (PSTN) access, mobile and remote access, and web conferencing and meetings. We cover these topics in detail in the following sections.

Cisco Webex Features

Cisco Webex is a cloud collaboration platform that provides messaging, calling, and meeting features. Cisco Webex Teams is a client application that connects to this platform and provides a comprehensive tool for teamwork. Users can send messages, share files, and meet with different teams, all in one place. Figure 6-1 lists the top collaboration priorities.

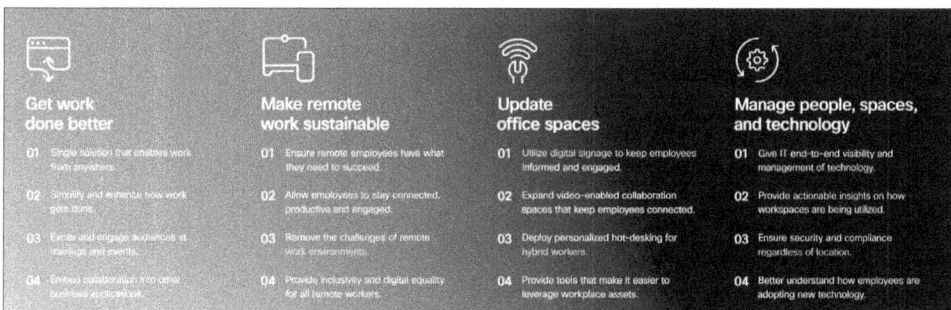

Figure 6-1 *Top collaboration priorities*

Cisco Webex Suite gives today's increasingly distributed organizations a seamless way to collaborate. It's one unified offering for calling, meetings, messaging, polling, events, and more.

The Webex Suite is comprehensive enough to address the collaboration needs of every type of business, yet adaptable to accommodate future needs. It delivers AI-driven intelligence that creates ever more engaging and inclusive collaboration experiences, enterprise-grade security that ensures your data is always protected, and frictionless deployment and management. Figure 6-2 shows the features of Webex Suite.

Figure 6-2   *Webex Suite*

Webex is one easy-to-use and secure app for calling, messaging, meeting, and getting work done. It has the following features:

- In-meeting reactions with emojis and hand gestures let you express yourself nonverbally and bring a little fun into your meetings.

- Immersive share lets you use your presentation or screen as your virtual background, giving participants an impressive viewing experience.

- Webex Assistant, your in-meeting digital assistant, provides live translations into 10 languages.

- With artificial intelligence (AI), Webex surfaces your most important messages to the top so you can be more productive. You can also personalize Webex spaces with colors, images, and co-branding.

- Move a 1:1 telephone call into a Webex video meeting and take advantage of AI transcriptions, notes and action items, and recordings.

Webex Cloud Calling

Cloud Calling enables your team to work from anywhere with complete call control capabilities that are easy to procure, onboard, and manage through a central management portal. You can experience enterprise-grade calling features and crystal-clear audio and video with robust security that is globally available in every major region at an affordable price. What's more, you can transition to the cloud at your own pace with migration strategies that are tailored to you, and you can even leverage on-premises investments. You can also discover how your teams work with advanced analytics and accurate performance indicators. This gives you timely and actionable data insights that can improve performance and productivity. Figure 6-3 shows a secure and reliable cloud call.

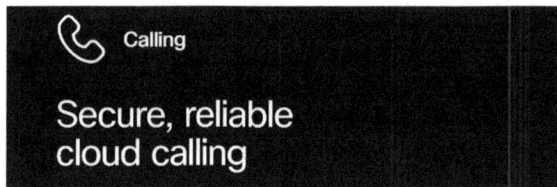

Figure 6-3   *Webex Calling*

A complete and connected cloud phone service that integrates with your collaboration tools, Cloud Calling and Collaboration provides businesses with the flexibility, reliability, and security needed to power hybrid work in today's global economy. Critical factors to consider when migrating to the cloud include the following:

- A complete collaboration experience
- Calling and device innovation
- Migration flexibility
- PSTN options

Cloud Calling covers all the bases—merging, call waiting, holding, forwarding, do not disturb, visual voicemail, and more. Figure 6-4 shows the Webex Calling features.

Webex Calling allows you to elevate a call to a meeting. You can move your call from one device to another or turn it into a video meeting instantaneously. Webex Calling also allows you to take more business calls with a phone menu, extensions, and intelligent call-routing features. All of this, with increased built-in security that allows you to stay connected and secure. Figure 6-5 shows the Webex voicemail feature.

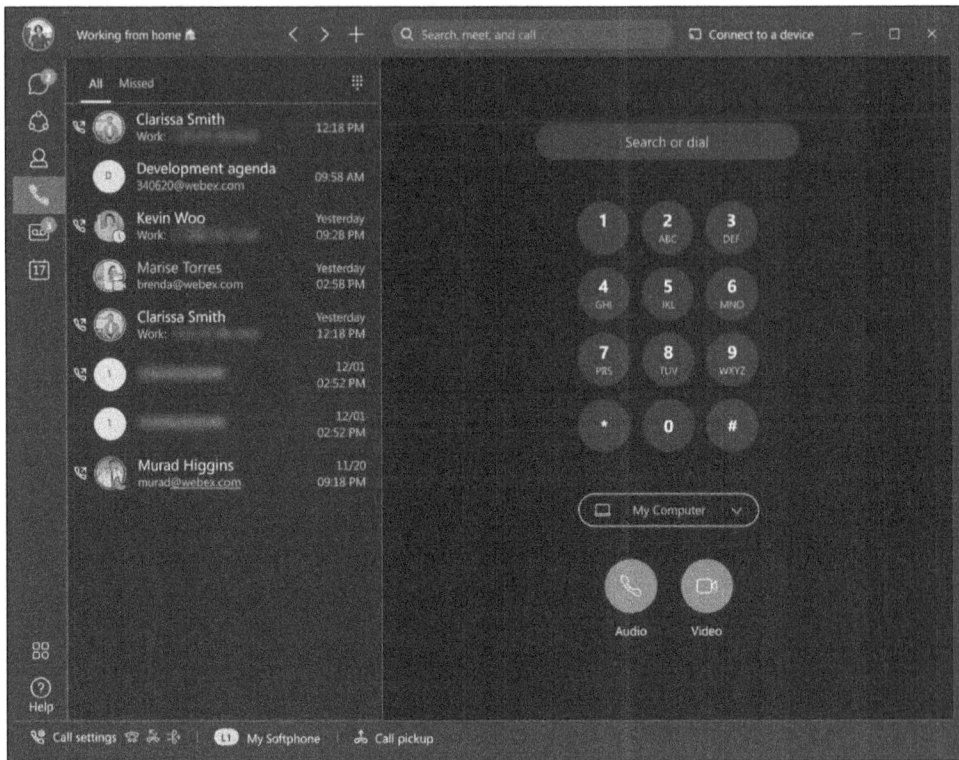

Figure 6-4   *Webex Calling features*

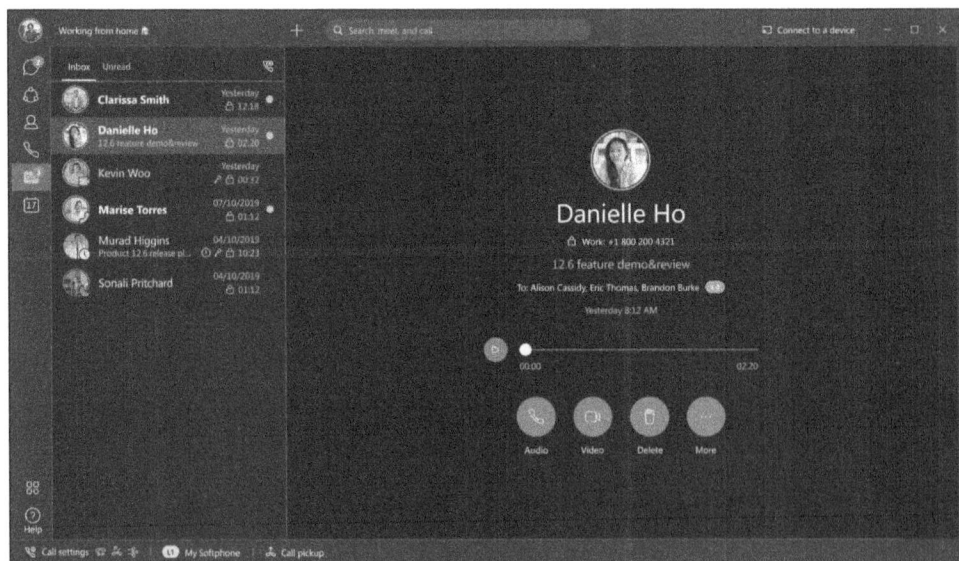

Figure 6-5   *Webex Calling voicemail*

Figure 6-6 shows the Webex Calling phone app.

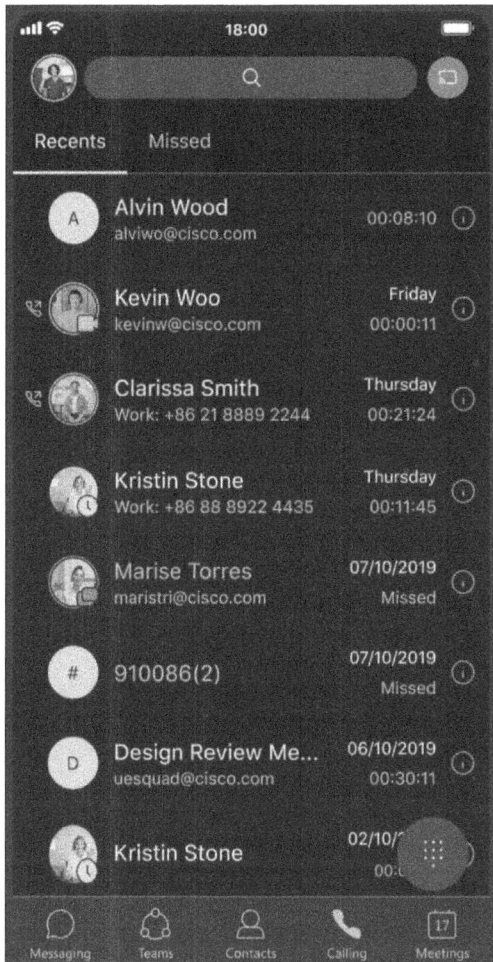

Figure 6-6   *Webex Calling phone app*

Webex Security Model

The Webex security model is built on the same security foundation deeply engraved in Cisco's processes. The Webex organization consistently follows the foundational elements to securely develop, operate, and monitor Webex services. We will discuss some of these elements in detail in the next part of this chapter. Figure 6-7 illustrates the Webex security model.

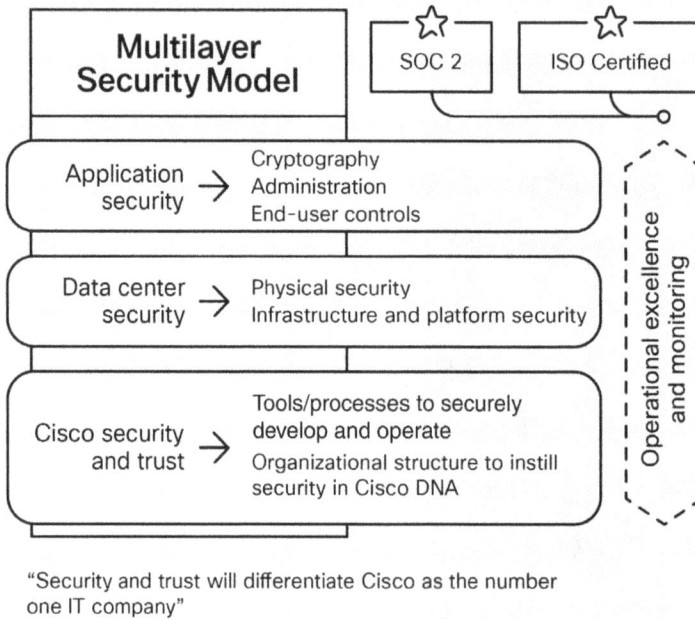

"Security and trust will differentiate Cisco as the number one IT company"

Figure 6-7   *Webex security model*

Webex Meetings

You can create more interactive and engaging meetings with innovations like emoji reactions, gesture recognition, immersive share, and next-gen polling by Slido, as well as take advantage of intelligent, AI-driven innovations like background noise cancellation, speech enhancement, recordings, and transcriptions so you can get more done with fewer meetings. Give everyone an equal seat at the table with inclusive features that enable everyone to be seen, heard, and understood with features like real-time language translation, breakout sessions, and moderated Q&A. Figure 6-8 shows the Webex Meetings feature.

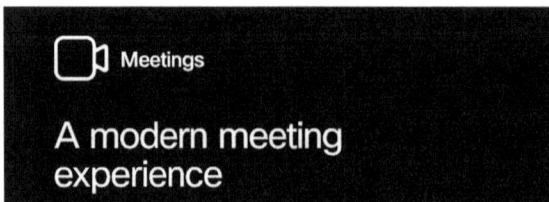

Figure 6-8   *Webex Meetings*

Customize Your Audio and Video Preferences

When you join a meeting from your computer, the app automatically detects the audio and video devices you have connected to your computer, such as a headset. You can change your settings right before you start or join a meeting, like if you want your video on or want to dial into a meeting with audio only. You can also make some of these preferences your default settings, if you'd like. Figure 6-9 shows Webex Meetings audio and video preferences.

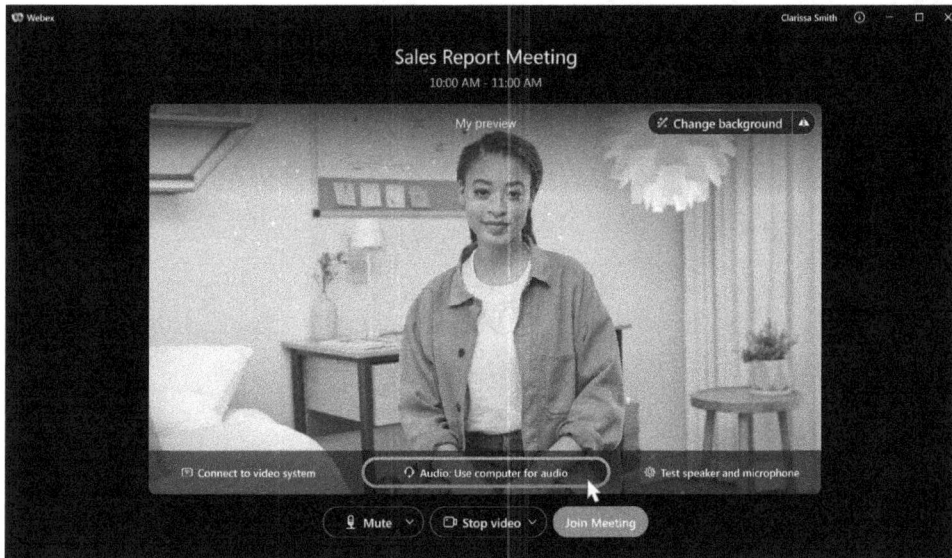

Figure 6-9 *Webex Meetings audio and video preferences*

You can customize your video settings as follows:

- Choose what camera to use.
- See yourself like you're looking in a mirror (Mirror My Video).
- Blur your background or use a preset or custom virtual background.

Figure 6-10 shows the Webex Meetings Settings menu.

You can also personalize your audio settings:

- Choose a headset, speaker, or microphone.
- Reduce disruptions with background noise removal and speech enhancement.

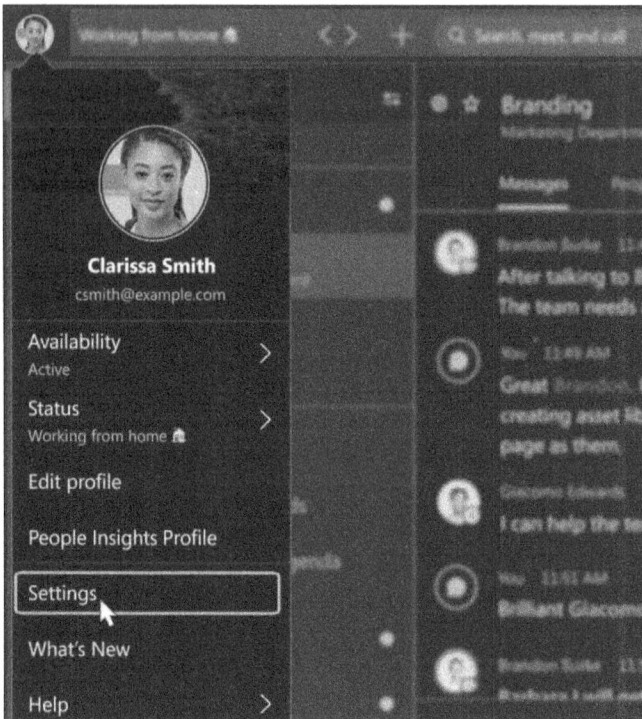

Figure 6-10 *Webex Meetings Settings menu*

Start Your First Meeting

With the Webex app, you can meet whenever you need to—right away or later. There are two ways to start or schedule your meetings in the app: either from the calendar or from your spaces. No matter which you choose, you can connect with video or just audio, record your meeting, set your virtual background, get rid of distracting background noise, and share your screen during your meeting.

From a Space

If you're already working together in a space, anyone can start an instant meeting to meet right away or schedule one for later. With these types of meetings, everyone in the space gets invited automatically and gets treated like a host. Therefore, during the meeting, everyone can let people in, mute people, and record. Since you're meeting in the same space where you're working, you get easy access to your messages, files, and whiteboards, and you can work on them while you're in the meeting.

From a Calendar

From your Meetings calendar, you can start a meeting right away in your Personal Room. You'll see this option if you have a host license, and it gives you a virtual conference room assigned just to you. Because it's your own room, your link is always the same.

If you don't see that choice, you can still schedule a meeting with anyone else. You don't need to be connected to them in the app, and they don't even need to have a Webex account. Plus, you or anyone you assign as a co-host can start the meeting, invite people to it, start breakout sessions, enable recording transcripts, and more. Figure 6-11 shows how to schedule a Webex meeting from the Webex app.

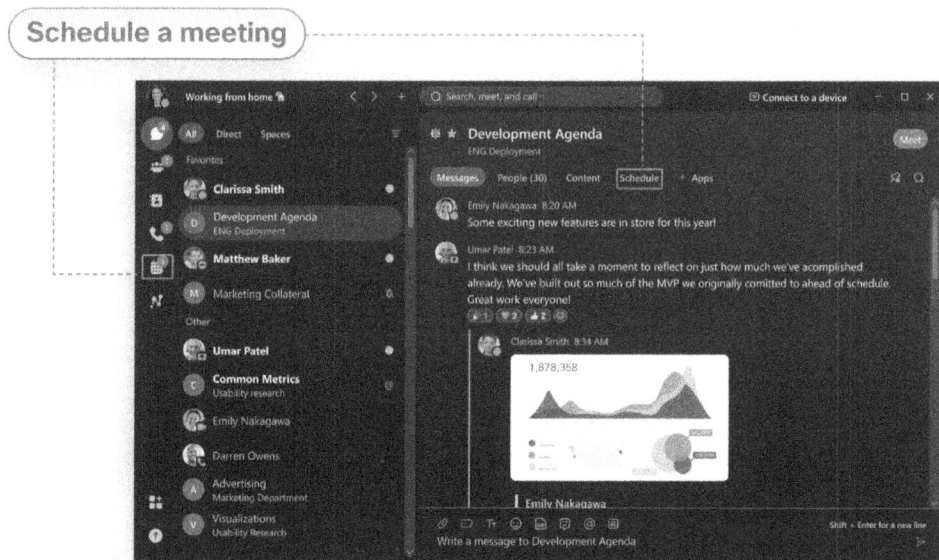

Figure 6-11   *Scheduling a Webex meeting*

Upcoming Meetings

Knowing what meetings you have can help you plan your workday. You can view details about your upcoming meetings in your meetings list, such as what the meeting is about, when it's happening, who's invited, and who scheduled the meeting. When it's time for a meeting to start, you can join it from the meetings list, too. Figure 6-12 shows upcoming meetings in Webex.

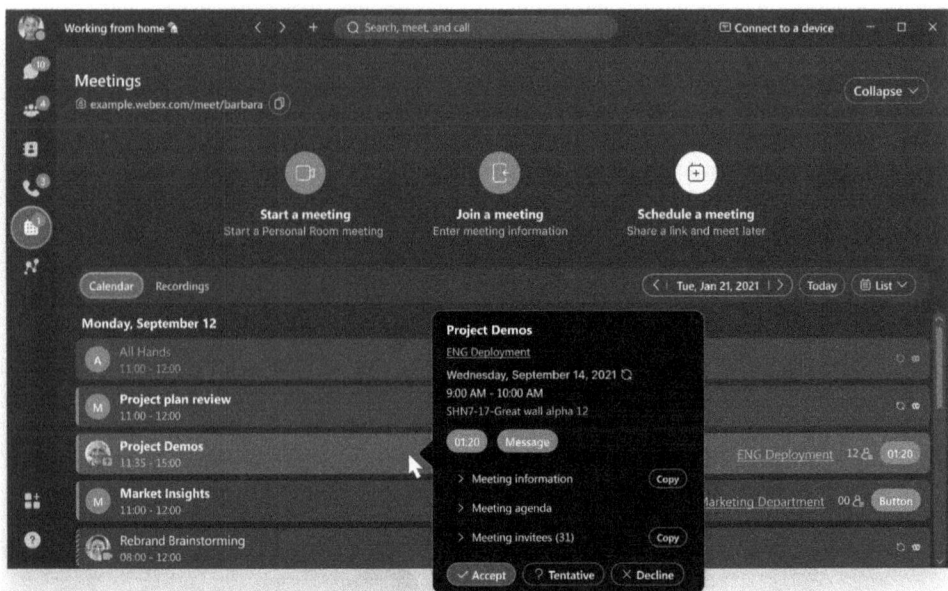

Figure 6-12   *Upcoming meetings in Webex*

Webex Meetings Security Update

Webex Meetings provides the highest level of security in the industry based on a simple product development methodology: secure by design, and not as an afterthought. Considering recent events in the video conferencing industry, where malicious actors have been disrupting users' meetings, Cisco has performed security audits of customers' site settings to help prevent such unwanted outcomes. Meetings are protected by passwords to provide the most secure experience for attendees joining using the Webex app on their desktop and mobile devices. Users who are signed into their Webex account will continue to join their meetings as quickly as before, and external users will be prompted for the meeting password before they can join meetings.

In addition, Webex has added additional security features:

- Automatically lock Personal Room after 10 minutes.

  Automatically locking your Personal Room meetings prevents unwanted people from joining your meetings. If you haven't already enabled it, Webex will now automatically lock your Personal Room 10 minutes after the meeting starts.

  When someone tries to join a locked meeting, they'll be asked to wait in your lobby, and you'll get a notification. You can decide if you want to admit them into the meeting or let them stay in the lobby. Figure 6-13 shows how Webex automatically locks a Personal Room Webex meeting.

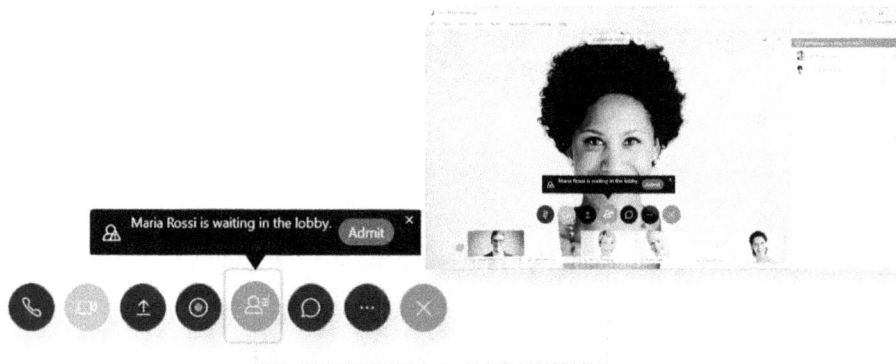

Figure 6-13 *Locking Personal Room Webex meeting*

- Enforce meeting password when joining from phone or video conferencing systems.

  Users joining your meetings using a telephone or a video conferencing system will now be required to enter a numeric meeting password before being admitted into the meeting. You'll find the numeric meeting password in the email invitation. The password cannot be disabled and overrides previously disabled password settings.

- When a meeting is in progress, the meeting host (and co-host) using Webex apps or Webex devices are presented with messages to inform them of new users in the lobby as well as controls to admit these users to the meeting or remove them from the meeting/lobby. Users in the meeting lobby are grouped and managed in three categories:

  - **Internal:** Signed-in (authenticated) users in your organization

  - **External:** Signed-in (authenticated) users outside of your organization

  - **Unverified users:** Unauthenticated guest users, whose identity is not verified

  Figure 6-14 shows participants in a meeting categorized as Internal, External, or Unverified.

Webex Messaging

Always-on messaging lets you minimize meetings, organize your thoughts, and actively engage—how you want and when you want—in an intelligent space that's personalized to you and your work style. With Webex, all your messages, contacts, files, content, and projects are stored and organized in a secure space—so you never miss a beat. Remove time barriers and silos that slow decision making and connect to all the people and business tools you need to do your job, from anywhere, anytime, on any device. Ensure a work–life balance with intuitive features that help you set boundaries. Set a custom status to show what you are working on, or set "do not disturb" to show when you are unavailable. Improve company culture with engaging and interactive features like animated reactions, GIFs, and more, which let participants express their personality. Figure 6-15 shows Webex Messaging.

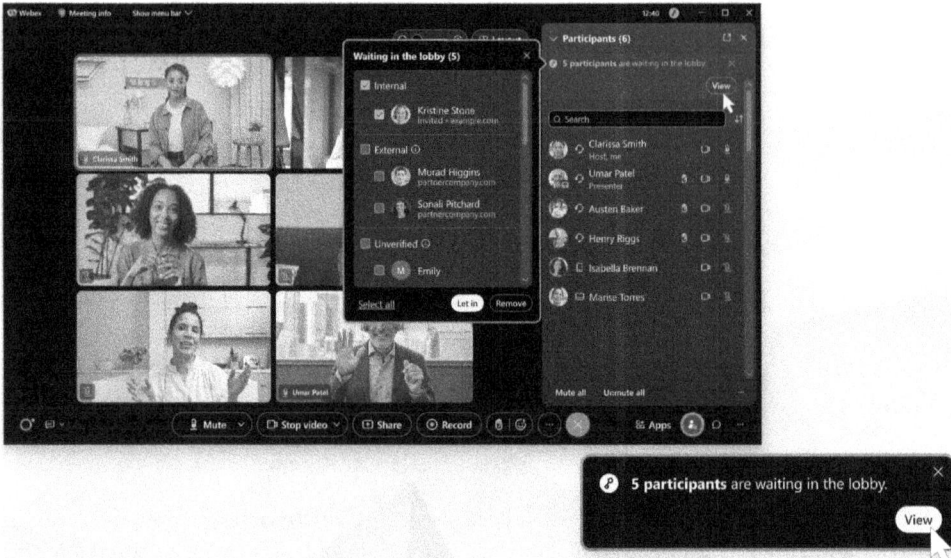

Figure 6-14   *Participants categorized as Internal, External, or Unverified*

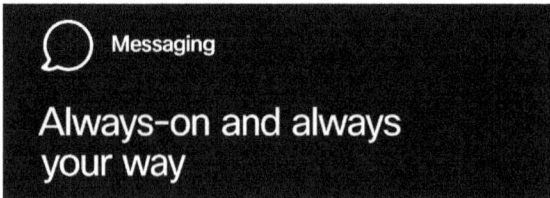

Figure 6-15   *Webex Messaging*

Send a Message

When you write your messages, you can send a quick one, or make it stand out with more text formatting and emojis. You can also share files, pictures, videos, and even GIFs. The Webex app keeps a list of all the content shared in a space, so you'll never lose track of them. Use @Mentions to make sure the right people see your message. Don't worry if you've made a mistake and need to edit it, or if you've pasted in the wrong space and need to delete the message entirely.

Your messages are persistent. The next time you message the group, your conversation picks right up where you've left it. And after you send a message, you can see who has read your message. Figure 6-16 shows the Webex Messaging features.

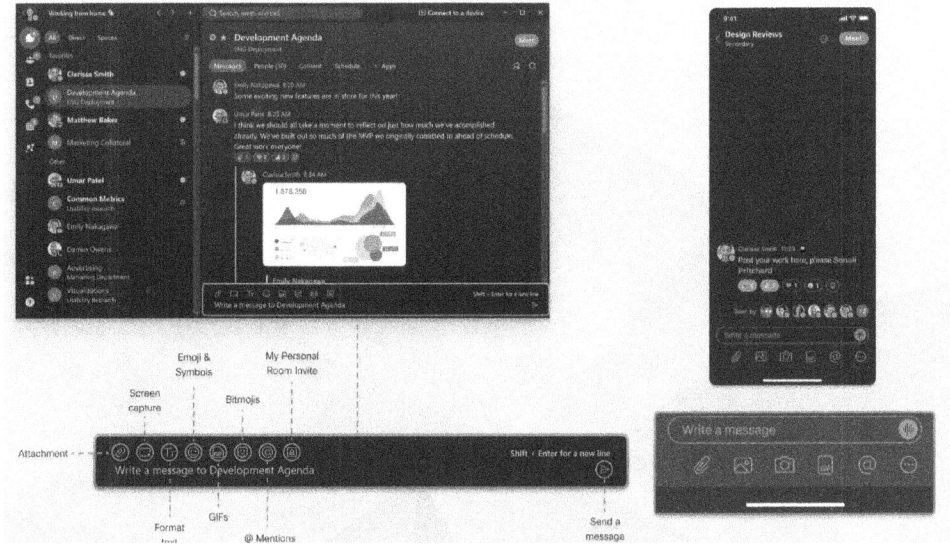

Figure 6-16 *Webex Messaging features*

Read and Respond to Messages

When you get a new message, you're notified right away. If you're too busy to respond but want to see someone's message, you can just take a quick peek instead. People won't know that you've seen the message.

You can also make it easy for yourself and others to follow a specific train of thought using threading, quotes, and even the ability to forward a message to someone else.

Organize Your Messages

Another way to help keep yourself productive is by organizing your messages. You can change appearance, mark favorites that will show on top, and see a compact view. You can also filter your messages so that you can focus on just your unread messages, for example, or just spaces where you've been @Mentioned. There are many more options to organize your messages. Figure 6-17 shows the options for organizing messages in Webex.

You can also flag important messages so that you can refer to them easily. Figure 6-18 shows how to flag important messages in Webex.

And if you're looking for a message or a file that was shared but you can't remember what space it was posted in, you can search for it. Figure 6-19 shows how to search for a message or file.

Figure 6-17   *Organizing messages in Webex*

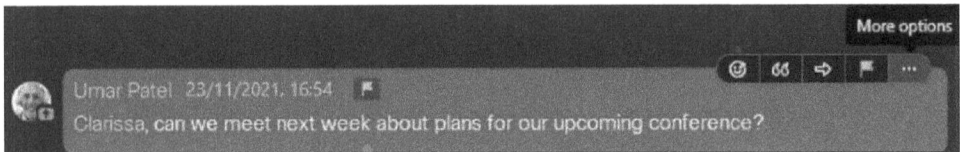

Figure 6-18   *Flagging messages in Webex*

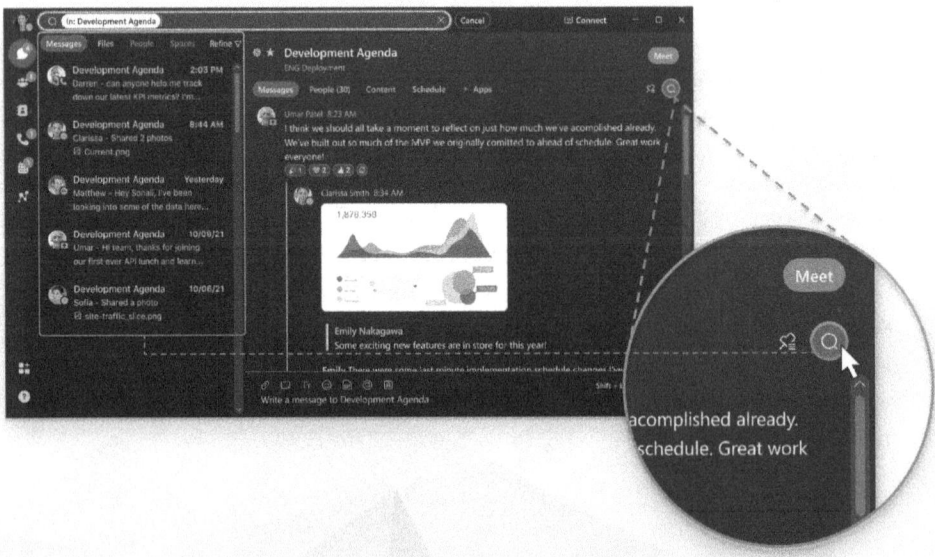

Figure 6-19   *How to search for a message or file*

Webex | App Security

Webex uses various security frameworks, including end-to-end encryption, to protect your data so your files and messages stay safe while in transit and when they're stored in the cloud. You can also manage who can access or view content in a space.

- Levels of encryption security

  - The Webex app encrypts messages, files, and names of spaces on your device before sending them to the cloud. When the data arrives at Cisco's servers, it's already encrypted. It's processed and stored until it's decrypted on your device. However, the app can't provide end-to-end encryption for messages and files linked to in-app automation tools like bots or integrations or to Adobe Acrobat PDF and Microsoft Word documents sent to spaces from Box.

  - Secure Hypertext Transfer Protocol (HTTPS) is used to encrypt data while in transit between your device and servers, which protects the identities of both senders and receivers.

  - The end-to-end encryption uses Advanced Encryption Standard (AES) 128, AES256, Secure Hash Algorithm (SHA) 1, SHA256, and RSA.

  - For audio, video, and screen sharing, Webex encrypts shared content using the Secure Real-Time Transport Protocol (SRTP).

- Security features in Webex spaces

  - You can add extra security by using moderators for teams and spaces. If teamwork is sensitive, you can moderate the space. Moderators can control who has access to the space and delete files and messages.

  - Also, if any spaces include people from outside your company, you'll see some areas in those spaces highlighted, like the border, background, the icon in the message area as well as their email addresses.

Figure 6-20 shows the security features in a Webex space.

- Privacy for files and messages

  - The Webex app uses advanced cryptographic algorithms to safeguard content you share and send. The only people who can view files and messages in a Webex space are those invited to that space or authorized individuals.

- Password security standards

  - IT teams can add features that use existing security policies like single sign-on (SSO) or synchronizing Webex with employee directories. Webex automatically recognizes when someone has left a company, so former employees won't be able to access company data using Webex.

  - Your company can also configure Webex so that it requires passwords and authentication that match your corporate security standards. The Webex app supports identity providers that use Security Assertion Markup Language (SAML) 2.0 and Open Authorization (OAuth) 2.0 protocols.

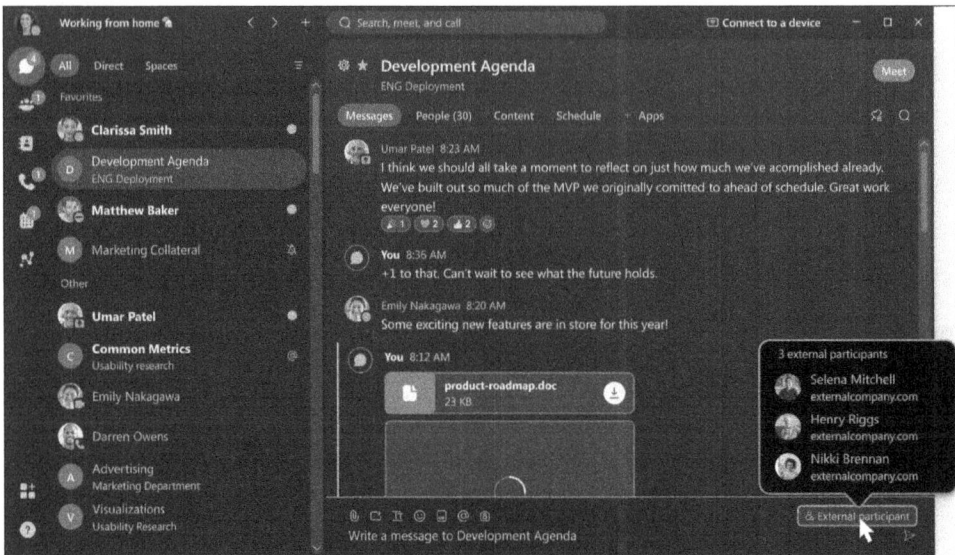

Figure 6-20   *Security feature in Webex space*

Webex Application Polling

Interact with participants, whether in the office or remote, before, during, and after meetings. Confirm participants' understanding of the meeting topics and address any areas of uncertainty. Streamline decision making by crowd-sourcing ideas from everyone and ensuring quick alignment on decisions.

Cisco Webex allows participants to view and upvote each other's questions. It also empowers everyone by creating a safe space for them to ask and answer questions anonymously. You can improve decision making by collecting feedback from everyone, not just the most vocal participants.

Cisco Webex also facilitates team bonding by allowing everyone to get to know their colleagues and coworkers better. You can create transparency across the whole company by enabling anyone to ask and answer questions, and you can build trust between leaders and employees by allowing them to ask any questions and address the most critical ones. Figure 6-21 shows Cisco Webex's Polling feature, which helps create a more engaging meeting.

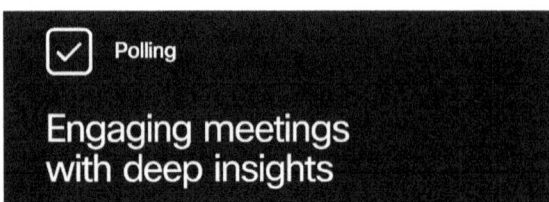

Figure 6-21   *Webex Polling*

Poll in Webex Meetings or Webex Webinars

Polling must be turned on for your meeting or webinar in **Advanced options > Scheduling options > Meeting options** or **Advanced options > Scheduling options > Webinar options.** Figure 6-22 shows Cisco Webex Polling on Windows.

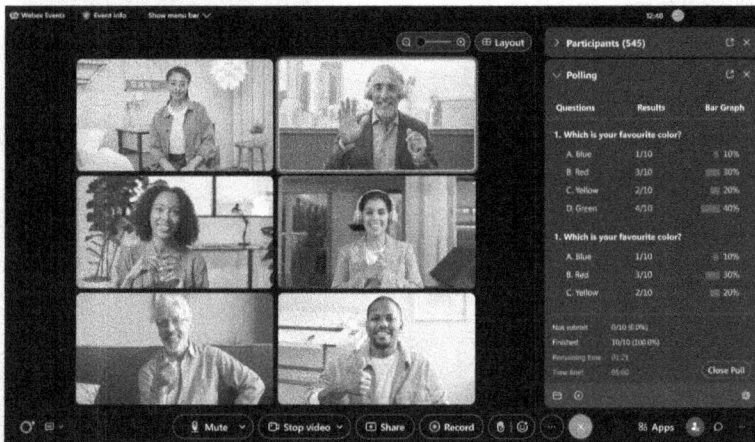

Figure 6-22   *Cisco Webex Polling on Windows*

Figure 6-23 shows Cisco Webex Polling on macOS.

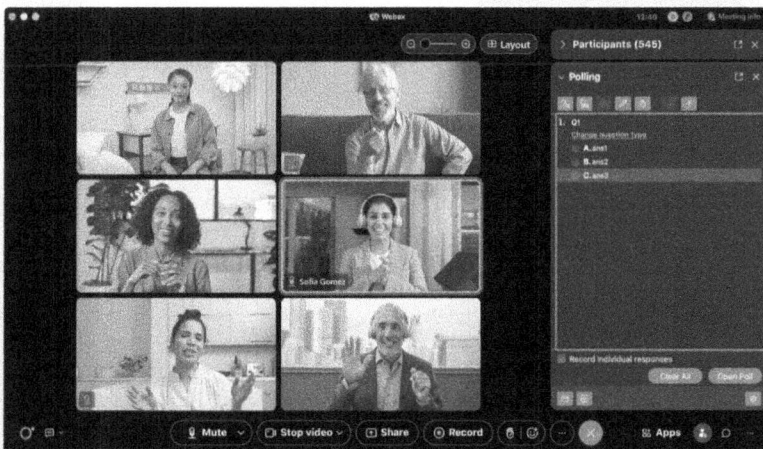

Figure 6-23   *Cisco Webex Polling on macOS*

Polls are a great way for meeting or webinar hosts to get input from participants. Use them to engage your audience, test knowledge, and ask for feedback.

Polls in Slido

Hosts can also use live polls with Slido to engage participants during a meeting or webinar. Figure 6-24 shows Cisco Webex Polling using Slido.

Figure 6-24   *Cisco Webex Polling using Slido*

Slido is available in Webex Meetings and Webex Webinars. You use can Slido in Webex Meetings on version 41.6 and later sites as well as in Webex Webinars on version 41.9 and later sites. Slido polls and Q&As in webinars are available for up to 10,000 attendees, while quizzes are available for up to 5,000 participants.

As a meeting or webinar host, you can create and launch polls directly from Meetings by clicking **Apps > Slido.** If you want to create polls before the meeting or webinar, add a guest collaborator to help you create and run the polls. Go to https://www.slido.com, click **Log In > Log in with Webex**, and enter your Webex username and password.

During the meeting or webinar, the host or guest collaborator can activate polls. Participants can view and answer the questions. There are a few different types of polls hosts can create, including single poll questions, quizzes, and surveys.

Here are the tasks you can perform as a host:

- Create a poll
- Create a survey

■ Edit or duplicate a poll

■ Activate a poll or activate a quiz

■ View poll results during a meeting

■ Reset a poll

■ Export and share poll results after a meeting

■ Delete a poll

In case you only want to use the Q&A during your meeting or webinar, you can turn off polls. Go to https://www.slido.com and click **Log In > Log in with Webex**.

Create a Poll in Slido

As a Webex Meetings or Webex Webinars host, you can create a poll to engage participants, gather their feedback, or test their knowledge. Figure 6-25 shows how to create a poll in Slido.

Figure 6-25   *Creating a poll in Slido*

Activate or Deactivate a Poll in Slido

As a Webex Meetings or Webex Webinars host, after you create a poll, you can let participants view and answer it. Figure 6-26 shows how to activate or deactivate a poll in Slido.

Figure 6-26   *How to activate or deactivate a poll in Slido*

Activate or Deactivate a Quiz in Slido

As a Webex Meetings or Webex Webinars host, after you create a quiz, you can let participants view and answer it. Figure 6-27 shows how to activate or deactivate a quiz in Slido.

Figure 6-27   *How to activate or deactivate a quiz in Slido*

Create a Survey in Slido

Surveys let Webex Meetings and Webex Webinars hosts ask multiple poll questions at the same time. You can group several polls, even of a different type, and let your participants respond to them at once. Figure 6-28 shows how to create a survey in Slido.

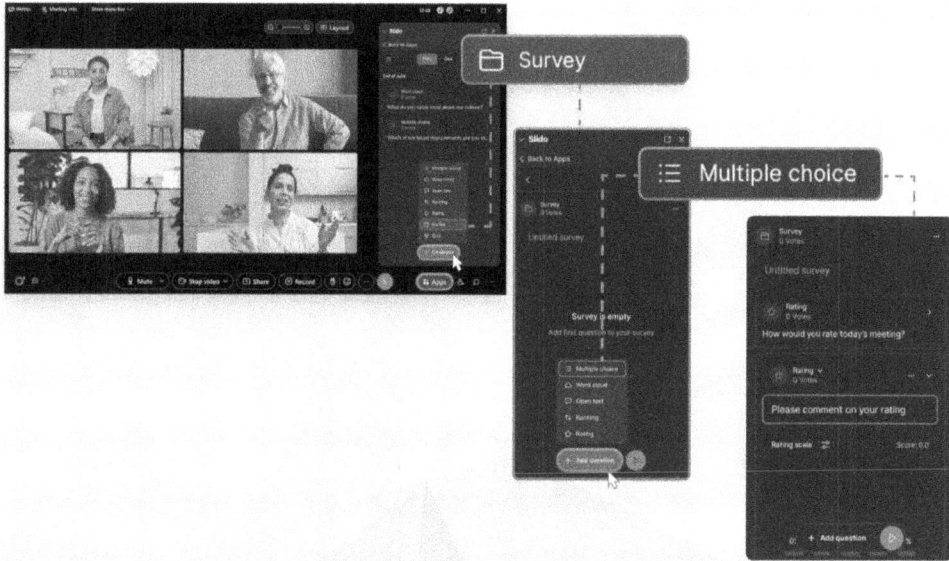

Figure 6-28   *Creating a survey in Slido*

Webex Events

The expanded Webex Events portfolio includes solutions for events of all types and sizes—from webinars to multi-session events, to conferences and community building. With the recent acquisition of Socio, Cisco has expanded its existing virtual event solutions to include end-to-end hybrid event management and new capabilities for ticketing, monetization, networking, and more.

Webex Events (formerly Webex Webinars) can be used to engage your audience through powerful, interactive online webinars. Figure 6-29 shows Cisco Webex Events (webinars).

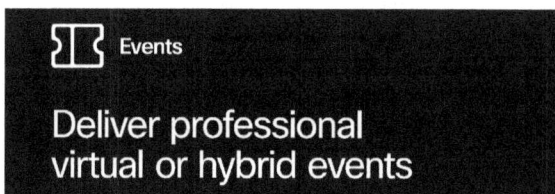

Figure 6-29   *Cisco Webex Events (webinars)*

Schedule Webex Webinars

As a host, you can schedule webinars. Webinars are interactive and highly engaging; if your event calls for a simpler attendee experience, webinars in webcast view are the way to go. You can get these scheduled quickly with the basics or take a little bit more time to customize your webinars using advanced options to tailor them to your needs. Figure 6-30 shows how to schedule Cisco Webex webinars.

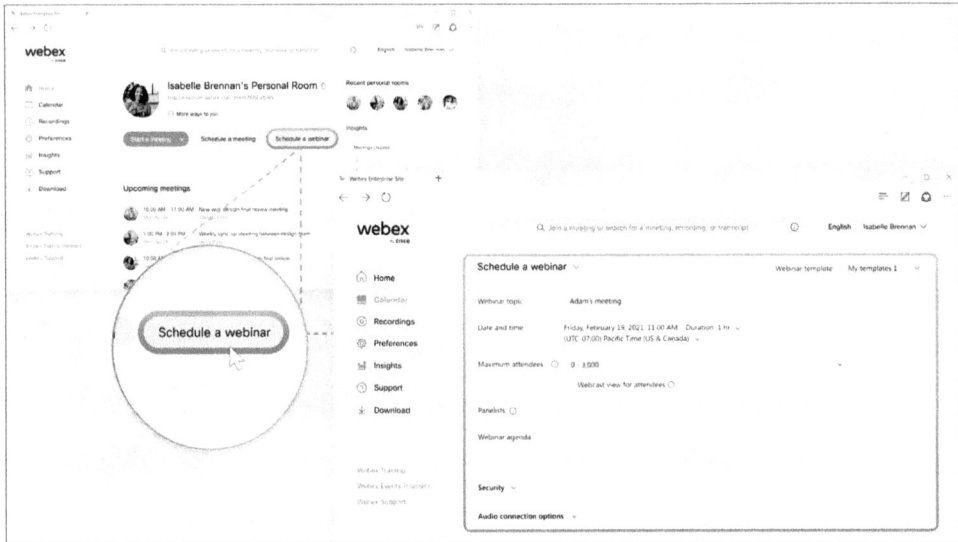

Figure 6-30 *How to schedule Cisco Webex webinars*

The number of people you can invite to a webinar depends on the license purchased. Webinars can include up to 10,000 people. A webinar in webcast view is required if you have more than 10,000 attendees.

After you schedule a webinar, you get a confirmation email as well as an email to forward to attendees.

Register for a Meeting or Webinar

You can require that attendees of Webex meetings and webinars register before they can join. This provides enhanced security and allows you to obtain information from your attendees. When you require that your attendees register for a meeting or webinar, you can do the following before and during the session:

- View a list of attendees to determine whether they have registered for the meeting or webinar.

■ Obtain attendees' names, email addresses, and other information before they can join the meeting or webinar.

■ Accept or reject individual registration requests.

Figure 6-31 shows how to manage Cisco Webex webinar registration.

Figure 6-31   *Manage Cisco Webex webinar registration*

If you invite someone to a meeting or webinar that requires registration, they receive an email that includes the following:

■ Information about the meeting or webinar

■ A link to register for the meeting or webinar

■ A random registration ID for the webinar, if you selected this option

Join a Webinar

You can join a Webex webinar on your computer, mobile device, browser, and more. Figure 6-32 shows how to join a Cisco Webex webinar.

Figure 6-32 *How to join a Cisco Webex webinar*

Webex | Record a Meeting

You can record meetings for people who can't attend or for those who want to refer to what was discussed. Your recordings can be saved either to the cloud or your computer as a local recording. Figure 6-33 shows how to record a Cisco Webex.

Figure 6-33 *How to record a Cisco Webex*

There are two ways to record meetings, webinars, and events. Your account type and Webex site configuration determine which recording method you can use, as detailed in Table 6-1.

Table 6-1 *Recording Options with Cisco Webex*

Recording Method	Webex Plan
Record meetings in the cloud	Webex Free plan: Not available
	Webex Starter, Plus, and Business plans: Available
	Enterprise plans: Configured by Webex site administrator
Record meetings on your computer	Webex Free, Starter, Plus, and Business plans: Available
	Enterprise plans: Configured by Webex site administrator

Share Content in Meetings, Webinars, and Events

You can keep everyone informed and engaged in Webex meetings, webinars, and events (classic) by sharing nearly any type of content. Share your entire screen, video from a USB camera, or specific files and applications that you choose. Figure 6-34 shows how to share content in Cisco Webex.

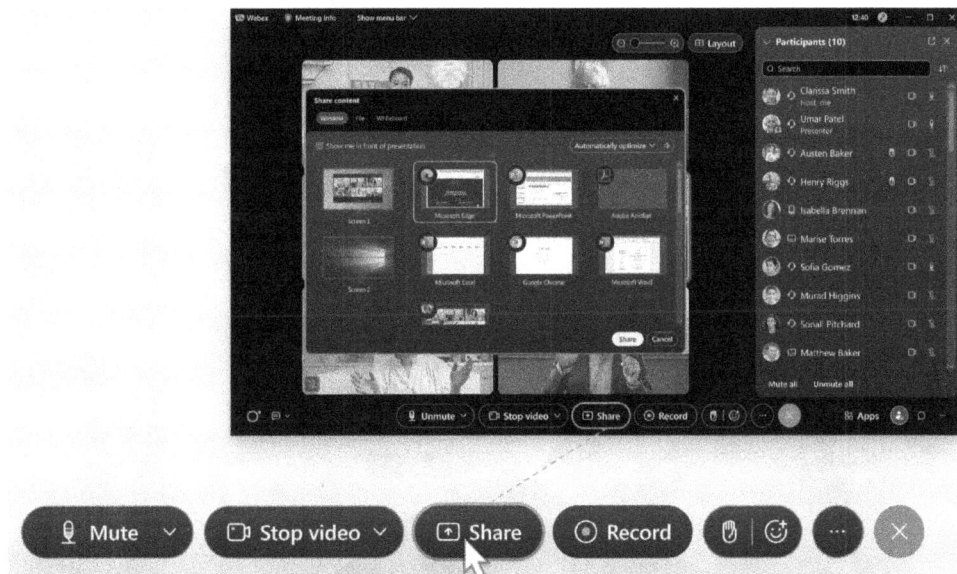

Figure 6-34 *How to share content in Cisco Webex*

Anyone in a meeting, as well as a presenter in a webinar or event, can share content. If you move an open window over the shared application, nobody can see it, but you can show your camera video over the shared application.

Sharing Multiple Applications

You can share multiple applications without having to stop what you're currently sharing. To share an additional app while currently sharing, click **Share** and then select **Share Content.** Figure 6-35 shows how to share multiple content in Cisco Webex.

Figure 6-35   *How to share multiple content in Cisco Webex*

When you're sharing content, you want to make sure you're sharing only what you want and that everyone in the meeting can see it. When you share your screen or an application, check what everyone else sees by opening a window that shows you what you're sharing.

While sharing, go to the tab in the meeting control bar at the top of the screen and click the down arrow. Figure 6-36 shows how to see what you are sharing.

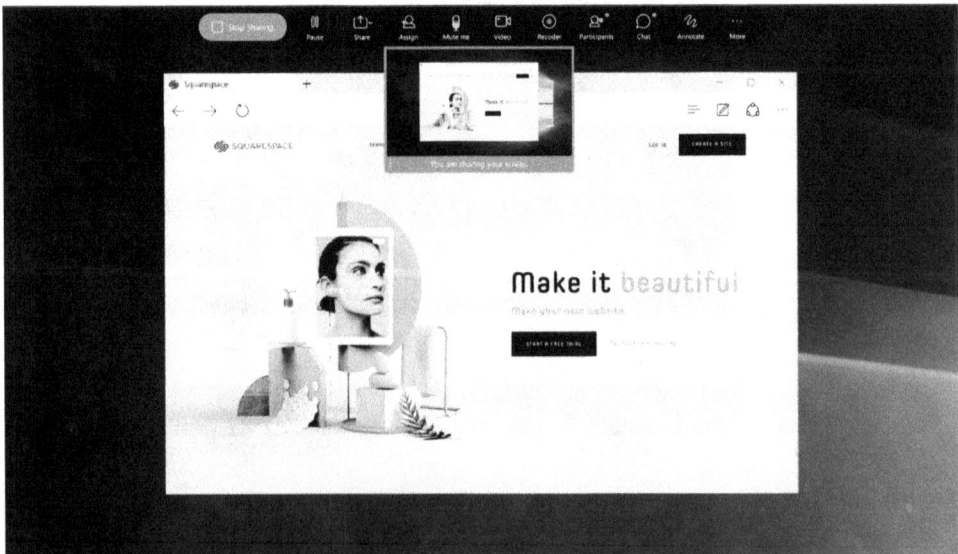

Figure 6-36   *How to see what you are sharing*

Webex Integrations

Webex integrates with hundreds of industry-leading apps and tools so you can get more done. Webex helps unlock frictionless collaboration with apps right inside Webex. Instead of toggling between a thousand windows, you can now use Webex collaboration experience with your favorite apps integrated right inside Webex meetings and messaging.

Simplify your daily routines, accelerate business outcomes, and automate everyday tasks using Webex App bots and integrations. Connect your favorite tools to Webex App and get notified when tasks are done, follow up on team status, or simply translate a message.

All Webex App users can browse through the available list in the Webex App Hub and choose a bot or an integration. The bots and integrations are grouped into categories (for example, customer relations and developer tools). Figure 6-37 shows the Webex App Hub and some of the available apps.

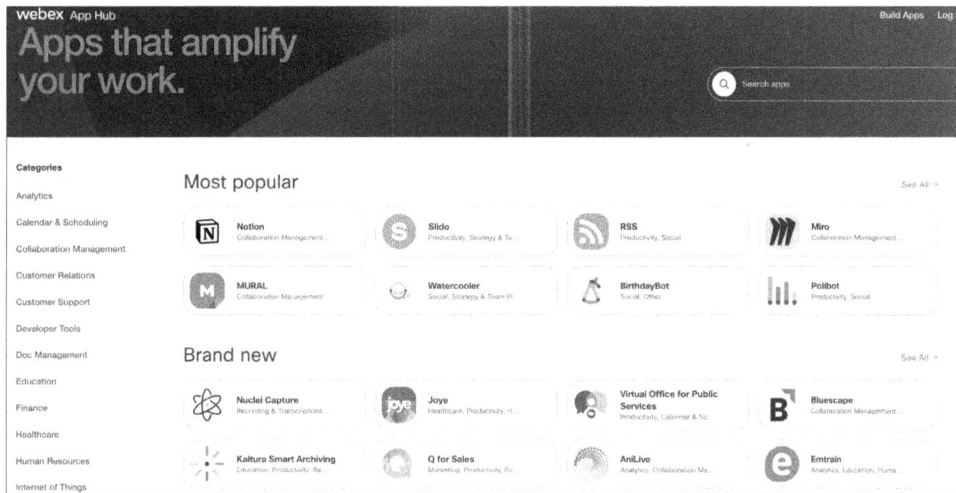

Figure 6-37   *Webex App Hub*

You don't need to know coding or use APIs to use bots or integrations. However, if you want to build your own, see developer.webex.com to learn how.

Integrations

You can use integrations to connect other tools to Webex App. For each integration you add, you are presented with a consent page that lists the functionality the integration needs to work in Webex App.

When you remove the integration, this access is also removed.

Functionality depends on the integration and how it is configured. The following are some things to know about integrations:

- They may be able to see the list of all space titles you're in.

- They may be able to post messages or content on behalf of the person who sets them up in a space.

- They may be able to respond to commands.

- They may be able to alert you whenever someone edits or configures something.

Bots

A bot acts like any other Webex App user. It has a special bot badge, though, so you can tell it isn't human. The bot can post messages, answer your questions, let you know when something happens, or do your bidding like an in-app assistant.

Keep in mind the following when you're working with a bot:

- A bot only reads the information you send to it directly. If you are in a group space, use an @mention when you want it to respond. If you are in a space with just the bot, then the bot reads every message.

- Some bots only respond to specific commands. Others can understand natural language questions and requests.

Support

If you're having issues with an integration or bot, you should reach out to the company that created it. You can find the company name below the bot or integration name in the Webex App Hub. If you notice anything urgent, report issues to devsupport@ webex.com. Cisco reviews every integration and bot listed in the Webex App Hub.

Add Bots and Integrations

If the tool you want to integrate requires you to create an account, create it before adding the integration. Here are the steps to follow:

Step 1.   Go to Webex App Hub and click **Log in** using your Webex App username and password.

Step 2.   Click your profile picture and select **My Webex Integrations** to see your current integrations.

Step 3.   Click **Webex App.**

Step 4.   Click the icon of the integration or bot you want to add or connect to:

- To add an integration, click **Connect.** Some integrations may have unique requirements; review the details in Webex App Hub.

■ To add a bot, click **Add to Space**. The spaces listed are spaces with two or more people or team spaces. However, you can start a conversation directly with the bot, create a space, and add the bot using the bot name and @ webex.bot. For example, add the Help bot using help@webex.bot.

Step 5.   Follow the prompts to add your bot or integration to a space in Webex App.

Figure 6-38 shows an example of some app integrations with Webex.

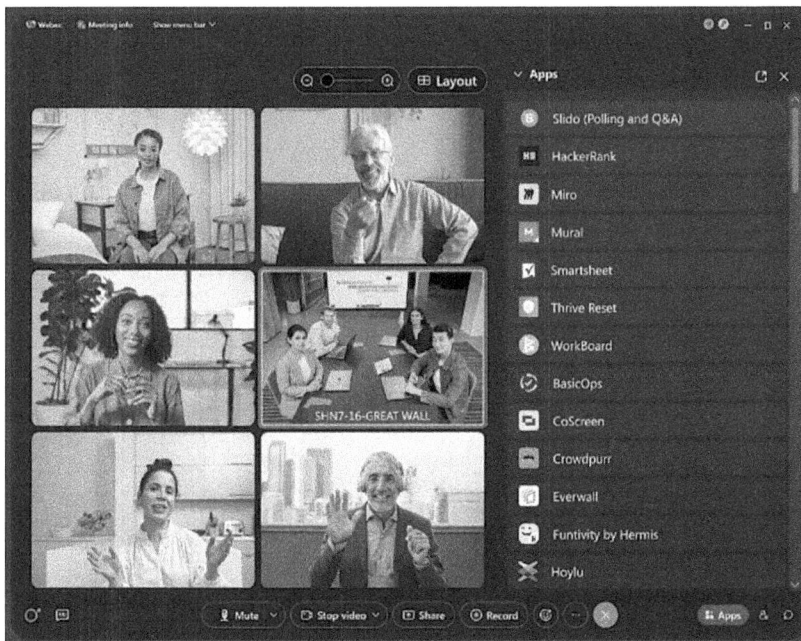

Figure 6-38   *App integrations with Webex*

Remove an Integration

For all the integrations listed on Webex App Hub, you can review the access permissions and remove the integrations by following these steps:

Step 1.   Sign in to Webex App Hub using your Webex App username and password.

Step 2.   Click your profile picture and select **My Webex Integrations** to see a list of all the integrations you have added.

Step 3.   Select the integration you want to remove and click **Disconnect**.

The integration is removed from all spaces and the access permissions are disconnected.

Remove a Bot

You can remove bots from teams and spaces in the same way you remove members from teams and spaces.

New feature additions are happening as we speak, making Cisco Webex a standout collaboration solution. Hopefully, the information covered in this section provided insight into some of the key features. In the next section, we will cover the Cisco Webex Cloud Service Architecture.

Cisco Webex Cloud Service Architecture

Webex Teams uses services that are located in several data centers. The services within these data centers can be broadly categorized as follows:

- **Identity services:** Storage of user identities, user authentication, single sign-on, and directory synchronization.

- **Webex Teams microservices:** Encryption key management, message indexing services for search functions and eDiscovery services, signaling services for Webex Teams apps, Webex devices, and API functions.

- **Content services:** Storage and retrieval of user-generated content such as messages and files.

- **Media services:** Media nodes for switching and transcoding for voice, video, and screen sharing content.

- **Anonymized data collection and analytics services:** Critical Webex Teams services are replicated across data centers for geographical redundancy. Within each data center, these Webex Teams services are hosted on virtual machines (VMs). These VMs can be moved for support and maintenance purposes, or new virtual machines can be installed as services expand.

Figure 6-39 shows an overview of the Webex Teams Cloud Service Architecture.

Typically, audio and video from Webex Teams or a Webex device transit from the user's location to media nodes in the Webex cloud. This is true for all call types (such as 1:1 calls and multiparty calls or meetings). All audio and video media streams are sent over the Secure Real-Time Transport Protocol (SRTP) using AES_CM_128_HMAC_SHA1_80 encryption.

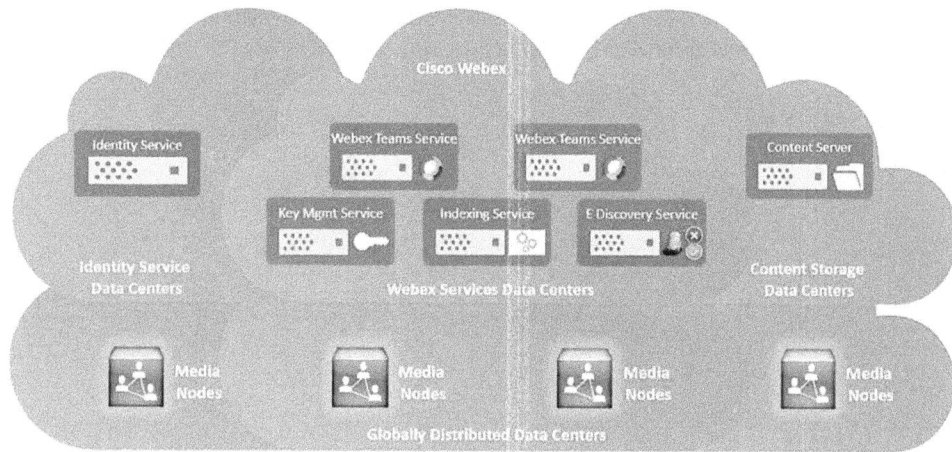

Figure 6-39 *Webex Teams Cloud Service Architecture*

UDP is recommended as the transport protocol for Webex Teams media, although most Webex Teams and Webex devices support TCP and HTTP (apps only) as a fallback protocol. TCP and HTTP are not recommended as media transport protocols because they are connection-oriented and designed for reliability, rather than timeliness. Using HTTP can also mean that media traffic must pass through a proxy server to reach media servers in the Webex cloud. Media quality can be impacted if the proxy server reaches a performance threshold when processing large numbers of high-bandwidth video streams.

Webex Teams Security Features and Deployment Practices

As enterprise customers increase their adoption of cloud-based services, the amount of Internet traffic generated by enterprise users also increases. Today, the ratio of the cost of enterprise WAN bandwidth (for example, MPLS) to that of Internet bandwidth can be as much as 200:1. Moving your cloud/Internet access to sites where your cloud users reside can provide significant savings in monthly bandwidth costs. Although this direct Internet access model is growing in popularity, many customers who deploy a centralized/regionalized Internet access model today have concerns that provisioning Internet access in each of their sites will perforate the security perimeter that surrounds their network. These security concerns can be addressed by limiting Internet access in these sites so that only traffic to and from approved cloud-based services is accessible via the site-based Internet connection.

Internet Access for Cloud-Based Services

You should provision Internet access as close as possible to the site where your Webex Teams and Webex devices reside. By providing local cloud/Internet access at each site for Webex devices, you can eliminate the need to transport Webex Teams traffic over the enterprise WAN to a regionalized/centralized Internet access point. Figure 6-40 and Figure 6-41 show the media flows for Webex Teams deployments with per-branch Internet access and centralized Internet access, respectively.

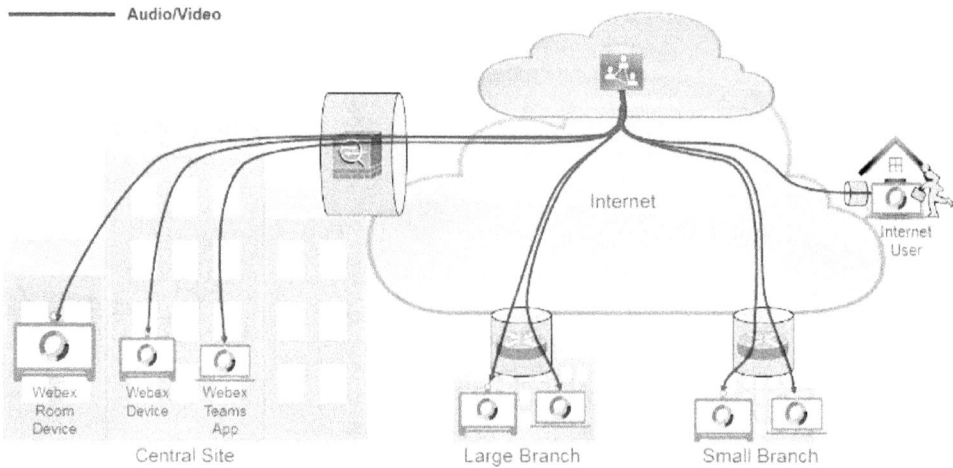

Figure 6-40   *Media paths for Webex Teams deployments with per-branch Internet/cloud access*

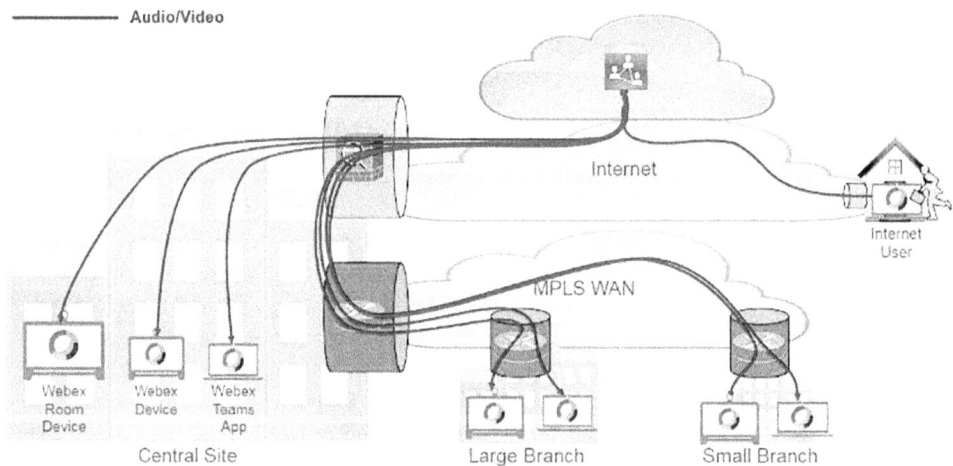

Figure 6-41   *Media paths for Webex Teams deployments with centralized Internet/cloud access*

Reducing Traffic to the Webex Cloud by Deploying Video Mesh Nodes

You can deploy Video Mesh Nodes in the enterprise network to provide local media processing. By processing audio and video media locally, the Video Mesh Nodes deliver a better quality experience for audio, video, and content sharing in meetings. A Video Mesh Node can also reduce or eliminate bandwidth consumption from the enterprise network to the Webex cloud. Webex Teams also provides automatic overflow to Media Nodes in the Webex cloud when large meetings/large numbers of meetings exhaust the locally available Video Mesh Node resources.

Figure 6-42 and Figure 6-43 show the media flows for Webex Teams deployments with per-branch Internet access and centralized Internet access, respectively, where a Video Mesh Node has also been deployed at the central site to provide local media processing. The Video Mesh Node processes media for local devices in meetings and, if needed, creates a cascade link to a Media Node in the Webex cloud for remote meeting participants.

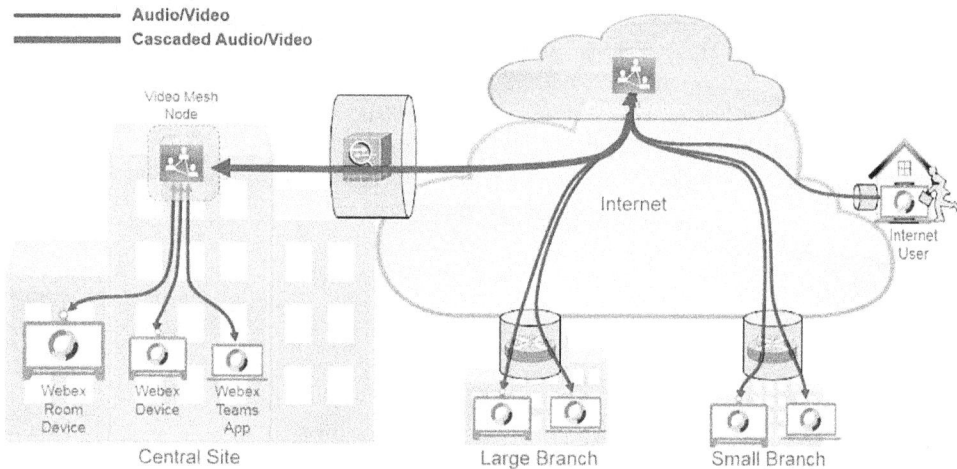

Figure 6-42 *Media paths for Webex Teams deployments with a central site Video Mesh Node and per-branch Internet access*

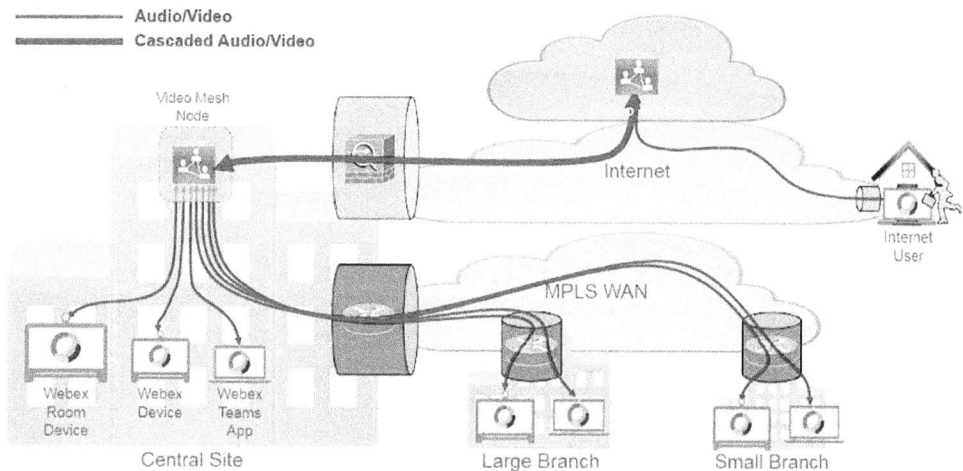

Figure 6-43 *Media paths for Webex Teams deployments with a central site Video Mesh Node and centralized Internet access*

Webex Teams Inspection Capabilities

Webex Teams supports SSL/TLS/HTTPS inspection, which allows enterprise proxies to do the following:

- Decrypt Internet-bound traffic.

- Inspect the traffic.

- Re-encrypt the traffic before sending it on to its destination.

The signaling traffic from Webex devices uses TLS for session encryption. Within a Webex Teams TLS session, messages and content such as files and documents are also encrypted, so SSL/TLS/HTTPS inspection has limited value because these messages and files cannot be decrypted and inspected. Some information is visible in the decrypted TLS session, such as API calls, obfuscated user IDs (such as a Universally Unique User Identifier [UUID], a 128-bit random value that represents the Webex Teams user ID), and so on. Figure 6-44 shows SSL/TLS/HTTPS signaling inspection by a proxy server.

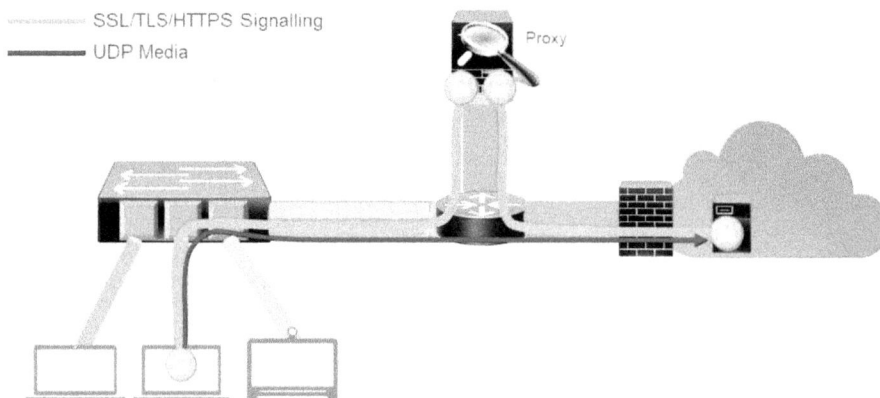

Figure 6-44   *SSL/TLS/HTTPS signaling inspection by a proxy server*

Webex Teams apps and Webex devices use certificate pinning to verify that they are connecting to Cisco's Webex service and to ensure that the session data is not intercepted, read, or modified while in transit. SSL/TLS/HTTPS inspection is a form of man-in-the-middle (MITM) attack.

Cisco pins server certificates to a few root Certificate Authorities (CAs) that have committed to not issue intermediate certificates through both the issuer's Certification Practice Statement and the root certificate containing a "pathLenConstraint" field in the Basic Constraints extension, which is set to zero (0) to indicate that no CA certificates can follow the issuing certificate in a certification path. This means that, ordinarily, Webex apps will not accept an impersonation certificate sent by a proxy for SSL inspection.

SSL/TLS/HTTPS Inspection for Webex Teams Desktop Apps

The Webex Teams apps rely on the certificates installed in the underlying OS Trust store to bypass the Webex Teams certificate pinning process. If the enterprise CA certificate exists in the OS Trust store, the Webex Teams app will trust certificates signed by the enterprise CA, when presented to it by the proxy server. This bypasses the certificate pinning process used by the Webex Teams app and allows a TLS connection to be established to the proxy server.

SSL/TLS/HTTPS Inspection for Webex Teams Devices

The Webex Teams devices download a list of trusted certificates during the onboarding process. To include your Enterprise CA certificate into the device trust list for your organization, open a service request (SR) with Cisco TAC.

For details on Webex Teams app and device support for SSL/TLS/HTTPS inspection, see the "Network Requirements for Webex Teams Services" article at https://help.webex.com/article/WBX000028782.

Webex Team Data Protection

Webex Teams uses the following mechanisms to protect data in transit:

- All signaling connections from Webex Teams and Webex devices are protected using an encrypted TLS session. TLS cipher suites use 256-bit or 128-bit symmetric cipher key sizes, and SHA-2 family hash functions. TLS cipher suites using 256-bit symmetric cipher keys are preferred. For example:

  TLS_EDHE_RSA_WITH_AES_256_GCM_SHA384

  TLS_ECDHE_RSA_WITH_AES_256_CBC_SHA384

- Only TLS version 1.2 is supported.

- Webex Teams TLS servers also support TLS_FALLBACK_SCSV (https://datatracker.ietf.org/doc/rfc7507/) to prevent TLS version downgrade attacks.

- All messages and content (files) sent by Webex Teams are encrypted before they are sent over the TLS connection. Encrypted messages and content sent by the Webex Teams use AES_256_GCM encryption keys.

- Media streams (voice, video, and screen share) from Webex Teams and devices are encrypted using SRTP with AES_CM_128_HMAC_SHA1_80 ciphers. SRTP ciphers are negotiated using SDES. For more information, see https://tools.ietf.org/html/rfc4568.

Figure 6-45 shows TLS connections from Webex Teams and Webex devices to the Webex cloud.

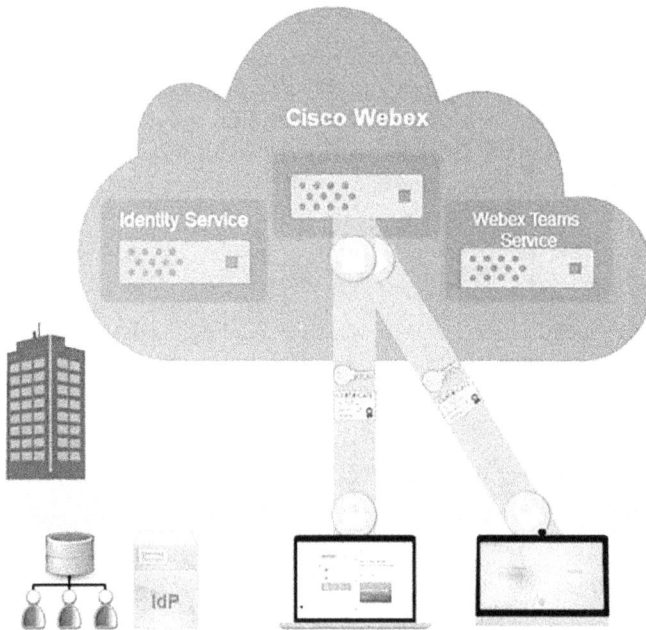

Figure 6-45 *TLS connections from Webex Teams and Webex devices to the Webex cloud*

Webex Teams and Webex devices make outbound connections only to the Cisco Webex cloud, and Webex Teams services only support TLS version 1.2.

Webex Teams supports the TLS Fallback Signaling Cipher Suite Value (SCSV) feature, which is used to prevent TLS version downgrade attacks, by indicating to the TLS server that the connection should only be established if the highest TLS version supported by the server is equal to, or lower than, that received by the app. Also, all Webex Teams data in transit (including the UUID) is encrypted using Transport Layer Security (TLS).

By default, all encrypted files and encrypted messages sent by Webex Teams to the Webex Teams Service are stored in U.S. data centers. The encrypted files and messages are stored in an encrypted database that is replicated for redundancy. For files, customers can choose to deploy an Enterprise Content Management service, such as Microsoft OneDrive or SharePoint Online for Webex Teams file storage and distribution.

Any customers who are concerned about Cisco storing their message and file encryption keys and content can choose to deploy an on-premises (encryption) Key Management Server (KMS), which is a component of the Webex Hybrid Data Security platform. The KMS controls and manages the encryption keys for content stored in Webex data centers. Encryption keys for content are created, distributed, and stored on the customer's premises. KMS has a secure (TLS) connection to the Webex cloud and can distribute keys to Webex Teams over a dedicated TLS connection between the KMS and Webex Teams. As shown in Figure 6-46, the on-premises KMS service can run on one or more Hybrid Data Security Nodes in your data center.

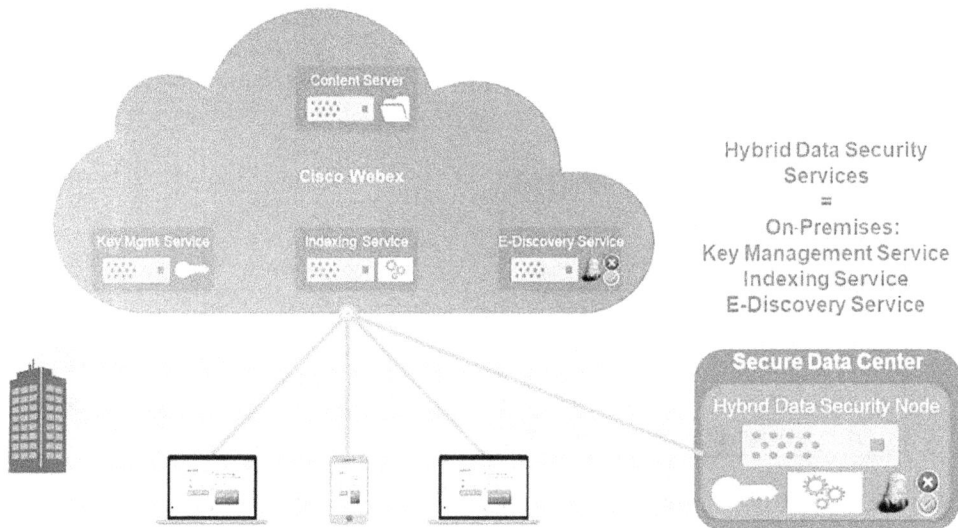

Figure 6-46   *On-premises hybrid data security services*

When Hybrid Data Security Nodes are deployed on the customer premises, encrypted files and content are stored in Webex Teams data centers, while their encryption keys are stored and managed locally. To read any file or message sent to the Webex cloud, two pieces of information are required:

■ The encrypted file or message

■ The encryption key used to secure it

All customer data within Webex Teams is encrypted and is inaccessible to Cisco personnel without authorization. Attempts to access encrypted customer content without authorization by any employee would be a violation of Cisco policy and would be investigated, and the employee would be subject to disciplinary action up to and including termination of employment.

In an effort to protect customers' interests, Cisco has outlined the steps for sharing requests for data. Details can be found at https://www.cisco.com/c/en/us/about/trust-center/transparency.html.

By default, all content (messages and files) sent to Webex Teams spaces is securely stored in Webex Teams data centers. Using Webex Teams APIs, customers have the option to archive a copy of this content with a third-party data archival company (for example, Actiance, Global Relay, or Verint Verba). Customers can retrieve and store content on their own archival system.

Cisco has also developed a Webex Teams API framework that allows enterprise customers to store all their files with their preferred Enterprise Content Management (ECM) provider instead of in the Webex cloud (for example, OneDrive, Box, or Google Drive).

Customers can also use the API for Enterprise Content Management to store files within their enterprise network. For more information, see the "Webex App | Microsoft OneDrive and SharePoint Online" article at https://help.webex.com/article/nuz39yeb. Figure 6-47 shows the Webex Teams API for Enterprise Content Management.

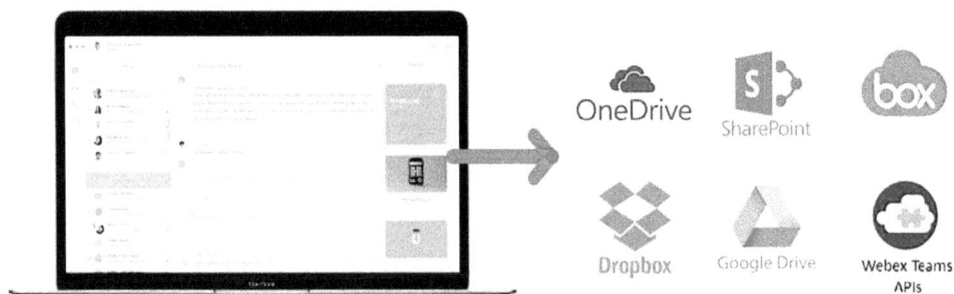

Figure 6-47   *Webex Teams API for Enterprise Content Management*

File version control is maintained by the ECM application. Webex Teams uses Microsoft standard Graph API for ECM integration to Microsoft OneDrive or SharePoint Online. For more information, see https://docs.microsoft.com/en-us/onedrive/developer/ rest-api/?view=odsp-graph-online.

Webex Teams Apps – Data at Rest Protection

Encryption of data at rest applies not only to content stored in the Webex cloud, but also to content stored by Webex Teams apps. The following content is securely stored by Webex Teams for Windows, macOS, iOS, and Android:

- Messages
- Preview files and files converted to Portable Network Graphics (PNG) file format
- Space encryption keys
- Profile pictures
- Space details
- Meeting details
- Whiteboard files
- OAuth tokens

Webex Teams apps on desktop and mobile devices store this content in an SQLite database that is encrypted using the AES-256-OFB algorithm. The master key for the SQLite database is encrypted by and stored in the platform OS secure store (for example, Windows Data Protect API, macOS/iOS Secure Enclave and Keychain, and Android Keystore).

Figure 6-48 shows the Webex Teams feature for the encryption of data at rest.

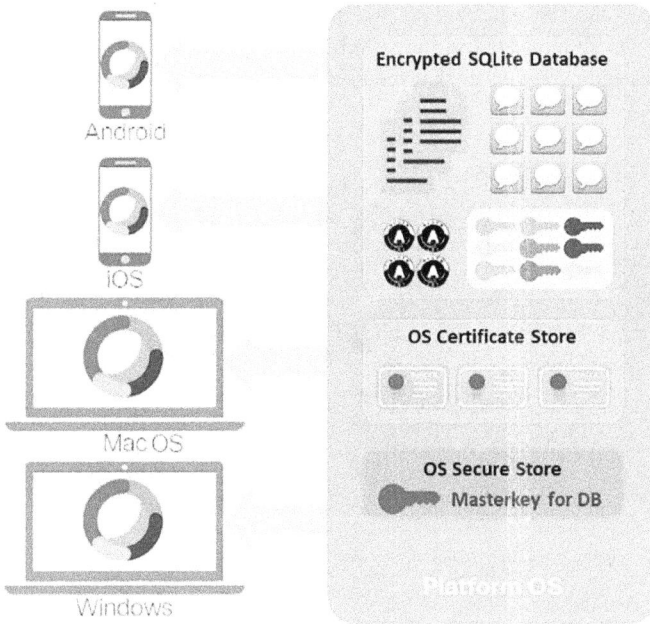

Figure 6-48 *Webex Teams encryption of data at rest*

Files downloaded by the Webex Teams app are decrypted prior to storage. The storage location of downloaded files is determined by the user (for example, the Windows Downloads folder).

Webex Teams App for Web – Data Storage

Webex Teams for Web (https://teams.webex.com) does not permanently store content. Messages, files, encryption keys, and tokens are deleted when the browser or browser tab is closed. One exception to this case is when the "Remember Me" option is selected by the user to bypass user authentication. In this case, the access and refresh tokens are stored and reused when Webex Teams is relaunched in the browser.

Webex Teams Indexing Service

The Webex Teams Indexing Service enables rapid searches of messages, files (filenames), people (usernames), and places (space names and team names) by Webex Teams users.

Typically, the Webex Teams Indexing Service resides in the Webex cloud (see Figure 6-49), but it can also be deployed on a customer's premises as a component of the Hybrid Data Security Service (see Figure 6-50). This service parses, stems, and hashes terms in all messages and filenames in spaces, as well as usernames and space names, to create a series of hashed indexes. These hashed indexes are stored in the Search Service in the Webex cloud. Indexing takes place for each message and file (name) posted by a Webex Teams user. Indexing involves decrypting the posted content, followed by the indexing process. Decrypted messages and filenames are deleted immediately after the indexing process is completed. User search requests use the Search service in the Webex cloud to find either content in spaces and team spaces that the user is a member of or names of other users and spaces.

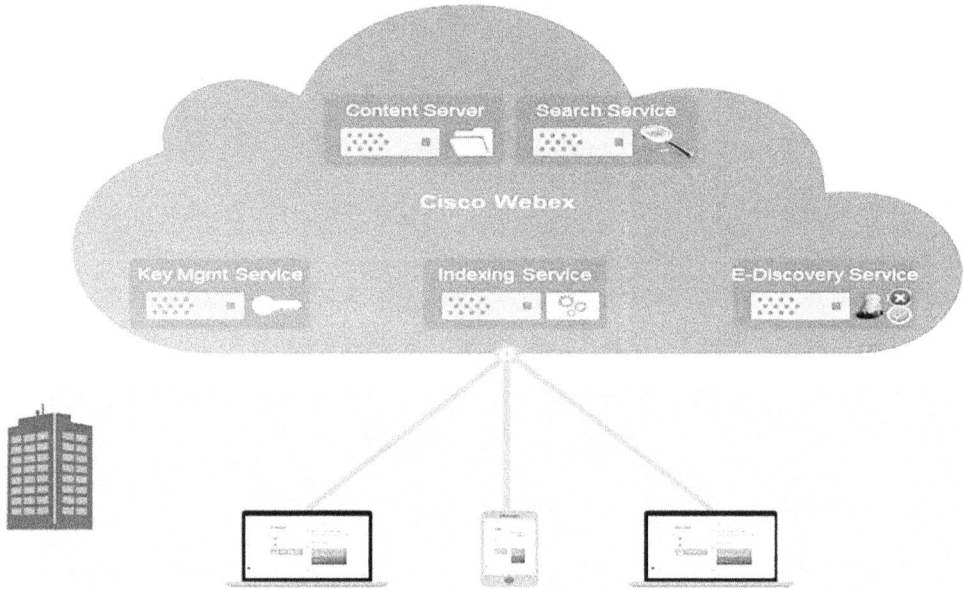

Figure 6-49 *Webex cloud-based indexing and search services*

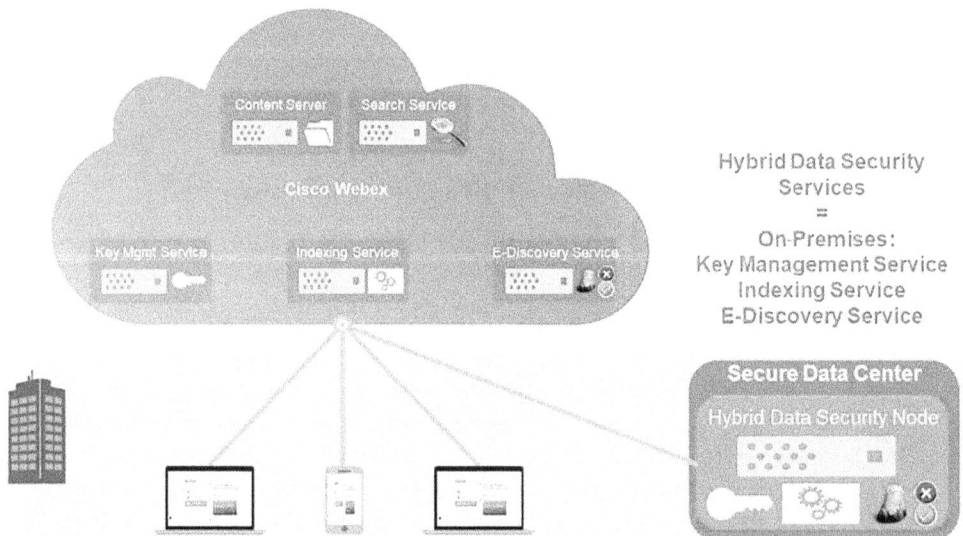

Figure 6-50 *Customer premises-based indexing and search services for Webex Teams hosted on a Hybrid Data Security Node*

When deployed on-premises, Hybrid Data Security (HDS) services provide an additional benefit, in that decryption of posted content for indexing takes place on the customer premises, not in the Webex cloud. Additionally, the encryption keys for messages and files are also owned, stored, and managed on the customer's premises as part of the Hybrid Data Security service.

KMS On-Premises

Webex Teams and Webex devices establish TLS connections to the Webex cloud. These encrypted connections are used for all communication to Webex cloud services and on-premises services such as the Hybrid Data Security service. To ensure that communication between Webex Teams and on-premises HDS services remain confidential, an additional encrypted connection is established between Webex Teams and the on-premises HDS service. This secure connection uses ECHDE for key negotiation and AES-256_GCM for authenticated encryption of data. Figure 6-51 shows the Webex Teams secure feature Webex cloud and HDS connections.

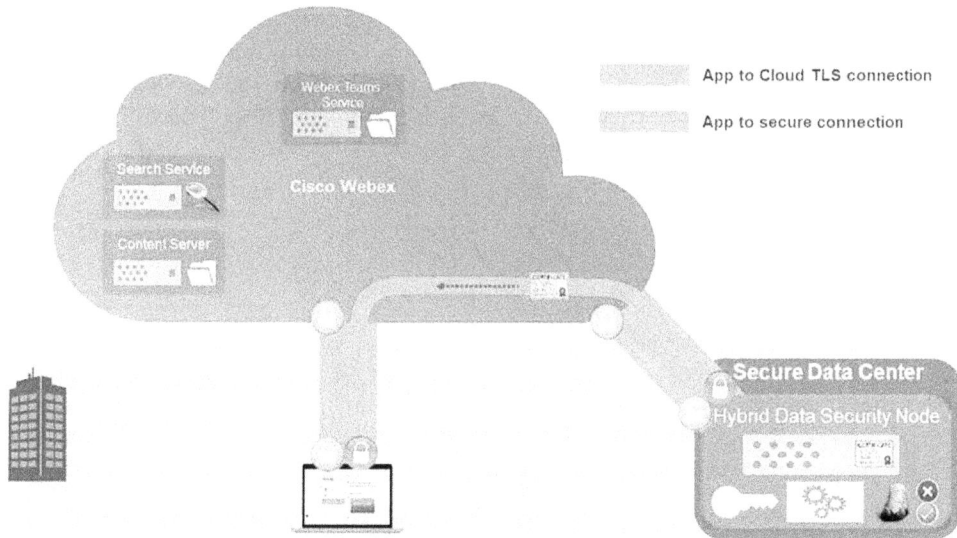

Figure 6-51   *Webex Teams – Webex cloud and HDS connections*

Key management services in HDS nodes automatically federate with the KMS services of other organizations when Webex Teams users from two or more organizations participate in a Webex Teams space. This KMS-to-KMS connection is established by using mutual TLS between the HDS nodes in each organization. Figure 6-52 shows KMS federation between two organizations using Webex Teams and HDS.

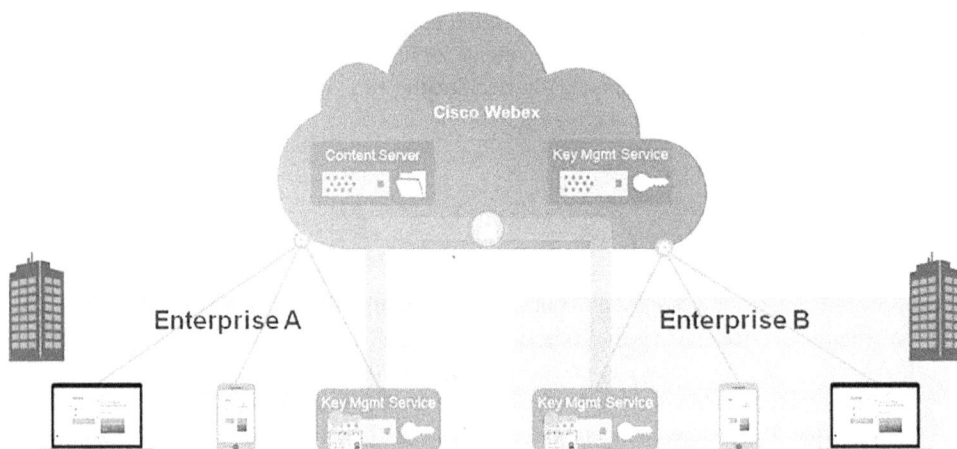

Figure 6-52 *KMS federation between two organizations using Webex Teams and HDS*

The Key Management Server (KMS) does not perform an encryption function; it creates and distributes encryption keys to Webex Teams that use end-to-end encryption for content (messages and files). The KMS does not create and distribute encryption keys for Webex Teams media streams; these keys are generated by the Webex Teams, devices, and media servers participating in a call or conference.

All encryption keys used by Webex Teams are securely stored. Encryption keys for messages and content shared in Webex Teams spaces and the details of these spaces are held in a database and encrypted before being stored. The space details include the space name, space owner or moderator, and participants.

For Webex Teams organizations using the Webex cloud KMS service, their encryption keys and space details are securely stored on Cisco-dedicated database servers. For Webex Teams organizations using the Webex Teams HDS service, their encryption keys and space details are securely stored in the organization's premises on customer-owned database servers (for example, Microsoft SQL or Postgres).

Access to KMS/HDS-related data is tenanted through a combination of the following:

- Access tokens that identify the user, the organization that they belong to, and the scope of Webex Teams services that they are authorized to access

- Data structures for Webex Teams spaces, meetings, and so on that define their authorized participants

The encryption keys for Webex Teams spaces and content (messages and files) are securely stored and cached by Webex Teams, which is helpful if the KMS goes down (especially for HDS).

For Webex Teams for iOS and Android, resetting user access in the Cisco Webex Control Hub deletes the cached content. Resetting user access also revokes the user's OAuth access token across all Webex Teams apps, requiring users to sign in again. For Webex Teams for Web, cached content is deleted when the user signs out or closes the browser or the browser tab.

As for file storage security during transcoding, files are never stored by the document transcoding application; they are processed by the application (converted to a PNG image). After the content is transcoded, the original document is deleted. Native document and file transcoding in the Webex cloud were introduced in 2019. File and document transcoding in the Webex cloud removes the requirement to use third-party transcoding services and improves transcoding performance.

For information about the encryption and security capabilities of Webex Teams, see: https://www.cisco.com/c/dam/en/us/td/docs/voice_ip_comm/cloudCollaboration/spark/whitepapers/cisco-wbxt-firewall-traversal-whitepaper.pdf.

For details of encryption and key management features and services supported today, see https://www.cisco.com/c/en/us/products/collateral/collaboration-endpoints/webex-room-series/datasheet-c78-740770.html.

Webex Teams Single Sign-On

Webex Teams supports any Identity Provider (IdP) that complies with SAML v2. Webex Teams works with the leading identity providers for both on-premises and Identity as a Service (IaaS) integration for the purpose of SAML v2 federated single sign-on. Cisco has created integration guides for some of these partners and has posted them on its Help site at https://help.webex.com/article/lfu88u. Integration guides or confirmed customer integrations are available for the following identity providers:

- On-premises identity providers:
  - Microsoft ADFS
  - Oracle Access Manager
  - Ping Identity
  - OpenAM
  - IBM Security Access Manager
  - CA Siteminder
  - F5 Big-IP
  - Shibboleth

- IaaS vendors:

  - Okta

  - PingOne

  - Salesforce

  - Microsoft Azure

  - Oracle Identity Cloud Service

  - Centrify

  - OneLogin

Multifactor Authentication

Webex Teams provides authentication through multifactor authentication (MFA) by integrating with SAML v2 identity providers that support this mechanism. Many organizations deploy MFA mechanisms across their enterprise for all services that require special additional factors during authentication—something you know, such as your password, and something you have, such as an x509 certificate, HMAC-based one-time password (HOTP), time-based one-time password (TOTP), device fingerprinting, or other supported mechanisms by the IdP.

IdP and MDM/MAM with Webex Teams

Enterprise customers are building new architectures to address the security of mobile devices, authentication, and authorization of cloud-based SaaS. Enterprise customers look to the identity provider vendors to provide authentication and authorization to web apps, as well as access control to mobile apps (also known as mobile application management, or MAM). These same IdPs also include mobile device management (MDM) features or integrations to make sure that trusted devices are used by employees when accessing applications. Many IDPs use features such as device registration or certificate-based authentication to achieve these goals.

Webex Teams Proximity and Device Pairing

Webex Teams desktop and mobile apps can use proximity to pair with Webex cloud-registered devices and on-premises Cisco video devices registered to Cisco Unified CM and Cisco TelePresence Video Communication Server (VCS). The device discovery and pairing mechanisms are similar for cloud-registered devices and Unified CM/VCS-registered devices; the content sharing and device control mechanisms both use TLS/HTTPS connections but differ in the paths they use between the Webex Teams app and the device.

Note   Webex Teams for web supports manual pairing only.

Proximity for Cloud-Registered Webex Devices

Cloud-registered Webex devices use ultrasonic signaling and tokens to pair with Webex Teams apps. Figure 6-53 shows that unique tokens are generated by the Webex cloud every 30 seconds and securely sent over TLS to the Webex device, which emits these tokens using ultrasound from the device speakers. A Webex Teams app within range of the ultrasound signal can use the received token to pair with Webex devices, by sending the token to the Webex cloud service. Once the device and app are paired, newly emitted tokens must be received by the Webex Teams app and sent to the Webex cloud service to maintain the paired connection.

One reason for using ultrasound for proximity detection is its limited range; ultrasound signals typically do not pass through walls, limiting the pairing token's range to the enclosed room that the endpoint is placed within.

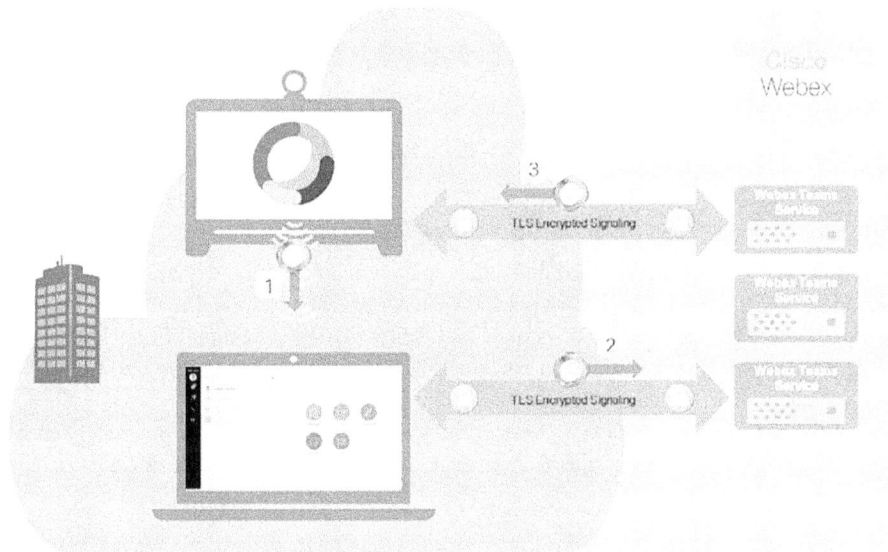

Figure 6-53 *Ultrasound pairing for Webex Teams and Webex devices*

Figure 6-54 shows that once the paired connection between the device and app has been established using the Webex cloud, the Webex Teams app can control the Webex device (for example, to make calls, mute, and so on) and also share content on the Webex device. Both the Webex Teams app and the Webex device use their existing TLS connections to the Webex cloud to exchange call control signaling and media for content sharing.

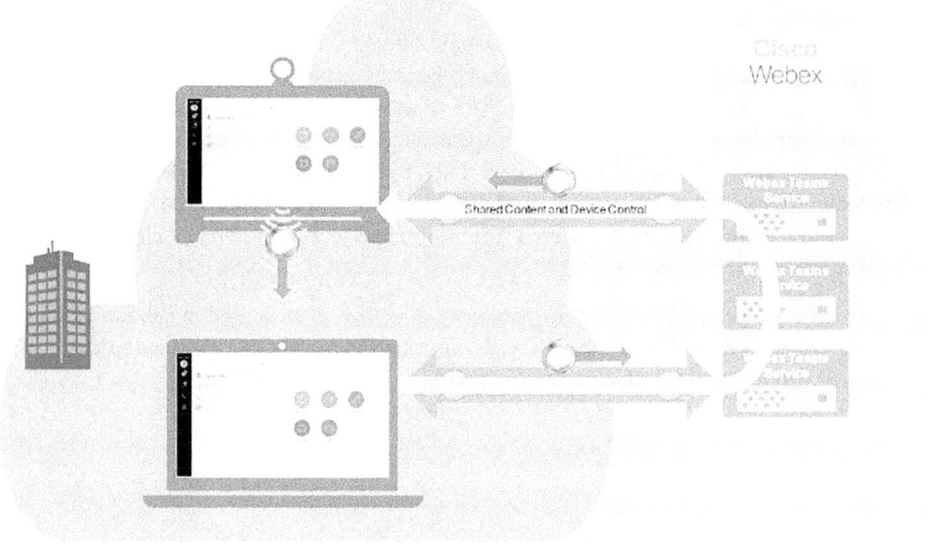

Figure 6-54   *Ultrasound pairing for Webex Teams and Webex devices post connection*

Proximity for On-Premises Registered Webex Devices

Figure 6-55 shows that Unified CM and VCS registered Cisco video devices use ultrasonic signaling and tokens for proximity pairing with Webex Teams apps. Unique tokens are generated by the device every 180 seconds and emitted using ultrasound from the device speakers. A Webex Teams app within range of the ultrasonic signal can use the received token to pair with a Unified CM or VCS registered Cisco Video device by sending the token to the device over an HTTPS connection. Once the pairing is complete, newly emitted tokens must be received by the Webex Teams app and returned to the device to maintain the paired connection.

For more information, see the "Configure On-Premises Devices for Cisco Webex Teams Users" article at https://help.webex.com/article/poqjhk.

When the paired connection between the Cisco video device and Webex Teams app has been established, the Webex Teams app can control the device (for example, to make calls, mute, and so on) and also share content (see Figure 6-26). The Webex Teams app and Unified CM or VCS registered video device use the directly established HTTPS connection to exchange call control signaling and media for content sharing.

There are differences in how the Webex Teams app connects to cloud-registered and on-premises devices. When connecting to an on-premises device, the content that is shared between the Webex Teams app and the video device is always encrypted. However, we don't enforce certificate verification when an HTTPS session is established with an on-premises device. Verifying certificates would prevent pairing with guest devices and would be complex to deploy and maintain. Figure 6-56 shows the Webex Teams discovery of on-premises devices option in Webex Control Hub; this option is disabled by default.

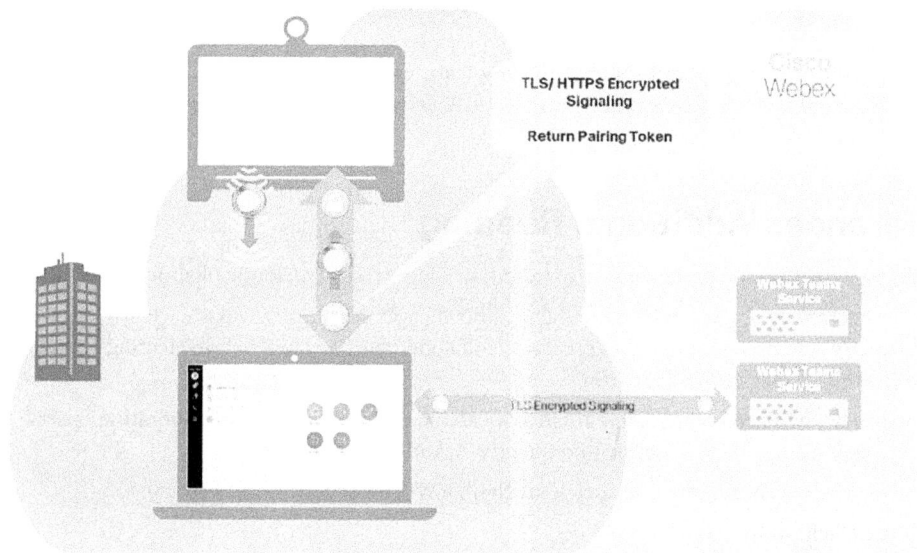

Figure 6-55 *Ultrasound pairing for unified CM/VCS registered devices and Webex Teams*

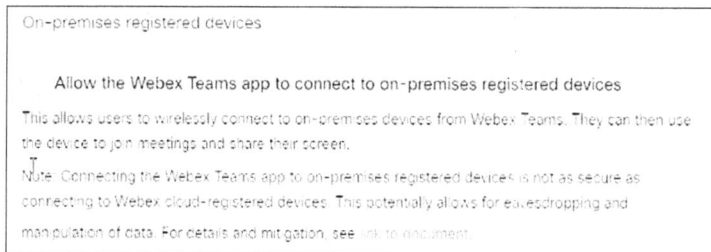

Figure 6-56 *Webex Teams discovery of on-premises devices option in Webex Control Hub*

Other Webex Device Discovery Mechanisms

Webex Teams apps can also use Wi-Fi to discover Webex devices and manually connect using a personal identification number (PIN). For more information, see the following articles:

- "Manage Wi-Fi Discovery of Webex Devices" (https://help.webex.com/article/nz9iowf)

- "Find and Connect to Nearby Cisco Webex Devices from Cisco Webex Teams"

- "Manually Connect to Cisco Webex Devices from Cisco Webex Teams" (https://help.webex.com/article/nf29igm)

Summary

In this chapter, we covered some of the key features and insights into Webex Teams architecture and some best practices to be used when you are deploying Webex in your network.

References/Additional Reading

https://www.cisco.com/c/dam/en/us/td/docs/voice_ip_comm/cloudCollaboration/spark/esp/Cisco-Webex-Apps-Security-White-Paper.pdf

https://www.cisco.com/c/en/us/products/collateral/conferencing/webex-meeting-center/white-paper-c11-737588.html

https://www.cisco.com/c/dam/en/us/td/docs/voice_ip_comm/cloudCollaboration/spark/esp/Webex-Teams-Security-Frequently-Asked-Questions.pdf

https://help.webex.com/en-us/article/nv2hm53/Webex-Security-and-Privacy

https://help.webex.com/

https://www.cisco.com/c/en/us/products/conferencing/web-conferencing/index.html

https://www.cisco.com/c/en/us/solutions/collaboration/webex-call-message-meet.html

Chapter 7

Internet of Things (IoT)

Before we can begin to see the importance of the Internet of Things (IoT), it is first necessary to understand the differences between the Internet and the World Wide Web (or Web)—terms that are often used interchangeably. The Internet is the physical layer or network made up of switches, routers, and other equipment. Its primary function is to transport information from one point to another quickly, reliably, and securely. The Web, on the other hand, is an application layer that operates on top of the Internet. Its primary role is to provide an interface that makes the information flowing across the Internet usable.

By comparison, the Internet has been on a steady path of development and improvement, but arguably hasn't changed much. In this context, IoT becomes immensely important because it is the first real evolution of the Internet—a leap that will lead to revolutionary applications that have the potential to dramatically improve the way people live, learn, work, and entertain themselves. Already, IoT has made the Internet sensory (temperature, pressure, vibration, light, moisture, stress), allowing us to become more proactive and less reactive. Figure 7-1 provides an overview of Cisco's IoT portfolio.

As the planet's population continues to increase, it becomes even more important for people to become stewards of the earth and its resources. In addition, people desire to live healthy, fulfilling, and comfortable lives for themselves, their families, and those they care about. By combining the ability of the next evolution of the Internet (IoT) to sense, collect, transmit, analyze, and distribute data on a massive scale with the way people process information, humanity will have the knowledge and wisdom it needs not only to survive, but to thrive in the coming months, years, decades, and centuries.

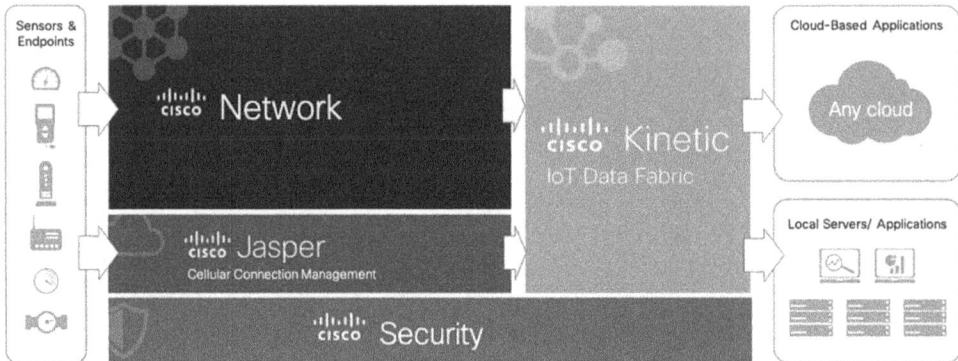

Figure 7-1   *An overview of Cisco's IoT portfolio*

The sheer size and variety of data traversing today's networks are increasing exponentially. This highly distributed data is generated by a wide range of cloud and enterprise applications, websites, social media, computers, smartphones, sensors, cameras, and much more—all coming in different formats and protocols. IoT contributes significantly to this rising volume, often by generating a high frequency of relatively small amounts of data.

How Do OT and IT Differ?

Operational technology (OT) is the hardware and software that monitor and control devices, processes, and infrastructure, and it's used in industrial settings. IT combines technologies for networking, information processing, enterprise data centers, and cloud systems. OT devices control the physical world, while IT systems manage data and applications.

IT is the technology backbone of any organization. It's necessary for monitoring, managing, and securing core functions such as email, finance, human resources (HR), and other applications in the data center and cloud.

OT is for connecting, monitoring, managing, and securing an organization's industrial operations. Businesses engaged in activities such as manufacturing, mining, oil and gas, utilities, and transportation, among many others, rely heavily on OT. Robots, industrial control systems (ICS), supervisory control and data acquisition (SCADA) systems, programmable logic controllers (PLCs), and computer numerical control (CNC) are examples of OT.

Operational technology can also be found in warehouses and outdoor areas such as parking lots and highways. Some OT examples include ATMs and kiosks, connected buses, trains, and service fleets, weather stations, and systems that allow a city to manage chargers for electric vehicles.

The key difference between IT and OT is that IT is centered on an organization's frontend informational activities, while OT is focused on the backend production (machines).

OT and IT network infrastructures have similar elements, such as switches, routers, and wireless technology. Therefore, OT networks can benefit from the rigor and experience that IT has built over the years with common network management and security controls to build a solid network foundation.

However, there are key differences:

■ **Form factor:** OT network devices come in smaller and modularized form factors so they can be mounted in different ways, such as on rails, walls, or light poles, in cars, or even embedded within other equipment.

■ **Hardening:** OT network infrastructure may need to be ruggedized when deployed in severe industrial conditions. The infrastructure must be resistant to shock, vibration, water, extreme temperatures, and corrosive air and chemicals.

■ **Network interfaces:** Depending on their purpose, OT devices may support networks such as LoraWAN or WiSun to connect industrial IoT (IIoT) devices.

■ **Protocols:** OT network devices connect IoT sensors and machines, which run communications protocols that are not commonly used in traditional IT networks. Therefore, industrial networking products must support a wide variety of protocols such as Modbus, Profinet, and Common Industrial Protocol (CIP).

IoT Challenges

The following is a list of some of the challenges IoT presents:

■ The process of connecting, securing, and managing diverse devices is complex.

■ A lot of data remains locked inside its sources.

■ Flexibility is needed to compute data at the edge, data center, and/or cloud.

■ There's no programmatic way to move the right data to the right apps at the right time.

■ There's no software control to enforce ownership, privacy, and security.

Cisco Kinetic Platform

To get real business value from all of your IoT data, you can use the power of the Cisco Kinetic platform to extract, compute, and move data from your connected things to various applications—and get maximum business benefit. Figure 7-2 shows how Cisco Kinetic integrates seamlessly between your data sources and apps.

You need to realize the full potential of your IoT data to drive better business outcomes. The data produced by all your "things" is a high-value asset that can change the trajectory of your business—if you can make full use of it. But that can be challenging when you're working with disparate things and a variety of applications that may live in edge or fog nodes, your data center, private clouds, and/or public clouds.

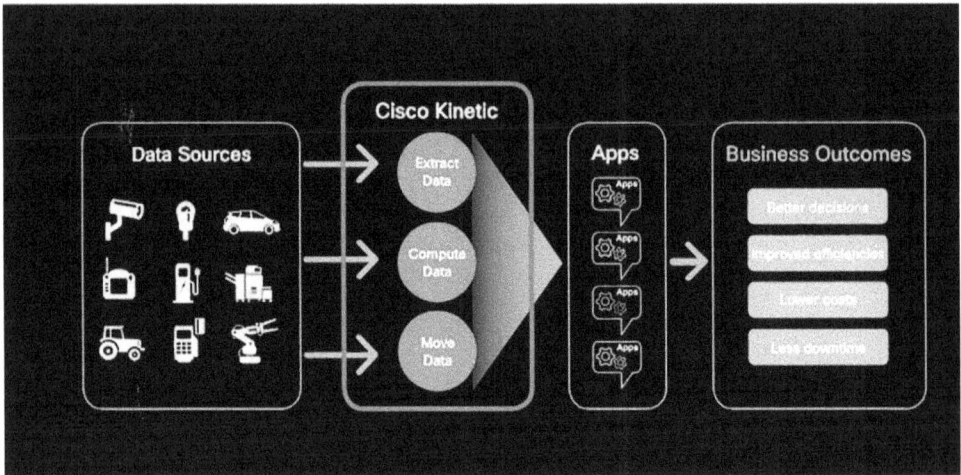

Figure 7-2   *How Cisco Kinetic integrates seamlessly between your data sources and apps*

Cisco Kinetic makes it easy to connect distributed devices ("things") to the network and then extract, normalize, and securely move data from those devices to distributed applications. The platform plays a vital role in enforcing policies defined by data owners, as to which data goes where, and when. Figure 7-3 illustrates how Cisco Kinetic can get data from devices in a highly distributed environment.

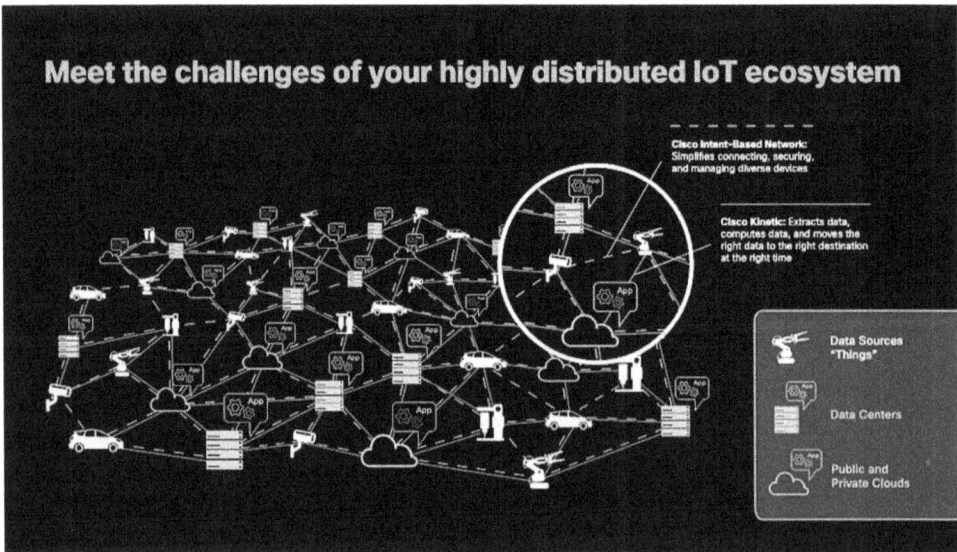

Figure 7-3   *How Cisco Kinetic can get data from devices in a highly distributed environment*

Cisco Kinetic is a new class of platform—an IoT data fabric. This distributed system of software streamlines your IoT operations by performing three key functions:

- It *extracts* data from disparate sources ("things"), regardless of protocol, and transforms it, making it usable by the applications that provide business value.

- It *computes* data anywhere, from edge to destination, to provide processing where it's needed. This enables fast decisions at the point of action, dramatically reduces latency, and makes the most efficient use of network resources.

- It *moves* data programmatically to get the right data to the right applications at the right time. The platform serves the need for data distribution in multicloud, multi-party, and multilocation situations, executing policies to enforce data ownership, privacy, and security.

The Kinetic platform is a scalable, open system, adaptable for a variety of use cases across a broad range of industries. Its modular design is well-suited for companies that want to get a fast start on their IoT journey and grow.

Why Cisco Kinetic

Table 7-1 describes the key features of Cisco Kinetic Platform.

Table 7-1   *Kinetic Platform Key Features*

Component	Function
Software connectors	Extract data from disparate sources using a wide variety of protocol adapters.
Data transformer	Converts data from disparate sources to a common format and precision to simplify the construction of and ingestion by applications.
Edge and fog processing	Performs complex rules on data in motion to intelligently reduce, compress, and transmit data in an optimal way.
	Adds compute power anywhere in the network, both at the edge and consolidating and processing data from multiple edge nodes, to further reduce it before sending it on to the next destination.
	Enables critical decisions to be made and appropriate actions to be taken without the expense and delay involved in processing everything at a higher location in the data flow topology.
Data models	Enable you to define the structure for various data types and collections of data you want to share.
Data controls	Enable you to define data flow policies—that is, which data goes to which apps at which time.

Component	Function
Northbound application connectors	Allow for subscription to data by authorized applications and services.
Cloud-based gateway management	Instantly provision remote Cisco 8x9 Industrial Integrated Services Router (IR8x9) gateways. Monitor and maintain health on an ongoing basis.
	Manage the Cisco IOx application environment configuration and software at scale from a single pane of glass.
	Deploy microservices to Cisco containers on Cisco gateways and manage application lifecycle and bulk updating when needed.

Understanding Cisco Kinetic Platform

Cisco Kinetic makes it easy to connect distributed devices ("things") to the network and then extract, normalize, and securely move data from those devices to distributed applications. The Kinetic platform also plays a vital role in enforcing policies defined by data owners, so they can control which data goes where, and when.

The platform includes three integrated modules:

- **Gateway Management (GMM):** Provision gateways at scale with a highly secure, low-touch workflow. Plus, view and control your gateways from a cloud-based dashboard.

- **Data Control (DCM):** Move the right data from diverse devices to the right cloud-based applications at the right time, according to policy set by the data owner.

- **Edge and Fog Processing (EFPM):** Compute data in distributed nodes. Make critical decisions near the point of action, and use network resources most efficiently.

Figure 7-4 lists the modules of Cisco Kinetic Platform.

Cisco Kinetic – Gateway Management Module

The Cisco Gateway Management Module (GMM) is a secure, scalable tool to provision, manage, and monitor IoT gateways. It is cloud-native, multitenant, and Cisco SBP (Service Billing Platform) enabled.

Use GMM to bring new gateways online in minutes instead of days—and easily manage them remotely with this secure cloud-hosted application. GMM streamlines provisioning and provides you with ongoing visibility and control of your Cisco-supported gateways from your desktop browser.

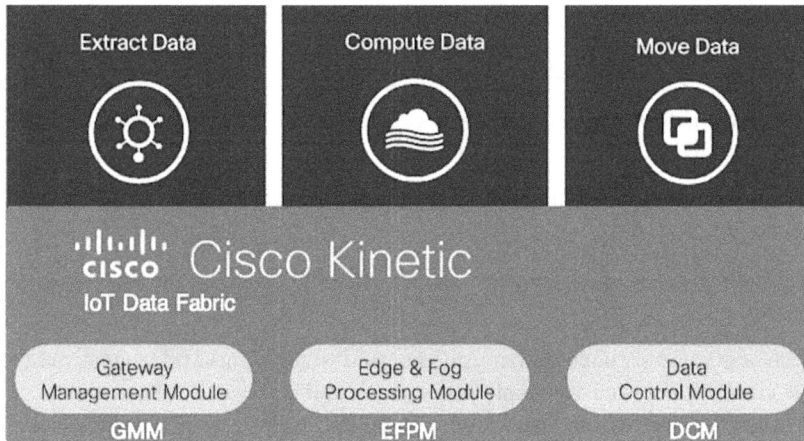

Figure 7-4   *Modules of Cisco Kinetic Platform*

For example, in a transportation use case, gateways installed along a roadway can be remotely managed using GMM. All required network configurations can be pushed from a single point in the cloud across all gateways based on user-defined templates. Figure 7-5 describes the GMM Module.

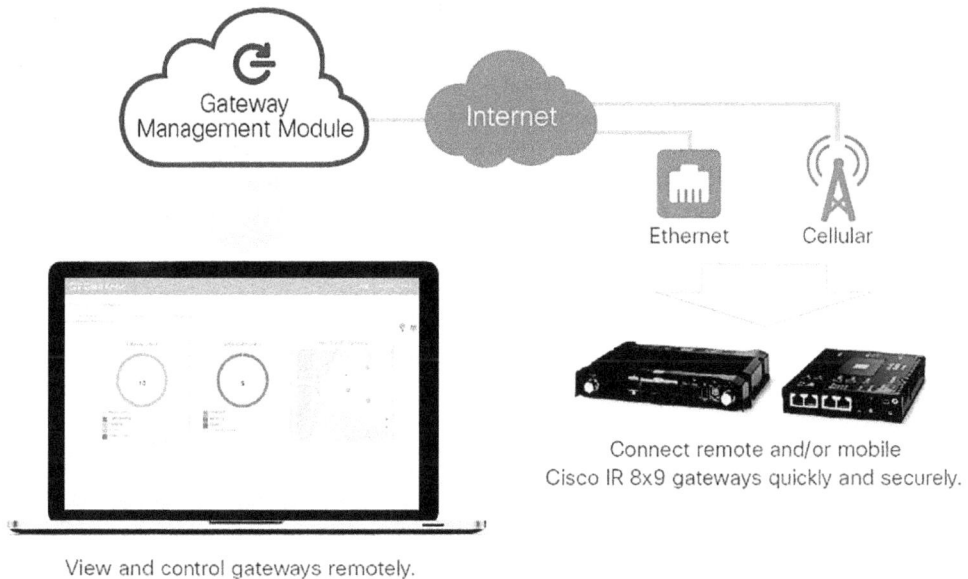

Figure 7-5   *GMM Module overview*

The following list explains some of the benefits provided by GMM:

- **Instant provisioning:** Dramatically reduce gateway onboarding time with simple setup.

    - Power up the gateway, plug it into the network, or use its cellular power to connect with GMM.

    - Enter the gateway's serial number in your browser-based Cisco GMM dashboard to securely "claim" it.

    - Select from your library of templates to automatically configure the gateway as it onboards.

    There's no configuration code to write, and no need to send a network engineer on site. The installation technician simply powers it on and makes sure it has a connection. You handle the rest from your cloud-based dashboard. There are no delays, and you can apply bulk operations to handle volume provisioning for even greater efficiency.

- **Manage gateways securely in various deployment models:** Whether you're adding gateways to an existing network or using them as standalone access points with cellular connectivity only, GMM streamlines your deployment. You can also extend your network security to mobile and remote gateways with an optional Cisco Flex VPN connection between these assets and your network and associated user access controls. Figure 7-6 illustrates the GMM deployment modules.

- **Cellular connectivity and strength:** Gain real-time visibility into the cellular connectivity and strength. Use this information to manage dual SIM connectivity when enabled on your gateways. This provides always-on connectivity for mission-critical remote and mobile applications. Plus, if your use case includes video recording in a vehicle, you can automatically offload files via Wi-Fi when in range of your network to avoid the higher cost of cellular data transfer. Figure 7-7 illustrates the GMM connectivity.

Cisco Kinetic – Data Control Module

Transform and filter sensor data and send the results to the cloud and/or other destinations, according to policies set by the data owner.

The benefits for Cisco DCM are as follows:

- Simplify management of operations at scale.

- Global view of all assets allows for better planning and management.

- Increase uptime and efficiency of IoT devices.

- Enforce data ownership and control of who gets your data.

- Scalable control of data by offering programmable filtering, throttling, and alerting from a single pane of glass.

- Triage and fix device issues remotely; avoid costly truck rolls.

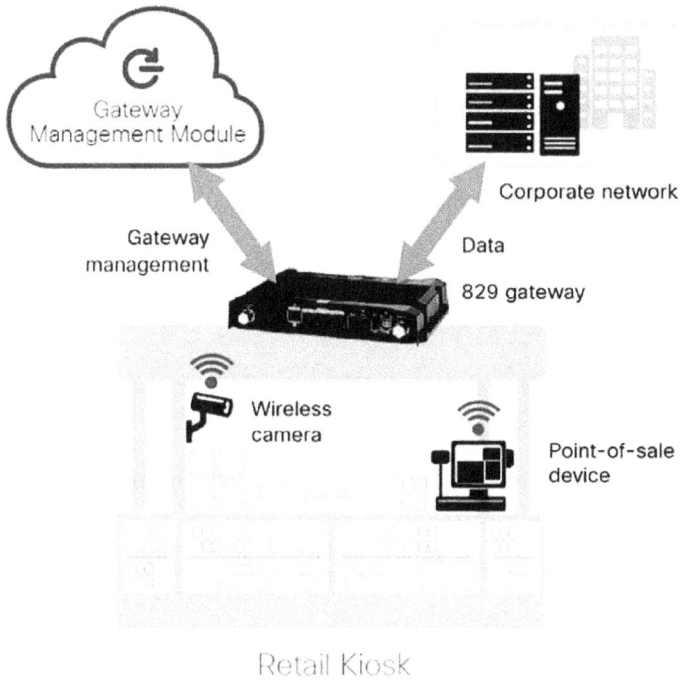

Figure 7-6   *GMM deployment modules*

Figure 7-7   *GMM connectivity*

Figure 7-8 illustrates the DCM dashboard.

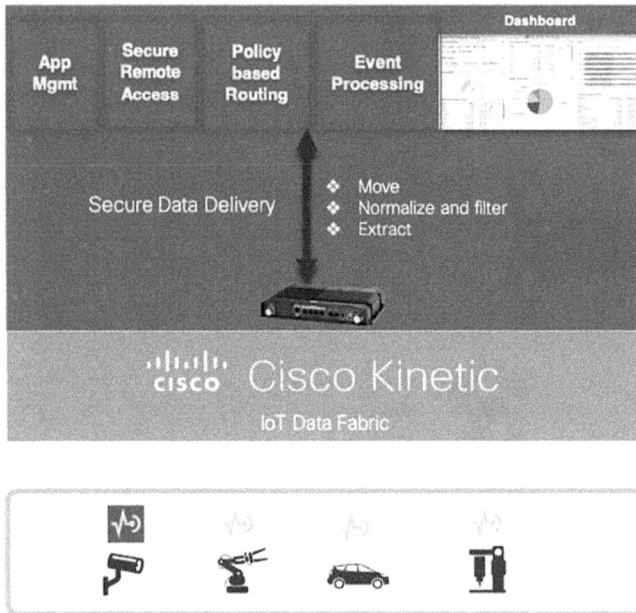

Figure 7-8   *DCM dashboard*

Cisco Kinetic – Edge & Fog Processing Module

Compute on distributed nodes of the network, from edge to destination.

The benefits of Cisco EFPM are as follows:

- Connect a wide range of devices; capture and transform data, normalizing it to make it usable.

- Support industrial environments without cloud connectivity or limited access.

- Respond in real time; apply rules to data in motion.

- Perform distributed micro-processing, where needed, from edge to endpoint.

- Securely and reliably deliver data at the edge or fog.

- Maintain historian data for future analysis.

- Visualize data in real time for faster responses to machine performance.

Figure 7-9 illustrates the EFP Module.

Figure 7-9   *EFP Module*

Introduction to Cisco IoT

The best decisions are made when the right people have access to the right information at the right time. The Internet of Things (IoT) has dramatically increased the volume and variety of data produced, opening the door to a wave of new possibilities. The key is to extract the data from its source, transform it so it is usable, and securely deliver the right data to the right applications to put it to work. Figure 7-10 illustrates the Cisco Edge Intelligence Solution.

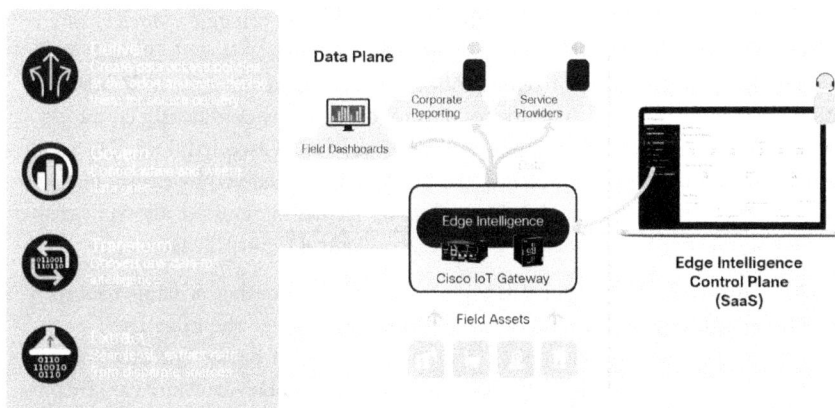

Figure 7-10   *Cisco Edge Intelligence Solution*

However, most solutions today are so complicated that organizations often cannot reap the full rewards of their data-gathering projects. The most important data is often at the remote edge of the network, where the core business operates, such as in oil rigs, delivery trucks, and utility substations and on roads. In addition, organizations lose insight into who has access to what data and often don't have the needed flexibility and simplicity to send the data everywhere it needs to go.

Cisco offers an unparalleled end-to-end IoT OD architecture to interconnect assets, applications, and data to uncover transformative business insights. Figure 7-11 illustrates Cisco IoT Solution Overview.

Network connectivity	Device management	Data control and exchange	Edge computing
Extend the network you know and trust to operational environments	Manage industrial assets and devices at scale with automated solutions	Efficiently move the right data to the right place at the right time	Push data processes to the edge to enable fast decision-making in the field

Security
Protect your business from end to end with
Cisco's industry-leading security portfolio

Figure 7-11   *Cisco IoT Solution Overview*

Edge Device Manager

Edge Device Manager is a core service in Cisco IoT used to manage industrial network devices such as IR1101, IR829, IR809, and IR807. Customers can bring new devices online with Zero Touch Deployment (ZTD) and easily manage them remotely with this service, for software upgrades, monitoring, and troubleshooting. With the included Cisco Validated Design (CVD) templates and eCVD templates, customers can now confidently configure one or thousands of devices quickly. When customers purchase Cisco IoT, Edge Device Manager is a service that always comes with the product and is enabled by device management licenses. Edge Device Manager has Cisco Control Center integration, allowing greater visibility and control of SIM-level details of the Cisco Control Center SIM.

The Cisco IoT Edge Device Manager (EDM) is a secure, cloud-native, scalable tool to provision, manage, and monitor IoT network devices. You can use the Edge Device Manager to bring new edge devices online in minutes instead of days—and easily manage them remotely with this secure cloud-hosted application. Edge Device Manager streamlines provisioning and provides you with ongoing visibility and control of your Cisco-supported edge devices from your desktop browser.

For example, in a transportation use case, network devices installed along a roadway can be remotely managed using EDM. All required network configurations can be pushed from a single point in the cloud across all network devices based on user-defined templates. Figure 7-12 provides an overview of Cisco EDM.

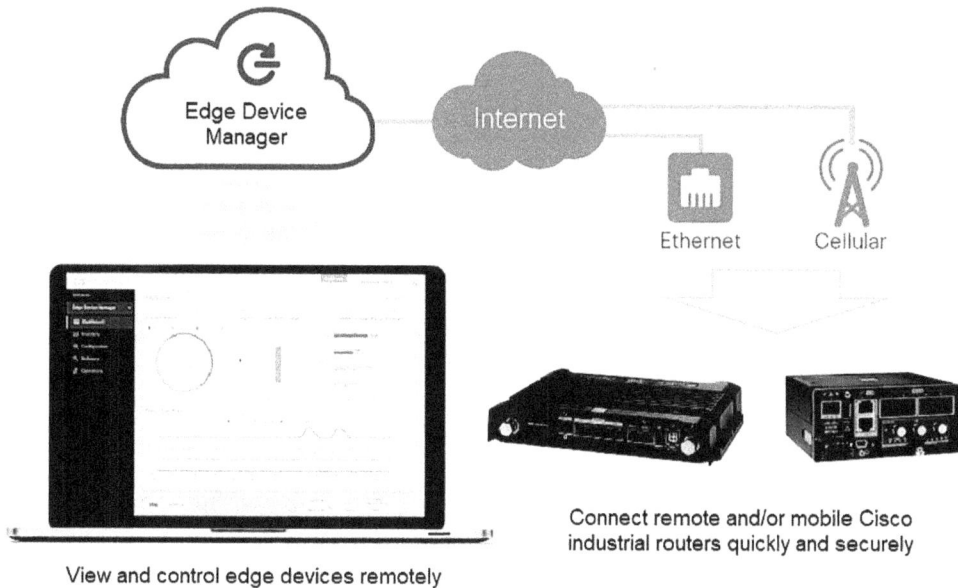

View and control edge devices remotely

Connect remote and/or mobile Cisco industrial routers quickly and securely

Figure 7-12   *Cisco Edge Device Manager Overview*

Cisco EDM includes the following main features:

- **Zero-touch deployment (ZTD):** Quick and easy provisioning of IoT network devices minimizes costly manual work. Using Secure Device Onboarding (SDO) and Cisco Plug and Play Connect, Cisco industrial routers can call home to Cisco IoT OD automatically, over cellular or Ethernet, for onboarding and provisioning upon power-up. An intuitive GUI enables you to create groups and apply configuration templates or custom template to one or thousands of devices. Other benefits of ZTD include the following:

  - Accelerate device setup and configuration.

  - Reduce deployment cost and project risk associated with time-consuming and error-prone manual configuration.

  - Avoid the training costs associated with more complex deployment models.

- **Device lifecycle management:** Properly maintain your network devices with the following:

  - Software upgrades

  - Configuration updates

- Device monitoring

- Device diagnostics

- Alerts and Events

■ **Cellular visibility:** Use Control Center integration to gain real-time visibility into cellular signal strength and aggregated cellular data usage.

■ **End-to-end security:** Ensure your data is protected with Cisco security at many levels. Enable certificate-based authentication during the device-claiming process.

■ **Device location:** View the location of your devices on a map and status summaries of device health, cellular usage, and more.

■ **User and organization management:** Gain greater control over user access and permissions with the following:

- Multitenancy

- Role-based access control (RBAC)

- Single sign-on (SSO) authentication with SAML

Supported Device Interfaces for Onboarding

The following interfaces are supported for IoT OD PnP onboarding using the default-configuration template. Only these supported interfaces provide monitoring data in the Dashboard page and in the device details Monitoring tab (**Inventory > *device* > Monitoring**). Currently, dual active/active LTE is not supported on any platform in the default template.

Table 7-2 details all the supported devices and interfaces used.

Table 7-2 *All Supported Devices and Interfaces Used*

Platform	Ethernet WAN	Cellular
IR807	FastEthernet0	Cellular0
IR809	GigabitEthernet0	Cellular0
IR829-LTE (single modem)	GigabitEthernet0, LAN (over SVI): GigabitEthernet 1, 2, 3, 4	Cellular0
IR829-2LTE (dual modem)	GigabitEthernet0, LAN (over SVI): GigabitEthernet 1	Cellular0/0 Cellular1/0
IR1101	GigabitEthernet0/0/0	Cellular0/1/0
IR1800	GigabitEthernet0/0/0	Cellular0/4/0

Onboarding Devices

Once your Edge Device Manager (EDM) account is set up, you can proceed with onboarding your various devices.

Onboarding IR devices

Use Edge Device Manager (EDM) to add network devices to IoT OD. Enter the device serial number and select the device group that is associated with the correct configuration template. You can then make any device-specific settings and add the device. The following example describes how to create a device group and apply an eCVD (Cisco Validated Design) template to an IR 1101 device. Figure 7-13 illustrates the IR device onboarding process.

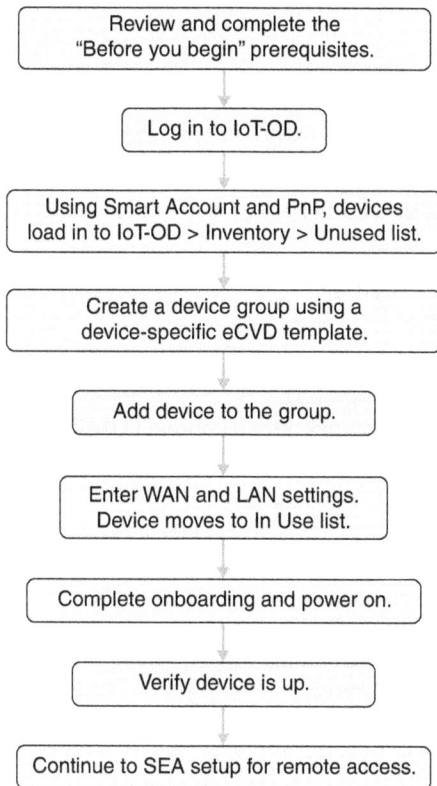

Review and complete the
"Before you begin" prerequisites.

Log in to IoT-OD.

Using Smart Account and PnP, devices
load in to IoT-OD > Inventory > Unused list.

Create a device group using a
device-specific eCVD template.

Add device to the group.

Enter WAN and LAN settings.
Device moves to In Use list.

Complete onboarding and power on.

Verify device is up.

Continue to SEA setup for remote access.

Figure 7-13   *IR device onboarding process*

Step 1.   Set up a new organization in Cisco IoT OD, or log in to an existing admin account.

Step 2.   Select the **Edge Device Manager** service in the left banner.

Step 3.   Pre-stage your network configuration by creating a device group and configuration template.

Device groups allow you to apply the same configuration template to groups of similar network devices. Any network device you add to the group will receive the group template. Any changes to that template will apply to all devices in the group.

   a. Click **Configuration**.

   b. In the **Groups** tab, click **Add Group**.

   c. Enter the group settings:

   ■ **Group Name:** Enter a meaningful name.

   ■ **Select Device Type:** Select the device model, such as the IR1101 series. Each device type has a different set of features that can be configured.

   d. Select a new base template. Select the **eCVD-IR1101-Basic** template.

Note   This configuration can be used as-is or customized later.

   e. Group Description (Optional). Describe the devices and configuration.

   f. Verify the settings and click **Create**. Your new group appears in the list.

Step 4.   Configure the group's WAN uplink settings.

This is only required if your deployment uses a private or custom Access Point Name that is not automatically recognized by the modem. There may be cases where a public APN is not in the modem's default list and would need to be added as part of the steps described next. If the APN name is required, you must also use Ethernet for the initial onboarding. After you add the device to IoT OD, Ethernet can be disconnected.

   a. Click the group name and then select **Edit Group**.

   b. Click the **Configuration** tab and select **Form View** (no Form View for IG 20 devices).

   c. Click **WAN**, enter the following settings, and click **Save**:

   ■ **Ethernet:** Select Enabled.

   ■ **Ethernet port WAN priority:** Select First.

- **Cellular 1:** Enabled.

- **Primary Cellular Access Point Name:** Enter the private/custom APN name.

- **First Cellular interface WAN priority:** Select Second.

Step 5.   Add a device to IoT OD and map it to an existing pre-staged device group.

   a. From the left pane, click **Inventory**.

   b. Click **Add Devices**.

   c. Select **Manual Add** and complete the following fields in the **Add Device** page:

- **Product ID (PID):** Select the product ID (model number) from the drop-down list.

- **Serial Number:** Enter a serial number.

- **Name:** (Optional) Enter a device name.

- **Latitude / Longitude:** (Optional) Enter the location of the device to display it on the dashboard map.

   d. Select the device group you just created. The configuration template for that group will be applied to the network device.

   e. Click **Next**.

   f. In the **Configuration** window, complete the settings and variables included in the template. The following settings are required to create a remote session with the subtended device.

WAN: Enable the following for your WAN back-haul settings:

- **Cellular:** Click **Enabled**. If you're using a public APN, leave the Primary Cellular Access Point Name blank (the name is automatically entered). For custom or private APNs, the APN name configured for the device group should appear.

- **Ethernet:** This should be Enabled for private or custom APNs, or if your device uses a wired network connection. For private or custom APNs, Ethernet is used to onboard the device. After the device is added, Ethernet can be disconnected and the private/custom cellular network will be used instead.

   g. Click **Next** after all settings are complete.

   h. Correct any errors before proceeding, if necessary.

   i. In the **Review** window, check that your settings are correct and click **Save**.

Step 6.   Connect the device to power and add it to your network.

When the device is powered on and connected to the network using either Ethernet or cellular, it will connect to IoT OD and be configured for use with IoT OD. The selected template configuration will also be applied. The device will go through the following states: **Unheard > Configuring > Up (Green)**. This can take 5–7 minutes.

SIM Card Activation and Seamless Device Onboarding

This feature will automatically activate your Cisco-provided AT&T SIM card, as long as you have set up an account with AT&T and entered the account credentials into IoT Operations Dashboard (OD). Once you enter your AT&T account credentials into IoT OD, you can preconfigure a group of devices to share the same SIM configuration with (comm plan and rate plan).

Once you complete these prerequisites, devices that are moved into the group will automatically provision into your AT&T account as soon as the IoT network devices are switched on for the first time. SDO accomplishes the following:

■ Automate device configuration for Day 1 operation (APNs, cellular config), replacing error-prone manual APN configuration.

■ Automate switching of device SIM from Cisco's holding account to customer's enterprise Control Center Account.

SDO Architecture

Figure 7-14 is a simplified graphic of the Secure Device Onboarding process.

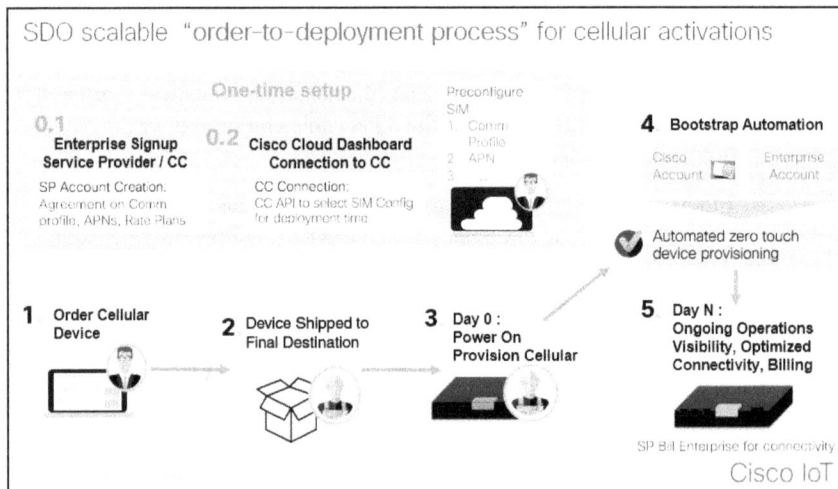

Figure 7-14 *Secure device onboarding process*

Secure Equipment Access

Use Secure Equipment Access (SEA) to remotely manage access and interact with both the gateways and connected devices. This can be used to directly troubleshoot or monitor the IoT devices in your deployment.

SEA provides browser-based access to equipment for all supported protocols: HTTP/S, SSH, RDP, and VNC. No additional software is required on the user laptop to access equipment. Specific users within in-house operations teams and external third parties can be assigned access to a group of equipment.

Here's an example:

- An elevator technician can use SEA to establish IP connectivity between his PC and an elevator in another city. He can then use a diagnostics application on his PC to troubleshoot an issue, determine a solution, and dispatch a repair technician with the right parts for that issue.

- An administrator can use a VNC connection to remotely access and control a Windows computer attached to the gateway.

- A device (such as a camera management server) can be accessed and used to configure and manage other devices (such as video cameras).

Summary Steps

Step 1. Log in to your Operations Dashboard account.

Step 2. A system administrator sets up device access.

Step 3. Onboard and configure gateways using the Edge Device Manager service.

Step 4. Add IoT devices to the gateways in SEA.

- Connected clients configured in EDM can be selected from a list. (**Note:** Connected clients for IG devices are auto-discovered.)

- Additional devices can be manually added in SEA.

Step 5. An operator administrator gives users SEA access to specific equipment.

Step 6. Operator users can then access the equipment.

Edge Intelligence

Edge Intelligence (EI) is edge-to-multicloud data orchestration software designed for connected assets. This software is deployed on Cisco industrial routers and compute gateways for simple out-of-the box deployment.

EI gives organizations full control over data—from its extraction to its transformation to its governance to its delivery. At each stage of data collection, EI streamlines the process so that it can be delivered easily at scale. For example, EI significantly speeds the labor-intensive process of developing and deploying applications that process data at the edge. It offers a plug-in for Microsoft Visual Studio Code. Organizations everywhere can easily create code and push applications out wherever they need to go without having to leave Microsoft Visual Studio.

EI provides the flexibility to integrate with multiple applications in multiple clouds. EI offers native integrations that simplify the entire process for Microsoft Azure IoT Hub and other MQ Telemetry Transport (MQTT) applications.

Edge to Multicloud Data Flow

EI helps you take control of your data throughout key aspects of its lifecycle, helping you simplify from start to finish. The following list and Figure 7-15 summarize this edge-to-multicloud lifecycle:

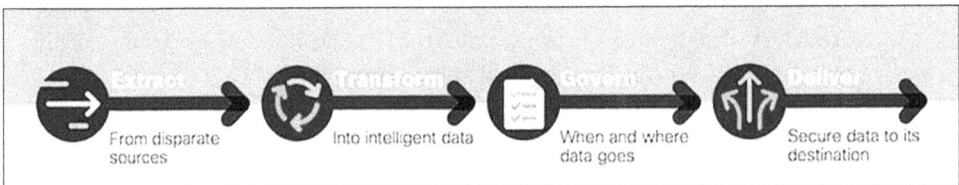

Figure 7-15 *Lifecycle of Edge Intelligence*

- **Extract:** You can automatically ingest data from any edge sensor using Cisco EI hosted on Cisco network equipment. EI has built-in industry-standard connectors, such as OPC Unified Architecture (OPC-UA), Modbus (TCP and Serial), and MQ Telemetry Transport (MQTT), that allow data to be extracted from disparate sources. The data is then converted to industry-standard formats to enable its full use.

- **Transform:** Once the data is extracted, EI enables real-time processing to filter, compress, or analyze data in a uniquely simple way. Via a plug-in, EI is fully integrated with one of the most popular tools, Microsoft Visual Studio Code. Developers can create, test, and deploy code without ever leaving the tool.

- **Govern:** EI provides a central point for the creation and deployment of polices that govern how edge data is processed and delivered.

- **Deliver:** Organizations have the data they need from multiple aggregated sources to gain actionable insights for the best decision making. You can then choose which data is sent to which destination and send it to multiple destinations/applications.

Overview of Configuration Lifecycle Management in EI

Creating an edge-to-multicloud data policy is a multistage process that can be completed in the EI UI. The key steps for EI management are shown in Figure 7-16.

1. Enable
EI Agents

3. Add Data
Destinations

5. Create & Deploy
Data Policy

2. Add & Configure
Assets

4. Create Data
Logic *(optional)*

Figure 7-16 *Process of EI management*

The progression begins with the extraction of the data from disparate sources and the transformation of the data using data policies. Finally, the deployed data policies deliver the data securely to the predetermined destinations.

Step 1. Enable EI agents. Deploy and configure the EI agents on the network device. They will then "call home" and show up in the EI cloud.

Step 2. Add and configure assets. Define the asset type, test it, and then configure the assets based on this asset type.

Step 3. Add data destinations such as Microsoft Azure IoT, MQTT Server, IBM Watson, Software AG Cumulocity IoT, or AWS IoT Core.

Step 4. Create and deploy the data policy, which sends data from the assets to the destinations. There are two options:

- **Data Rules:** Sends data from assets to destinations without transformation.

- **Data Logic:** Uses JavaScript scripts developed in Microsoft Visual Studio (VS) code to transform data before it is sent to a destination (if local processing of data is required).

Figure 7-17 summarizes the creation and deployment of data policies using the EI.

Enable and Manage EI Agents

Cisco Edge Intelligence is enabled by installing the EI agent software on your Cisco network devices. The EI agent is a Cisco IOx app that runs on Cisco network devices such as the IR809, IR829, IR1101, and IC3000.

In this release, enable the EI agent on your network devices using the Cisco Kinetic Gateway Management Module (GMM), Cisco Field Network Director (FND), Cisco IoT Operations Dashboard (OD), or the Local Manager. EI agent details cannot be modified from EI.

Table 7-3 details the steps for enabling EI agents.

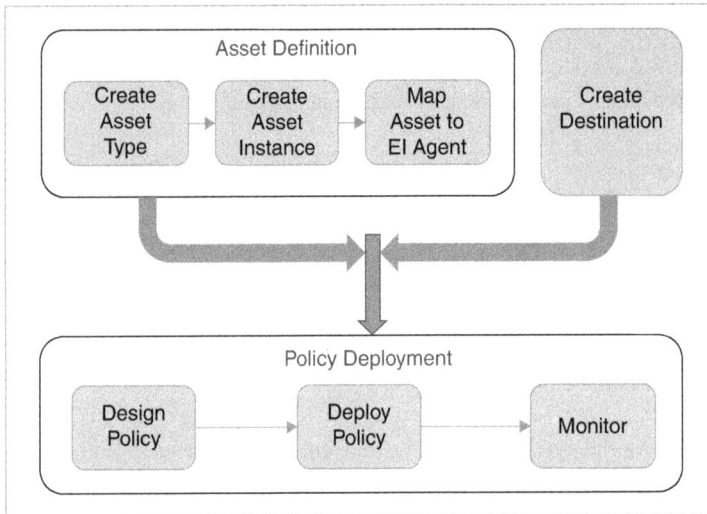

Figure 7-17   *Creation and deployment of data policies using the EI*

Table 7-3   *Steps for Enabling EI Agents*

Step	Description
Download EI agent (IOx application).	Go to the Cisco Software Download page to download the EI Agent.
Gather input parameters.	You need to gather the following specific parameters from the EI web-based management backend: ■ Access Token ■ Upstream Configuration URL
Upload and install EI agent using GMM, FND, EDM, or Local Manager.	

Asset Management Workflow

To integrate IoT edge data into applications, you must first extract the data from assets. The main steps are as follows:

Step 1.   Add an asset type. An asset type is a template that defines the type of business asset and sensor attached to it.

■ Configure the connection settings. Connection settings define how the associated assets connect to the EI agent running on a network device.

■ Create a data model. The data model defines the format of the data being generated from assets (how the data is represented in the asset).

- Test and verify the data model. The data model can be tested before saving it.

- Save the asset type.

Step 2. Add assets:

- Assets are physical instances that will be attached to a gateway.

- Asset instances are assigned to an asset type to define the connection settings and data model.

- Asset details and custom attribute values are also added.

Step 3. Map the asset to the associated EI agent.

Step 4. Map physical instances of assets to their attached gateways.

Add Data Destinations

Add data destinations to define where data policies send data, such as Azure IoT or MQTT. The data destination defines the connection details.

A destination must be set before you can design and deploy data policies.

Add an MQTT Server Destination

EI has customized screens for specific MQTT-based cloud destinations such as IBM Watson and SAG Cumulocity IoT based on the MQTT parameters typically required for those implementations. A generic MQTT destination can be used for different configurations.

For example, a SAG Cumulocity destination that requires TLS and peer verification can be configured in EI. You can use a generic MQTT connection, however, to connect to a SAG Cumulocity IoT instance without TLS. For generic MQTT connections, make sure the configuration matches the destination instance requirements such as parameters, message format, and so on.

To add an MQTT Server destination, complete the required fields.

Step 1. From the left menu, click **Data Destinations.**

Step 2. In the right pane, click **Add Data Destination** and select **MQTT.**

Step 3. Complete the fields in the Add Data Destination – MQTT Broker page and click **Save.**

Deploy Data Rules

Data rules are deployed and run on the EI agent software installed on edge devices. At least one asset must be mapped to each EI agent where the data rule is deployed.

Step 1.   From the left menu, click **Data Policies > Data Rules**.

Step 2.   In the Data Rule entry, click **Deploy / Undeploy**.

Step 3.   In the **Data Rule** section, select the EI agent(s) and click **Deploy**.

Step 4.   Scroll down to Deployment Status:

   ▪ **Deployment Pending** (yellow): The data policy is in the process of being deployed.

   ▪ **Deployed** (green): Deployment is successful on all EI agents. Data is flowing from all assets to the data destination as configured.

   ▪ **Error** (red): The policy deployment is unsuccessful. There is at least one EI agent where the deployment failed. The data flow from assets to data destination is not successful for some configured assets.

Deploy Data Logic

Use data logic to transform the data from assets before it is sent to a data destination. Data logic scripts are created in VS code and synchronized with your organization's Cisco IoT account, where they can be deployed to an EI agent. This means the script will run on the Cisco network device where the EI agent is installed, receive data from assets, transform that data according to the data logic script, and send the results to a data destination. Here are the steps to follow:

Step 1.   In Cisco EI, configure the EI agents, asset types, asset instances, and data destinations that will be used by the data logic.

Step 2.   In VS code, develop and debug the data logic script.

Step 3.   In VS code, click **Push to Production** to save the data logic to Cisco EI.

Step 4.   In Cisco EI, deploy the data logic to an EI agent:

   ▪ Click **Data Polices > Data Logics**.

   ▪ Click **New / Not Deployed**.

   ▪ In the Data Logic entry, click **Configure**.

   ▪ (Optional) Click the **Configuration** tab to change the data destination, or view the script or Input Asset Type details.

   ▪ Click **Deploy**. This takes you to the **Deployment** tab.

   ▪ Select one or more EI agents and click **Deploy**. This takes you to the **Status** tab, which shows the list of deployed EI agents.

Licensing

Cisco Edge Intelligence is licensed as a subscription. Licenses are divided into two groups: base functionality and industry-specific device adapters. A base license defines the general set of agent capabilities available for the agent and is required for each Cisco network device that will run an Edge Intelligence agent. An additional industry-specific device adapter license may be purchased for each agent when industry-specific device connectivity is needed.

One base license must be purchased for each hardware device that will run the Cisco Edge Intelligence agent. Additional device adapter licenses may be purchased for specific industry use cases.

Summary

Cisco all-in-one IoT gateways provide simple, essential connectivity for assets at mass scale. The solution offers low upfront costs with an affordable monthly cloud subscription. The gateways take just a few minutes to deploy with minimal IT support. It's a fast and simple Day 0 set up: plug in and power on, with no staging required. The SIM provisioning is automated with Cisco Control Center integration with no manual intervention.

The Cisco IoT gateways portfolio consists of ruggedized and non-ruggedized options, allowing you to connect outdoor and indoor assets. Simply connect your unconnected assets to eliminate digital blind spots in your operations.

The IoT gateways are managed centrally through a simple, easy-to-use cloud management tool, the Cisco IoT Operations Dashboard. With this dashboard, you can remotely deploy, monitor, and troubleshoot the gateways. It enables you to gain insights into network usage and carry out updates remotely without sending anyone onsite. You receive automatic alerts if a device goes down so that you can take quick action. All of this is done remotely and at scale.

The gateways have essential security built in to secure the hardware, interfaces, and all communications to the data center. With Cisco networking, organizations benefit from end-to-end security, from the edge all the way to the headend in the data center. They can remotely monitor and diagnose the operational assets connected to an IoT gateway using Cisco's Secure Remote Access, eliminating the need for any truck rolls.

Chapter 8

Cisco Cloud Security

More applications and servers are moving to the cloud to take advantage of cost savings, scalability, and accessibility. Because of this, you've lost some of the visibility and control you once had. You don't know who is doing what and when in the cloud. Your data is now hosted in the cloud, which brings up concerns about what information is there, who's accessing it, where it's going, whether it's being exfiltrated, and so on. Despite multiple layers of security, malware infections and other advanced threats still loom.

With Cisco Cloud Security, you can adopt the cloud with confidence and protect your users, data, and applications, anywhere they are. Unlike traditional perimeter solutions, Cisco Cloud Security blocks threats over all ports and protocols for comprehensive coverage. Cisco Cloud Security also uses API-based integrations so you can amplify your existing security investments. It's simple to use and deploy, so you can start defending your organization in minutes.

This chapter will cover the following solutions:

- Cisco Cloudlock
- Cisco Umbrella
- Cisco Secure Cloud Analytics
- Cisco Duo Security

Shadow IT Challenge

You can't enable, manage, secure, or block what you can't see. Organizations, departments, and individual users are all embracing the cloud and leveraging new apps to help improve productivity, but the majority of new apps are being adopted without any involvement from IT or Security. This results in a big shadow IT challenge with the typical organization accessing hundreds of cloud apps that IT isn't aware of. The lack of a coordinated cloud-enablement strategy typically leads to a broad set of productivity, expense,

314   Chapter 8: Cisco Cloud Security

security, and support issues. You need full visibility into cloud activity and the ability to block unwanted apps to enable cloud adoption in a secure and organized fashion.

True visibility is more than just app identification. The first step is identifying the full spectrum of cloud apps that are in use in your organization, but that isn't enough. You need to understand who the vendor is, what the app does, how many users are accessing it, the volume of requests, and what level of risk it represents. Figure 8-1 lists key questions that all organizations have.

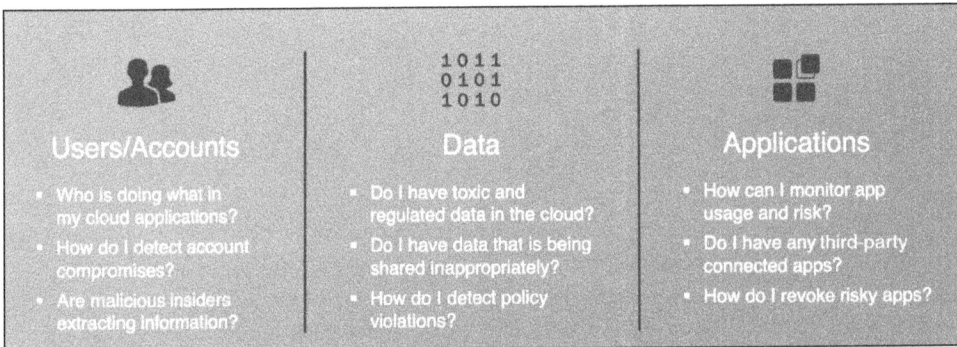

Figure 8-1 *Key questions organizations have*

On average, 24,000 files are exposed per organization, with the majority done using non-corporate email addresses. Figure 8-2 illustrates data exposure per organization.

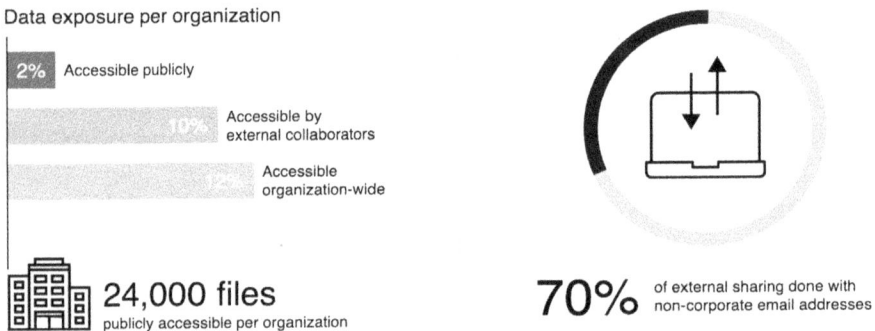

Figure 8-2 *Data exposure per organization*

Cisco Cloudlock

Cisco Cloudlock is a cloud-native cloud access security broker (CASB) that helps you move to the cloud safely. It protects your cloud users, data, and apps. Cloudlock's simple, open, and automated approach uses APIs to manage the risks in your cloud app ecosystem. With Cloudlock, you can more easily combat data breaches while meeting compliance regulations. Figure 8-3 illustrates Cisco Cloudlock solution.

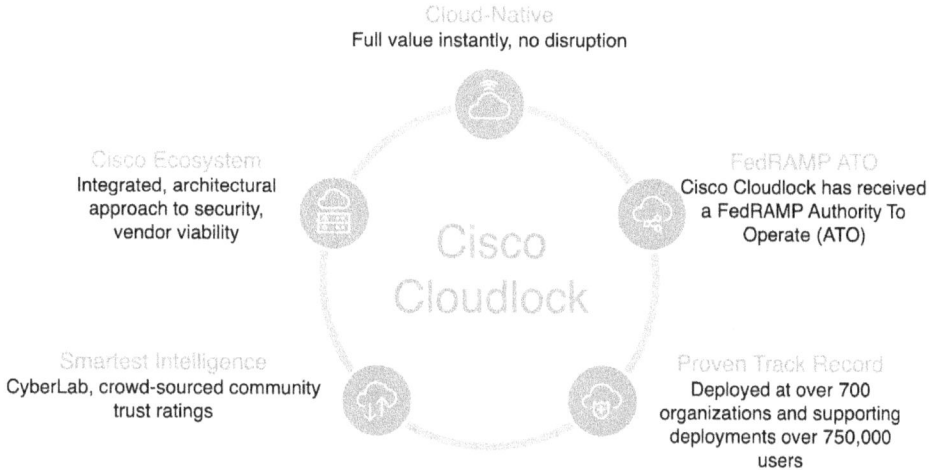

Figure 8-3 *Cisco Cloudlock solution*

Cloudlock discovers and protects sensitive information for users, data, and applications. Figure 8-4 provides an overview of Cisco Cloudlock.

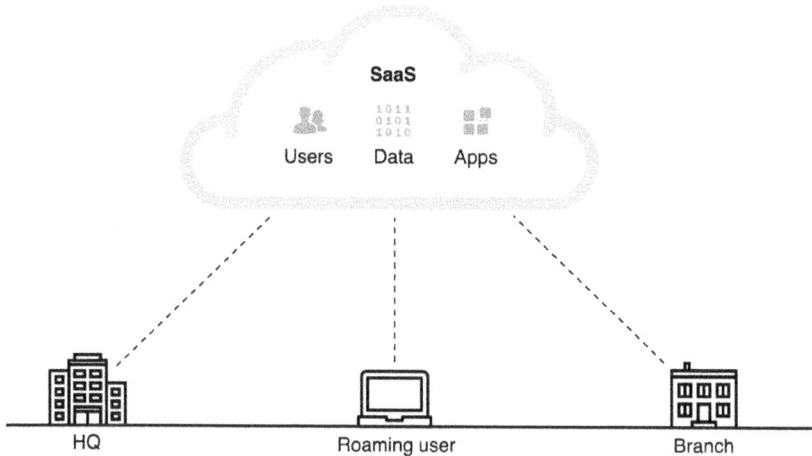

Figure 8-4 *Cisco Cloudlock overview*

User Security

Cloudlock uses advanced machine learning algorithms to detect anomalies based on multiple factors. It also identifies activities outside allowed countries and spots actions that seem to take place at impossible speeds across distances.

You can defend against compromised accounts and malicious insiders with User and Entity Behavior Analytics (UEBA), which runs against an aggregated set of cross-platform activities for better visibility and detection.

Data Security

Cloudlock's data loss prevention (DLP) technology continuously monitors cloud environments to detect and secure sensitive information. It provides countless out-of-the-box policies as well as highly tunable custom policies.

Identify Sensitive Data in Cloud Environments

Cisco Cloudlock continuously monitors cloud environments with a cloud data loss prevention (DLP) engine to identify sensitive information stored in cloud environments in violation of policy. With Cisco Cloudlock, security professionals enforce out-of-the-box policies focused on common sensitive information sets, such as PCI-DSS and HIPAA compliance, as well as custom policies to identify proprietary data, such as intellectual property. Advanced capabilities such as custom regular expression (RegEx) input, threshold settings, and proximity controls ensure high true-positive and low false-positive rates.

Cloudlock protects against exposures and data security breaches using a highly configurable DLP engine with automated, policy-driven response actions. Cloudlock has over 80 predefined policies. Figure 8-5 illustrates some of the Cisco Cloudlock predefined policies.

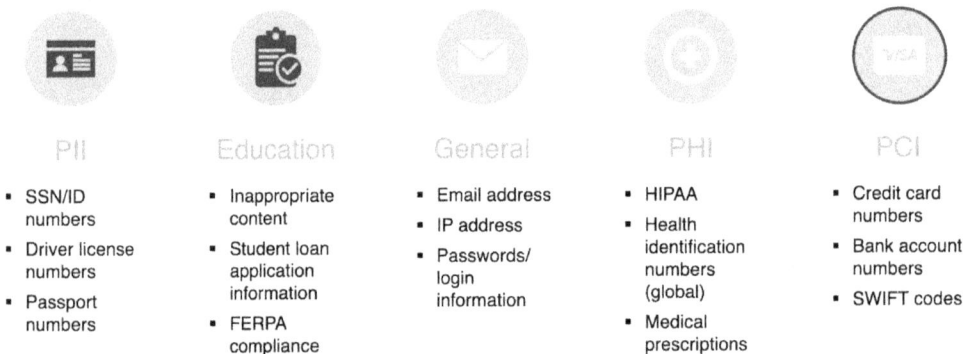

PII	Education	General	PHI	PCI
• SSN/ID numbers	• Inappropriate content	• Email address	• HIPAA	• Credit card numbers
• Driver license numbers	• Student loan application information	• IP address	• Health identification numbers (global)	• Bank account numbers
• Passport numbers	• FERPA compliance	• Passwords/login information	• Medical prescriptions	• SWIFT codes

Figure 8-5   *Cisco Cloudlock predefined policies*

Mitigate Increased Risk of Data Exposure in Cloud Applications

Combating data leakage in the cloud is a formidable challenge given the collaborative nature of cloud environments and the ease with which they enable users to access, create, and share sensitive information. Organizations are struggling to bridge the gap between legacy data protection tools and the often-limited level of visibility and control within cloud environments, particularly when accessed by external users or employees off of the corporate network.

Mitigate Risk Through Automated Responses

Cisco Cloudlock takes cloud DLP beyond discovery by offering configurable cross-platform automated response actions. Through an API-driven CASB architecture, Cisco Cloudlock supports deep, integrated response workflows that leverage the native capabilities of the monitored application, such as automated field-level encryption in Salesforce.com and automated file quarantining in Box. Cisco Cloudlock enables efficient risk reduction without the resource-intensive operation of many data protection tools. Figure 8-6 shows the Cisco Cloudlock dashboard.

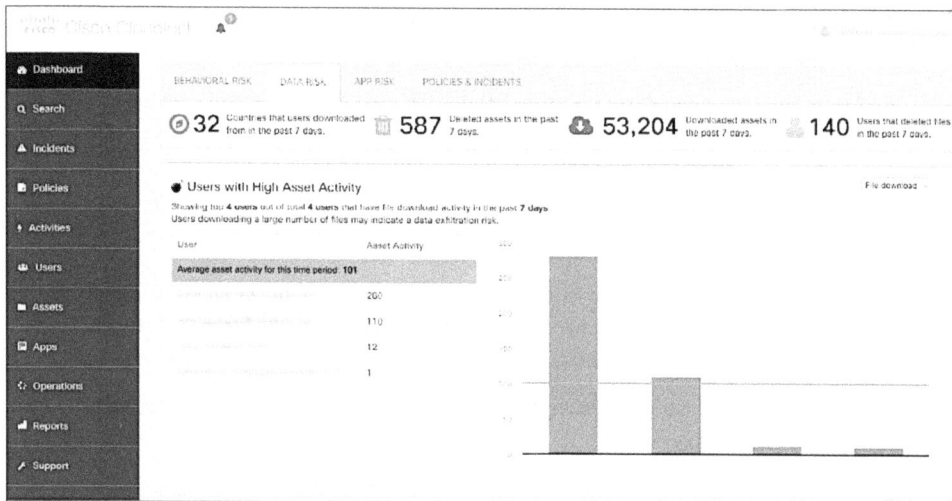

Figure 8-6   *Cisco Cloudlock dashboard*

App Security

The Cloudlock Apps Firewall discovers and controls cloud apps connected to your corporate environment. You can see a crowd-sourced Community Trust Rating for individual apps, and you can ban or allow-list them based on risk. Cloudlock Apps Firewall discovers and controls malicious cloud apps connected to your corporate environment and provides a crowd-sourced Community Trust Rating to identify individual app risks.

The following are Cloudlock use cases for user and entity behavior analytics, Cloud DLP, and Cloudlock Apps Firewall:

- **Analyze and take action:** Analyze application risk in order to block access to risky applications so they don't introduce unnecessary cost or risk to your organization.

  - Continuously monitor cloud environments for sensitive information and exposures.

  - Enforce cross-platform automated response actions to mitigate risk rapidly.

- **Application governance:** Categorize applications as sanctioned or unsanctioned and baseline cloud usage in order to prevent the loss of your company's IP and to remain compliant.
  - Integrate with SIEM solutions for simplified incident investigation and incorporation in broad security analysis.
- **Alerting:** Proactively notify you about any apps in your environment that are very high-risk so that you can triage them before they do any damage in order to protect company data.
  - Pinpoint sensitive data within cloud apps through custom and out-of-the-box DLP policies.
- **Anomaly detection:** Alert you when there are spikes in traffic passing between a user and a discovered app, so that you can investigate and potentially ban the app in order to protect company data.
  - Reduce false positives through advanced DLP capabilities such as threshold and proximity controls.
- **Reporting:** Exportable reports of cloud services in use with detailed risk analysis and insight into data usage, user specifics so you can have this information at your fingertips, share with stakeholders.
  - Activate automated end-user notifications to educate employees and reduce future DLP violations.

Figure 8-7 illustrates Cisco Cloudlock use cases.

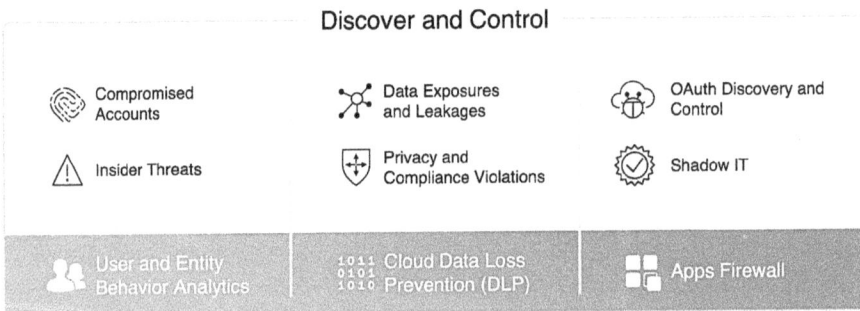

Figure 8-7   *Cisco Cloudlock use cases*

Enabling Cloudlock via WSA (11.5)

Figure 8-8 illustrates Cisco Cloudlock enablement workflow using WSA.

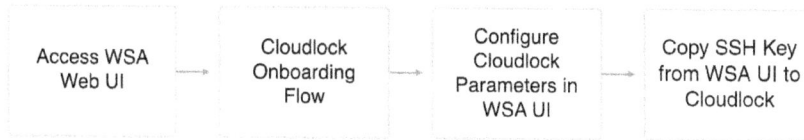

Figure 8-8   *Cisco Cloudlock enablement workflow using WSA*

Figure 8-9 shows the Cisco Cloudlock onboarding page for signing in and signing up.

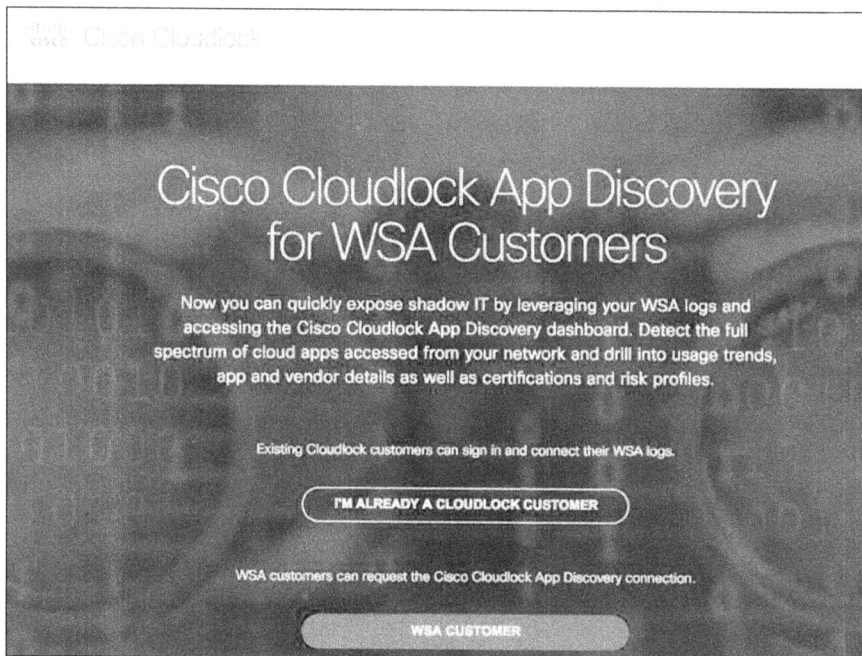

Figure 8-9   *Cisco Cloudlock onboarding page (sign-in and sign-up)*

The new radio button for Cloudlock log subscription has the following features:

■ It is preselected when it is triggered from the Cloudlock settings page.

■ Preselected fields and parameters are sent to Cloudlock.

■ The admin enters SCP-related information and clicks Submit.

Figure 8-10 illustrates Cisco Cloudlock log subscription configuration.

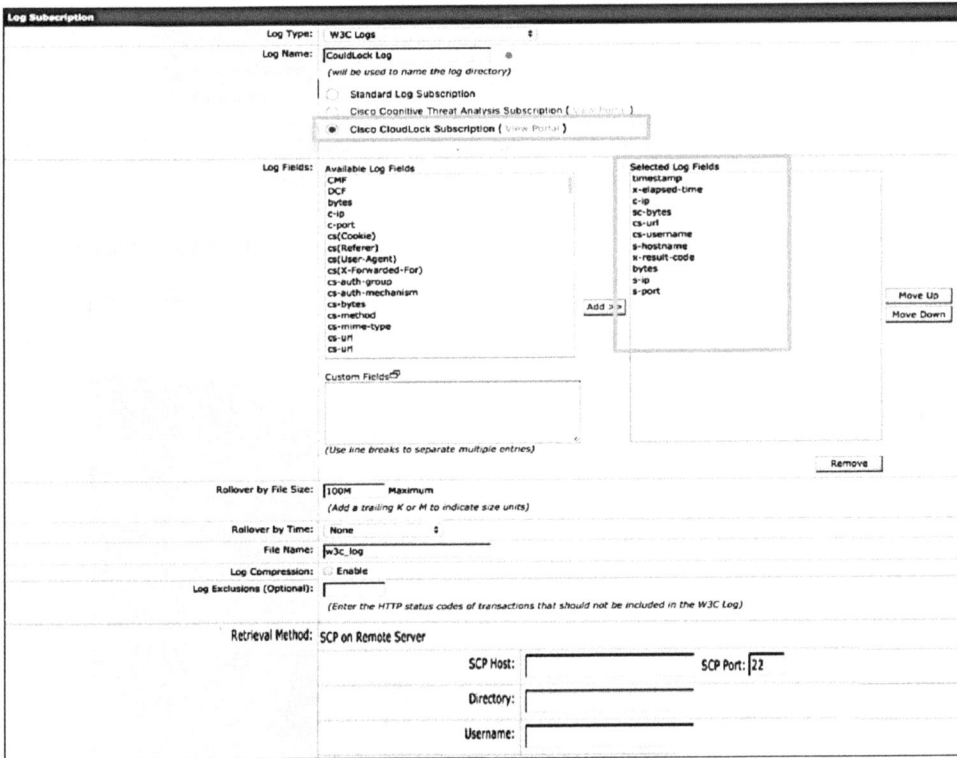

Figure 8-10 *Cisco Cloudlock log subscription configuration*

Figure 8-11 shows the Cisco Cloudlock settings configuration page.

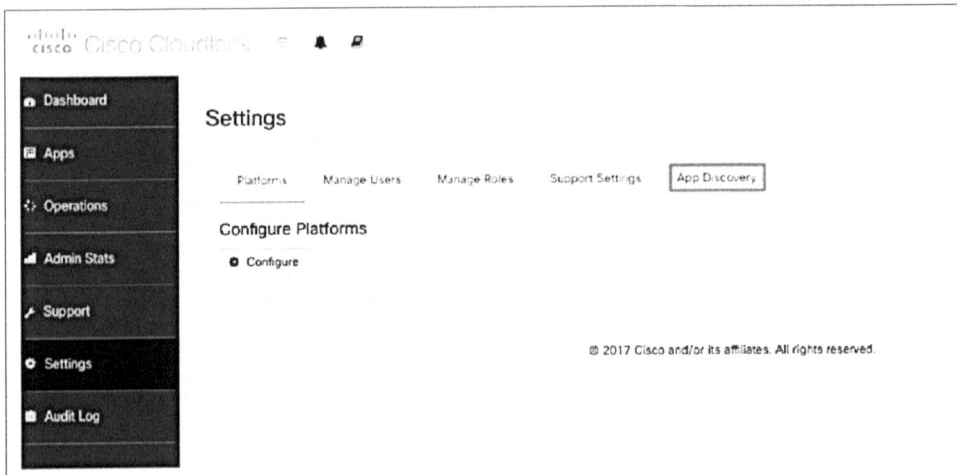

Figure 8-11 *Cisco Cloudlock settings configuration*

Figure 8-12 shows the Cisco Cloudlock "Add a New Log Source" process.

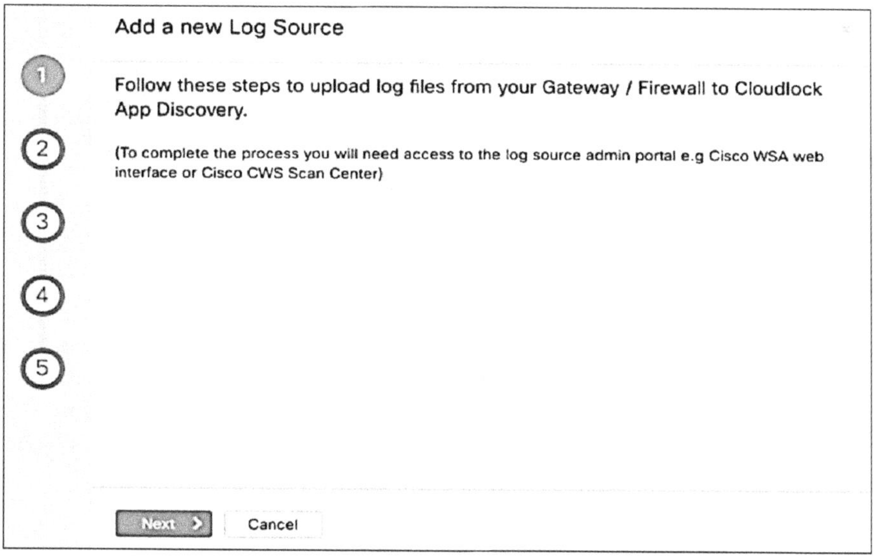

Figure 8-12   *Cisco Cloudlock "Add a New Log Source" process*

Figure 8-13 shows the Cisco Cloudlock "Add a New Log Source" SCP configuration process.

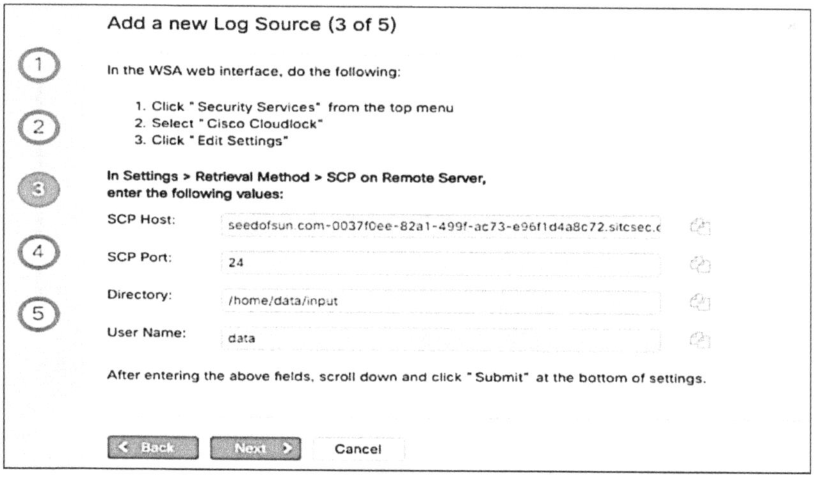

Figure 8-13   *Cisco Cloudlock "Add a New Log Source" SCP configuration process*

The Evolution of Cloud Security Service

Figure 8-14 illustrates the timeline of Cisco Cloudlock and Umbrella integration.

2006	2012	2015	2019
– as a recursive DNS provider (OpenDNS)	– DNS-layer security (OpenDNS Umbrella)	– by Cisco	– to integrate more security functions into a single service

Figure 8-14   *Cisco Cloudlock and Umbrella integration*

To help organizations embrace direct Internet access, in addition to DNS-layer security and interactive threat intelligence, Cisco Umbrella now includes secure web gateway, firewall, and CASB functionality, plus integration with Cisco SD-WAN, delivered from a single cloud security service. Figure 8-15 illustrates multiple security functions in a single cloud security service Cisco Umbrella.

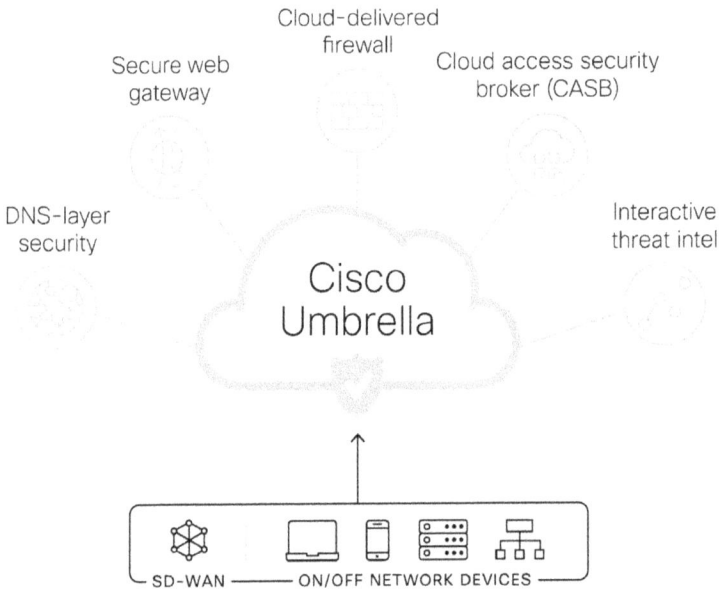

Figure 8-15   *Multiple security functions in a single cloud security service Cisco Umbrella*

DNS-Layer Security

Umbrella's DNS-layer security provides the fastest, easiest way to improve your security. It helps improve security visibility, detect compromised systems, and protect your users on and off the network by stopping threats over any port or protocol before they reach your network or endpoints.

Secure Web Gateway

Umbrella's secure web gateway logs and inspects web traffic for full visibility, URL and application controls, and protection against malware. Use IPsec tunnels, PAC files, or proxy chaining to forward traffic to our cloud-based proxy to enforce acceptable use policies and block advanced threats.

Firewall

Umbrella's firewall logs all activity and blocks unwanted traffic using IP, port, and protocol rules. To forward traffic, simply configure an IPsec tunnel from any network device. As new tunnels are created, policies are automatically applied for easy setup and consistent enforcement everywhere.

Cloud Access Security Broker

Umbrella exposes shadow IT by providing the ability to detect and report on cloud applications in use across your organization. For discovered apps, you can view details on the risk level and block or control usage to better manage cloud adoption and reduce risk. Figure 8-16 illustrates Cisco Cloudlock's "shadow IT" visibility.

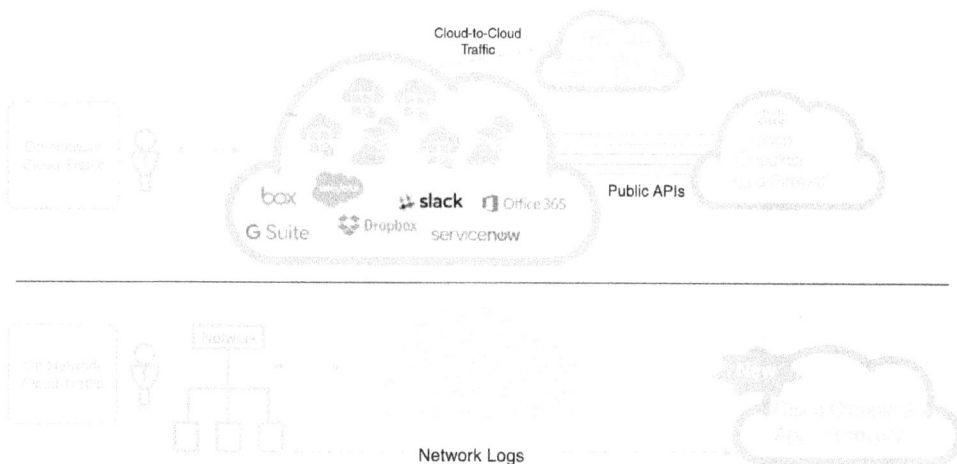

Figure 8-16 *Cisco Cloudlock's "shadow IT" visibility*

Interactive Threat Intelligence

Our unique view of the Internet gives us unprecedented insight into malicious domains, IPs, and URLs. Available via a console and API, Umbrella Investigate provides real-time context on malware, phishing, botnets, trojans, and other threats, enabling faster incident investigation and response.

Integration with SD-WAN

The Umbrella and Cisco SD-WAN integration deploys easily across your network for powerful cloud security and protection against Internet threats. Cisco's integrated approach secures cloud access and efficiently protects your branch users, connected devices, and app usage from all direct Internet access breakouts. The App Discovery dashboard and Umbrella's logs can be used for visibility.

Leveraging Umbrella Log Files for Shadow IT Visibility

You can now use your DNS logs to discover the cloud apps your users are accessing because Cisco provides in-product integration between Umbrella and Cloudlock. The Umbrella user interface can now be configured to include both the Cloudlock App Discovery dashboard and drill-down reports based on your existing Umbrella DNS activity.

Dashboard for Visibility and Trends

The dashboard shows the level of cloud service activity and risk in your organization. It also provides a summary by app category that is sorted by risk level. This gives insight into potential policy and compliance violations if employees use a new cloud service instead of an approved app. Figure 8-17 illustrates the Cisco Umbrella App Discovery dashboard.

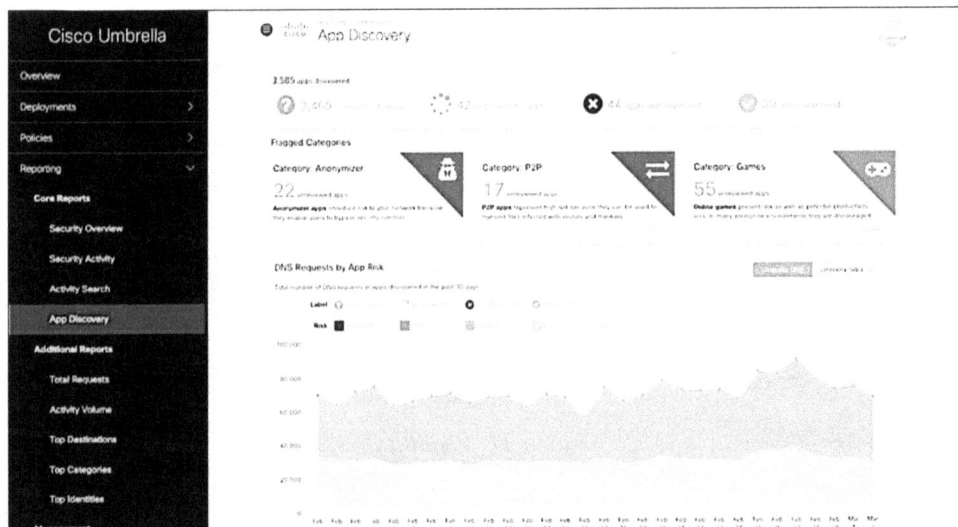

Figure 8-17   *Cisco Umbrella App Discovery dashboard*

Overview and Trending Information

The App Discovery dashboard provides an overview of the number of app requests by date and risk level to show patterns and changes over time. The most recent set of discovered and unreviewed apps is highlighted for easy access, and a chart showing the number of apps in each major category is provided with a breakdown by risk level. These summary charts allow point-and-click access to more detailed information on the category or individual application to simplify common administrator tasks.

Application Details

Preset application-level reports provide a list of apps labeled either Unreviewed, Under Audit, Approved, or Not Approved. You can easily apply filters to create custom views that help you understand and track by category, usage, type, or status. Figure 8-18 shows an example of a Cisco Umbrella application-level report.

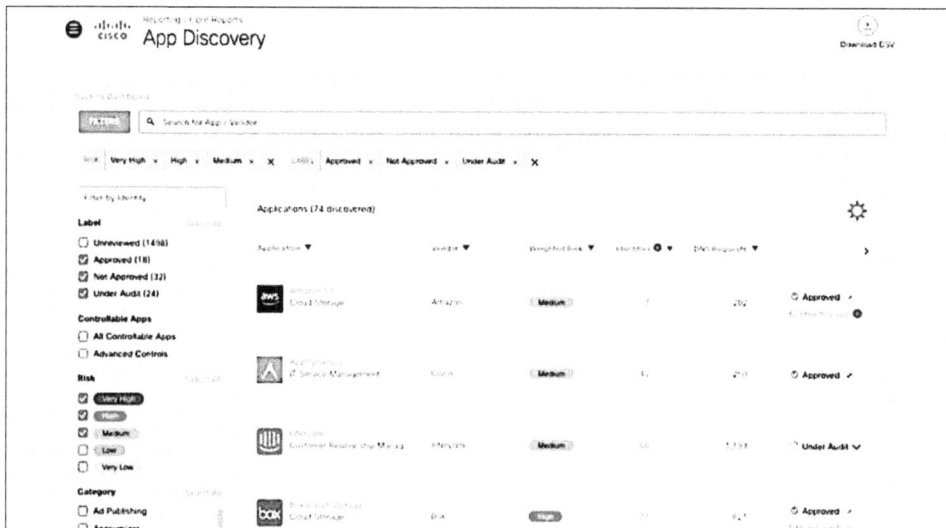

Figure 8-18 *Cisco Umbrella application-level report*

Optimization

With hundreds of apps in use and new ones being adopted on a regular basis, organizations need an automated way to view key vendor and app details and compare risk elements and compliance certifications. It's also important to be able to view which identities are using which applications to enable monitoring and to help with policy formation or incident investigations. This information is provided in the app detail pages, which can be accessed from the dashboard or any of the aforementioned App Grid reports. All of this insight will help you to make informed decisions about the cloud apps you want to approve in your environment.

Utilize the 30 application categories to organize the apps in use and filter by risk level or number of requests to understand your current exposure. Then make informed decisions about categories and assign the individual apps to the Approved, Under Audit, or

Not Approved group. Figure 8-19 shows an example of a Cisco Umbrella categorized application-level report.

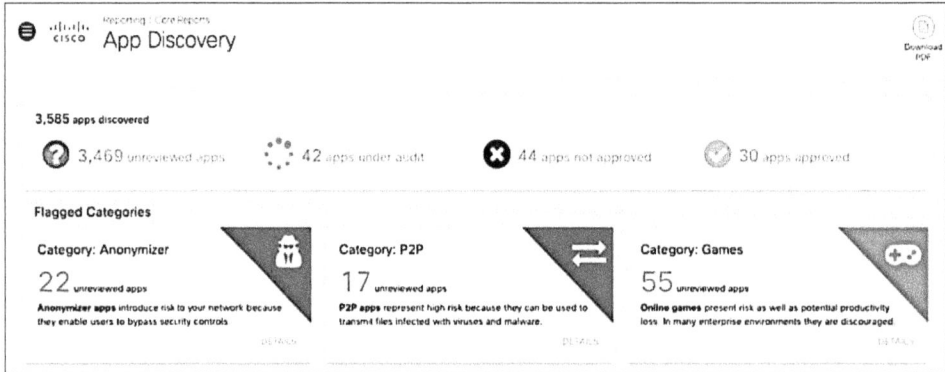

Figure 8-19   *Cisco Umbrella categorized application-level report*

Figure 8-20 shows apps by category and risk.

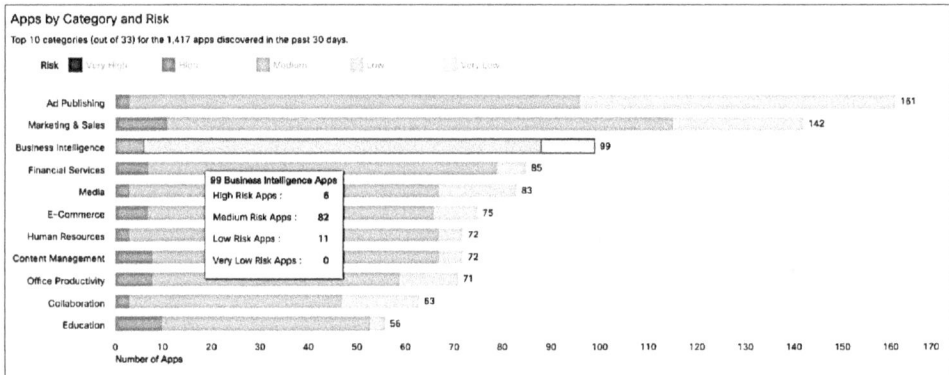

Figure 8-20   *Apps by category and risk*

Application Blocking

Once the organization has visibility into the full spectrum of apps in use and details on the usage and risk levels, it is natural to want to block either entire categories or specific applications that don't match the cloud adoption or security strategy. The blocking capabilities in Umbrella allow you to select a category or individual application and block it for all users, specific groups, individuals, or networks.

You can easily block the available apps by clicking the link in the application listing or detail pages as well as enforce this control for any network, group, or individual user accessible by Umbrella policies. Figure 8-21 illustrates the configuration steps to control an application.

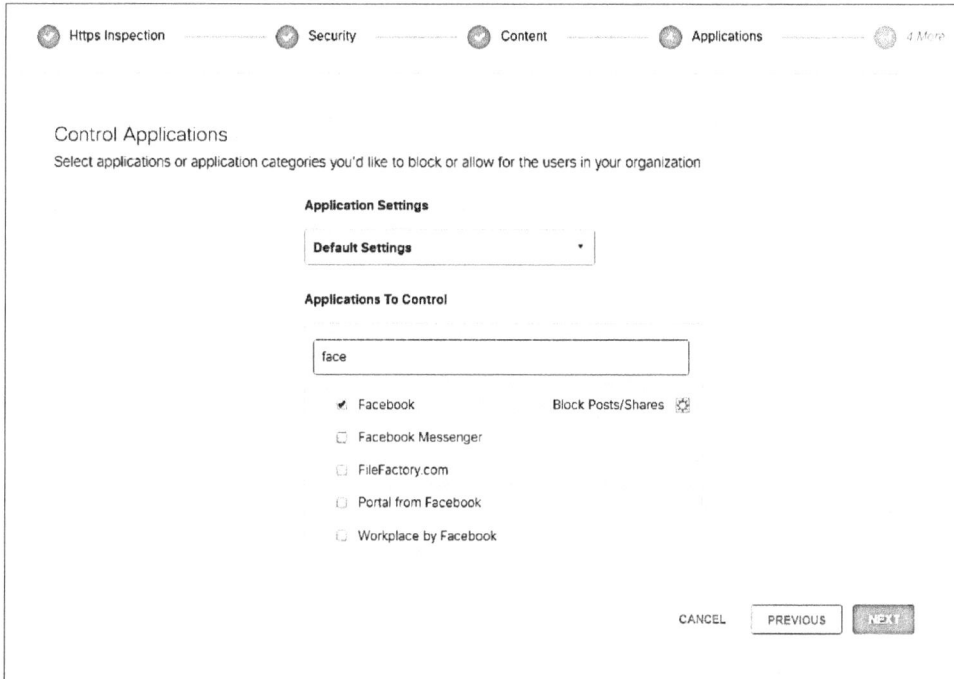

Figure 8-21   *Configuration steps to control an application*

Enabling Healthy and Efficient Cloud Adoption

Users are aggressively adopting cloud applications to improve collaboration and productivity. This activity should be enabled and encouraged due to the many benefits, but you need the ability to monitor cloud app usage on an ongoing basis and compare vendors and apps to provide guidance and control. Armed with a list of sanctioned and unsanctioned apps, you can intelligently manage the volume of cloud apps in use and help enable end users trying to make decisions about new apps. Figure 8-22 shows the Cisco Cloudlock Composite Risk Score.

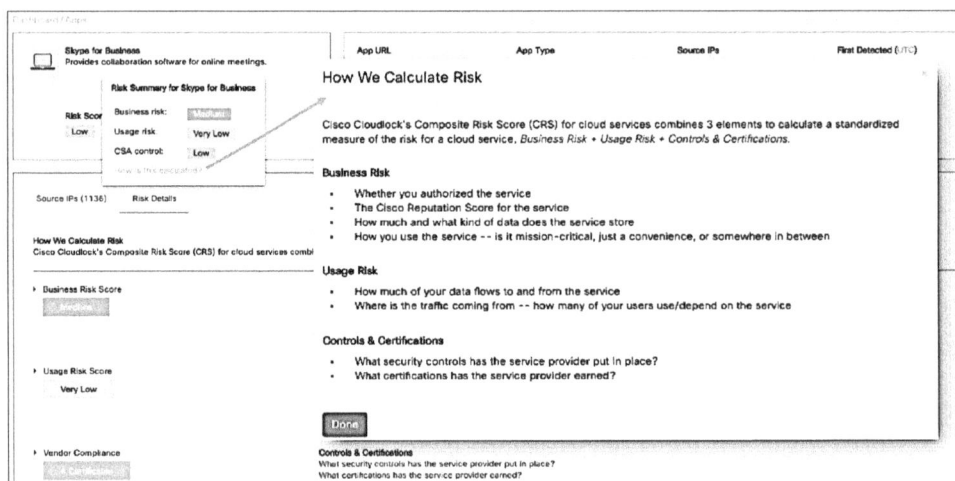

Figure 8-22 *Cisco Cloudlock Composite Risk Score*

Cisco Umbrella

Security is shifting and converging in the cloud. You may hear different names for this trend, such as secure Internet gateway (SIG), edge security, secure access service edge (SASE), and more. It can get confusing. Regardless of what you call it, it denotes multiple security functions integrated into one cloud service, the flexibility to deploy security services how and where you choose, the ability to secure direct-to-Internet access, cloud app usage, and roaming users, plus, no appliances to deploy.

Today's work environment allows employees to work from any device, anywhere and anytime. As remote users work directly in cloud apps, perimeter security appliances and VPNs are no longer always going to protect devices and data. Therefore, Cisco continues to enhance its secure Internet gateway (SIG), Cisco Umbrella, to protect users when off the network and off the VPN. Formally launched at the RSA Conference in February 2017, Cisco Umbrella now processes more than 120 billion DNS requests per day, with more than 85 million daily active users. The recently announced Cisco Security Connector app for iOS enables company-managed iPhones and iPads to be protected by Cisco Umbrella, whether on Wi-Fi or the cellular network.

Cisco Umbrella is a cloud-delivered security platform that secures Internet access and controls cloud app usage across networks, branch offices, and roaming users. Unlike disparate security tools, Umbrella unifies secure web gateway, cloud-delivered firewall, DNS-layer security, and cloud access security broker (CASB) functionality into a single cloud platform. Umbrella also integrates with Cisco SD-WAN to provide security and policies for direct Internet access (DIA) at branch offices. Umbrella acts as a secure onramp to the Internet and delivers deep inspection and control to support compliance and provide the most effective protection against threats for users anywhere they connect. Figure 8-23 provides an overview of Cisco Umbrella SIG.

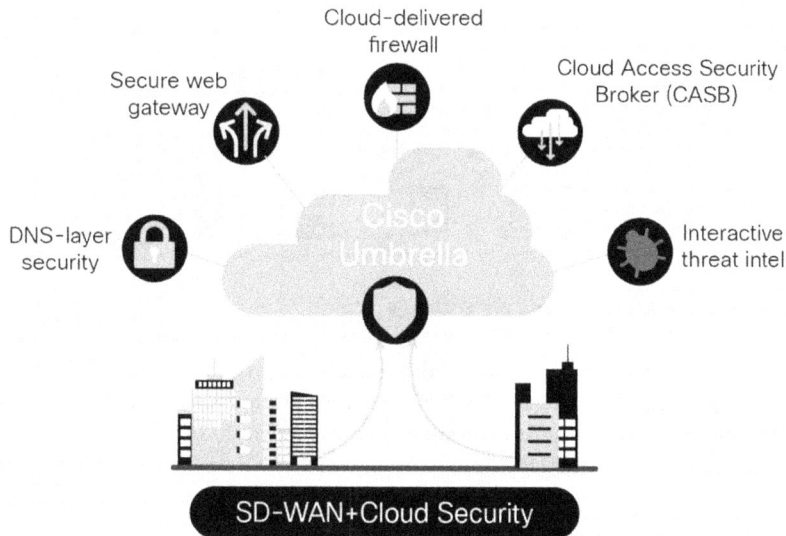

Figure 8-23 *Cisco Umbrella SIG overview*

Benefits

The following components are integrated seamlessly in a single, cloud-delivered platform:

- **DNS-layer security:** DNS requests precede the IP connection, enabling DNS resolvers to log requested domains over any port or protocol for all network devices, office locations, and roaming users. You can monitor DNS requests, as well as subsequent IP connections, to improve accuracy and detection of compromised systems, security visibility, and network protection. You can also block requests to malicious destinations before a connection is even established, thus stopping threats before they reach your network or endpoints. Figure 8-24 illustrates Cisco Umbrella DNS-layer security.

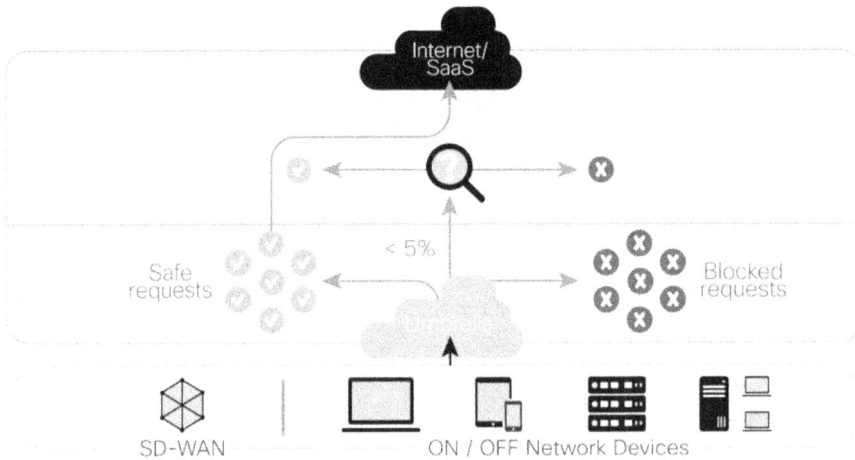

Figure 8-24 *Cisco Umbrella DNS-layer security*

■ **Secure web gateway:** A cloud-based full (or selective) proxy that can log and inspect your web traffic, including uploaded and downloaded files, for greater transparency, control, and protection against malware and other hidden threats. You can view detailed reporting with full URL addresses, network identity, allow or block actions, plus external IP addresses. You can also create policies for content filtering by category or specific URLs to block destinations that violate policies or compliance regulations. Figure 8-25 illustrates Cisco Umbrella as a secure web gateway.

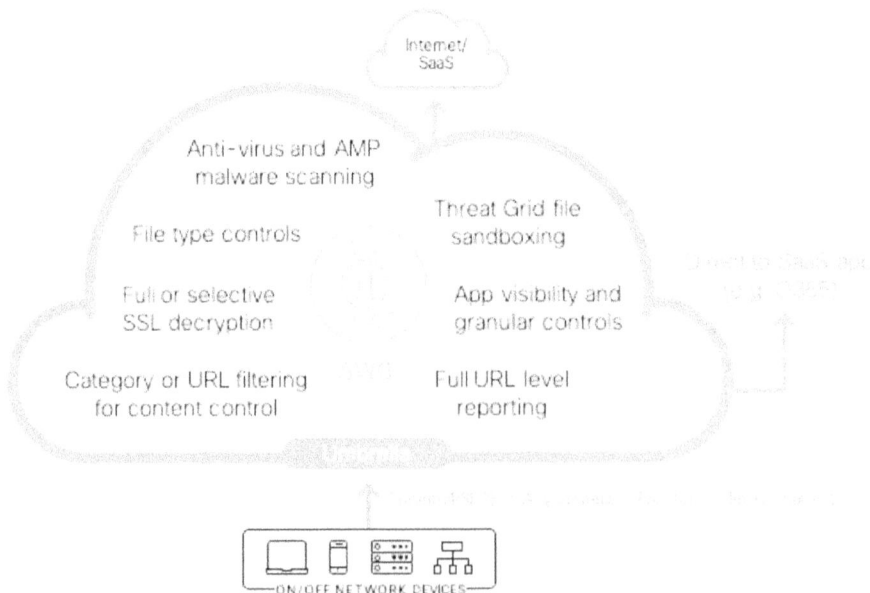

Figure 8-25 *Secure web gateway*

■ **Cloud-delivered firewall:** All Internet activity is logged and unwanted traffic is blocked using customizable IP, port, and protocol rules. To forward traffic, simply configure an IPsec tunnel from any network device. As new tunnels are created, security policies can automatically be applied for better visibility and control of all Internet traffic, including easy setup and consistent enforcement throughout your environment. Figure 8-26 illustrates Cisco Umbrella as a cloud-delivered firewall.

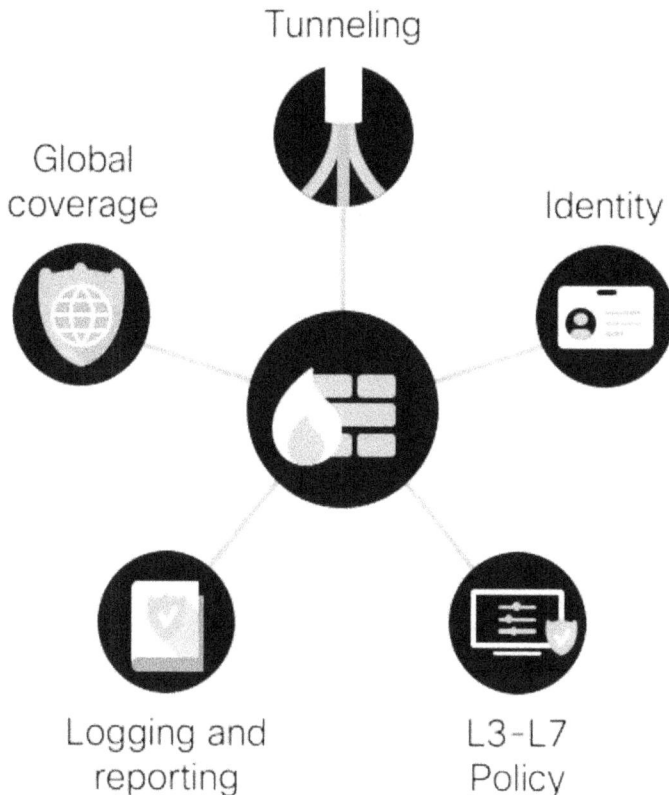

Figure 8-26   *Cloud-delivered firewall*

■ **Cloud access security broker (CASB):** You can detect and report on the cloud applications in use across your environment as well as automatically generate overview reports on the vendor, category, application name, and the volume of activity for each discovered app. Drill-down reports include web reputation score, financial viability, and relevant compliance certifications to enable better management of cloud adoption, reduce risk, and provide more control to block the use of offensive or inappropriate cloud applications in the work environment. Figure 8-27 illustrates Cisco Umbrella as a cloud access security broker.

Out of band/API	Inline/Proxy
• Cloudlock UEBA	• Umbrella App Discovery & blocking
• Cloudlock DLP	• Umbrella Advanced App Control
• Cloudlock Apps Firewall – OAuth-connected apps	– Block uploads Dropbox/Box – Block attachments Webmail

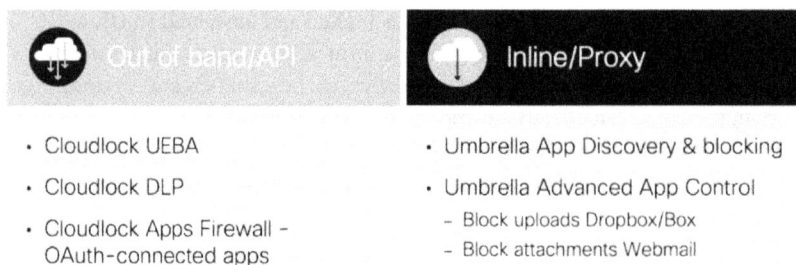

Figure 8-27 *Cloud access security broker*

■ **Interactive threat intelligence access:** Umbrella utilizes threat intelligence from Cisco Talos, one of the largest commercial threat intelligence teams in the world, to uncover and block a broad spectrum of malicious domains, IPs, URLs, and files used in attacks. Cisco feeds volumes of global Internet activity into a combination of statistical and machine learning models to identify new attacks staged on the Internet to help organizations respond to the rise in threats, incidents, and breaches. You can view unparalleled threat intelligence in Cisco's web console or integrate with your existing security tools for faster remediation. Figure 8-28 illustrates Cisco Umbrella utilizing threat intelligence.

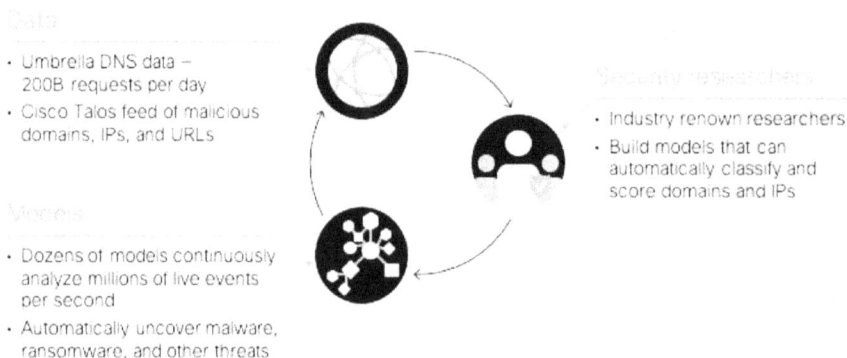

Data
- Umbrella DNS data –
  200B requests per day
- Cisco Talos feed of malicious
  domains, IPs, and URLs

Models
- Dozens of models continuously
  analyze millions of live events
  per second
- Automatically uncover malware,
  ransomware, and other threats

Security researchers
- Industry renown researchers
- Build models that can
  automatically classify and
  score domains and IPs

Figure 8-28 *Threat intelligence*

■ **SD-WAN integration:** You can deploy across your network and gain powerful cloud-delivered security to protect against threats on the Internet and when accessing the cloud. You can also create flexible security policies based on the level of protection and visibility you need—all in the Umbrella dashboard. Cisco's integrated approach can efficiently protect your branch users, connected devices, and application usage from all DIA breakouts.

Deployment Options

The following are some key points concerning the deployment of Cisco Umbrella:

■ To deploy Umbrella's DNS-layer security, you can provision any network device (router, DHCP server, and so on) by pointing external DNS to Cisco's IP addresses. You can also use your existing Cisco footprint—SD-WAN (Viptela), Integrated Services Router (ISR) 1K and 4K Series, Meraki MR, and wireless LAN controllers—to quickly provision protection across hundreds of routers and access points.

■ Off-network protection is available for laptops that use Windows, macOS, Chrome OS, and supervised Apple devices that run iOS 11.3 or higher.

■ To enable the secure web gateway or cloud-delivered firewall functionality, the following options are available:

   ■ For cloud-delivered firewall, you create IPSec tunnels to forward all Internet traffic to Cisco's platform.

   ■ For secure web gateway, you can forward web traffic via proxy chaining or PAC files.

   ■ IPSec tunnels.

■ If the end user IP address needs to be visible, you can deploy Umbrella Virtual Appliance (VA) within the customer environment.

■ To set up policies based on username, deploy an AD connector within the customer environment.

■ For roaming users, deploy the roaming client or use Cisco AnyConnect.

Umbrella Integrations

Umbrella, while providing multiple levels of defense against Internet-based threats, is the centerpiece of a larger architecture for Internet security. Figure 8-29 illustrates Cisco Umbrella integrations.

This section will explore the integrations that occur with other products in the Cisco portfolio and the role each plays in securing the business flows.

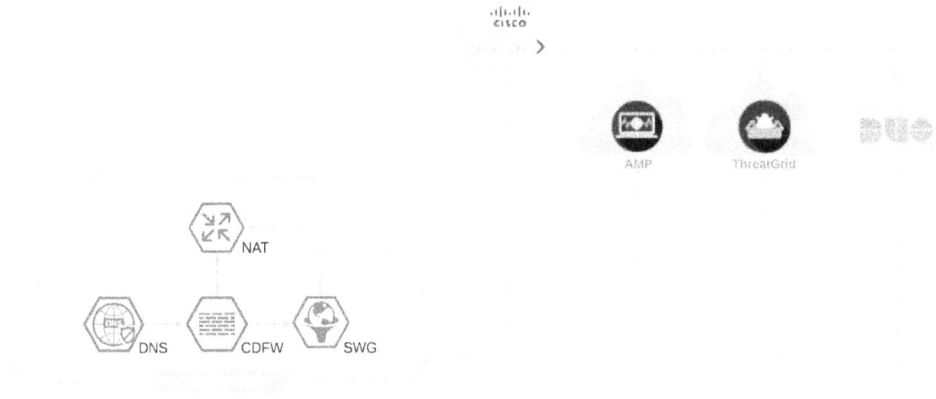

Figure 8-29   *Cisco Umbrella integrations*

Backhauling Internet-bound traffic from remote sites is expensive and adds latency. Many organizations are upgrading their network infrastructure by adopting SD-WAN and enabling DIA. With the Umbrella and Cisco SD-WAN integration, you can simply and rapidly deploy Umbrella IPsec tunnels across your network and gain powerful cloud-delivered security to protect against threats on the Internet and secure cloud access. This market-leading automation makes it easy to deploy and manage the security environment over tens, hundreds, or even thousands of remote sites. Umbrella's DNS security also can be deployed with a single configuration in the Cisco SD-WAN vManage dashboard. When you need additional security and more granular controls, Cisco's integrated approach can efficiently protect your branch users, connected devices, and application usage at all DIA breakouts. Umbrella offers flexibility to create security policies based on the level of protection and visibility you need—all in the Umbrella dashboard. Figure 8-30 illustrates Cisco Umbrella integration with SD-WAN.

The Cisco SecureX platform connects the breadth of Cisco's integrated security portfolio and additional third-party tools for a consistent, simplified experience to unify visibility, enable automation, and strengthen security. It aggregates data from a multitude of Cisco and partner products for improved intelligence and faster response time. You can immediately visualize the threat and its organizational impact and get an at-a-glance verdict for the observables you are investigating through a visually intuitive relations graph. It enables you to triage, prioritize, track, and respond to high-fidelity alerts through the built-in Incident Manager. Then you can take rapid response actions across multiple security products, such as isolate hosts, block files and domains, and block IPs, all from one convenient interface. SecureX empowers your security operations center (SOC) teams with a single console for direct remediation, access to threat intelligence, and tools such as Casebook and Incident Manager. It overcomes many challenges by making threat investigations faster, simpler, and more effective. Figure 8-31 shows Cisco Umbrella integration with SecureX.

Figure 8-30 *Cisco SD-WAN integration*

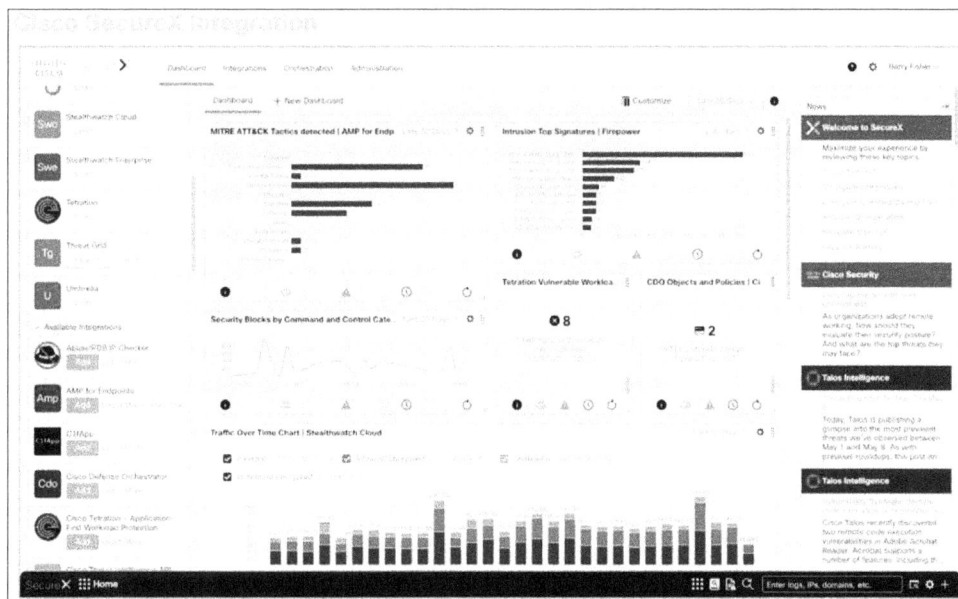

Figure 8-31 *Cisco SecureX Integration*

Umbrella is not an open proxy and therefore must trust the source forwarding web traffic to it. This can be accomplished by assigning either a network or tunnel identity to a web policy. Policies created in this fashion apply broadly to any web traffic originating from the network or tunnel. However, to create more granular policies for users or groups, Security Assertion Markup Language (SAML) should be implemented or AnyConnect should be installed on the devices. Identities obtained from SAML can be matched to users and groups that have been provisioned by manually importing a CSV file from Active Directory. This can also be done automatically by using Active Directory–based provisioning with the Umbrella AD Connector. Duo Access Gateway acts as an identity provider (IdP), authenticating your users using existing on-premises or cloud-based directory credentials and prompting for two-factor authentication before permitting access to your service provider application. Figure 8-32 illustrates Cisco Umbrella integration with Duo.

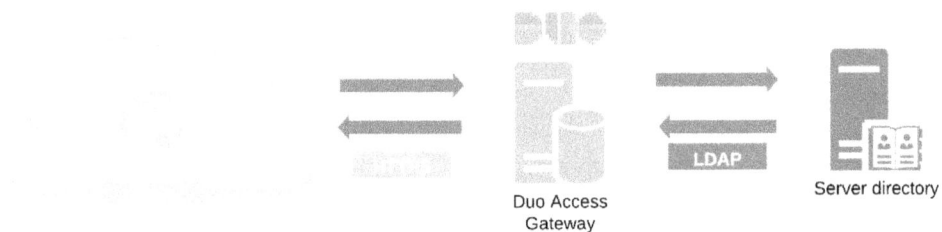

Figure 8-32   *Cisco Duo integration*

Umbrella Packages

Cisco offers various Umbrella packages based on the functionality needed to address your cybersecurity challenges. Table 8-1 details the various Cisco Umbrella packages and their features.

Table 8-1   *Cisco Umbrella Packages and Features*

Package	Features
DNS Monitoring	Used for visibility into recursive DNS activity across your organization. This does not include any security blocks or content web filtering policies.
DNS Security Essentials	Easy to deploy, simple to manage DNS-layer security that blocks Internet threats (phishing, malware, ransomware, botnets or C2 callbacks, cryptojacking, and so on). Includes the following features: ■ User-based policies with Active Directory integration ■ Web filtering ■ Custom domain block/allow lists ■ App Discovery and Control based on domain ■ Indefinite logs retention ■ APIs for network devices, management, reporting, and enforcement

Package	Features
DNS Security Advantage	Includes everything in the DNS Essentials package, plus the following: ■ IP-layer enforcement for C2 callbacks that bypass DNS ■ Access threat intelligence in the Investigate web-based console and API for deeper context during investigations ■ Proxy risky domains with customizable URL blocking and file inspection using antivirus engines and Cisco Advanced Malware Protection (AMP)
Secure Internet Gateway (SIG) Essentials	Includes DNS Advantage plus deeper inspection and control to block threats and support corporate compliance. Combines multiple security services, including: ■ DNS-layer security ■ Secure web gateway ■ Firewall ■ Cloud access security broker (CASB) Also includes Cisco SD-WAN (Viptela) implementation to provide a unique combination of performance, security, and flexibility.

Cisco Secure Cloud Analytics

Only 56 percent of security alerts are investigated, and more than half of those are not remediated, according to the Cisco 2017 Annual Cybersecurity Report. Responding to these alerts is an overwhelming job, and most organizations do not have the security staff to keep up. Companies of all sizes face the challenge of securing their public cloud environments as well as their on-premises infrastructure.

Adding effective security measures for public cloud workloads—with solutions that can reduce the number of false positives—is a critical task. However, the public cloud infrastructure differs from an on-premises infrastructure. A public cloud offers fewer network-monitoring capabilities, even as it undergoes a very high change rate in assets. To provide effective security while reducing the number of false positives, a new approach is necessary.

Imagine that an employee's cloud credentials are compromised, through phishing or another method. Can you tell if that employee begins logging in from another country? Cisco Secure Cloud Analytics (formerly Stealthwatch Cloud) provides the actionable security intelligence and visibility necessary to identify these kinds of malicious activities in real time. You can quickly respond before a security incident becomes a devastating breach. Figure 8-33 illustrates Cisco Secure Cloud Analytics integrating with the network.

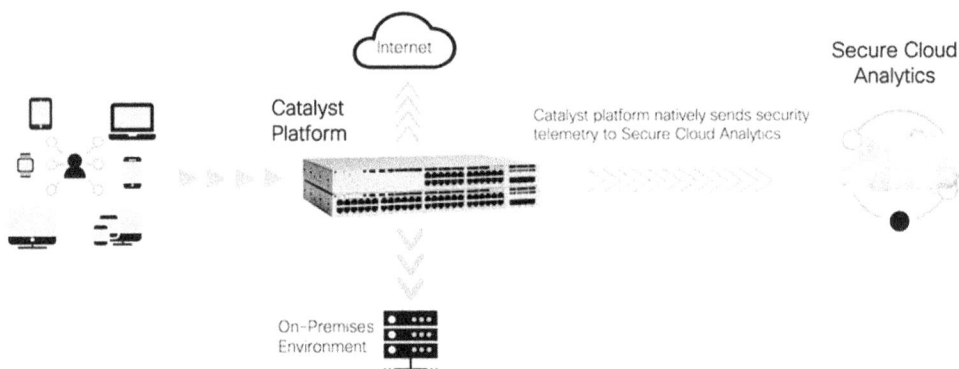

Figure 8-33   *Cisco Secure Cloud Analytics integration*

The following are some of key challenges your business faces as it grows in the cloud:

- The transition to the cloud is complicated. In their quest to remain agile, businesses have flocked to the public cloud, a place where they can migrate workloads into managed, serverless, and containerized environments that offer faster and more flexible deployments, higher efficiency, and more scalable ways to grow their operations. According to the Cisco Annual Internet Report, Cloud data centers will process nearly 95% of workloads in 2021. And while your organization and cloud footprint continue to grow, so do your compliance concerns and your attack surface. In fact, 94% of cybersecurity professionals report that they are at least moderately concerned about public cloud security.

- As their cloud footprint expands, businesses are increasingly more worried about ensuring compliance and the risk of threats, which is why maintaining proper cloud security posture is critical. Over the past 5 years, some big-name companies have fallen victim to attacks that stem from improper cloud management and resource configuration. With sensitive workloads and data up in the cloud, it is critical that you have the proper tools in place to monitor and protect this information.

- It doesn't help that most IT tasks are divided into various functions. Your SecOps organization is responsible for threat hunting and monitoring the network for attacks and malicious behavior, while your DevOps team is responsible for rapidly building and deploying applications in the cloud. These groups are separately trying to tackle a wide variety of challenges in the public cloud, and often they don't work together as closely as they should. As organizations mature, they often pursue a strategy that enables close collaboration between SecOps and DevOps teams.

Cisco Secure Cloud Analytics has many benefits. With Cisco Secure Cloud Analytics, security teams can confidently monitor and protect their cloud workloads and perform quick security posture assessments of their cloud environments using a cloud-native, API-driven solution that works the way a DevOps team would expect. With just one intuitive solution, both SecOps and DevOps can share information on cloud workloads and resolve compliance or configuration issues before an attack takes place. The following table and Figure 8-34 outline the key benefits of Cisco Secure Cloud Analytics:

Rapidly detect advanced threats that may be taking advantage of misconfigured assets in the cloud

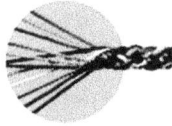

Strengthen and maintain your cloud security posture through live event viewing

Gain comprehensive visibility of activity occurring within your cloud resources

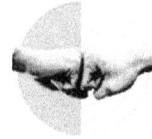

Enable quick corrective action on security policies and configurations through seamless communication across your SecOps and DevOps teams

Figure 8-34   *Cisco Secure Cloud Analytics benefits*

- Gain actionable intelligence through visibility of your environment, from the private network to the public cloud

- Rapidly detect advanced threats and indicators of compromise

- Grow your security with your business while lowering operational overhead

- Greatly reduce false positives with higher fidelity alerts supported by underlying observations

- Attain a stronger security posture across the enterprise, including the public cloud

With Secure Cloud Analytics, you can detect external and internal threats across your environment—from the private network to the branch office to the public cloud. Secure Cloud Analytics is a SaaS solution delivered from the cloud. It is easy to try, easy to buy, and simple to operate and maintain. When data is received, it requires very little additional configuration or device classification. All the analysis is automated.

Understanding Secure Cloud Analytics

Cisco Secure Cloud Analytics is a SaaS-based network detection and response (NDR) offering that give CISOs more confidence in their ongoing journey into the cloud. This solution is already built to protect your public cloud resources, as it provides comprehensive visibility into all of your public cloud traffic. It is a true multicloud solution and can ingest native telemetry from Amazon Web Services (AWS), Microsoft Azure, and Google Cloud Platform (GCP). It even has the ability to detect threats in encrypted traffic without active packet inspection. Figure 8-35 illustrates the inclusion of Cloud Insights into Cisco SecureX.

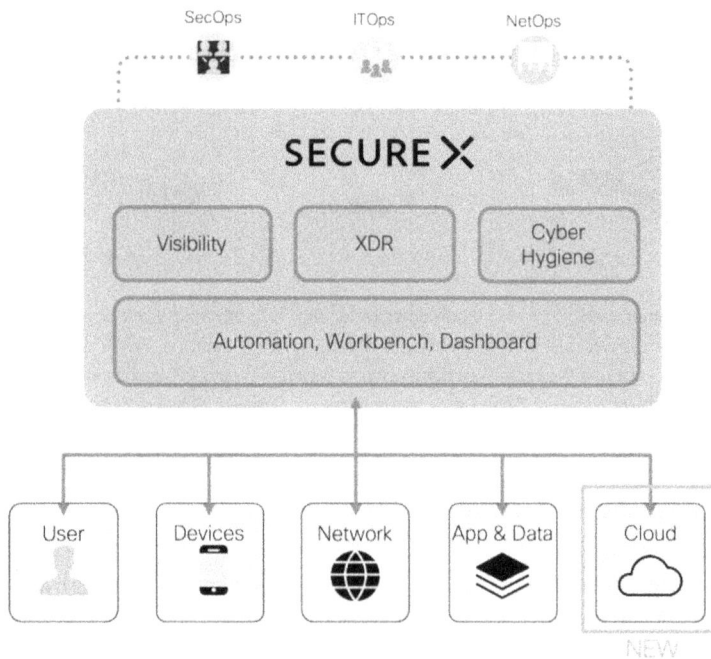

Figure 8-35 *Cloud Insights in Cisco SecureX*

Secure Cloud Analytics is a highly flexible event viewer that offers a wealth of information about your business's cloud deployment, resource configuration, alignment to industry standards and regulations, and much more. Here is a breakdown of how these features will help your business:

- **Encourage collaboration through simple reporting on cloud security posture:** Secure Cloud Analytics enables your DevOps and SecOps groups to work cohesively, as one team. It identifies a critical gap that often exists between these functions. Your SecOps team is focused on threat hunting and protecting the business. It must monitor the network for alerts and address suspicious behavior in a timely manner. DevOps is responsible for implementing changes to code and configuring cloud resources but often lacks visibility into what SecOps is discovering about the network. The event viewer allows the SecOps teams to identify vulnerabilities and gather critical information about configurations in the cloud and seamlessly deliver this information to DevOps to ensure that proper adjustments are made and that cloud workloads stay secure. Integrated with Cisco SecureX and other third-party platforms, Secure Cloud Analytics makes it easier than ever for teams to communicate their findings and make fluid adjustments in the public cloud.

- **Maintain compliance and meet standards unique to your industry:** There is no one team solely responsible for ensuring compliance or meeting segmentation rules; however, these new features enable teams to find and share information about public cloud traffic easily. The event viewer allows users to monitor cloud posture as it relates to various industry best practices. Users can investigate all cloud accounts and be alerted on those that are not compliant with industry standards like PCI, HIPAA, and CIS frameworks or custom internal policies. Robust filtering and query searches allow the user to zero in on misconfigured or vulnerable assets that cause any compliance concerns.

- **Seamlessly monitor and protect your public cloud resources:** The bread and butter of Secure Cloud Analytics is its ability to classify your network devices and monitor their *behavior* to detect threats. This process is known as *dynamic entity modeling*. Upon deployment, Secure Cloud Analytics starts to establish a baseline for learned "normal" behavior. While it does provide some alerts out of the box, the most powerful alerts are triggered when it begins to understand the network and sees some deviation from the behavioral norm. It automatically groups your cloud resources into roles such as EC2 instances, S3 buckets, AWS load balancers, and more. It generates alerts like Geographically Unusual Azure API Usage and AWS Lambda Invocation Spike, which are designed specifically to spot vulnerabilities in your cloud configurations.

How Secure Cloud Analytics Works

The deployment and working of Secure Cloud Analytics is described in the following sections.

Deployment

Secure Cloud Analytics supports two deployment types to support your network:

- **Public cloud monitoring:** Agent-less monitoring of workloads by ingesting native cloud logs, and API integration to deliver threat detection and configuration monitoring.

- **Private cloud monitoring:** Virtual Cisco Secure Cloud Analytics sensor deployment to ingest network flow data, SPAN/mirror port traffic, and NGFW log information. (In this book, we only focus on public cloud monitoring.)

You can deploy either or both at the same time and review the configuration and alerts from both in a single Secure Cloud Analytics web portal UI. The web portal displays all sensors and monitored cloud deployments from the same page, so you can quickly review the state of your monitoring.

Dynamic Entity Modeling

Secure Cloud Analytics uses dynamic entity modeling to track the state of your network. In the context of Secure Cloud Analytics, an *entity* is something that can be tracked over time, such as a host or endpoint on your network, or a Lambda function in your AWS deployment. Dynamic entity modeling gathers information about entities based on the traffic they transmit and activities they perform on your network. Secure Cloud

Analytics can ingest native cloud log data and industry-standard telemetry as well as user cloud provider APIs to identify entities and the types of traffic entities usually transmit. Secure Cloud Analytics updates these models over time, as the entities continue to send traffic, and potentially send different traffic, to keep an up-to-date model of each entity. Figure 8-36 illustrates the interaction between various cloud-native security functions.

Figure 8-36   *Interaction between various cloud-native security functions*

From this information, Secure Cloud Analytics identifies the following:

- The roles for the entity, which are descriptors of what the entity usually does. For example, if an entity sends traffic that is generally associated with email servers, Secure Cloud Analytics assigns the entity an Email Server role. The role/entity relationship can be many-to-one, as entities may perform multiple roles.

- Observations for the entity, which are facts about the entity's behavior on the network, such as a heartbeat connection with an external IP address, an interaction with an entity on a watchlist, or a remote access session established with another entity. Observations on their own do not carry meaning beyond the fact of what they represent. A typical customer may have many thousands of observations and a few alerts.

Alerts and Analysis

Based on the combination of roles, observations, and other threat intelligence, Secure Cloud Analytics generates alerts, which are actionable items that represent possible malicious behavior as identified by the system.

To build on the previous example, a New Internal Device observation on its own does not constitute possible malicious behavior. However, over time, if the entity transmits traffic consistent with a domain controller, then the system assigns a Domain Controller role to the entity. If the entity subsequently establishes a connection to an external server that it has not established a connection with previously, using unusual ports, and transfers large amounts of data, the system would log a New Large Connection (External) observation and an Exceptional Domain Controller observation. If that external server is identified as on a Talos watchlist, then the combination of all this information would lead Secure Cloud Analytics to generate an alert for this entity's behavior, prompting you to take further action to research and remediate the malicious behavior.

When you open an alert in the Secure Cloud Analytics web portal UI, you can view the supporting observations that led the system to generate the alert. From these observations, you can also view additional context about the entities involved, including the traffic they transmitted, and external threat intelligence if it is available. You can also see other observations and alerts that entities were involved with, and you can determine if this behavior is tied to other potentially malicious behavior.

Public Cloud Monitoring Configuration for Amazon Web Services

Cisco Secure Cloud Analytics public cloud monitoring is a visibility, threat identification, and compliance service for Amazon Web Services (AWS). Secure Cloud Analytics consumes network traffic data, including virtual private cloud (VPC) flow logs, from your AWS public cloud network. It then performs dynamic entity modeling by running analytics on that data to detect threats and indicators of compromise. Secure Cloud Analytics consumes VPC flow logs directly from your AWS account using a cross-account IAM role with the proper permissions. In addition, Secure Cloud Analytics can consume other sources of data, like CloudTrail and IAM (Identity and Access Management), for additional context and monitoring. Figure 8-37 illustrates the Cisco validated design for AWS three-tier architecture.

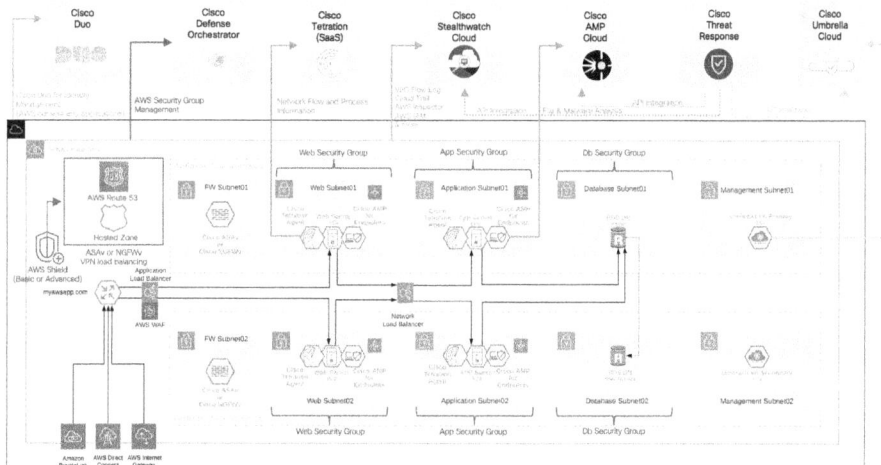

Figure 8-37 *Cisco validated design for AWS three-tier architecture*

To configure an S3 bucket to store your flow logs as well as Secure Cloud Analytics to ingest these flow logs, follow these steps:

1. In AWS, enable VPC flow logging for a VPC and then configure an S3 bucket to which you export the flow logs.

2. In AWS, configure an IAM access policy and IAM role to allow Secure Cloud Analytics the permission to access and ingest the flow logs.

3. In the Secure Cloud Analytics web portal UI, update the configuration with the S3 bucket and IAM role to enable AWS flow log data ingestion.

Public Cloud Monitoring Configuration for Google Cloud Platform

Cisco Secure Cloud Analytics public cloud monitoring is a visibility, threat identification, and compliance service for Google Cloud Platform (GCP). Secure Cloud Analytics consumes network traffic data, including VPC flow logs, from your GCP public cloud network. It then performs dynamic entity modeling by running analytics on that data to detect threats and indicators of compromise. Secure Cloud Analytics consumes VPC flow logs directly from your GCP account using a cross-account IAM service account with the proper permissions.

Single GCP Project Configuration

To configure GCP to generate and store flow log data for a single project as well as Secure Cloud Analytics to ingest that data, follow these steps:

1. In GCP, configure a service account with the proper permissions to view flow log and other data and then save the JSON credentials.

2. In GCP, enable flow logging and the Stackdriver monitoring API for metrics gathering.

3. In the Secure Cloud Analytics web portal UI, upload the service account JSON credentials.

If you have a high-throughput GCP environment, you can optionally configure Pub/Sub for a single project to deliver flow log data to Secure Cloud Analytics, as follows:

1. Determine if your deployment is high throughput.

2. Configure a Pub/Sub topic to ingest flow log data as well as a Pub/Sub subscription for the topic to deliver the flow log data.

Multiple GCP Project Configuration

To configure GCP to generate and store flow log data for multiple projects as well as Secure Cloud Analytics to ingest that data, follow these steps:

1. In GCP, configure a service account with the proper permissions to view flow log and other data and then save the JSON credentials. Configure the additional projects to use a single service account.

2. In GCP, configure the additional projects to use the service account.

3. In GCP, enable flow logging and the Stackdriver monitoring API for metrics gathering.

4. In the Secure Cloud Analytics web portal UI, upload the service account's JSON credentials.

If you have a high-throughput GCP environment, you can optionally configure Pub/Sub for multiple projects to deliver flow log data to Secure Cloud Analytics, as follows:

1. Determine if your deployment is high throughput.

2. Configure a Pub/Sub topic to ingest flow log data as well as a Pub/Sub subscription for the topic to deliver the flow log data.

3. Configure additional Pub/Sub topics and subscriptions for the additional projects.

Public Cloud Monitoring Configuration for Microsoft Azure

Cisco Secure Cloud Analytics public cloud monitoring is a visibility, threat identification, and compliance service for Microsoft Azure. Secure Cloud Analytics consumes network traffic data, including Network Security Group (NSG) flow logs, from your Azure public cloud network. It then performs dynamic entity modeling by running analytics on that data to detect threats and indicators of compromise. Secure Cloud Analytics consumes NSG flow logs directly from your Azure storage account and uses an application to gain additional context. Figure 8-38 illustrates the Cisco validated design for Azure three-tier architecture.

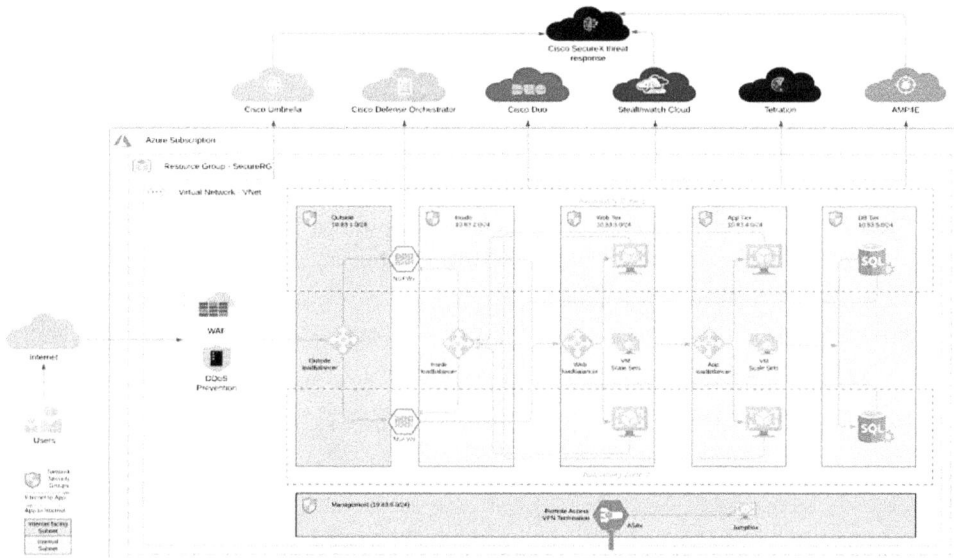

Figure 8-38 *Cisco validated design for Azure three-tier architecture*

To configure Azure to generate and store flow log data as well as Secure Cloud Analytics to ingest that flow log data, follow these steps:

1. In Azure, have at least one resource group to monitor.

2. In Azure, obtain your Azure AD URL and subscription ID.

3. In Azure, create an AD application and then associate roles with the application.

4. In Azure, create a storage account for the flow log data and then generate a SAS URL.

5. In Azure, enable Network Watcher and flow logs.

6. In Azure, if you want additional visibility on activity taken, configure your storage account to store activity logs.

7. In Secure Cloud Analytics, upload Azure credential and flow log storage information, including the AD URL, subscription ID, application ID and key, and blob service SAS URL.

Watchlist Configuration

Watchlists control whether or not traffic from a specific entity will generate an alert. You can configure entries such that traffic involving those entities always causes the system to generate an alert. You can also configure those watchlist entries to expire after a configured period of time, at which point traffic involving those entities no longer causes the system to generate an alert.

Configuring the AWS CloudTrail Event Watchlist

You can configure a watchlist to generate an alert for specific AWS CloudTrail events generated for specific AWS accounts. Follow these steps to add an entry to the AWS CloudTrail Alert Watchlist:

Step 1.   Select **Settings > Alerts > AWS CloudTrail Watchlist**.

Step 2.   Select an AWS Account ID from the drop-down or select to generate an alert if the system detects the CloudTrail event in any of your monitored AWS accounts.

Step 3.   Enter a CloudTrail event. See AWS documentation on CloudTrail events for more information on the supported events.

Step 4.   Click **Create**.

Configuring the GCP Logging Watchlist

You can configure a watchlist to generate an alert for specific GCP events generated for specific GCP projects. To add an entry to the GCP Logging Watchlist, follow these steps:

Step 1.   Select **Settings > Alerts > GCP Logging Watchlist.**

Step 2.   Click **New Watchlist Item.**

Step 3.   Enter a GCP action. See the GCP documentation for more information on the available actions.

Step 4.   Select a GCP project ID from the drop-down or select to generate an alert if the system detects the action in any of your monitored GCP projects.

Step 5.   Click **Create.**

Configuring the Azure Activity Log Watchlist

You can configure a watchlist to generate an alert for specific Azure events. Follow these steps to add an entry to the GCP Logging Watchlist:

Step 1.   Select **Settings > Alerts > Azure Activity Log Watchlist.**

Step 2.   Click **New Watchlist Item.**

Step 3.   Select a subscription ID from the drop-down or select to generate an alert if the system detects the action in any of your monitored Azure projects.

Step 4.   Enter an operation (or action). See Azure documentation for more information on the available actions.

Step 5.   Click **Create.**

Dashboard Overview

The Dashboard menu option presents several different ways to view your network at a high level:

■   The dashboard provides a summary of alerts, entities on your network, and traffic statistics.

■   The AWS visualizations present AWS-related spider graphs, with your AWS resources, security groups, and IAM permissions as nodes.

■   View the overall health of your network from the dashboard.

■   View the open alerts and supporting observations and other context to determine whether network behavior is malicious.

- View the models to detect historical patterns in entity, network, and other related behavior over time.

- View reports in the Help menu to understand the breadth and depth of traffic monitored by the system.

Figure 8-39 illustrates the Secure Cloud dashboard.

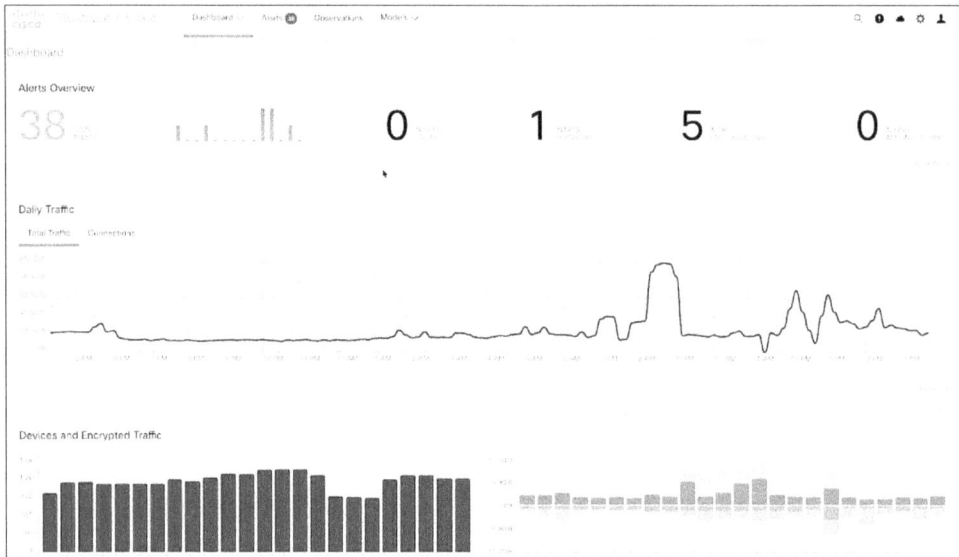

Figure 8-39   *Secure Cloud dashboard*

Cisco Duo Security

The landscape of authentication is clearly changing. Just a few years ago, security experts started preaching a risk-based access model—evaluating users, their devices, and the applications they access to determine a login's legitimacy. The corporate network wasn't the ultimate source of security anymore. Instead, risk could be managed using stronger security controls such as multifactor authentication (MFA).

Now, with the concept of de-perimeterization firmly established, access security is building on the foundation of MFA. IT professionals are realizing that security adoption is as important as the technology itself—and that forgoing passwords is a major usability improvement. It is also clear that remote work is here to stay, and access security must respond to new and evolving use cases. In the face of so much change, it's more important than ever that organizations have a streamlined, effective security stack that runs like clockwork.

In this section, we'll examine these industry shifts and look at how accessing security for everyone, from any device, anywhere is possible with Duo.

Since its founding in 2010, Duo has stood out in the cybersecurity industry by offering users people-focused endpoint verification solutions that make effective security easy. With user-friendly tools for authentication (including MFA and passwordless single sign-on), device trust, and adaptive context-based access, Duo quickly became a sought-after security software provider—and an obvious choice for joining Cisco Secure's powerful digital security portfolio. Duo Security has been a part of Cisco Secure since 2018, and its secure access product portfolio has continued to expand both in breadth and in its ability to solve emerging security challenges, like those faced in remote and hybrid workplace migrations.

Today, Duo provides Cisco Secure with streamlined endpoint verification tools, secure remote access platforms, cutting-edge visibility tools for administrators, and much more. Duo's dynamic and effective zero-trust solutions offer users security resilience by providing both product reliability and flexibility. Because of Duo's ability to integrate with any device, identity provider, application, or infrastructure, Cisco Secure clients can confidently deploy these sophisticated products to add zero-trust security into any setting. Figure 8-40 illustrates the capabilities of Duo Security.

| Confirm user identities in a snap. | Monitor the health of managed and unmanaged devices. | Set adaptive security policies tailored for your business. | Secure remote access without a device agent. | Provide security-backed, user-friendly SSO. |

Figure 8-40 *Capabilities of Duo Security*

Zero-trust takes security beyond the corporate network perimeter, protecting your data at every access attempt, from any device, anywhere. It's the future of information security, and Duo is your rock-solid foundation.

Multifactor Authentication from Duo

Two-factor authentication (2FA) is a specific type of MFA that strengthens access security by requiring two methods (also referred to as authentication factors) to verify your identity. These factors can include something you know, such as a username and password, and something you have, such as a smartphone app, to approve authentication requests.

2FA protects against phishing, social engineering, and password brute-force attacks and secures your logins from attackers exploiting weak or stolen credentials. You can ensure users are who they say they are at every access attempt, and you can regularly reaffirm their trustworthiness. MFA is the foundation for zero-trust. Duo verifies that your users are who they say they are, before they access your data—and with multiple second-factor options, including one-touch Duo Push, users can easily authenticate in seconds.

MFA from Cisco's Duo protects your applications by using a second source of validation, such as a phone or token, to verify user identity before granting access. Duo is engineered to provide a simple, streamlined login experience for every user and application, and as a cloud-based solution, it integrates easily with your existing technology. Figure 8-41 illustrates the Duo App MFA.

We know the most effective security solution is one your users actually use. Duo's 2FA solution only requires your users to carry one device—their smartphone, with the Duo Mobile app installed on it. Duo Mobile is available for both iPhones and Android, as well as wearables such as the Apple Watch. With support for a large array of authentication methods, logging in via push notification is fast and easy with Duo Mobile. We strongly recommend using Duo Push or WebAuthn as your second factor because they're secure and can protect against man-in-the-middle (MITM) attacks, but with Duo's flexibility and customizability, you'll be able to find the adaptive authentication method that meets the unique needs of your diverse user base.

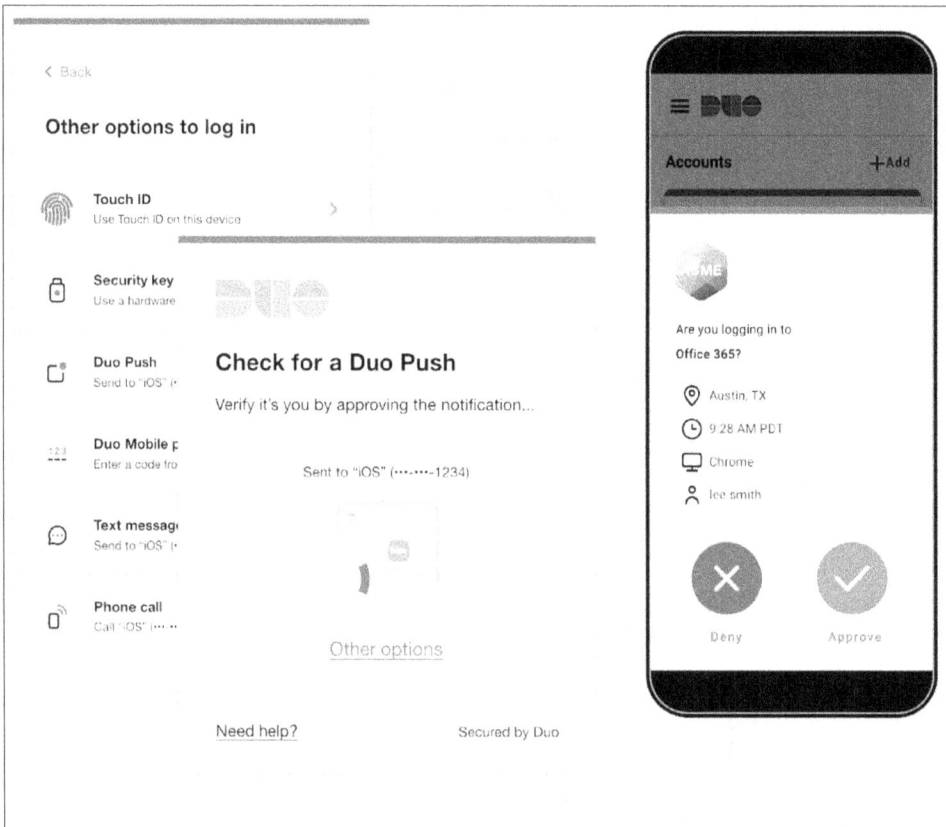

Figure 8-41 *Duo App multifactor authentication*

Types of 2FA

A number of different second factors can be used to verify a user's identity. From passcodes to biometrics, the available options address a range of use cases and protection levels:

- **SMS 2FA:** SMS two-factor authentication validates the identity of a user by texting a security code to their mobile device. The user then enters the code into the website or application to which they're authenticating.

- **TOTP 2FA:** The time-based one time password (TOTP) 2FA method generates a key locally on the device a user is attempting to access. The security key is generally a QR code that the user scans with their mobile device to generate a series of numbers. The user then enters those numbers into the website or application to gain access. The passcodes generated by authenticators expire after a certain period of time, and a new one will be generated the next time a user logs in to an account. TOTP is part of the Open Authentication (OAuth) security architecture.

- **Push-based 2FA:** Push-based 2FA improves on SMS and TOTP 2FA by adding additional layers of security, while improving ease of use for end users. Push-based 2FA confirms a user's identity with multiple factors of authentication that other methods cannot. Duo Security is the leading provider of push-based 2FA.

- **WebAuthn:** Created by the FIDO (Fast IDentity Online) Alliance and W3C, the Web Authentication API is a specification that enables strong, public key cryptography registration and authentication. WebAuthn (Web Authentication API) allows third parties like Duo to tap into built-in capabilities on laptops, smartphones, and browsers, letting users authenticate quickly and with the tools they already have at their fingertips.

Duo Device Trust Monitor

With Duo, you can monitor the health of every device across your organization in real time, whether it's corporate-managed or not. With Duo's device trust features, you can customize access requirements at the device level, and because it's a cloud-based solution, you'll stay ahead of the latest security threats. Identify risky devices, enforce contextual access policies, and report on device health using an agentless approach or by integrating with your device management tools.

You can't protect what you can't see. Gaining visibility into devices is the first step in establishing device trust, and it's an essential aspect of a strong zero-trust strategy. Duo provides visibility into every single device on your network and enforces health checks at every single login attempt.

With Duo, you can verify device health before granting access, to prevent exposing your applications to potential risk. Duo provides detailed information about both corporate and unmanaged devices, so you can easily spot security risks like out-of-date or jailbroken devices. Figure 8-42 shows Duo Device Trust Monitor dashboard.

Duo helps you spot potential risks so you can meet compliance and adjust your access parameters for any situation. With powerful reporting capabilities and an admin-friendly dashboard, Duo makes it easy to monitor your security policies and spot anomalous login activity.

Duo Trust Monitor analyzes and models authentication telemetry in order to highlight risk as well as adapt its understanding of normal user behavior. Table 8-2 provides a sampling of some of the telemetry Duo Trust Monitor considers.

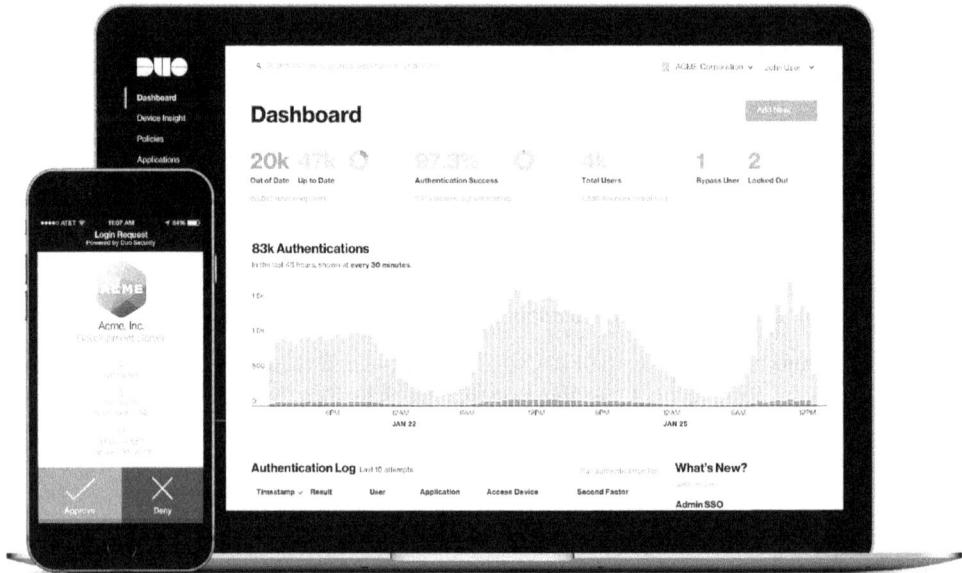

Figure 8-42 *Duo Device Trust Monitor dashboard*

Table 8-2 *Sampling of Duo Trust Monitor's Telemetry*

Data Type	Definition or Example
User	jsmith
Timestamp	Current server timestamp in seconds
Application	Cisco AnyConnect VPN, Office 365
Factor	Push, SMS, passcode
IP address of access or auth device	The IPv4 address of the user to be authenticated

Data Type	Definition or Example
Access or authentication device characteristics	Various, pending use of Duo Device Insight, Duo Device Health Application, and Trusted Endpoints
Authentication result	Granted, failure, fraud

Duo Trust Monitor may leverage up to 180 days' worth of historical Duo data to define a baseline. However, organizations don't need this much data for Duo Trust Monitor to be useful. We recommend customers enable the feature after using Duo in their environment for at least six weeks.

Duo Trust Monitor uses a variety of tactics to build out a threat model. Duo Trust Monitor evaluates the effect of each component over time and learns which combinations provide the most security value.

Table 8-3 illustrates a sampling of some of the models present within the feature.

Table 8-3 *Duo Trust Monitor's Models*

Model	Description
Novelty	Presence of a new variable in the access attempt. This includes a brand-new device or location or an attempt to access an application for the first time.
Rarity	Rarity covers the cases where a variable isn't new but is exceedingly infrequent, such as a variable present in 1% of access attempts.
Attack Pattern	Known patterns in the world of access security, such as unrealistic geo-velocity logins and brute-force attacks. Duo Trust Monitor surfaces attempts that fit these patterns.
Known Signal	Examples of inherently risky signals include a user marking an attempt as fraud or an admin applying bypass status to a user.
Compounding Risk	Access attempts that include more anomalous variables or distinct threat models combine to be more risky than those with fewer.
Administrator Designated	Duo Trust Monitor's risk profile enables Duo administrators to set priority assets. These assets are then prioritized in the feature's risk assessment.

When first setting up Duo Trust Monitor, administrators should designate their organization's risk profile. The Risk Profile flow enables administrators to select a prioritized set of Duo-protected applications, user groups, and locations/IPs.

Setting the risk profile is required to surface and view events. If an administrator creates a risk profile that selects every application, group, and location, Duo Trust Monitor still functions, but the feature will not prioritize any anomalies specifically over others.

To set up a risk profile, follow these steps:

Step 1.   Log in to the **Duo Admin Panel** and navigate to **Trust Monitor > Risk Profile.**

Step 2.   Click **Create Risk Profile.**

Step 3.   Begin by selecting applications. Scroll through the list of all applications protected by Duo in your organization's environment and then select the high-value applications to include in the risk profile.

Figure 8-43 illustrates application selection while creating a risk profile.

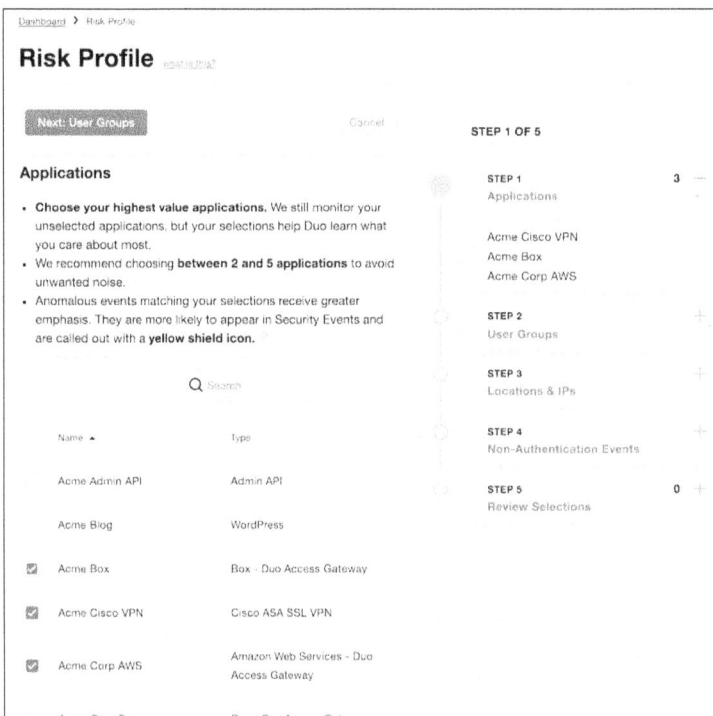

Figure 8-43   *Application selection while creating a risk profile*

Step 4.   Your next step is selecting the priority user groups. Highly credentialed power users, contractors, and users in bypass mode are often selected, but the exact configuration will vary by organizational structure. We recommend selecting three to eight groups.

Figure 8-44 illustrates the user group selection while creating a risk profile.

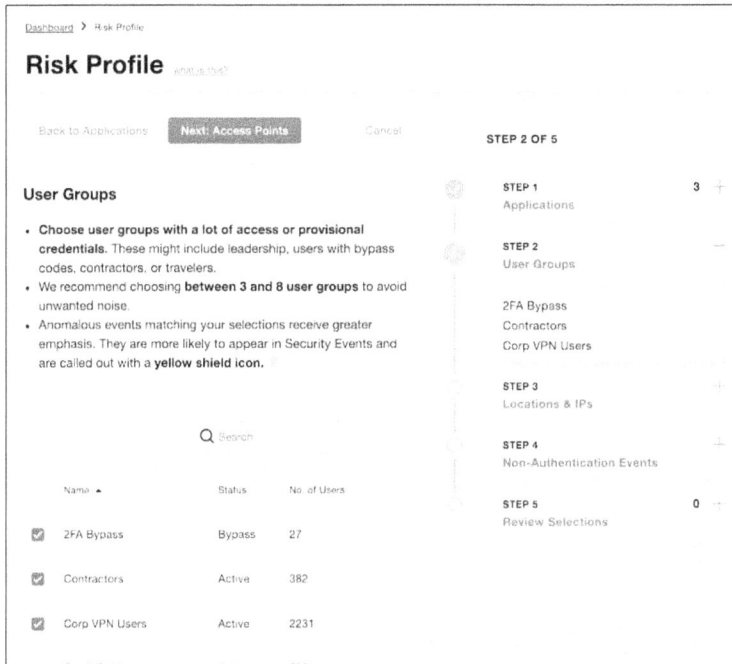

Figure 8-44 *User group selection while creating a risk profile*

Step 5. In this step of configuring the risk profile, you set trusted IPs or select risky countries. Typical selections would be countries where your organization doesn't do any business or have any users, meaning an access attempt from those countries would warrant some suspicion. For low-risk IPs, companies may enter corporate network blocks or trusted IP ranges. To reiterate, this tool merely prioritizes anomalies; events from a trusted network or country can still be surfaced in the Security Events dashboard.

Figure 8-45 illustrates the trusted location and IP selection while creating a risk profile.

Step 6. If you want Trust Monitor to surface non-authentication events that may be considered high risk, such as when a Duo admin applies bypass status to a user, enable that in this step.

Step 7. Review your application, group, location/IP, and non-authentication event selections. If you need to make corrections, you can use the **Back to ...** buttons to revisit each of the selection's steps. If everything looks okay, click **Apply Configuration.**

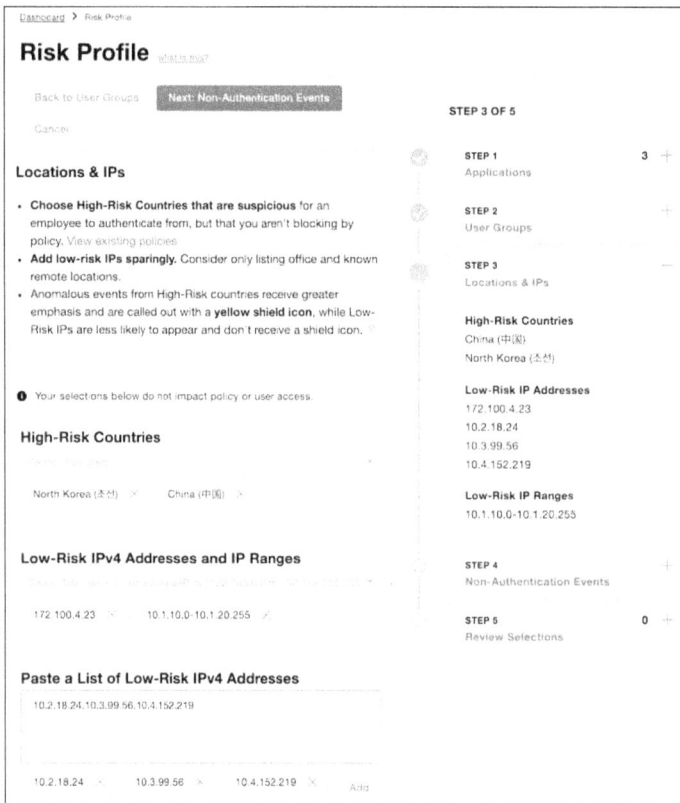

Figure 8-45 *Trusted location and IP selection while creating a risk profile*

Enforce Adaptive Policies

With Duo, you can assign granular and contextual access policies, limiting exposure of your information to as few users and devices as possible, and you can grant your users just the right amount of access. Duo's advanced policy enforcement capabilities let you define security requirements at the user, device, and application levels, based on contextual factors such as location and update status.

A true zero-trust strategy changes the level of access or trust based on contextual data about the user or device requesting access. It also limits access to only users who really need it. With Duo, you can set up detailed policies in minutes via a simple, intuitive administrator dashboard, and you can manage rules globally or for specific applications or user groups.

Every user has a different use case for access to your applications, and Duo handles them all with ease. Detect user location, device, role, and more at every login, set security policies based on these attributes, check for anomalous access, and continuously monitor policy efficacy—all without interrupting your users' daily workflows. Figure 8-46 illustrates adaptive policies in Duo.

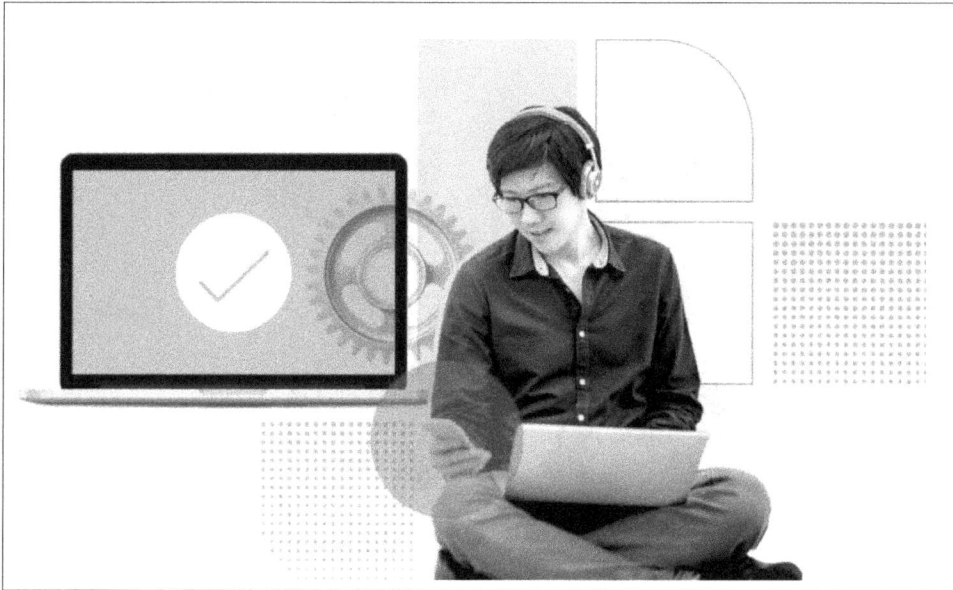

Figure 8-46   *Adaptive policies in Duo*

With Duo, you can protect against potentially compromised or risky devices accessing your applications and data as well as apply security policy across every device—managed or unmanaged. Duo lets you define permissions based on OS and individual device settings and automatically notify (or even block) users when their software is out of date.

With Duo, you can take a big step toward zero-trust by making sure the right people have access to the right tools. Duo's application-specific controls make it easy to onboard contract employees, change access permissions, protect high-value information with stringent security policies, and more.

Secure Access for Every User

For today's workforce, the "office" could be anywhere: home, a coffee shop, even an airplane. Duo protects every device and every application, so your users can keep working with the tools they love, anywhere, anytime. Flexibility and peace of mind? With Duo, you can have both.

You can provide appropriate permissions for every user accessing any application, anytime and from anywhere. You can also enable your mobile workforce without compromising your company's data. Duo provides modern remote access solutions and protects existing IT infrastructure, making it easy to onboard new employees and contractors, thus allowing employees to work on the go. Figure 8-47 illustrates remote access enablement with Duo.

Figure 8-47   *Remote access enablement with Duo*

Secure VPN-Less Remote Access for Any Environment

Everyone's IT stack is unique, and Duo can help protect everything—even surpassing the need for VPN connectivity. Helping to secure both on-premises and cloud environments (like Microsoft Azure, Amazon Web Services, and Google Cloud Platform), Duo's VPN-less remote access proxy, the Duo Network Gateway, can streamline and facilitate remote access in your organization.

Simple, Secure Single Sign-On

Today's workforce relies on an incredible variety of programs and platforms for productivity, and it can be difficult to provide on-demand access to these tools without compromising on security. Luckily, Duo safely puts essential applications at your users' fingertips. Whether you're looking for a new SSO solution or want to protect an existing one, Duo enables a streamlined login experience that's backed by airtight information security:

■ Reduce the risk of credential theft by enabling users to securely access their applications with a single username and password.

■ Duo's cloud-based single sign-on (SSO) grants users secure access to all protected applications (on-premises or cloud-based) through a uniform, frictionless interface that's accessible from anywhere.

■ SSO from Duo provides users with an easy and consistent login experience for any and every application, whether it's on-premises or cloud-based. Cloud-based and hosted by Duo, it's easy to set up and manage.

Figure 8-48 illustrates single sign-on enablement with Duo.

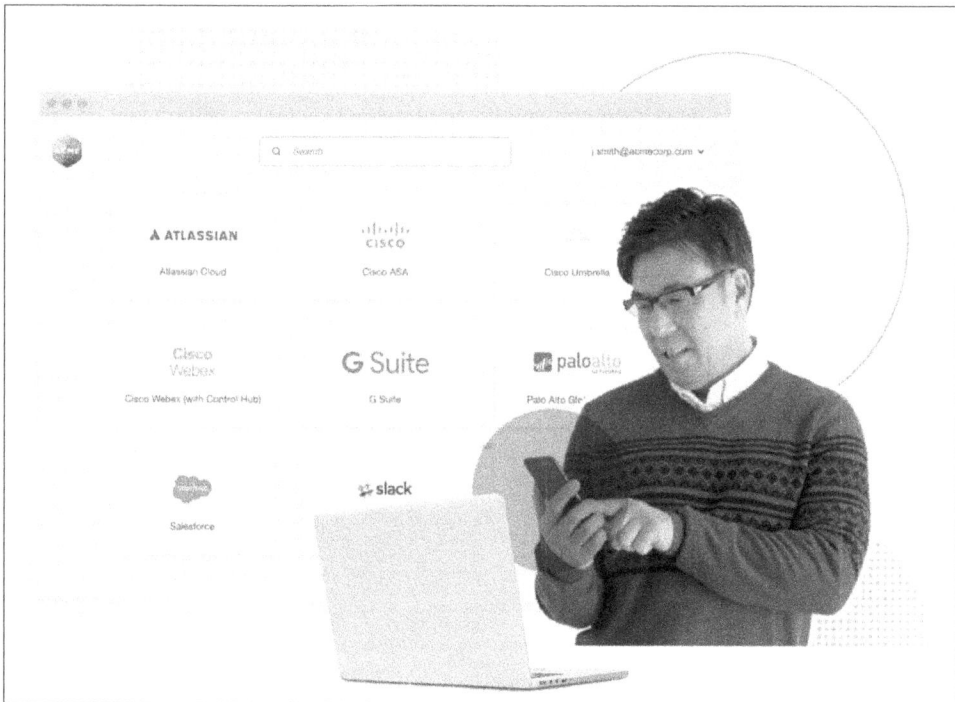

Figure 8-48   *Single sign-on enablement with Duo*

You can implement SSO with the tools people are actually using. Whether your applications are on-premises or cloud-based, they're all conveniently integrated for easy access—and with Duo's granular access policy options, you can provide just the right level of access for each.

Duo's cloud-based SSO is designed to complement Cisco's multifactor authentication solution, but its zero-trust platform integrates with dozens of other SSO and identity provider tools, allowing you to secure application access in the way that works best for your business.

Summary

Securing the public cloud is an increasingly difficult challenge for businesses. As a result, IT departments are searching for a cloud-delivered security solution that provides sufficient end-user security.

Cisco Cloud Security products extend protection to all aspects of your business. Cisco Umbrella helps secure cloud access, and Cisco Cloudlock safeguards the use of SaaS applications.

In addition, Cisco Secure Cloud Analytics (Stealthwatch Cloud) monitors your IaaS instances and alerts on suspicious activities. Cisco Cloud Security products deliver a broad, effective security solution for your multicloud world.

Index

Numbers

I

394 Metric Browser, Docker

O

T

*SLAs (service level
    agreements), 114–115*
target integration, 109–110
WSA, enabling Cisco Cloudlock with,
    318–321

X

Xamarin mobile applications,
    monitoring, 169
XenServer, 105–106
Xeon Scalable processors, 120

Y-Z

Zero Touch Deployment. *See* ZTD
    (Zero Touch Deployment)
zoning interface, SANs, 33
ZTD (Zero Touch Deployment)
    EDM (Edge Device Manager), 299
    GMM (Gateway Management
        Module), 298

www.ingramcontent.com/pod-product-compliance
Lightning Source LLC
Chambersburg PA
CBHW080134220326
41598CB00032B/5063